When Media Goes To War

When Media Goes To War

Hegemonic Discourse, Public Opinion, and the Limits of Dissent

Anthony DiMaggio

WHEN MEDIA GOES TO WAR
Anthony DiMaggio

Published in agreement with Monthly Review Press, New York for publication and sale only in the Indian Subcontinent (India, Pakistan, Bangladesh, Nepal, Maldives, Bhutan & Sri Lanka)

First Published in India 2012

ISBN 978-93-5002-188-0 (Pb)

Published by
AAKAR BOOKS
28 E Pocket IV, Mayur Vihar Phase I, Delhi 110 091
Phone : 011 2279 5505 Telefax : 011 2279 5641
info@aakarbooks.com; www.aakarbooks.com

Printed at
Mudrak, 30 A, Patparganj, Delhi 110 091

Contents

To Mary and to my family for always being there for me,
unconditionally, and without hesitation

Acknowledgments

I'd like to thank colleagues and friends from Illinois State University and North Central College for aiding in my professional development: Jamal Nassar, Carlos Parodi, Manfred Steger, and Ali Riaz. My appreciation as well to John Wilson for your mentoring, and Erik Abderhalden, Gary Gletty, Matt Hindman, Zach Wolfe, Stephen Caliendo, Jake Van Laar, David Fernandes, and Erica Thurman for all your help in my journalistic and intellectual career.

Thanks also go out to those at the University of Illinois, Chicago, who helped me the last four years: Doris Graber, Dennis Judd, Andy McFarland, Andy Rojecki, Barry Rundquist, Ike Balbus, Victor Margolin, Gregy Holyk, Bob Bruhl, Evan McKenzie, Matt Powers, and Zach Gebhardt.

I would have never been as successful as I am today without help from friends and peers in the progressive community who have published, read, and reviewed my work, including Jeff St. Clair, Chris Spannos, Mike Yates, Michael Parenti, Bob McChesney, Danny Schechter, Peter Phillips, Yahya Kamalipour, Lee Artz, Peter Hart, Alexander Cockburn, Noam Chomsky, and Paul Street.

Organizations and publications that helped me along the way include *Counterpunch*, *Z Magazine*, and the Open University of the Left.

Most important, I'd like to thank my family and friends for being there: Mom, Dad, Sam, Marty, Alissa, Jon, Dan, Grant, Kevin, Tony, and Steve. Thanks also to Paul Fasse for being one of my best friends over the years, and for all your help on this book and the last one. Without your assistance and comments I would never have been able to finish these projects, and I'm indebted to you forever for all you've done. Finally, I'd like to thank my wife, Mary, for putting up with me during the long hours I put into this book. Your love, infinite patience, and support are what keep me going. I love you very much, and thank you for everything.

INTRODUCTION

Propaganda and the News in a Time of Terror

In July of 2007, the editors of the *New York Times* staked out a claim for the paper as a leading "antiwar forum." July marked the first time the *Times* openly supported a withdrawal from Iraq, although that support came over two and a half years after the general public had turned against the war as no longer "worth it."[1] The reasons provided for the editors' antagonism were instructive. Though hailing America's altruistic goals of "building a stable, unified . . . democratic Iraq," the *Times* lamented that President Bush had "neither the vision nor the means" to accomplish the mission. In the face of overwhelming evidence that Iraq did not possess weapons of mass destruction (WMD), the editors retracted earlier reporting from the paper that portrayed Iraq as a dire threat. The invasion was now seen as "unnecessary"—its management "incompetent." The editorial derided "the [Iraqi] political leaders Washington has backed" as "incapable of putting national interests ahead of sectarian score settling" and assessed the failure to stabilize Iraq in terms of its costs for the United States. The "sacrifice" of American "lives and limbs" was also seen as "sapping the strength of the nation's alliances and its military forces" at a time when the world needed a "wise application of American power and principles."[2]

Although one can easily argue that much of the mainstream press is now opposed to the Iraq war, criticisms in liberal newspapers like the *Times* are largely dedicated to issues of procedure over substance. The occupation is seen as tremendously costly in terms of dollars spent, with the U.S. military overextended and unable to effectively project power. President Bush is denigrated for lacking the vision necessary to fight the Iraq war. But he is not criticized for illegally invading a sovereign nation, for maintaining a material interest in Iraqi oil, or for responsibility in the deaths of over one million Iraqis since 2003.[3] Though American political leaders may be deemed incompetent in achieving their goals, the goals themselves are beyond reproach. Claims about the benevolence of government intentions reveal much about the media's bias toward officialdom at a time when distrust for political leaders is common.

When criticisms of substance are made by the *Times* editors, they have been one-sided or displayed contempt for democracy in Iraq. The *Times* made post-hoc condemnations of the Bush administration for manipulating WMD intelligence, yet these criticisms were too late to have prevented the United States from entering into a conflict based on false pretenses.[4] More critical coverage of the WMD issue should have been expected from the media prior to going to war, as plenty of critical intelligence was available in 2002 and early 2003.

The *New York Times*'s attacks on Iraq's elected officials as ineffectual and unenlightened reveals much about the paper's paternalistic commitment to "democracy promotion." That the United States—by dissolving Iraq's army, government, intelligence agencies, and police—might have been responsible for creating the conditions for civil war in Iraq was apparently unfathomable to the editors of the "paper of record." Although the July editorial admits that Americans share blame for dissolving Iraq's governing infrastructure, the occupation is defended as promoting stability and security, rather than the main cause of instability and insecurity.

The *New York Times* editorial above is important because it represents the limits of dissent in the American press. This book dissects those limits in greater detail, stressing the government and mass media's use of propaganda in the "war on terror." Most intellectuals are uncomfortable with the claim that the media manipulate political information. As a result, few undertake either the study of propaganda or its harmful effects for democracy. The aims of this book are straightforward: I examine how the U.S. media frame foreign policy in accord with the views of political officials. I demonstrate this point by examining media coverage of U.S. relations with Iraq, Iran, and Afghanistan. The propaganda role of the American press is analyzed through a number of issues, including withdrawal and civil war in Iraq, Iran's alleged nuclear weapons development, and U.S. escalation in Afghanistan. Official propaganda is not physically forced upon news editors and journalists; rather, they willingly adopt such propaganda by restricting public debate to the spectrum of agreement and disagreement expressed by America's bipartisan political elites. This study demonstrates the incredible consistency of journalists, editors, and news outlets in internalizing and disseminating official views, and at the expense of dissenting public views.

When Media Goes to War also dissects the coverage of Iraq in the foreign media, distinguishing their reporting from that in the American press. By questioning the moral foundation of the "war on terror," these outlets demonstrate their independence from U.S. propaganda. Finally, this work reviews the effects of American media on the public regarding the issues of Iraq, Iran, and Afghanistan. The indoctrinating effects of media are not always uniform or long-lasting. Many Americans do reject official foreign policy views, although there are clear limits to the public's independence from the propaganda state.

Edward Herman and Noam Chomsky's landmark work, *Manufacturing Consent: The Political Economy of the Mass Media,* remains vital to the study of the press. Herman and Chomsky formulate "an analytical framework that attempts to explain the performance of the U.S. media in terms of basic institutional structures and relationships within which they operate. It is our view that, among other functions, the media serve, and propagandize on behalf of, the powerful societal interests that control and finance them."[5] Media propaganda functions, Herman and Chomsky argue,

> to inculcate and defend the economic, social, and political agenda of privileged groups that dominate the domestic society and the state. The media serves this purpose in many ways: through selection of topics, distribution of concerns, framing of issues, filtering of information, emphasis and tone, and by keeping the bounds of debate within acceptable premises.[6]

In *Manufacturing Consent*, Herman and Chomsky describe five filters through which propaganda messages are created by media and disseminated to the American public. These filters include: 1. "concentrated [business] ownership, owner wealth, and profit orientation of the dominant mass media firms"; 2. "advertising as the primary income source of the mass media"; 3. "the reliance of the media on information provided by government, business, and 'experts' funded and approved by these primary sources and agents of power"; 4. the use of official and elite-based "'flak' as a means of disciplining the media"; 5. and "anti-communism as a national religion and control mechanism." While anti-socialist and anti-communist rhetoric continue to be a mainstay of media commentary today, the fifth filter can also be interpreted to include anti-terrorism as another means of silencing criticism.

Though the corporate media remain formally independent from government, informally, media outlets are dominated by official sources. Reporters overwhelmingly rely upon government voices in constructing news stories. Sometimes media and government propaganda are one and the same, as in the case of the uncritical dissemination of speeches outlining U.S. foreign policy from government officials. A case in point is media transmission of presidential propaganda following the 9/11 terrorist attacks. Previous studies have found that media outlets marginalized the possibility of a peaceful settlement of the conflict with Afghanistan. Americans were rarely exposed to peaceful proposals for averting war, although peace may have been possible if the United States had presented evidence of Osama bin Laden's involvement in 9/11 in order to extradite him to the United States.[7]

The president is often able to dominate public opinion in times of war. President George W. Bush's effectiveness was displayed most dramatically following September 11, 2001. Speaking before the public and Congress about the necessity for war, Bush warned of the dangers of the al-Qaeda network. He spoke of the need to "close immediately and permanently every terrorist training camp in Afghanistan" and destroy a group that was intent on "imposing its radical beliefs on people everywhere." The U.S. response to the 9/11 attacks, Bush promised, would involve a "lengthy campaign" continuing indefinitely into the future.[8] U.S. media outlets, as documented in scholarly analysis, were overwhelmingly sympathetic to Bush's plans for war.[9]

The American public was already strongly sympathetic to an attack on Afghanistan. In the month following the attacks, 90 percent of Americans supported using force against the perpetrators of the acts, and 70 percent supported going to war with Afghanistan.[10] Presidential rhetoric played a significant role in *increasing* support for war from an already sympathetic public. Eighty-three percent of those who viewed the President's speech to Congress felt it made them "more confident in this country's ability to deal with this crisis." As Figure 1 demonstrates, those exposed to Bush's speech were significantly more likely than those who did not

FIGURE 1.0: Support for War After 9/11

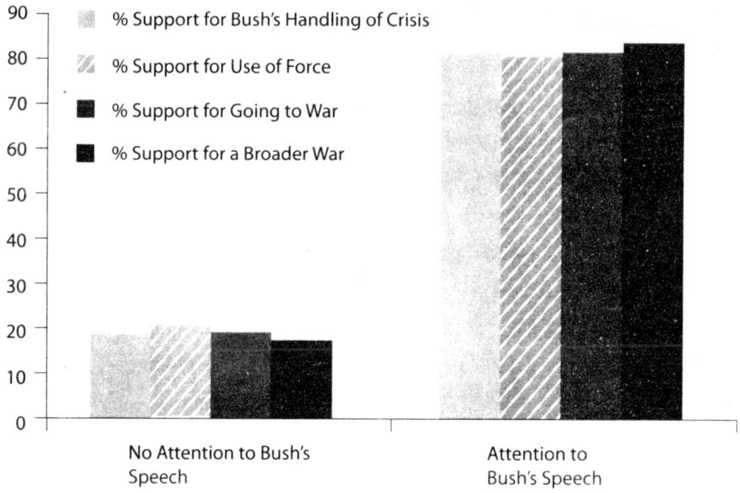

Source: See the September 2001 survey from CBS, available through the *Inter-University Consortium for Political and Social Research* (http://www.icpsr.org).

watch it to support Bush's handling of the crisis, the use of force against Afghanistan, and the use of force against other states that may have supported al-Qaeda.[11] These data represent strong evidence that political leaders and sympathetic media outlets can be very successful in their efforts to "manufacture consent" for specific foreign policy initiatives.

The concept of hegemony is particularly useful in understanding media propaganda. Hegemony was originally developed by the Italian Marxist Antonio Gramsci in the early twentieth century. Gramsci defined hegemony by distinguishing between the use of "coercion and consent" in modern democracies. Societal elites typically exercise leadership over subordinate groups and individuals through ideological controls, rather than through coercion. Hegemony is "rooted in an economically dominant, or potentially dominant, mode of [capitalist] production."[12] The role of the "dominant fundamental [political and economic] group" is not to force subordinates into submission through the use of violence. Quite the opposite, "consent is 'historically' achieved through the prestige, and consequent confidence, which the dominant group enjoys because of its position and function in the world of [economic] production."[13] In Gramsci's application, hegemony presupposes "an active and practical involvement of hegemonized groups."[14] As we shall see, one such group is journalists.

The relevance of hegemony to studies of media seems clear when discussing reporting on foreign conflicts. Media outlets exercise varying levels of hegemonic dominance over much of the general public, with many news viewers (particularly the most affluent of Americans) actively consenting to official doctrines that are established by political officials. Journalists and editors not only sympathetically report on the activities of political elites, but are, for all intents and purposes, a part of the elite themselves. The hegemonic approach to media studies focuses on the "pressures toward commodification of news media and its consequences for the way in which power is distributed through the material conditions of the capitalist system."[15] Hegemony theorists contend that reporters and editors have been co-opted within a system where they actively subscribe to the norms that drive the capitalist system of economic production, thereby circumventing the need for regular suppression and censorship from business owners above them.

Media programming actively constructs reality in preference of pro-capitalist, pro-official interpretations of the world.[16] Hegemonic media practices are reflexively accepted by reporters without critical reflection. They are buttressed by journalists' reliance on official sources.

Communication scholar Robert McChesney stands at the forefront of the hegemonic critique of mass media.[17] McChesney faults corporate media for failing to provide a "rigorous accounting of people in power" or to "provide reliable information" through pursuit of a "wide range of informed opinions" on important issues. While media outlets define themselves through professional "objectivity" and neutrality, reporters are typically "oblivious to the compromises with authority they routinely make," as seen in such subtle acts as the equation of the "spread of 'free markets' with the spread of democracy" within news stories.[18]

Gramsci originally developed hegemony as an explanation for why the masses failed to rise up against capitalist government throughout Europe, but scholars today appropriate hegemony to argue that capitalist media challenge the state. This perversion of hegemony is most clearly evident in the work of Todd Gitlin, who argues that the media not only "specializes in formulating and conveying the national ideology," but also "take[s] account of certain popular currents and pressures, symbolically incorporating . . . groups out of power—radical students, farm workers, feminists, [and] environmentalists . . . [which] can contest the prevailing structures of power and definitions of reality."[19] Gitlin's analysis neglects the fact that hegemony was originally conceived as a foundational critique of the capitalist state, not as a means of exploring how competing factions within the capitalist state may dispute the best application of military force and the most effective promotion of capitalism abroad.[20]

Gitlin's argument that "hegemonic routines of news coverage are vulnerable to the demands of oppositional and deviant groups [such as antiwar groups]" finds little support in this book.[21] Chapter 2, for example, examines how the views of progressive-left antiwar protestors are systematically censored from mass media coverage. Mainstream critics of the war may be strongly represented in media coverage, but none of their attacks on the war substantively challenge the "right" of the United States to invade sovereign nations, or characterize U.S. policy as aggressive, terrorist, illegal, or imperial. These claims *are* made by progressives (and much of the general public), but they are ignored in the mass media. Chapters 7 and 8 chronicle the conditions under which the public expresses criticisms that morally challenge the foundations of U.S. actions abroad. However, contrary to Gitlin's claims, little evidence exists that reporters or editors play a conscious role in fostering mass resistance to government propaganda.

If we are to discuss propaganda, we must have a clear definition of the concept. Herman and Chomsky's five filters do not represent the crux of what constitutes propaganda; rather, they represent the *means* by which propagandistic messages are conveyed by media. Chomsky defines propaganda as the limiting of debate to those "acceptable" views that are voiced by the major political parties. As Chomsky explains, media "reflexively adopt the presuppositions" that drive official debate in Washington.[22] In a "democratic propaganda system," the mass media

> does not proclaim the party line—so that it can be easily refuted—but presupposes it, thus helping to establish it even more deeply as the very precondition of discussion, while also providing the appearance of a lively debate.[23]

Sadly, few scholars explore the ways in which media employ propaganda.[24] Many of the most prominent studies of media in mainstream academia fail to cite *Manufacturing Consent* or examine how media reporting is propagandistic.[25] In a rare reflection, Eric Herring and Piers Robinson explain, "Most commonly, Chomsky [and his propaganda model are] not denounced, misinterpreted or engaged with. He is simply ignored."

Why have most scholars ignored or condemned the propaganda model *before* subjecting it to serious empirical testing? An answer to this question seems obvious for those who contemplate it: most scholars fall ideologically within the bipartisan ideological framework of which Herman and Chomsky are so critical. As political scientist John Zaller argues, "Most American social scientists are moderate/centrist in their personal views, which makes us reluctant to structure our arguments in terms of a book as non-centrist as *Manufacturing Consent* seems to be."[26]

It seems clear that most critics of Herman and Chomsky's propaganda model either have not bothered to actually read *Manufacturing Consent* or have not bothered to seriously engage in the arguments made by the authors. The vast majority of the academic attacks on the authors are lacking in insight, systematically distorting Herman and Chomsky's arguments and findings. Again, the reason for such attacks seems obvious: most scholars reject any personal responsibility for challenging a media system that serves concentrated political and economic power.

Mainstream academics openly dismiss claims that the media should be responsible for challenging official propaganda, instead maintaining that media need only "convey the policy recommendations of leading political figures, and to indicate, after the dust has settled, whether the advice succeeded or failed."[27] W. Lance Bennett, Steven Livingston, and Regina Lawrence argue that critical media reporting is dependent upon the emergence of bipartisan disputes between Democrats and Republicans: "The U.S. press system generally performs well—presenting competing views and vigorous debate—when government is already weighing competing initiatives in its various legal, legislative, and executive settings."[28]

Hostility toward the creation of a press that is independent of government propaganda is common in academia. Scholars are reluctant to dispute the "legitimacy" of elected leaders on issues with which both parties agree.[29] Extending debate outside bipartisan views is seen as possible only in an "ideal world," while reporters are seen as lacking the moral authority or "wisdom" to defy government propaganda.[30] Some scholars simply redefine what counts as a free, independent press in order to excuse media dependence on the state. Where contemporary definitions of "independence" require that an actor or institution "not look to others for one's opinions or for guidance in conduct," scholars redefine independence to include the domination of media by the major parties.[31] Political scientist Scott Althaus, for example, presents "evidence for press independence" as including media challenges to the 1991 Gulf war as potentially resulting in a "quagmire."[32] W. Lance Bennett and Steven Livingston cite journalists' questioning of the "government['s] misjudgment [in 2003] regarding the Iraqi embrace of liberation by American troops and subsequent rise to democracy" as confirmation of a media independence.[33]

It is difficult to see how the examples cited above constitute independence from government. How can media be "independent" of government propaganda when journalists' very critiques of war are restricted to those that exist within accepted partisan frameworks? Independence is defined as freedom *from* government influence and actions, not as reliance *on* them. The arguments above remain deeply cynical in their opposition to critical expectations that media serve an adversarial role against government manipulation. One crucial component is missing from each of these condemnations of independent media—namely an active role for the American public in democratic deliberation. Scholars maintain that media's criticism of government is dependent upon the room allowed by disagreements between political officials, rather than those allowed by mass opposition to government. That we might expect media to question official actions by reacting to public discontent (rather than simply to official discontent), does not factor into the worldview of most scholars.

Government officials, it seems, are expected to be self-regulating, with each party holding the other accountable for its transgressions, and no independent role allowed for media or the public. Such expectations are extremely problematic for those who are committed to citizen-based democracy. In a democracy, it is the public's opposition, not opposition from adversarial political officials, that represents *the most* important component of dissent. When the people's moral challenges to U.S. power are systematically cut out of media reporting (as I detail in chapters 1, 2, 7, and 8), media become little more than lapdogs of the state.

In refusing to criticize media propaganda, mainstream scholars also condemn those who offer such attacks. Such condemnations, however, are typically based on misrepresentations and distortions. Some scholars erroneously claim that *Manufacturing Consent* relies on "anecdotal evidence," despite the extensive quantitative research that appears in the work.[34] Others falsely claim that the propaganda model fails to take into account more nuanced roles that media play. Daniel Hallin argues that the propaganda model is "flat and static" because media do not serve "as a simple mouthpiece for a unified power elite."[35] This comment completely misrepresents *Manufacturing Consent*, which is dedicated precisely to showing how media coverage of the Vietnam War became increasingly open to pragmatic criticisms of the use of force after a divided elite began to disagree about the effectiveness of the war. Media criticisms of the Vietnam War, as explored in *Manufacturing Consent*, represent a strong example of communication between elites who debated whether the war was "winnable."[36]

Academics also create false dichotomies between conservative right and radical left media critics, placing themselves responsibly between such "extremes." Timothy Cook argues that "neoconservative" studies conclude that "the news media have become dominated by a 'new class' of Northeastern journalists," ensuring a liberal media bias, whereas "neo-Marxist" studies (such as Herman and Chomsky's) argue that capitalist ownership of the press ensures conservative dominance of the media.[37] Similarly, W. Lance Bennett claims:

> Liberal news audiences and critics tend to be unhappy with the news as well. Media scholars such as Edward Herman and Noam Chomsky argue that when it comes to the important national interest issues of economics, military, and foreign policy, the press is more conservative than liberal and more lapdog than watchdog.[38]

These descriptions of the propaganda model are little more than caricatures, serving to deter rather than provoke thoughtful debate. Herman and Chomsky's model is explicitly based on the prominence of liberal, adversarial bias in the press, among other types of biases. As Chomsky clarifies:

> According to the propaganda model both liberal and conservative wings of the media fall within the same framework of assumptions, so that if the system functions well, it ought to have a liberal bias, or at least appear to. Because if [media] appears to have a liberal bias, that will serve to bound thought even more effectively.[39]

Another attack that is leveled against Herman and Chomsky is that they impose their own biases on a non-ideological media system. This approach promulgates the myth of an "objective" American media. Kurt and Gladys Lang charge Herman and Chomsky with having "selected their cases [in *Manufacturing Consent*] to make a political point," as compared to other scholars claiming to adhere to standards of "objectivity."[40] The refusal of mainstream academics to admit to their own ideological biases, however, does not mean those biases do not exist.

Similarly to Herman and Chomsky, mainstream scholars express controversial political views in their works. These views, however, are taken for granted as inherently true, due to the unwillingness of most scholars to challenge them. Every time scholars discuss terrorism as a part of the actions of other states but not those of the United States, they reveal their commitment to the orthodoxy of state power.[41] Every time an academic assumes the United States is promoting democracy abroad while U.S. leaders violently attack democratically elected governments, they demonstrate the subjectivities of their discipline.[42] Such contentions, as we will see in this book's conclusion, are extremely controversial throughout the rest of the world, where U.S. power is not viewed so benevolently.

A final attack on the propaganda model faults it for failing to take into account the professional values of journalists, which supposedly ensure partial or full media independence from the state. Kurt and Gladys Lang take issue with Herman and Chomsky's alleged failure to "inquire into how events becomes news" and their neglect of journalistic norms and values.[43] Michael Schudson dismisses Herman and Chomsky's comparisons of the Soviet *Pravda* newspaper with the *New York Times*, in terms of both papers' dissemination of propaganda. The analogy, Schudson maintains, is "misleading," "mischievous," and "sophomoric," since U.S. reporters are non-ideological, compared to Soviet reporters who express partisan views.[44]

The possibility that journalists may report the world through an ideological prism that rewards power has received little attention in mainstream studies. Schudson discusses the need "to recognize news as a social and cultural institution [that] is far more complicated than anything one could reduce to an articulate political ideology."[45] Edward Epstein argues against notions that "news is largely predetermined by newsmen's economic and social class. . . . The trouble with this approach is that it tacitly assumes that newsmen have a stable set of values or ideologies to which they are inextricably attached and which they carry with them to the news organization they work for."[46] Supposedly, journalists are "nonpartisan" and "detached" in their efforts to "make sure facts are doing the talking, not the reporter's own preconceived notions."[47]

There is good reason to question attacks on the propaganda model for its focus on macroeconomic and political structures, rather than on micro-level processes involving journalistic routines, values, and norms. Herman and Chomsky admit that "no simple model [including theirs] will suffice to account for every detail of such a complex matter as the working of a national media. A propaganda model, we believe, captures essential features of the process, but it leaves many nuances and secondary effects unanalyzed."[48] Despite the authors' admissions of the limits of the propaganda model, available evidence suggests that it accounts for journalistic norms quite effectively. Contrary to the earlier claims from mainstream scholars that journalists are non-ideological, chapters 4 and 5 present ample evidence that reporters introduce blatantly ideological views into newscasts regarding events in Iraq, Iran, and Afghanistan. Journalists' claims that they are objective need to be seriously examined. The outcome of reporting is what matters, not the self-perceptions or rationalizations of journalists.

I have referred to several chapters above, but it is useful to lay out a more formal outline of what is to follow. The outline for this book is laid out below, with brief descriptions provided for each chapter. Readers will find that the chapters effectively stand on their own, and that they may skip around, reading sections that most interest them without losing sight of major concepts and themes. Each chapter focuses on different political issues, but all relate to the study of media propaganda. These issues are described below.

Chapter 1 examines U.S. and U.K. media coverage of the Iraq withdrawal question. Media outlets examined in both countries include the *New York Times*, *Washington Post*, NBC, ABC, CBS, and CNN in the United States and the *Times* and *Independent* of London in the United Kingdom. This chapter finds that the outlets studied in Britain are often relatively less propagandistic than those studied in the United States, and the reporting is less tailored to the debate between British political elites. After reading this chapter it should be clear that there is significantly more diversity in U.K. media outlets than in U.S. media.

Chapter 2 expands the discussion of Iraq withdrawal. It focuses on the American press, examining how media frame antiwar movements. Numerous outlets are examined, including the *New York Times*, *Los Angeles Times*, *Washington Post*, *Washington Times*, *Chicago Tribune*, CNN, Fox News, *Time*, *Newsweek*, and *U.S. News and World Report*. An analysis is undertaken to measure the extent to which moral and foundational criticisms (those framing the Iraq war as illegal under international law, driven by oil interests, or as exacting too great a toll on Iraqi civilians) and procedural criticisms (framing the war as too costly or unwinnable) appear in coverage of Iraq withdrawal. A study of media coverage of the September 15, 2007, antiwar protest in Washington is also undertaken.

Chapter 3 answers a simple question: To what extent are human rights violations highlighted in American media coverage in allied and enemy states? Herman and Chomsky claim that the victims of state violence in enemy states (designated "worthy" victims) receive more attention than the victims of violence in allied states (designated "unworthy" victims). This chapter finds that Herman and Chomsky's prediction regarding worthy and unworthy victims holds in the case of U.S. media coverage of Iraqi and Turkish Kurds, as well as in regard to the 2007 congressional dispute over the Turkish government's responsibility for the Armenian genocide. Media coverage of civilian casualties is differentiated into two categories: worthy victims in the case of enemy states, specifically regarding Saddam Hussein and his repression of Iraqi Kurds, and unworthy victims killed by the United States and its allies.

Chapter 4 provides a background to the study of journalistic values and practices. Sympathetic media coverage of war in Iraq is seen as a product of socialization and indoctrination, rather than primarily as a result of government coercion. Differences are highlighted between journalistic norms driving media coverage in the United States and United Kingdom. U.K. media outlets such as the *Guardian*, *Independent*, and *New Statesman* are characterized as less reliant on propaganda in their framing of foreign policy issues.

Chapter 5 dissects American and British media coverage of Iran and its civilian nuclear program. The chapter focuses specifically on three British outlets, including the *Guardian*, *New Statesman*, and *Economist*, and a number of American ones, including the *Washington Post*, NBC, *Newsweek*, *Time*, and the *Chicago Tribune*. There has been much controversy in the West regarding the program, as Western leaders maintain that the civilian nuclear program is a cover for the development of nuclear weapons. International weapons inspectors and U.S. intelligence bodies maintain the opposite, that there is no evidence of a nuclear weapons program. Media coverage of the Iranian program is analyzed so as to ascertain how journalistic routines and practices influence propagandistic reporting on Iran.

Chapter 6 reviews reporting on Iraq across the globe. Few studies have been done thus far on cross-national media. This chapter addresses two questions: To what extent are people all over the globe subject to different levels of media attention directed at the Iraq war? How different do media throughout the world depict events in Iraq? Surprisingly little is known about these issues, due to the heavy emphasis of academics on United States and allied media. I sample thirteen English and Spanish language newspapers, including those in the United States, Canada, Mexico, Spain, the United Kingdom, Hong Kong, Australia, South Africa, New Zealand, Thailand, Pakistan, Singapore, and Israel.

My analysis demonstrates that national newspapers cover the Iraq war more or less intensely and sympathetically based on their level of political and economic involvement in the capitalist campaign. Those countries that were/are most heavily involved in the intervention devote the most attention to the conflict and are the most sympathetic to allied war aims, whereas countries that are not directly involved generally devote less attention and are less sympathetic to the conflict.

Chapter 7 addresses a few simple questions. How does the public respond, if at all, to changes in information regarding U.S. involvement in Iraq and Iran? Does opinion change in rational, predictable directions? What major factors influence the mass public in turning against war? Increases in the war's financial and human costs, increases in violence in Iraq, and downturns in the U.S. economy play important roles.

Chapter 8 addresses the media's effects on public attitudes toward war, focusing on the role of individual attention to politics, formal education, and consumption of media on public opinion of the conflicts in Iraq, Iran, and Afghanistan. Increased consumption of news is significantly associated with increased trust in media, while strong trust in media is strongly related to trust in government. Increased consumption of media and politics, and higher levels of education, produce "indoctrinating" effects, whereby the individuals in question become more supportive of elite political views.

Chapter 8 also demonstrates the power of media in influencing public opinion on Iraq, Iran, and Afghanistan. The media may produce very powerful short-term effects on perceptions of foreign threats. In the long term, however, media effects on the public are often limited and superficial as the public begins to reject elite wartime rhetoric.

The conclusion to this book, provided in chapter 9, concerns the historic discussion undertaken by academic and political elites regarding the need to "manufacture consent" for public policy. The role of media in diverting public attention from political issues of substance is also reviewed. Mass media outlets need to step outside the bounds of bipartisan propaganda to promote a meaningful dialogue on foreign policy issues. When the views of the general public stand outside of those expressed by the political parties regarding these issues, incorporation of the public's perspectives is absolutely vital for a democratic media.

Finally, this book ends with a postscript that extends my analysis to media coverage in the age of President Barack Obama. I conclude that media coverage of U.S. foreign policy did not change significantly with the election of a Democratic president. Reporting and editorializing on Iran, Iraq, and Afghanistan under Obama remain well within the confines of bipartisan debate in Washington. Coverage of Iran systematically demonizes the Khameni regime, and reporting on Iraq continues to stress U.S. "humanitarian" goals in light of limited withdrawal. Discussion of the Obama administration's "surge" in Afghanistan remained generally positive as of early to mid 2009, although critical coverage increased in late September once U.S. political officials began to consistently and publicly criticize the conflict as unwinnable.

CHAPTER ONE

Withdrawal Pains: Iraq and the Politics of Media Deference

It makes no sense to tell the enemy when you plan to start withdrawing. All the terrorists would have to do is mark their calendars and gather their strength—and begin plotting how to overthrow the government and take control of the country of Iraq. I believe setting a deadline for withdrawal would demoralize the Iraqi people, would encourage killers across the broader Middle East, and send a signal that America will not keep its commitments. Setting a deadline for withdrawal is setting a date for failure—and that would be irresponsible. . . . Our troops are carrying out a new strategy [in Iraq]. . . . The goal of this new strategy is to help the Iraqis secure their capital, so they can make progress toward reconciliation, and build a free nation that respects the rights of its people, upholds the rule of law, and fights extremists and radicals and killers alongside the United States in this war on terror.

—GEORGE W. BUSH, May 1, 2007

Nouri al-Maliki's government will not survive because he has proven that he will not work with important elements of the Iraqi people. The Prime Minister is a tool for the Americans and people see that clearly. . . . We don't have a democracy here, we have foreign occupation. The British have given up and they know they will be leaving Iraq soon. They are retreating because of the resistance they have faced. . . . The British have realized this is not a war they should be fighting or one they can win. The Mahdi army [the al-Sadr inspired Shia militia] has played an important role in that. The British put their soldiers in a dangerous position by sending them here but they also put the people in their own country in danger. They have made enemies among all Muslims and they now face attacks at home because of their war.

—MOQTADA AL SADR, August 19, 2007

There is no shortage of controversy on the issue of the United States' withdrawal from Iraq.[1] Officials such as former president George W. Bush argued passionately that the United States must remain in Iraq to fight terrorism, promote human rights, and prevent civil war. Enemies of the occupation such as Moqtada al-Sadr maintain that the United States and its allies increase instability in Iraq and alienate the Iraqi public.

Statements from al-Sadr and Bush demonstrate the intensity of the fight over Iraq withdrawal. Many American officials vehemently oppose withdrawal deadlines. In mid-2007, Democratic political leaders stressed the need for "success" in Iraq and refused to commit to any coherent timetable for *complete* withdrawal.[2] President Barack Obama favors de-escalation, not full withdrawal of troops, claiming that troops may remain in Iraq until the end of his first term or later.[3] Conversely, the majority of Americans and Iraqis support a timetable for total withdrawal from Iraq.[4] Moqtada al-Sadr's opposition to the United States is shared by most Iraqis. Understanding the wide range of views on the occupation, however, does little to explain how these views are covered in the media systems of the United States and United Kingdom.

The invasion and occupation of Iraq is an issue of major importance. Major resources are allocated for the war effort by both countries, and there remains much congressional and parliamentary deliberation over this issue. The mass media play a crucial role in determining which voices are included in the public dialogue and which are neglected or excluded. Media influence how the debate over foreign policy is conducted by controlling what the public sees and hears.

Democratic theory posits that a wide-ranging debate is essential for the formulation of government policy. The mass media are supposed to present the largest diversity of views possible to educate citizens and political leaders regarding the nuances of political issues. Media independence (or lack thereof) from government can be measured by how media institutions treat controversial views that are not in line with the rhetoric of the Democratic and Republican parties.

Very few studies review American media reporting of international issues alongside the coverage of other countries. This chapter addresses the lack of comparative media research by examining reporting of Iraq in both the United States and United Kingdom. Only by making such comparisons between countries can one better understand the various ways in which news stories are framed, depending upon the national context in question. After undertaking this examination, I conclude that there remain dramatic differences between the British and American press in terms of their reliance on, and dissemination of, official propaganda.

DIVERGING VIEWS ON MEDIA DELIBERATION

Before we examine coverage of withdrawal from Iraq, it is important to discuss contemporary debates on mass media and its relationship with government and the American people. A number of critics argue that the media fails to hold political leaders accountable to the public. Attacking television, Internet, print, and radio alike, these critics frame media as overwhelmingly uniform in reporting foreign politics. Conversely, some speak more optimistically of an independent or "semi-independent press," whereby media deliberation is balanced by covering competing voices in the Democratic and Republican parties. Supposedly, reporting of partisan disagreement is evidence that media adequately promote criticism of government.[5] In contrast, those who speak of media propaganda stress that reporting must extend beyond the narrow confines of bipartisan debate for it to be independent.

A pertinent issue in media studies is the question: "Who deliberates?"[6] How are important issues framed? How issues are framed influences not only public policymaking but also citizens' everyday experiences.[7] Robert Entman describes framing as the "process of selecting and highlighting some aspects of a *perceived* reality."[8] Murray Edelman discusses how the images of political leaders and political enemies are socially constructed to reinforce specific views at the expense of others.[9] Edelman argues, "Audience interpretations [of news reports] . . . are manifestly constrained in some measure by what is reported, what is omitted, and perhaps most fundamentally, by the implications in news reports respecting limits upon the ability of citizens to influence policy."[10] "Agenda setting" studies examine the power of media to emphasize certain themes and concerns at the expense of others. Frank Baumgartner and Bryan Jones, for example, find a strong pro-business tone in reporting discussing economic and financial issues in the pesticide industry.[11]

Agenda-setting studies find that business and government sources tend to dominate news reporting. John Kingdon distinguishes between "visible and hidden participants" in the agenda-setting process. Visible actors include high-profile political leaders such as the president, federal appointees, members of Congress, media outlets, and political parties.[12]

Political and business leaders play a more prominent role in setting policy and in establishing the limits of public deliberation. The public plays, at best, a secondary role.

Studies also employ the concept of framing to examine the effects of media on audiences. Shanto Iyengar and Donald Kinder find strong evidence that the most commonly focused-upon "problems" in media content affect television viewers' assessments of the nation's most important issues.[13] Michael Parenti argues that news frames tend to highlight orthodox economic and political views instead of unorthodox ones. News frames favor business over labor, government officials over protestors, and put more trust in American leaders over foreign ones.[14]

Some research in political science examines the political economy of the mass media.[15] Charles Lindblom discusses the prevalence of "class indoctrination," in which a "favored class" of people "successfully indoctrinate much of the entire population in certain of its own favored attitudes, beliefs, and volitions." Indoctrination "by the most favored class is, of course, never a complete success."[16] This process is discussed at greater length in chapters 7 and 8.

Contemporary media scholars argue that criticisms of American foreign policy are most common when conflict emerges between the two parties. One prominent study analyzes debate over the use of torture in Iraq, demonstrating that criticisms of the United States for engaging in such behavior did not materialize in media coverage until after prominent political figures addressed the issue. The study looked specifically at how media were hesitant to use the word *torture* to discuss the United States' actions at Abu Ghraib, since no major political leader was willing to use the word, whereas coverage later focused heavily on torture when Senator John McCain publicly took a stand against it in his 2005 efforts to outlaw the practice.[17] Other studies of coverage of Vietnam, Iraq, and other American military efforts find that media outlets "index" their criticisms of government to fit those criticisms already made by political leaders.[18]

To date, there are very few systematic studies of how media operate across national borders. This study reviews reporting of Iraq in both the United States and United Kingdom's media, since these powers are the most heavily involved in the invasion and occupation. Little is known about how the American media operate when compared to other countries. In *Comparing Media Systems*, Daniel Hallin and Paolo Mancini claim that "media systems have historically been rooted in the institutions of the nation-state, in part because of their close relationship to the political world."[19] Concerning British media, Hallin and Mancini contend that although British broadsheet papers retain "different political orientations," they also retain "closeness" to the British party system.[20] Subsequent research reinforces the importance of this "parallelism" between the media and political systems of specific countries.[21] David Edwards and David Cromwell study propaganda in the British media. The authors convincingly argue in *Guardians of Power* and *Newspeak in the 21st Century* that British news groups "constitute a propaganda system for elite interests."[22] Little attention has been directed, outside of Edwards and Cromwell's work, to examining the question of media propaganda in recent years.[23]

MEDIA COVERAGE OF IRAQ WITHDRAWAL

In this section, I review the openness of American and British media to criticisms of the Iraq war. Focusing on the question of withdrawal, I postulate that the British media is relatively less propagandistic than the American press in its reporting. British media are expected to cite international voices and non-state actors with greater frequency than American media. British media outlets are expected to be less dependent on the views of domestic officials than their counterparts in the United States. Additionally, greater differences should be evident between individual British media outlets—when compared to American outlets—when reporting on Iraq withdrawal. The specific theoretical reasons for my expectations are discussed at length at the end of this chapter.

In the case of Iraq withdrawal, one expects that media coverage will be "indexed" to the attention political leaders pay to this issue. Following from this trend, American media attention to withdrawal is expected to dramatically increase following the first attempts by Democrats to set a timetable for partial withdrawal. This first effort occurred in June of 2006, as well as after the November 2006 midterm election, when Democrats gained majority status in Congress. As with the American press, stories in the British press covering Iraq withdrawal are expected to increase significantly following former prime minister Tony Blair's first announcement (in May of 2006) of plans for a partial withdrawal of troops. As the major agenda-setting actor in the British press, Blair's statements should provide an important cue for reporters to follow, and serve as a catalyst for increased coverage of withdrawal following his withdrawal declaration.

The January 2005 to mid-2007 period is crucial in regard to the question of withdrawal. This time frame can be split into two periods that are important in understanding public and political deliberation on withdrawal. The first period is from January 2005 to June of 2006, when the American public began to oppose the war as not "worth it" and support a withdrawal timetable. The second period, from June 2006 through mid-2007, is when deliberation about withdrawal among American officials radically intensified. By June of 2006, congressional Democrats began to address the possibility of some sort of withdrawal by introducing a required timetable. By late 2006 to early 2007, a Democratic majority emerged in Congress that made withdrawal a major political issue.

The April 2004 to mid-2007 period is vital when reviewing British stories on Iraq withdrawal. This period is also split into two. The first period is from April 2004 through April 2006, when the majority of the British public began to favor withdrawal. The second period begins in May of 2006, when Blair announced for the first time intentions to withdraw a limited number of British troops, through mid-2007, when Prime Minister Gordon Brown announced plans for a larger withdrawal.

It must be conceded that the earlier periods of public discontent are not marked by a total absence of elite opposition to occupation. A limited number of political leaders did discuss withdrawal at this time. For example, Rep. John Murtha supported withdrawal in November of 2005, but his calls were met by animosity from Republicans and by strong reservation from most Democrats. In the case of the United Kingdom some members of both the Liberal Democratic and Labour parties did call for withdrawal before Blair's mid 2006 announcement. However, the Liberal Democratic Party was in the minority in Parliament, retaining only 8 percent of the total seats in the House of Commons before the 2005 parliamentary election, and just 9.5 percent after the election. Furthermore, the Labour Party's majority control of government ensured that the Liberal Democratic Party had no formal power to force a withdrawal initiative without the support of Labour leaders. Most of the major Labour leaders were vehemently opposed to considering withdrawal prior to Blair's mid-2006 announcement, which is evident in the pro-occupation statements of Tony Blair, former home secretary John Reed, former foreign secretary Jack Straw, and former secretary of state Margaret Beckett. Because of limited political opposition in both countries in earlier periods, one would still expect some coverage of withdrawal.

An examination of news stories on Iraq reveals that reporting closely follows deliberation among the Democratic and Republican parties. Figure 1.1 and Table 1.1 summarize major trends in the *New York Times* and *Washington Post* coverage of Iraq withdrawal and demonstrate that emphasis on withdrawal increased dramatically from June 2006 onward.

Although there is substantial month-to-month variation in the number of stories printed in both papers on withdrawal, attention to withdrawal clearly increased following the first introduction of the Iraq bill in mid-2006, and radically increased during and after the November 2006 midterm election. Attention to Iraq withdrawal following the June congressional withdrawal bill outnumbers pre-June coverage by over two and a half times in the *New York Times* and is twice as prevalent in the *Washington Post.* Editorial opinions in both papers also became more supportive of withdrawal from Iraq only after the 2006 election.

By March of 2007, the *Washington Post* was still cautioning against withdrawal, lambasting those advocating troop cuts as ignoring the security needs of the Iraqi people. Calls for withdrawal, the editors argued, did not "answer the question" of "what might happen if American forces were to leave." Those who advocated withdrawal failed to "explain how continued United States interests in Iraq, which holds the world's second-largest oil reserves and a substantial cadre of al-Qaeda militants,

FIGURE 1.1: U.S Media and Iraq Withdrawal

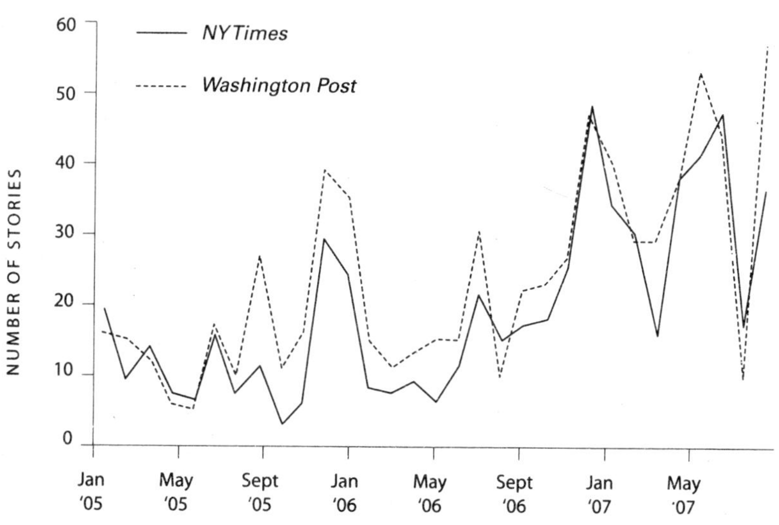

Source: Lexis Nexis

TABLE 1.1: American Newspapers on Iraq Withdrawal

Average Number of News Stories on Iraq Withdrawal		
Newspaper	Pre-Introduction Period (1/2005–5/2006)	Post-Introduction Period (6/2006–7/2007)
NEW YORK TIMES	11.2	28.8
WASHINGTON POST	16.2	32.7

Source: Lexis Nexis

would be protected . . . in fact, it [withdrawal] may prohibit United States forces from returning once they leave."

By July of 2007, however, the paper had somewhat warmed to partial cuts in troops, as it discussed the "emerging consensus" of both parties that "the Pentagon cannot sustain the current level of forces in Iraq beyond next spring [2008] without rupturing current deployment practices and placing new demands on the already stretched Army and Marine Corps."[24]

Similarly, the *New York Times* refused to advocate withdrawal until well after the 2006 election, and over two years after the American public initially concluded the war was no longer worth it, in late 2004. In a July 2007 editorial, the paper conceded that it had "put off" advocating withdrawal for some time, preferring to "wait for a sign that President Bush was seriously trying to dig the United States out of the disaster he created by invading Iraq without sufficient cause, in the face of global opposition, and without a plan to stabilize the country afterward."[25] Both papers' ideological stances remain closely indexed to the positions of the parties. While the *Washington Post*'s editorial stance corresponded much more closely to the Republican platform, the *New York Times*'s stance strongly followed the claims of Democrats who chastised the administration for failing to adequately fight the war and for alienating American allies.

A similar trend is discernible regarding the major networks. Table 1.2 summarizes an analysis of the news features and minutes dedicated to withdrawal; the average number of stories in nightly newscasts on ABC, NBC, and CBS increased by 350, 116, and 40 percent in the period following the 2006 introduction of the Democrats' withdrawal bill.[26] The average number of minutes in network stories featuring withdrawal are 330, 200, and 85 percent higher in ABC, NBC, and CBS stories in the period after June of 2006.

TABLE 1.2: American Television News and Iraq Withdrawal

Average Number of Minutes Per Month on Iraq and Withdrawal 1/2005–7/2007

Network	Pre-2006 Introduction	Post-2006 Introduction
ABC	2.4	10.4
NBC	3.6	10.8
CBS	6.6	12.2

Average Number of Features Per Month on Iraq and Withdrawal 1/2005–7/2007

Network	Pre-2006 Introduction	Post-2006 Introduction
ABC	0.6	2.7
NBC	1.2	2.6
CBS	1.7	2.4

Source: Vanderbilt News Archive

Although media in the United States heavily tailor their coverage of withdrawal to the actions of political leaders, this happens less consistently in the British press. Figure 1.2 demonstrates this point clearly. Stories in the Rupert Murdoch–owned and centrist-to-conservative leaning *Times* of London increased significantly following Blair's announcement of plans for partial withdrawal in mid-2006, but attention to withdrawal in the left-leaning *Independent* is much weaker in conforming to this pattern.

A close inspection of the *Times* of London reporting on Iraq reveals much fluctuation, but a clear increase in attention to withdrawal following Blair's initiative. Table 1.3 indicates that the average number of stories mentioning withdrawal after Blair announced withdrawal outnumbered those prior to his announcement by nearly two to one.

Conversely, coverage of withdrawal in the left-leaning *Independent* varies so widely that the reporting in the periods preceding and following Blair's announcement are less distinguishable. A closer examination of both the *Times* of London and *Independent* reveals that the papers are more distinct in their ideological orientations than are the *New York Times* and *Washington Post*. The editors at the *Times* of London

FIGURE 1.2: British Media & Iraq Withdrawal

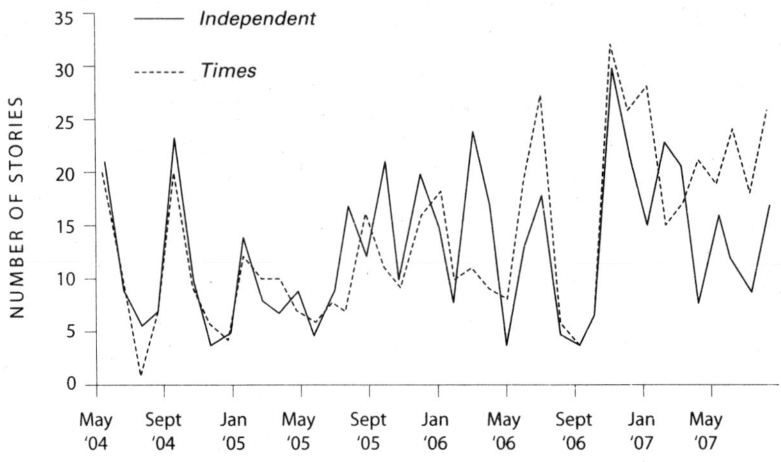

Source: Lexis Nexis

express an outlook on withdrawal that straddles the positions taken by the British Labour and Conservative parties. The paper was loath to advocate withdrawal prior to Blair's mid-2006 announcement of limited withdrawal. The *Times* remained tenacious in its opposition to withdrawal even after Blair's announcement; its editors argued in May of 2006: "There can be no question of any rapid withdrawal of British forces while the [sectarian] militias are struggling for power."[27] By October of 2007, however, the paper became more open to the Blair policy, conceding that "a timetable that sees an estimated 1,000 men and women return from Iraq before Christmas, with another substantial withdrawal by Easter, will suit all concerned."[28]

The reporting and editorial style of the *Independent* is distinct from the pattern displayed by the *New York Times*, *Washington Post*, and *Times* of London. Statistically, both American newspapers are extraordinarily simi-

TABLE 1.3: Average Number of British News Stories Per Month Mentioning Iraq and Withdrawal

Newspaper	Pre-Blair Announcement Period (4/2004–4/2006)	Post-Blair Announcement Period (5/2006–7/2007)
TIMES	10.25	19.25
INDEPENDENT	11.9	14.7

Source: Lexis Nexis

TABLE 1.4: Similarities and Differences in American and British Media Coverage (Jan 2005 – Jul 2007)

Paired Papers	Montly Overlap in Stories on Withdrawal
NYT & WASHINGTON POST	89%
TIMES & INDEPENDENT	65%
NYT & TIMES	72%
WASHINGTON POST & TIMES	72%
NYT & INDEPENDENT	28%
WASHINGTON POST & INDEPENDENT	34%

Source: Lexis Nexis

lar in their month-to-month fluctuations in reporting on withdrawal. These distinctions are represented in Table 1.4, which depicts the percent overlap in each pair of papers' monthly coverage of stories on withdrawal.[29] There is a nearly 90 percent overlap in the month-to-month fluctuations in the stories on withdrawal in the *New York Times* and *Washington Post*. This is strongly differentiated from the reporting of both the *Independent* and *Times*, of which there is a smaller overlap. Looking at coverage across countries, one can see that the differences between the *Independent* and *Times* of London are even greater than those between the conservative *Times* and American newspapers. The *Times* of London's overlap in monthly withdrawal coverage with the *New York Times* and *Washington Post* is far stronger than that seen between the *Independent* and the two American papers. In other words, there are major differences in coverage in both the United States and United Kingdom, most specifically in the foremost liberal paper in each country (the *New York Times* and *Independent*). Coverage in the *Times* of London is closer to that in the *New York Times* and *Washington Post* than it is to the *Independent*.

A review of British and American media coverage reveals the radically different priorities of each news organization. Table 1.5 summarizes major news events covered during months when reporting on withdrawal peaked in the *New York Times* and *Washington Post*.

One can see that news coverage increases during months when Democratic and Republican political leaders engage in discussion of the war, or when politically centered events such as the November 2006 midterm election or the release of the Iraq Study Group report draws the

TABLE 1.5: Peaks in Iraq Withdrawal Coverage in the *New York Times* and *Washington Post* 1/2005–7/2007

Month(s)	Stories on Withdrawal	Major Events
July 2007	36 *(NYT)* 57 *(Post)*	Congressional Withdrawal Bill on Iraq Defeated
Nov 2006	48 *(NYT)* 47 *(Post)*	Midterm Election; Democratic Congressional Majority Emerges; Iraq Study Group Report Released
May 2007	47 *(NYT)* 44 *(Post)*	Senate Rejects Withdrawal Resolution; Democrats Recant on Troop Deadline Demand
April 2007	41 *(NYT)* 53 *(Post)*	Withdrawal Debate Continues in Congress in Run-Up to Congressional Vote
March 2007	38 *(NYT)* 38 *(Post)*	Congress "Gears Up" for Debate on Withdrawal from Iraq
March 2007	29 *(NYT)* 39 *(Post)*	House Debate Over Withdrawal

Source: Lexis Nexis

attention of reporters and editors. Importantly, only one month prior to the June 2006 introduction of the first congressional withdrawal bill appears in the table of peaks in Iraq withdrawal coverage. That month experienced extensive coverage because of congressional debate over withdrawal, not because of public opposition to war. Headline coverage of American public opinion and opposition to war is minimal in the early to mid-2005 period. Revealingly, there is not a single story from January and June of 2005—the two months where polls revealed most Americans felt the war was not worth it and first favored a general timetable for withdrawal—that focuses on public opposition to war.

The peaks in Iraq withdrawal coverage in the *Times* of London are similar to those seen in the American press. Table 1.6 shows that attention spikes during months when British political and military leaders discuss withdrawal or when British leaders interact with American leaders on the issue of withdrawal. As with the American press, peaks in the *Times* are concentrated overwhelmingly during the period when Blair and other leaders take up the issue of withdrawal. No months prior to Blair's 2006 announcement appear in Table 1.6, despite strong public opposition in this earlier period.

TABLE 1.6: Peaks in Iraq Withdrawal Coverage in the *Times* of London 4/2004–7/2007

Month	Stories on Withdrawal	Major Events
Oct 2006	32	British General Calls for Withdrawal
Dec 2006	28	Bush Says No to Withdrawal; Bush-Blair Summit on Iraq Announced
Jun 2006	27	British Partial Withdrawal Begins
July 2007	26	Gordon Brown Distances from Bush Stance on Iraq Withdrawal
Nov 2006	26	British Military Leaders Announce Desire for Total Withdrawal within a Year; United States Midterm Election
May 2007	24	Brown Plans Withdrawal; Bush Vetoes Withdrawal Bill

Source: Lexis Nexis

The extensive tailoring of coverage to official debate in Washington and London is no "natural" consequence of press-state relations. Other practices exist, in which reporters prioritize events outside of official actions. The coverage of the *Independent* demonstrates this. In reporting on Iraq, the paper emphasizes a wide diversity of events in months when withdrawal coverage peaks. Such events include, as Table 1.7 demonstrates, not only major initiatives and statements from American and British officials, but also events in Iraq.

Significantly, four of the six peak months include major events in Iraq. The *Independent* has consistently retained a record of substantive opposition to the Iraq war. We can see this trend in a piece run by the *Independent* in May of 2004, the same month that a majority of British citizens first favored a withdrawal plan. The editorial, titled "The US and Britain Must Now Prepare an Orderly End to Their Occupation of Iraq," framed allied troops in Iraq as "aggressors." American and British forces were lambasted for having "bombarded and then invaded" Iraq "without the cover of a UN resolution," and for having "increasingly treated Iraqis as second-class citizens, whether by ill-treating those they have detained or . . . by their shameful failure to record the thousands of

TABLE 1.7: Peaks in Iraq Withdrawal Coverage in the *Independent* 4/2004–7/2007

Month(s)	Stories on Withdrawal	Major Events
Oct 2006	30	American General Announces a Possible Withdrawal Plan
Feb 2006	24	100th British Soldier Dies in Iraq
Sept 2004	23	Liberal Democrats Demand Withdrawal; Italian Hostage Crisis Coverage Peaks
Jan 2007	23	The Surge Begins
May 2004–Sept 2005	21	British Public Opinion Shifts in Favor of Withdrawal; 100,000 British Citizens Meet to Protest the War; British-Controlled Basra Bursts into Riots
Feb 2007–Nov 2006	21	Blair Announces Plan for Eventual Withdrawal of Half of British Troops; British Defense Secretary Announces Plan to Withdraw Thousands of British Troops; 2006 United States Midterm Election

Source: Lexis Nexis

civilian dead." In calling for an "exit strategy," the paper's editors were unequivocal: American and British forces were "unwelcome, oppressive intruders" and, "far from fostering security and stability, they are a block to peace and a focus for attack."[30] Such fiercely anti-occupation rhetoric stands in marked contrast to the pro-war orientation of the British Labour Party, and significantly exceeds the rhetoric of leaders of the Liberal Democratic Party.

The *Independent*'s news stories are characterized by a generous mix of editorializing and reporting. The paper's reporters covering Iraq, including Patrick Cockburn and Robert Fisk, openly interject their opinions into reports they file from Iraq. Stark differences are evident between the *New York Times* and *Independent*. While the *New York Times* files stories by titles such as "Chaos Overran Iraq Plan in '06, Bush Team Says," the *Independent* reports stories such as, "Iraq Aftermath: Can't Blair See That This Country Is About to Explode? Can't Bush?"[31] The framing of the

TABLE 1.8: Partisan and Non-State Actors
4/2004–7/2007 (*Independent*); 1/2005–7/2007 (*NYT*)

New York Times		*Independent*	
Type of Source	% of all Sources	Type of Source	% of all Sources
Democrat	31%	Labour	21%
Republican	33%	Liberal Democrats	5%
Independent	<1%	Conservative/Tory	4%
Labor Leaders	0%	Labor Leaders	1%
Antiwar Protestors	3%	Antiwar Protestors	6%

Source: Lexis Nexis

papers is quite different. One reflects the approach of American reporters merely repeating the analysis of American leaders, and the other assesses the war as a "fraud."[32] Fisk attacks British officials for falsely conveying the impression in the earlier days of the occupation that Iraq's security was improving: "Much of Iraq has fallen outside the control of America's puppet government in Baghdad, but we are not told. Hundreds of attacks are made against US troops every month. But unless an American dies, we are not told."[33]

Does news coverage in both countries balance the voices of competing parties in government? How do these media cover non-state actors? Table 1.8 shows that both the *New York Times* and *Independent* closely quote politicians commensurate with their percentage of seats in government. In the United States, the *New York Times* made significant efforts to split coverage evenly between Democratic and Republican sources, while devoting little attention to antiwar protestors. Similarly, the *Independent* molds its reporting to reflect the power distribution among the United Kingdom's three major parties. However, the *Independent* is twice as likely to quote antiwar protestors than the *New York Times*, suggesting that British coverage is less reliant on official sources in dissenting against the war.[34]

Aside from the antiwar figures quoted in the *Independent*, one can also classify many of the paper's reporters as antiwar. This would radically increase the presence of non-state, antiwar critics appearing in the *Independent*. After examining the polemical reporting of the *Independent*'s reporters, their antiwar leanings become more obvious. In one description of the state of the Iraq occupation, reporter Patrick

Cockburn addresses "the true extent of Britain's failure in Basra." He poses the following questions about the war: "Why is the British Army still in south Iraq and what good does it do there? The suspicion grows that Mr. Blair did not withdraw them because to do so would be too gross an admission of failure and of soldiers' lives uselessly lost. It would also have left the US embarrassingly bereft of allies."[35] In more stark language, Robert Fisk portrays Iraq as hell on earth:

> Baghdad is a city that reeks with the stench of the dead . . . the corpses are stacked, a bloody reminder that Baghdad is racked by a wave of killing and kidnapping. . . . The smell of the dead pours into the street through the air-conditioning ducts. Hot, sweet, overwhelming. Inside the Baghdad morgue, there are so many corpses that the fridges are overflowing. . . . Tony Blair says it is safer here. He is wrong. Every month is a massacre in Baghdad. Thieves, rapists, looters, American troops at checkpoints and on convoys, revenge killers, insurgents, they are shooting down the people of this city faster than ever.[36]

Fisk's antiwar posturing has no equivalent within the American media. Though many American journalists may similarly oppose the Iraq war, their criticisms of the war do not appear in media reports in the United States media.

PROPAGANDA AND IRAQ: AMERICAN CABLE NEWS

If the mass media is thoroughly dominated by official sources, this should be observable in television news stories. The analysis of CNN below examines ten months of stories (from July 2006 to April 2007, including 44 programs) from the weekly show *This Week at War*. The program is devoted primarily to the war in Iraq and United States interests in the Middle East. This ten-month period is relevant because it represents an even split of five months before the November 2006 midterm election, and five months after. This time frame encompasses both the periods before and after the emergence of the Democratic majority in Congress.

An assessment of *This Week at War* suggests that the network's news analysis is heavily skewed toward official sources. News coverage is highly routinized, relying on a few major types of themes, including regular updates on the service men and women of the week killed in Iraq; stories emphasizing the grief of their families; emphasis on sectarian violence in

Iraq; postulation about what the United States can do to decrease that violence; and far less coverage of the responsibility of American soldiers for causing Iraqi civilian deaths. Importantly, not a single antiwar activist from the family of a soldier killed in Iraq was interviewed on the program, reinforcing the false impression that military families never vocally oppose war.

As Table 1.9 indicates, the most prominent people mentioned in CNN programs are those in the executive and legislative branches and in the military. Thirteen of the top-twenty most mentioned figures are of this sort. In contrast, only two officials on the list are foreign allied leaders—former Pakistani President Pervez Musharaf and Iraqi Prime Minister Nouri al-Maliki. The remaining five spots are reserved for officially designated enemies of state: Islamist leaders Musab al-Zarqawi and Osama bin Laden, Iranian president Mahmoud Ahmadinejad, and Iraqi leaders Moqtada al-Sadr and Saddam Hussein. In summary, most who are mentioned in CNN's *This Week at War* are overwhelmingly either American officials or those who are demonized by them.

There was no room in the most-mentioned list for domestic or foreign antiwar protestors, representatives of transnational humanitarian groups, dissident scholars, or even liberal-left political leaders such as John Murtha and the late Edward Kennedy who favored withdrawal.

CNN stories rely extensively on interviews with specific types of guests, including current and former government officials, Washington-based think tanks, national reporters based in New York and Washington, and retired military leaders. Table 1.10 indicates that Washington insiders constitute a combined total of 82 percent of all guests who appeared on *This Week at War*.

Conversely, foreign officials, domestic business leaders, academics, and antiwar activists constitute less than 2 percent of all guests. Domestic non-state and non-media actors (including scholars, antiwar activists, and representatives of civil society groups) constitute only 5 percent of all guests, and none of those guests expressed antiwar views on the program. Although alternative media pundits and analysts and non-Washington-based think tank specialists constitute a sizable 10 percent of all guests, none of them spoke out against the war when interviewed.

CNN's *This Week at War* did not interview a single antiwar protestor or activist in the ten months examined. This represents a tremendous degree of discipline in systematically cutting out antiwar figures. The closest the program came to incorporating antiwar voices was an inter-

TABLE 1.9: CNN: This Week at War: Most Prominent People 6/2006–4/2007

Ranking	Number of Mentions
1. George W. Bush	473
2. Nouri al-Maliki	115
3. Osama bin Laden	98
4. Donald Rumsfeld	95
5. Ayman al-Zarqawi	63
6. Condoleezza Rice	62
7. Saddam Hussein	61
8. Mahmoud Ahmadinejad	56
9. Moqtada al-Sadr	56
10. David Petraeus	54
11. Robert Gates	54
12. John McCain	40
13. George Casey	40
14. Bill Clinton	30
15. Pervez Musharraf	28
16. Dick Cheney	27
17. John Abizaid	27
18. Hillary Clinton	26
19. James Baker	25
20. Nancy Pelosi	23

Source: Lexis Nexis

view with Lawrence Korb, former assistant defense secretary and a member of the Washington-based Center for American Progress. Korb is clearly no activist or protestor, and his criticism of the Bush administration for failing to ensure National Guard troops were fully prepared before deployment to Iraq is not in the same league as the comments of antiwar *Independent* reporters Patrick Cockburn and Robert Fisk, or antiwar activists like Cindy Sheehan. Unlike Korb, these figures take forceful stands against the legitimacy of the occupation and question American motivations for occupying Iraq.[37]

Aside from ignoring antiwar protestors, *This Week at War* also fails to interview any Iraqi officials or American citizens (people on the street)

TABLE 1.10: CNN: This Week at War 6/2006–4/2007

Guest Breakdown

Type of Guest	% of Total Guests
Gov./Former Gov. Official (United States)	17%
Gov./Former Gov. (Foreign)	<1%
Military (United States)	26%
Think Tank Specialist (Washington-Based)	23%
Think Tank Specialist (Non-Washington-Based)	3%
Reporters/Editors (Nat'l and DC Based)	16%
Non-Agenda-Setting Media Figures (International, Local, Alternative)	7%
Academic (United States)	5%
Academic (Foreign)	0%
Business Leaders (United States)	2%
Business Leaders (International)	<1%
Protestors/Activists (United States)	0%
Protestors/Activists (International)	0%

Quoted Sources

Source	% of Times Quoted
Government/Former Gov. Official	43%
Foreign Gov. Official (Allied)	5.5%
Foreign Gov. Official (Enemy)	1.4%
United States Military	28%
Foreign Military (Allied)	1.4%
Foreign Military (Enemy)	0%
Military Families	17%
Person on Street (United States)	0%
Person on Street (Foreign)	<1%
Antiwar Protestors/Activists (United States)	0%
Antiwar Protestors/Activists (Foreign)	0%
Islamist Figures	2%
IGO/NGO members	<1%

Source: Lexis Nexis

who oppose the occupation. No representatives of domestic, Iraqi, or international human rights organizations or non-governmental organizations appeared as guests. In addition, no dissident American or foreign scholars opposing the war were interviewed. The closest that *This Week at War* came to interviewing anyone matching these criteria was their interview of Shirouk Abaychi of the Iraq Foundation, which is a multifaceted organization focusing on a multitude of activities such as producing seminar papers, conducting workshops, and "civil society strengthening."[38] It is not a human rights group, nor does it explicitly take an anti-occupation stance. Furthermore, when interviewed, the program's director shared her views about the escalating sectarian crisis in Iraq but never expressed any skepticism of the United States occupation.[39]

The same pattern of privileging government and government-affiliated actors is discernible when reviewing the list of quoted sources in Table 1.10. Government and military officials constitute 71 percent of all sources quoted in *This Week at War*. If one combines the members of military families (none of which expressed any sort of dismay with the war), government, military, and military-affiliated sources account for 88 percent of all those quoted. Foreign government, military, and non-state are rarely quoted, and domestic non-state actors such as antiwar activists and "people on the street" receive literally no attention. Although allied political leaders do account for over 5 percent of all sources, that number is less than the percentage of allied sources quoted in British media sources.

CRITICISMS OF THE IRAQ WAR ON CNN

How are criticisms of the Iraq war framed when they emerge in the press? This question is addressed at length in chapter 2, and discussed below. A brief review of the content of *This Week at War* shows that support for the war is common in reporting while criticisms of the war are pragmatic in orientation rather than substantive. The need to achieve "progress" in the pacification of Iraq is commonly emphasized.[40] Reports stress the importance of the occupation, emphasizing an American role in promoting stability. Anger directed at the occupation is transformed in an Orwellian fashion into support for the American military presence. In one example, host John Roberts discusses widespread Iraqi opposition to the occupation with a guest in a September 2006 program: "Sixty-five percent of Iraqis say that they want United States forces to leave [Iraq] immediately . . . why would people in Iraq want United States forces to leave immediately, particularly since all of the analysis and a lot of statements from people there in Iraq, senior positions in Iraq, are saying if the United States pulled out, the whole place would devolve into civil war almost immediately?"[41]

Tactical criticisms of the occupation were prevalent in the period examined. In one program, CNN correspondent Michael Ware complained that Islamist forces in Iraq have escalated their attacks on the United States and civilians, and that "there's simply not enough American troops to combat them."[42] CNN senior political analyst Bill Schneider addressed the Democratic Party's claims that the war has not been efficiently fought: "What's the Democrats' plan? What's their strategy? Do they have a plan for victory in this war?"[43] CNN host John Roberts posited that the United States Army was "stretched too thin," and that "despite all of the best efforts of the United States military and the efforts to stand up Iraqi forces," the country has "push[ed] toward chaos."[44] Military leaders echod the claims of CNN reporters. Major General Donald Shepperd argued, "We need more troops to do the things that we are now doing in Iraq, which is . . . securing peace and security in Baghdad. . . . But you can't do that and you can't defeat the insurgency . . . and you can't train the Iraqis to take over all at the same time with the number of troops we have in the country right now." Failure to effectively fight the Iraq war means, as one retired general put it, that the occupation was "counterproductive" in its efforts.[45]

THE *INDEPENDENT* AND IRAQ: A CHALLENGE TO OFFICIAL PROPAGANDA

The *Independent*'s coverage is far less parochial than that of the *New York Times*. Whereas the *New York Times* is heavily propagandistic in its choice to marginalize international sources, the *Independent*'s reporting balances national and international voices. Table 1.11 summarizes the frequencies in which domestic and foreign sources are quoted in both papers. The *Independent*'s coverage of withdrawal is split nearly in half between domestic and foreign sources, whereas the *New York Times* is heavily tilted toward domestic sources.

There are tremendous discrepancies between what the *Independent* and *New York Times* deem the most important news sources. Although both papers' stories are dominated by official sources, no single source dominates *Independent* coverage to the extent that they dominate the *New York Times*. The top-twenty most quoted sources in the *Independent* and

TABLE 1.11: Domestic vs. Foreign Quoted Sources
4/2004–7/2007 (*Independent*); 1/2005–7/2007 (NYT)

New York Times		*Independent*	
% Domestic	% Foreign	% Domestic	% Foreign
86%	14%	55%	45%

Source: Lexis Nexis

New York Times are dramatically distinguished in Table 1.12. Quotes from George Bush are in first place, appearing in 21 percent more stories in the *New York Times* than in the *Independent*. The same can be said of nearly every individual who ranks in the top quoted sources.

Almost every top-ranking source in the *New York Times* was quoted in twice as many stories than the corresponding top-ranking source in the *Independent*. Essentially, individual national elites were less likely to dominate the *Independent*'s coverage, leaving more room for a diversity of sources.

There are other significant differences between the two papers as well. Whereas nineteen of the top-twenty sources in the *New York Times* were domestic officials in the executive branch, Congress, and the military, thirteen of the top-twenty sources in the *Independent* were foreign, rather than domestic officials. This represents further evidence of parochial American media coverage, as opposed to more cosmopolitan British reporting. Major foreign leaders such as former British prime minister Tony Blair, Iraqi President Jalal al-Talabani, former Iraqi prime minister Ayad Allawi, and former Iraqi prime minister Ibrahim al-Jaafari appear far less frequently in the *New York Times*. By contrast, Iraqi political leaders rank among the most quoted sources in the *Independent*.

The neglect of Iraqi sources ensures that anti-occupation developments in Iraq receive little attention in the American press. Worship of domestic sources means that the initiatives of Iraqi leaders demanding an end to the occupation are neglected. Although a majority of Iraq's parliament passed both a non-binding petition and a draft bill demanding that the United States set a plan for withdrawing (in May and June of 2007) such demands were marginalized by outlets like CNN and the *New York Times*. For example, the Iraqi pro-withdrawal draft bill just described received no headline attention in the *New York Times* during the entire month of June, when it was passed. While the pro-withdraw-

TABLE 1.12: Most Quoted Sources in British and American News 4/2004–7/2007 (*Independent*); 1/2005–7/2007 (*New York Times*)

New York Times		*Independent*	
Ranking	% of Stories Appearing in	Ranking	% of Stories Appearing in
1. George W. Bush	38%	1. George W. Bush	17%
2. Harry Reid	17%	2. Tony Blair	14%
3. Nancy Pelosi	9%	3. John Reid	6%
4. Carl Levin	9%	4. Menzies Campbell	5%
5. John Murtha	8%	5. Nouri al-Maliki	3%
6. John Warner	8%	6. Des Browne	3%
7. Dick Cheney	6%	7. Richard Dannatt	3%
8. Hillary Clinton	6%	8. Charles Kennedy	3%
9. Mitch McConnell	6%	9. Gordon Brown	3%
10. Dana Perino	6%	10. Ibrahim al-Jaafari	2%
11. John Kerry	6%	11. John Murtha	2%
12. Dan Bartlett	5%	12. Condoleezza Rice	2%
13. Tony Snow	5%	13. Jalal Talabani	2%
14. John McCain	4%	14. Harry Reid	2%
15. Barack Obama	4%	15. Donald Rumsfeld	2%
16. Stephen Hadley	4%	16. Dick Cheney	2%
17. Donald Rumsfeld	4%	17. Edward Kennedy	2%
18. Rahm Emanuel	4%	18. Ayad Allawi	2%
19. Chris Dodd	4%	19. Silvio Berlusconi	2%
20. Nouri al-Maliki	4%	20. Hillary Clinton	2%

Source: Lexis Nexis

al petition from May of 2007 was the subject of a single story in the *New York Times*, coverage was heavily tilted in favor of the American perspective. Only one Iraqi political leader was quoted discussing the bill—parliamentary member Saleh al-Igili—and he provided no reasons for why Iraqis support withdrawal. Though withdrawal coverage did increase in November of 2008, it was only because the Bush administration committed to a Status of Forces Agreement requiring a removal of troops by 2011.

No reason was provided in the May 2007 *New York Times* story (mentioning the Iraq parliament's withdrawal bill) for why the Iraqi people oppose the occupation. Rather, the report framed Iraqi demands as in line with the Bush administration's agenda. The story's reporter claimed that "the petition brings the majority of Iraqi legislators into agreement with the Bush administration: both argue that an American withdrawal should depend on the readiness of Iraqi troops." Although the story failed to report any reasons why Iraqis oppose the occupation, it did provide reasons for why the United States should remain. The U.S. Army's Major General Benjamin Mixon was quoted demanding *more* troops be sent to Iraq, claiming, "I do not have enough soldiers right now in Diyala Province to get [the] security situation moving. . . . We have plans to put additional forces in that region. . . . We just can't think about pulling out of here just like that."[46] Although this withdrawal story represents just one example of *New York Times* reporting, it effectively demonstrates that even in the instances when Iraqi politics is addressed, American officials remain the effective voices in setting the parameters of debate.

Although officials dominate American news stories on foreign policy, one might still object that this is not conclusive evidence of propagandistic news coverage. Many argue that government officials deserve an important place in media reporting, and that American news outlets are merely concentrating attention on those with the most power to set government policy. Although there is nothing inherently wrong with directing media attention to official sources, media coverage goes far beyond simply allowing officials to be heard. Rather, officials are successful in dominating the news to the point where they create reality. Government officials do not merely retain a preferred or privileged position in news reporting, they actively manufacture stories, effectively blocking out opposing views due to their tremendous power to mold stories.

Political and military leaders are tremendously successful in manufacturing news stories in the *New York Times*, but far less efficient in doing so in the *Independent*. Table 1.13 suggests that no sources are as successful in creating *New York Times* stories as official ones. Seventy-two percent of withdrawal stories in the *New York Times* originate from the statements of domestic government and military officials, rather than events in Iraq. A full 84 percent of all the stories in the paper originate from both domestic and allied government and military statements. Conversely, only 9 percent of the stories on withdrawal in the *New York Times* originate from events in Iraq or the United States. This is a significant revelation, considering that many readers and viewers of the news expect stories to reflect the reporting of journalists who travel to the Middle East and chronicle events in the region, rather than simply parroting what officials say about those events.

The routine of simply reporting official announcements in the United States is hardly natural. Other standards of journalism do exist, standards that place news events at the center of reporting. The *Independent*'s reporting on withdrawal differs greatly from that of the *New York Times* in several ways. Domestic government and military statements account for only 26 percent of all story sources, as contrasted with 72 percent of American story sources.[47] Even when domestic and allied government and military statements are included, they only account for just over half (53 percent) of all British story origins, compared with 84 percent of American story origins.

In contrast with the American press, over 10 percent of *Independent* stories originate from the statements of non-government officials, as opposed to less than 2 percent of *New York Times* stories. Much of the *Independent*'s

TABLE 1.13: News Story Origins
4/2004–7/2007 (*Independent*); 1/2005–7/2007 (*New York Times*)

New York Times		*Independent*	
Story Source	% of Total Sources	Story Source	% of Total Sources
Gov. Statements	66%	Gov. Statements	22%
Allied Gov.	12%	Allied Gov.	22%
Military	6%	Military	4%
Allied Military	0%	Allied Military	5%
Enemy Gov.	1%	Enemy Gov.	0%
Events (in Iraq)	6%	Events (in Iraq)	21%
Events (in Britain)	0%	Events (in Britain)	6%
Events (in the U.S.)	3%	Events (in the U.S.)	6%
Expert Statements	3%	Expert Statements	5%
Non Gov. Statements (U.S.)	<1%	Non Gov. Statements (U.S.)	<1%
Non Gov. (Britain)	0%	Non Gov. (Britain)	7%
Non Gov. (Iraq)	<1%	Non Gov. (Iraq)	3%

Source: Lexis Nexis

coverage is based on events occurring in the United States, Britain, and Iraq. A sizable 33 percent of all stories on Iraq withdrawal originate from events, as compared with only 9 percent in the *New York Times*.

EXPLAINING DIFFERENCES BETWEEN THE BRITISH AND AMERICAN PRESS

Although the reporting of the *Times* of London is strongly tailored to accommodate official statements and actions, it is unfair to classify the *Independent* as a propaganda agent on par with the *Times*, *New York Times*, or *Washington Post*. The newspaper is relatively less constrained by government dogma, although it is often dominated by government sources and propaganda. As he was stepping down as prime minister, Tony Blair attacked the British press as a "feral beast, just tearing people and reputations to bits."[48] Although Blair had received quite positive coverage from British papers such as the *Times* and *Telegraph* throughout his tenure, he singled out the *Independent* for its sustained attacks on the Iraq war. Blair's critical reaction should hardly be a surprise, given the antiwar views appearing in the *Independent*.

Although this chapter has shown that there are differences between British and American media, one is still left to explain *why* the coverage is different. Although this chapter cannot systematically answer this question, five explanations are postulated below, and explored in later chapters.

Media Concentration

Media critics in the United States deride the rapid consolidation of corporate media outlets, as fewer and fewer corporate conglomerates purchase more and more television, radio, Internet, and print outlets.[49] It may be the case that more diverse markets, in which media outlets are owned by a larger number of separate interests, allow for more eclectic patterns of deliberation. The cases of New York and London are instructive. Both cities have roughly comparable populations, with 8.2 and 7.5 million people respectively as of 2006. Both are global cities, and represent the economic and financial centers of the United States and United Kingdom. The cities retain radically different media markets, however, in terms of levels of ownership concentration of news outlets. Outside of tabloid and financial papers, London retains three major print newspapers: the *Daily Telegraph*, *Times*, and *Independent* (with major distribution of a fourth paper, the *Guardian* of Manchester), whereas New York has only one: the *New York Times*. The existence of four times as many major print newspapers may provide more space for a diversity of views.

Demographic Concerns

Closely related to market concentration are business concerns over catering to target markets. Since its purchase by Rupert Murdoch's News Corporation in the 1980s, the *Times* became known as a center-right paper in its political orientation, although the paper moderated its ideology following the emergence of "new Labour" and the ascendancy of former prime minister Tony Blair. Brian McNair chronicles Rupert Murdoch's swing during the mid-1990s from supporting conservative British political leaders to "new Labour" as driven by pragmatic and financial concerns. Though Murdoch "remained a conservative right-winger at heart, he calculated that the political environment [following Blair's victory], and public opinion with it, had shifted so far that it was in his commercial interests to favour 'new' Labour over the old and discredited Conservatives."[50]

If the *Times* and other formerly right-wing papers now view it as more profitable to cater to centrist readers, the *Independent* views its target market as composed of center-to-left readers, liberals, and even left radicals. The paper was formed in the mid-1980s as a response to the growing disenchantment of former *Daily Telegraph* reporters with the conservative-leaning ideology of that paper. As one of the most prominent reporters for the *Independent*, Robert Fisk left the *Times* in 1988 as a result of the paper's censorship of one of his stories regarding the United States attack on Iran Air Flight 655. Since his migration, Fisk has helped ensure that the *Independent* retains a reputation as the United Kingdom's preeminent progressive newspaper on foreign policy issues.

Cultural Norms, Socialization, and News Routines

Media studies emphasize the importance of reporters' news "routines" in constructing stories. Timothy Cook includes in this routinization "the strategic ritual of objectivity."[51] Unlike their American counterparts, British reporters are not subject to the rigid socialization of American journalism schools, which require conforming to journalistic norms of "objective" reporting. While schools promoting journalistic "neutrality" emerged in the United States simultaneously alongside the rapid commercialization, consolidation, and corporatization of American newspapers, the United Kingdom failed to undergo an identical transformation.

To this day, values of "objectivity" do not resonate quite as strongly with many British journalists as they do with American reporters. Robert Fisk describes the chasm between American and British reporting as follows: "I think we are dealing here with a problem in American journalism school, which thank god we Brits don't go through. We do politics and history and other subjects at [the] university. . . . My paper sends a correspondent to live abroad to tell us what happens there, not to tell us what two sides are saying, I can read that on the wire. . . . I want to know what the reporter thinks. If you send a reporter to a region, you send him there because you think he is intelligent, fair, [and a] decent reporter; you don't have to ask him to give 50 percent of every paragraph to each side."[52] In short, "objectivity" does not appear to be as highly valued a cultural norm in the United Kingdom's media system.

Transnational Political-Economic Linkages

A country's position in the global political-economic system may strongly influence its media coverage of foreign issues. The British media's concern with the opinions of foreign leaders may relate to its history of political and economic consolidation with other members of the European community. The United Kingdom's incorporation into the European Union may have encouraged media and political elites to take a more cosmopolitan outlook when it comes to foreign relations and foreign policy formulation. Such a political context is different from that of the United States. Although the United States has entered into multilateral agreements throughout its history, none approach the level to which British politics is intertwined with that of other nations and transnational governing institutions of the European Union countries. Simply put, a country like the United Kingdom can seldom afford to ignore the views of neighbor countries with which it retains close relations.

Economic and Military Power

A state's economic and military power may also influence its media reporting. As the world's leading economic and military power, the United States has traditionally relied on the exercise of hard power to an extent greater than other nations lacking its economic and military capabilities. The economic stakes of United States military intervention in the Middle East as a result are much greater than those of allied countries that have committed no resources to the occupation of Iraq. Although the United Kingdom clearly had much at stake in the occupation of Iraq, its troop concentrations were relatively low compared with the United States (a few thousand British troops as contrasted with 150,000 American troops as of early 2009) and its forces occupied a smaller part of the country than the United States. British troops were completely withdrawn from Iraq by September of 2009. In short, the United Kingdom invested significantly less in the conflict in terms of financial, military, and human resources, and this may translate into a lower level of pressure exerted upon media outlets refusing to conform to official statements and agendas.

All five of these explanations should be subjected to extensive examination, and applied to a far wider range of countries, to evaluate how well they explain a state's media coverage of its government's foreign policy and coverage of global issues. Many of these explanations are explored at greater length in the following chapters.

CHAPTER TWO

There Are No Protestors Here: Media Marginalization and the Antiwar Movement

> A colleague and his friend had just returned from inside Fallujah and said that, along with one correspondent for Al-Jazeera, they had been the only two reporters inside the city. He claimed that most of what he'd been witness to wasn't making the news, such as the heavy United States casualties along the road between Baghdad and Fallujah, as well as inside Fallujah. He informed us that the military had ordered families to leave the city, and commenced bombing them while they made their attempt to exit. He told unbelievable stories, making the United States onslaught sound more like a Mongol invasion of barbaric proportions, complete with pregnant women being sliced open by United States Marines, deliberate targeting of children and elderly, and bombings of ambulances.[1]
>
> —DAHR JAMAIL, unembedded journalist in Iraq, April 2004

> During the course of the roughly four hours we were at that small clinic, we saw perhaps a dozen wounded brought in. Among them was a young woman, eighteen years old, shot in the head. She was having a seizure and foaming at the mouth when they brought her in; doctors did not expect her to survive the night. Another likely terminal case was a young boy with massive internal bleeding. I also saw a man with extensive burns on his upper body and wounds in his thighs that might have been from a cluster bomb; there was no way to verify in the madhouse scene of wailing relatives, shouts of "Allahu Akbar" [God is great], and anger at the Americans.[2]
>
> —RAHUL MAHAJAN, unembedded journalist in Fallujah, April 2004

Critical news reporting poses a major threat to official narratives that claim altruistic motivations and humanitarian intent. Few would disagree, that Rahul Mahajan's and Dahr Jamail's descriptions of American military operations in Iraq pose a major challenge to the Bush administration's claims that the United States is playing a positive role in stabilizing the country. If American journalists claim to "objectively" report the news, do reports like those above receive much attention in stories on Iraq? These stories should receive attention in a media system priding itself in reporting critical accounts of the war.

This chapter examines media coverage of those who substantively challenge the occupation of Iraq. Scholars argue over how dependent media institutions are on government. Examining the range of views excluded from reporting will assist in furthering our understanding of the media's "adversarial" role in questioning government. Intellectuals consider the news media to be an important player in politics. In his much cited *The Press and Foreign Policy*, Bernard C. Cohen argues that "[news] correspondents are authentic participants in the politics of foreign policy-making."[3] Communication scholar Shanto Iyengar describes news frames as taking two forms: episodic and thematic. News is framed through specific "episodes," as seen in coverage of an antiwar protest, for example. Stories may also be framed through "thematic" approaches emphasizing general social trends, such as increasing inequality or persistence of unemployment.[4] This study examines media framing from both episodic and thematic perspectives, reviewing how media outlets portray dissenting views expressed at antiwar protests and by antiwar critics.

Reporters and editors are generally hesitant to portray political leaders—particularly the president—in a negative light. In *Making News: A Study in the Construction of Reality*, Gaye Tuchman asserts that reporting during Watergate threatened images of the president as a respected public official. The "president as crook" framework that was established was a major problem for the media:

> Delegitimating the presidency threatens the very basis of news work. Challenging the legitimacy of offices holding centralized information dismantles the news net. If all officialdom is corrupt, all its facts and occurrences must be viewed as alleged facts and alleged occurrences. Accordingly, to fill the news columns and airtime of the news product, news organizations would have to find an alternative and economic method of locating occurrences and constituent facts acceptable as news.[5]

Previous works found that the favorableness of media coverage to social movements depends to a great extent on how well those movements are accepted by government. In *Silencing the Opposition: Antinuclear Movements and the Media in the Cold War*, Andrew Rojecki concludes that media sympathy for the nuclear test ban movement was contingent upon presidential sympathy to the movement. A lack of elite cohesion in opposition to progressive-left movements allows for increased media openness in covering these movements. Rojecki finds that "antinuclear movements made their greatest strides in situations of political uncertainty. In those times, when the administrations [Eisenhower, Kennedy, and Reagan] were divided and provided less certain cues [regarding their feelings on the nuclear test ban], the movements gained credibility, not necessarily because their messages were more credible, but because the official message was devalued."[6] Rojecki found that *New York Times* coverage of the test ban movement doubled during the Kennedy presidency, when a nuclear ban received strong rhetorical support, as opposed to during the Eisenhower years, when official support was less clear.[7] Similarly, Robert Entman found that negative media attention to the antinuclear movement "discouraged involvement by those ordinary citizens who supported the remedy [of limiting nuclear proliferation] but remained outside the groups' activities."[8]

HEGEMONY, MASS MEDIA, AND SOCIAL MOVEMENTS

Scholars approach the question of media coverage of social movements from a variety of perspectives. Todd Gitlin examines media coverage of antiwar protests and activism through a cultural lens. He stresses the processes by which reporters are socialized to reinforce dominant institutional norms and routines. Media play a fundamental role in "the distribution of ideology . . . every day, directly or indirectly, by statement and omission, in pictures and words, in entertainment and news and advertisement, the mass media produce fields of definition and association, symbolic and rhetoric, through which ideology becomes manifest and concrete."[9] Ideological monopolies over media content are secured through journalistic routines that "are structured in the ways journalists are socialized from childhood, and then trained, recruited, assigned, edited, rewarded, and promoted on the job; they decisively shape the ways in which news is defined, events are considered newsworthy, and 'objectivity' is secured."[10]

Gitlin employs hegemonic theory in analyzing media. In coverage of dissent, the American media represent the interests of "an alliance of powerful groups in search of an enduring basis for legitimate authority."[11] Included among this group are government officials, economic leaders, business owners, prominent intellectuals and scholars. Under hegemonic theory, these groups forge alliances in utilizing media to promote dominant class interests. The major ideological underpinnings reinforcing hegemony are considered beyond challenge in media reporting and deliberation. "Out of bounds" areas include the private ownership of capitalist industry, as well as assumptions that the United States is unconditionally committed to promoting democracy abroad.[12]

Gitlin's *The Whole World Is Watching: Mass Media in the Making and Unmaking of the New Left* is perhaps the most influential book on the topic of media and social movements. In this work, Gitlin demonstrates how media elevate the antiwar movement in the public mind, while also attempting to discount the movement by promoting a series of negative stereotypes against its members. He discusses an incident at the *New York Times*, where one reporter who was deemed too sympathetic to the anti-Vietnam War movement was pulled from covering protests. Other reporters were sent out and expected to find evidence of domestic protestors' ties to the Soviet Union, although such efforts were typically fruitless.[13] *New York Times* reporters were subject to potential censorship in subtle ways. One former editor for the paper recounts that, during the Vietnam War, publisher Arthur Hays Sulzberger systematically reviewed the content of news stories filed by journalists in the field: "I wanted our reporters to do their work without feeling that the publisher was constantly looking over their shoulders. In truth, however, he [Sulzberger] was. He read the paper closely and he had a very personal feeling about what he saw there—if the *Times* looked silly, he felt that he looked silly."[14]

ALTERNATIVE HEGEMONIC THEORIES OF THE PRESS

Gitlin certainly enjoys no monopoly over the application of hegemony to the study of media. Edward Herman and Noam Chomsky contend that dissident voices are marginalized by "the reliance of media on information provided by government, business, and 'experts' funded and approved by these primary sources and agents of power."[15] Chomsky argues that those who refuse to conform to the parameters of debate set by partisan political and economic leaders are systematically denied media exposure. Of course, disagreement may not be limited only to those battles between Democratic and Republican officials. One may also speak of propaganda as the limitation of reporting and debate to disagreements between political *and* economic/business leaders. As Herman and Chomsky claim, critical sources speaking outside of political-economic elite circles "may be avoided not only because of their lesser availability and higher cost of establishing [their] credibility, but also because the primary [official] sources may be offended and even threaten the media using them."[16]

The major point of departure between Gitlin's and Herman and Chomsky's theories relates to their descriptions of media openness to dissident views. Gitlin argues that the "hegemonic frame" is more flexible than Herman or Chomsky believe. Gitlin claims that major "shifts" in the hegemonic frame can and do take place during certain historical periods. The major shift in media coverage during the Vietnam War, Gitlin concludes, came in 1968 when:

> editors at the *New York Times* and other establishment news organizations turned sympathetic to moderate antiwar activity. The Tet Offensive shattered the official rationale that the war should be pursued because it was *not only just,* but winnable. The observed and reported facts of Tet subverted the Johnson administration's own claims [regarding the war]. . . . At this point, the normal routines for constructing news and reproducing hegemony became, from the point of view of much of the political elite, unreliable.[17]

Gitlin describes hegemonic vulnerability as the result, in part, of the fuzziness notions of "objectivity" in covering social movements:

> When movements mobilize, reporters may be pulled into the magnetic fields generated by their alternative or oppositional world views. Now the routines of objectivity prove somewhat adaptable . . . reporters tend to be pulled into the cognitive worlds of their sources. . . . When movements become newsworthy, reporters who cover them steadily are subject to a similar pull. . . . Because the idea of "objectivity" and the standards of "newsworthiness" are loose, the hegemonic routines of news coverage are vulnerable to the demands of oppositional and deviant groups.[18]

Gitlin claims that reporting on dissent seemed to open up prior to the Iraq war, as newsreaders found "largely respectful coverage" immediately prior to the 2003 invasion.[19]

Gitlin contends that the mass media can take on a strongly adversarial role toward the government by challenging the justness of war; however, this contention should be empirically evaluated. Public discontent against the Iraq war represents a relevant case in which to study Gitlin's claim. By late 2004, most Americans turned against the Iraq war.[20] By mid-2005, most Americans supported a general timetable for the reduction of some or all troops, and by mid-2006 to early 2007, talk was emerging among Democrats about passing legislation to set such a timetable.[21] Finally, an increasing number of op-eds and editorials throughout the mass media began to criticize the Bush administration for its handling of the war by late 2004, and continued to do so in later periods.[22]

Herman and Chomsky disagree with Gitlin that reporting became substantively critical following the 1968 Tet offensive. They claim that pragmatic criticisms of the war as "unwinnable" do not constitute a serious challenge to policy. Such "criticisms" are *pro-war* in that they fault political leaders for not fighting conflicts effectively. Chomsky claims that the Tet offensive did indeed qualify as a "turning point" in American history, but not in the way assumed by Gitlin. Post-Tet media coverage was intended to "restore the basic doctrines of the faith: the war must now be understood as a noble effort gone astray. We may say that the war began with 'blundering efforts to do good'" although the war had deteriorated into a "disastrous mistake."[23] In the end, the war was seen by reporters and editors as an error or mistake. This contrasts greatly with Gitlin's claim that media portrayed the conflict as unjust. The general American public may have seen the conflict as "fundamentally wrong or immoral" after Tet, but this does not mean that media held the same view.[24]

MEDIA, IRAQ PROTESTS, AND WITHDRAWAL

Contrary to Gitlin, Herman argues that major American newspapers consistently "give little voice to civil society." The mass media is seen as playing a lapdog role in marginalizing and demonizing antiwar protestors: "Where protests are large enough, they may be covered, but the media regularly give undercounts of numbers, unfavorable placement, disproportionate attention to counter-protestors and protestor violence . . . and they rarely attempt to convey the messages and analyses of the protestors, let alone give editorial support to the protestors."[25] All of these claims are reviewed below, as I examine media reporting of the September 15, 2007, antiwar protest in Washington, D.C.

PROTESTING IRAQ: MEDIA COVERAGE OF THE MOVEMENT

Members of the group Iraq Veterans Against the War led a march of tens of thousands of activists from the White House to the Capitol to deliver a petition demanding that Congress cut off funding for the Iraq war. After a symbolic "die-in" in which thousands of protestors laid down on the Capitol grass to show their solidarity for those killed in Iraq, a number of Iraq veterans crossed a police barricade to deliver their antiwar petition to Congress. Inspired by the veterans' actions, dozens of other protestors peacefully crossed the police line, knowing that they would be arrested and taken away up the steps of the Capitol building. In all, over a hundred activists were arrested under "disorderly conduct" charges, as thousands cheered them on with chants of "Arrest George Bush" and "Stop the War."

The September 15 protest retains a special symbolism in that it represents a dramatic shift in antiwar activism toward more vigilant, nonviolent resistance. Antiwar activist Cindy Sheehan voiced this new opposition well, explaining that protestors had grown tired of simply marching and congratulating each other on their antiwar placards. Antiwar efforts would now focus on nonviolently "shutting the city down."[26]

The veterans' protest narrative is potentially powerful for those Americans unfamiliar with the eclectic nature of the antiwar movement. In a country where "supporting the troops" is often assumed to mean supporting war, increased coverage of antiwar veterans threatens to destroy conventional dogmas. However, the American public's access to information about the antiwar movement is greatly restricted. A systematic review of local and national media coverage of the event reveals a picture of the protest that is virtually unrecognizable to those who attended. On nearly every major point, the mainstream press distorted the news and conveyed serious misrepresentations of the reality on the ground.

A LACK OF ISSUE SALIENCE

Media attention to the September 15 antiwar protest was minimal when compared to other stories reported at the time. Though the protest was covered by most major media outlets, it was regarded as unworthy of front-page placement. As the papers closest to the protest, the *Washington Times* and the *Washington Post* did run small, bottom-page pictures with captions on page 1 about the protest, but neither ran a front-page story, instead printing pieces on pages A7 and A8 respectively. Other papers also buried the story: the *New York Times* on A21, the *Los Angeles Times* on A16, and the *Chicago Tribune* on A4.[27]

Headlines that were deemed more deserving than the antiwar protest of front-page attention concerned baby boomer retirement, pig disease in China, and a scandal involving Democratic fundraiser Norman Hsu in the *Washington Post*, an article on cheating in professional football in the *Chicago Tribune*, and stories on renovations in a Washington D.C. marketplace and the Colorado Episcopalian church's controversy over gay and lesbian representation in the *Washington Times*.[28] The media's uniformity in downgrading antiwar protestors contradicts reporters' claims that they are independent from the influence of pro-war officials.

It is not the case that journalists and editors consider the issue of Iraq withdrawal to be unworthy of front-page coverage. Rather, they do not seem to feel that antiwar activists carry enough legitimacy to sustain front-page coverage of withdrawal. Presidents and other political leaders do receive front-page coverage regarding the topic of withdrawal. For example, the day before the antiwar protest in Washington, a large picture of President Bush appeared on the front page of the *New York Times* alongside a story about withdrawal. The story elaborated upon a presidential plan announced "to begin withdrawing some troops from Iraq gradually," assuming that the United States was able to secure a "free and friendly Iraq" and deter Iran's alleged meddling.[29] The page one story was accompanied by another story on page A8, which provided the text of a speech made by President Bush defending the Iraq war as the vital front in the "war on terror."[30] Other papers such as the *Washington Post*, *Chicago Tribune,* and *USA Today* have also run front-page stories with vague presidential promises about eventual withdrawal, and newspapers produced many front-page stories on withdrawal based on debate between the Congress and president over withdrawal.[31] The lesson seems clear:

unlike the president, antiwar activists are not legitimate agenda setters in defining the terms of wartime debate.

THE MYTH OF LEFT-RIGHT POLITICAL CONFLICT

As Herman warns, media outlets continue to allot "disproportionate attention to counter-protestors" and misrepresent protest numbers. Television media coverage of the September 15 march created a false image of the protest—one in which there was supposedly intense conflict between pro and antiwar activists. Coverage on Washington's local News Channel 8 cut back and forth between protestors opposed to the war and counter-protestors along the march route's sidelines.[32] This coverage gave the impression that the demonstration centered on conflict between the two groups. On *CNN Newsroom*, anchor Suzanne Malveaux situated the debate in terms of "both sides" that are "convinced they're right." She aired a debate between pro-war military mother Deborah Johns and antiwar mother Tina Richards who spoke at the protest rally. The CNN story, while providing an estimate of 1,000 pro-war protestors, failed to present a comprehensive number for the antiwar side.[33] This trend was quite common to many news sources, as will be discussed later in this chapter.

Conservative media coverage emphasized prowar groups over antiwar ones. *Fox News Live*, for example, focused on the plans of pro-war organizations Free Republic and Gathering of Eagles to protest the antiwar protestors. While *Fox* emphasized pro-war groups, even that emphasis was subsumed by sensationalistic coverage of O. J. Simpson's arrest and a British child's abduction, as both of these tabloid stories were the primary subject of the newscast, while the mentions of the pro-war groups appeared as a blurb on the bottom of the screen.[34]

Print coverage also followed a left-right dichotomy. The *Washington Times* conveyed the impression that antiwar and pro-war groups were of a similar size, by claiming that pro-war and antiwar protestors were "equally energized," and that antiwar "crowds appeared significantly smaller than the tens of thousands of organizers had promised." The paper, like CNN, projected a 1,000-person pro-war turnout, while failing to provide a number for antiwar activists except for low-ball estimates.[35]

Both the *Washington Post* and the *Washington Times* pursued a false balancing of sources. The *Washington Post* ran the headline "Dueling

Demonstrations," suggesting that the protest coalesced primarily around confrontation between the two groups. The paper printed an equal number of statements (seven each) from both pro-war and antiwar individuals, while citing two pro-war groups participating in the protest (Free Republic and Gathering of Eagles), and only one antiwar group (ANSWER). The *Washington Times* printed six statements from pro-war individuals, and only four from antiwar figures.[36] These depictions left the impression that the demonstration was composed more of pro-war advocates.

The left-right depiction as applied to the September protest is problematic, primarily for two reasons. First, antiwar protestors *vastly* outnumbered pro-war ones, as tens of thousands of activists showed up to challenge the war, whereas a maximum 1,000 pro-war protestors—possibly fewer—attended the event.[37] One would not know how lopsided the turnout was, however, from media coverage. The *New York Times* and *Los Angeles Times*, for example, reported inaccurately that "several thousand" antiwar protestors attended, although the number was really in the tens of thousands.[38] The *Washington Post* uncritically repeated pro-war activists' claims that antiwar protestors, rather than the pro-war protestors, were the "vocal minority."[39] The paper ran a photo of pro-war protestors that was four to five times the size of the antiwar picture run alongside it, reinforcing pro-war prominence.

Second, contrary to media reports of high-levels of political conflict, the overwhelming majority of antiwar protestors ignored the verbal attacks of pro-war protestors, choosing instead to walk by the demonstrators *without* engaging them. Conflict with pro-war activists was only a minuscule part of the protest, and certainly not a main goal of those opposing the war. Antiwar protestors came to the capital to demand that political leaders reconsider their support for the war, not to engage in heated arguments with a small but vocal group of war supporters.

PREDOMINANCE OF THE LAW-AND-ORDER FRAME

Edward Herman's claim that "disproportionate attention" is focused on "protestor violence" is also reaffirmed. Media sensationalism has been well documented in previous studies. In a review of television news stories in four local markets and four continental time zones, Matthew R. Kerbel found that "local news presents us with an endless assortment of fire, murder, assault, shootout, and accident stories."[40] To that list one can add reporting of antiwar protests.

Media coverage often gave the impression that the protests were chaotic, violent, and lacking seriousness. D.C.'s *Local News 8* highlighted a scene whereby a prowar protestor punched the station's video camera, while *CNN Newsroom* reported that the demonstration, although peaceful, was "noisy," "loud, angry, and did get physical."[41] The *New York Times* and *Washington Post* described the event as "raucous," "unruly," and "chaotic."[42] The *Chicago Tribune* claimed that the "event took on an almost circus-like atmosphere," in part because protestors were calling for the impeachment of President Bush.[43]

D.C. police officers certainly played a central role in influencing news frames of the September antiwar protest. They were depicted as providing security during the protest, rather than preventing antiwar protestors from entering the Capitol building to deliver the antiwar petition. The *New York Times* reported that "officers struggled to keep demonstrators from breaking through their ranks and began arresting those who tried."[44] The *Washington Times* emphasized the "heavy" law enforcement presence, as "heated exchanges between the two camps" were mediated "by barricades manned by lines of police officers."[45]

Evidence on the ground suggested that the law and order frame did not adequately represent the spirit of the protest. The majority of antiwar marchers ignored the small pro-war group. Although D.C. police were surely helpful in preventing any potential conflicts or violence between protestors on both sides, this role was of relatively minor importance for a peaceful protest. Even those protestors who chose to cross the police line at the Capitol building did so in an organized, orderly, and peaceful manner, one by one, and did not resist arrest when detained by the police.

Gitlin argues that during the 1960s antiwar protests "what was most distinctly newsworthy was clash and arrests." In short, "arrests certif[ied] protest events."[46] In the case of media coverage of the September 15 protest, however, one sees the opposite trend. The veterans' participation in that protest was omitted from most media reporting reviewed in this chapter. Only the *Los Angeles Times* presented this event as pivotal to the protest, reporting that Iraq Veterans Against the War organized the "die in" in front of the Capitol building.[47] Images of the arrest of antiwar veterans do not comport well with stereotypes framing the troops as prowar. Seemingly, pictures of war veterans confronting D.C. police are incongruent with what many reporters expect to see during antiwar demonstrations. Sensationalistic headlines and images may make for good news stories, but they have to be the right kind of stories. Images of veterans arrested in opposition to war—although dramatic and newsworthy—make a mockery of official promises to promote democracy in Iraq.

ABSENCE OF SUBSTANTIVE ANTIWAR ARGUMENTS

Herman's claim that the media fails to emphasize substantive antiwar claims is also corroborated. Michael Parenti asserts that "the cumulative impact of press coverage" of 1960s antiwar protests "was to create the impression that these 'kids' were violent, extremist, and dangerous to society." Reporters, Parenti claims, display "discomfort with reporting criticisms of the United States as an imperialist power"; they "prefer frames stressing [American] opposition to aggression, promotion of national security, and punishing of designated enemies of state."[48]

Major criticisms of the American occupation as terrorist, imperialist, illegal, or driven by lies and a lust for oil are omitted from the news. Of all the news stories from the September 15 protest reviewed, only three moral arguments against the war appeared—one from the *Los Angeles Times* and two from the *New York Times*.[49] Two of the statements from the protestors criticized the Bush administration for its "false assertions about Iraq" (*New York Times*) and for a policy that "will continue to kill thousands of US service members and hundreds of thousands of Iraqis" (*New York Times*). In a rare moment of critical media reflection, one antiwar activist was quoted arguing, "The Iraqi people do not see us as peacemakers. They see us as occupiers and murderers" (*Los Angeles Times*). These claims were the exception rather than the norm in news stories.

EDITORIAL COVERAGE IN LIGHT OF ANTIWAR PROTESTS

Editorials surrounding the September 15 protest were also biased in favor of war. A review of Beltway political debate the day after the protest provides insight into the quality of deliberation. Despite the appearance of tens of thousands of protestors in the capital, not a single antiwar activist was granted editorial space in a Washington newspaper the day after the demonstration. Of the *Washington Times*'s three op-eds addressing Iraq, all were sympathetic to the Bush administration. A front-page article in the "Commentary" section by the late conservative William F. Buckley complained about a lack of adequate information about military progress in Iraq, but recommended that when it comes to the occupation Americans should "stick it out."[50] Buckley's article was printed next to a large cartoon of General Petraeus presenting a progress report suggesting that the "areas of hostility" to American troops in Iraq radically decreased from 2006 to 2007, and that "ethno-sectarian deaths" had fallen significantly. The cartoon referred to Congress as the only major "area of hostility" remaining in light of American success. The message was clear: only a lack of American resolve was preventing victory in Iraq.

A second op-ed by Congressman Elton Gallegly was accompanied by a cartoon of Uncle Sam facing a dark doorway with an "Exit?" sign above his head. Gallegly argued, "Despite many mistakes in the execution of the Iraq war after Saddam Hussein's removal, I believe the consequences of failure in that country would be disastrous to United States national security."[51] A third editorial on the "Forum" page of the *Washington Times* by Ken Connor was titled "Battling Divisions Over the Surge." Despite a title suggesting a discussion between antiwar and prowar voices, the article simply stated that the Bush administration's surge, "by a number of objective measures, has been a success. Since the surge went into effect, incidents of ethno-sectarian violence and deaths are down, the number of weapons caches found and cleared is up, IED explosions and car bombings are down, and the number of al Qaeda leaders captured or killed is up."[52] Connor's message was unequivocal: the only assessment one could draw from the surge was that the United States must remain in Iraq.

A fourth op-ed in the paper (indirectly discussing Iraq) by Frank Salvato attacked antiwar activists associated with the Democratic Party for challenging General Petraeus's assessments of the occupation. The article, titled "Accepting Thuggery," attacked the Democratic allied MoveOn.org for an ad it ran suggesting that General Petraeus misled Congress and betrayed the American public, and for MoveOn's claim that "every independent report on the ground situation in Iraq shows that the surge strategy has failed."[53]

The *Washington Post*'s op-eds and editorials were similarly sympathetic to the Bush administration's militaristic posturing. A front-page story by retired General Wesley Clark in the "Outlook" section was accompanied by a black-and-white photo of four American soldiers. The caption for the photo read: "The Next War: It's Always Looming, But Has Our Military Learned the Right Lessons From This One to Fight It and Win?" Clark's piece looked forward to "the most likely next conflict" with Iran, "a radical state that America has tried to isolate for almost 30 years and now threatens to further destabilize the Middle East."[54] Regarding Iraq, the *Washington Post* ran two op-eds, one from former secretary of state Henry Kissinger, and another from regular columnist Jim Hoagland.[55] Kissinger's piece warned that an "abrupt withdrawal" would encourage "sectarian conflict [that] could assume genocidal proportions" while "terrorist base areas could reemerge." Hoagland's piece was similarly alarmist, warning of the "horrific bloodbath in Iraq if American troops are withdrawn precipitously."

It is important to note that the above analysis of media commentary in the *Washington Times* and *Washington Post* does not represent the entire range of debate in the American media. While the *Washington Post* and *Washington Times* are known as prowar papers, there are other media outlets—such as the *Los Angeles Times* and *New York Times*—that editorialized by mid-2007 in favor of a timetable for withdrawal. Despite this trend, it is still an open question as to what types of criticisms of the war appear in national media.

The bounds of media commentary are limited to strategically critical claims that the war is unwinnable, and even this claim sits uncomfortably with many in the media. A case in point is the contempt for MoveOn.org. Media outlets shamed MoveOn.org for alleging that Petraeus was dishonest and misled Americans over the progress of the occupation. Attacks on military leaders for failing to effectively pursue the war do receive attention in media discourse. Those who attend antiwar protests and criticize the war in Iraq as terrorist, illegal, imperialistic, or motivated by oil, however, stand so far outside the boundaries of "legitimate" debate that their claims do not even receive consideration by reporters.

ANTIWAR ARGUMENTS IN THE *NEW YORK TIMES* AND BEYOND: A COMPREHENSIVE ANALYSIS

Tom Matzzie of MoveOn.org is the quintessential mainstream antiwar activist. He challenges the Iraq war within the conventional framework of assumptions expressed by the Democratic Party. His criticisms are personalized so as to challenge the Bush administration's management of the occupation, rather than its legitimacy.[56] He frames the Iraq war as a "mess," rather than fundamentally illegal under international law, and he questions the Bush administration's claims about "progress" in Iraq, rather than challenging the administration for self-interested motives driving the occupation.[57] Matzzie is a comfortable face for media outlets that refuse to report antiwar views residing outside the ideological boundaries of the Democratic Party.

Although the *New York Times* seldom pays attention to antiwar activists and groups in their stories on withdrawal, figures like Matzzie are consulted when stories are run, as they lend a "legitimate" face to the antiwar movement. A review of one of the *New York Times*'s few stories focusing on antiwar activism and withdrawal demonstrates this point rather starkly. The story, titled "Antiwar Groups Use New Clout to Influence Democrats on Iraq," exclusively cites mainstream members of the antiwar movement. Matzzie's group, MoveOn.org, is heavily referenced, as it retains intimate ties with Democrats in Congress, and worked closely with them in sponsoring legislation regarding a withdrawal timetable. Of course, MoveOn.org is not the only antiwar group appearing in the *New York Times*. Others include the umbrella group Americans Against Escalation in Iraq (AAEI), Votevets.org, and the National Security Network (NSN)—described by the paper as "a collection of liberal-leaning military and foreign policy experts headed by Rand Beers, former national security advisor to the presidential campaign of Senator John Kerry." NSN even "deployed former generals and officials to persuade individual lawmakers" over the need to change course in Iraq.[58]

The *New York Times* emphasis on reformist and mainstream antiwar groups is instructive. It demonstrates which antiwar groups are not considered acceptable actors in the debate over war. If the AAEI "coalition's strength," as the *New York Times* proclaims, "is its diversity, bringing together groups like MoveOn.org and organized labor on one end and former veterans," then why bother to incorporate the views of other dissident groups on the fringe of the more "respectable" antiwar movement?[59] While antiwar groups such as ANSWER, United for Peace and Justice (UFPI), and others are primarily responsible for gathering hundreds of thousands of protestors to Washington, these groups are downplayed in reporting. Newspaper articles focus primarily on the tactics of antiwar groups, rather than the underlying reasons for their opposition to extended occupation. When groups such as UFPI and Gold Star Families for Peace (the group cofounded by radical antiwar activist Cindy Sheehan) are reported by the *New York Times*, their major antiwar claims are rarely given attention.[60]

While the anecdotal evidence above suggests media discomfort with non-mainstream antiwar views, a comprehensive review of stories featuring Iraq and withdrawal demonstrates a consistent pattern of omission of progressive views. Despite the fact that media coverage has generally become more open to the topic of withdrawal after the 2006 midterm election, papers like the *New York Times* exclude substantive, and even procedural, antiwar arguments in favor of prowar claims.

Reactions to the occupation of Iraq and the surge range from profound exuberance to strategic questioning. Debate emphasizes how effective the United States is in pacifying Iraqi resistance, not whether the United States has a right to occupy a country in which the majority of the people oppose the war. By late 2007, *Time* magazine portrayed the American occupation as a borderline failure, although it advocated a "stay the course" approach: "Too much American blood has been spilled in Iraq for the United States to continue without wholesale progress being made."[61] In anticipation of General Petraeus's congressional report on the surge, the editors of the *Chicago Tribune* repeated the Bush administration's mantra regarding the dangers of withdrawal: "The potential for a cataclysm is so great that many of the same Iraqis who fervently wish American 'occupiers' would leave will grudgingly acknowledge that United States troops *must* stay, lest the violence grow worse."[62]

The *Chicago Tribune*'s editors represent the extreme conservative end of the mainstream spectrum of debate on Iraq. They refuse to even admit that the United States is conducting an occupation. Widespread Iraqi public and political opposition to the occupation is deemed irrelevant, as American leaders must selflessly drag an unwilling Iraqi public along, allegedly for their own good. The paper's paternalism continued in the wake of the Petraeus report.[63] The *Tribune*'s editors explained: "Petraeus made a good case that the surge is a military success. His forces have delivered progress toward pacification, though it's far from complete."[64]

On the other end of the mainstream spectrum of debate, the *New York Times* dubbed the war too costly and unwinnable, advocating a long-term plan for drawdown. The paper's editors ridiculed the Bush administration for failing to "contain the bloodletting" and for continuing the occupation despite having "no achievable military goal." They attacked the administration for its "vacuous slogans about victory" and their pursuit of a "pointless war" that has "dragged on for too long." They criticized

Republicans for "shortchanging the Pentagon on troops and armor."[65] In the *Chicago Sun-Times*, Justin Logan claimed in response to the United Kingdom's plan to remove troops from Iraq that the withdrawal "must be seen as a harbinger of defeat for the United States' mission." The United States will suffer from a "loss of credibility," with withdrawal serving "as a cautionary tale about the perils of nation building and the inadvisability of foreign policy adventurism."[66]

When withdrawal is advocated in liberal mainstream media sources, it falls far short of the expectations set by the American public. Although majority support for withdrawal dates back to mid-2005,[67] it took the *Los Angeles Times* and *New York Times* until two years later to advocate the same.[68] Similarly, it took *Time* until July of 2007 to advocate "an orderly withdrawal of about half the 160,000 troops currently in Iraq by the middle of 2008. A force of 50,000 to 100,000 troops would dig in for a longer stay."[69] The majority of Americans, however, supported a much shorter time frame for withdrawal. One Gallup poll conducted a month after the *Time* story revealed that 66 percent favored the removal of most troops within nine months, as opposed to *Time*, which advocated the removal of only half of the troops within roughly the same period.[70] A *CBS–New York Times* poll from October of 2007 found that 72 percent supported a total withdrawal within less than two years, as contrasted with *Time*, which supported an indefinite occupation consisting of 50,000 to 100,000 troops.[71]

Whereas American leaders are denigrated by the liberal mainstream press for being unrealistic in their expectations for success in Iraq, Iraq's political leaders are a more popular target for moral criticisms. Media outlets portray American leaders as naive in their expectations for military success, but Iraqi leaders are seen as both incompetent and malicious in their intentions. The editors at the *Chicago Tribune* criticize the "absence of effective Iraqi political leadership" and complain about an "Iraqi army [that] has yet to prove it is an effective fighting force."[72] The paper's editors lament over "Iraqi leaders [who] were expected to seize this moment of reduced violence [allegedly as a result of the surge] to forge a unified Iraq. Instead they are as divided as ever." Iraqi leaders fail to do "enough to eliminate militia control of local security forces," as various Iraq militias are attacked in the American press for escalating ethnic-sectarian tensions.[73]

While the above criticisms of Iraqi officials are largely tactical, moral condemnations are also common. The *Washington Post*'s editors declared that Iraqi leaders simply "won't deliver on the long list of 'benchmarks' the [Bush] administration has set."[74] *Time* denounced Iraqi officials as "criminally negligent" in their "callous disregard" after they took a four-week break from parliamentary activity in August of 2007.[75] The *Chicago Tribune*'s editors lambaste Iraqi politicians for their "refusal to deal in good faith to build a united Iraq" as one columnist from the paper claims that Iraqi prime minister Nouri al-Maliki "imperils" the United States' mission.[76] Editors at the *New York Times* decry "recalcitrant Iraqi leaders" who refuse to "take the necessary steps to rescue their country."[77] These attacks on Iraqi leaders are significantly different from those made against American officials. While American reporters question the efficacy of the occupation, challenges to the Bush and Obama administrations' motives are nonexistent.

SUBSTANTIVE ANTIWAR CLAIMS IN THE *NEW YORK TIMES*

Table 2.1 summarizes the percentage of *New York Times* stories from early 2005 through mid-2007 in which antiwar claims appear in news featuring withdrawal from Iraq.[78] Since reporters claim to be "objective," not placing their own views into news stories, this study reviews the types of sources they quote and the substance of the comments their sources make. This study finds that the percentage of quoted sources in the *New York Times* that morally challenge the war is nearly nonexistent. Those who condemn the Iraq war as illegal receive not a single mention in *New York Times* reporting.

Similarly, the paper refused to quote anyone arguing that the war is imperial in nature. Those antiwar intellectuals, protestors, and citizens who claim that the war was motivated by oil interests are also completely ignored. This is not to say that the oil topic is omitted from reporting. The *New York Times* did run a story in January 2006 referencing claims that the United States invaded Iraq because of oil. The story did not bother to quote any antiwar critic, but rather cited President Bush, who argued that those suggesting this possibility were not "honest critics."[79] In another article from May 2007, the paper reported "deep reservations" about a "draft version of a national oil law and related legislation" and "misgivings that could derail one of the benchmark measures of progress in Iraq laid down by President Bush."[80] American support for passing a partial pri-

TABLE 2.1: Substantive Arguments for Withdrawal
New York Times (1/1/2005–5/31/2007); No. Articles = 139

Reason for Withdrawal	% of Articles Claim Appears
American Casualties (too high)	<1%
Iraqi Casualties (too high)	0%
American Imperialism	0%
Iraqi Nationalism (as a motivation for opposing occupation)	1.4%
American Oil Interests	0%
Invasion and Occupation as Illegal	0%

Source: Lexis Nexis

vatization bill, however, was not portrayed as a primary motivation of the occupation, but rather innocently as a means of achieving "progress" in reconstructing Iraq. Conversely, major newspapers grant the president prominent coverage when he claims that the United States must remain in Iraq because of oil interests.[81] In short, it does not appear that the newsworthiness of the oil issue, in and of itself, determines the nature of media coverage. When the president claims that the war is not for oil, media uncritically report the claim. When the president claims that war is for oil, outlets also report the claim uncritically.

Antiwar critics that emphasize Iraqi civilian and American military casualties are quoted in none and less than one percent of stories, respectively. An elaboration upon the few stories that do discuss casualties is informative. In one piece from mid-June 2006, Senator John Kerry was quoted arguing that the war is "a mistake"; it is the "wrong war, [at the] wrong place, [at the] wrong time." Democratic Senate majority leader Harry Reid adds, "This war has taken too long, is too expensive, and has cost too many lives." Finally, Democratic senator Russell Feingold concludes, "If the policy [in Iraq] is wrong, we owe it to those who are injured, to those who are still there and those who will go and that will die in the future, to correct that mistake."[82]

Kerry's support for phased withdrawal in 2006 led congressional Democrats to situate him at the liberal end of the range of expressible views on the war. Although Kerry finally "found his resolve," as the *New York Times* reported, he had "not made his fellow Democrats any happier," as they perceived his criticisms as representing a potential danger to their chances for electoral success.[83] Their attack on Kerry is significant in its demonstration of the Democrats' contempt for public opposition to the war.

A final criticism that receives almost no media attention covers Iraqi opposition to the occupation. One of the few *New York Times* stories that address Iraqi opposition to the occupation cites religious leader Moqtada al-Sadr, from whom Iraq's Shia population draws inspiration. The April 2007 story focused on Sadr's decision to remove his ministers from the thirty-eight-member Iraqi cabinet because of its reluctance to demand a timetable for American withdrawal. Though the story did mention popular protests demanding an end to the occupation, the story did not reference the Iraqi public's opposition to the war. Rather, the story quoted Prime Minister Nouri al-Maliki, who argued that withdrawal depends on "the readiness of our armed forces to handle the entire security portfolio in all provinces."[84] Conditions in the military battle—not the feelings of the Iraqi public—were deemed vital for determining a withdrawal date.

PROCEDURAL AND AMBIGUOUS CRITICISMS

Although the propaganda model stresses that tactical criticisms of the war are prominent in the news, this study finds that the *New York Times* fails to incorporate even these limited criticisms into stories on withdrawal. Table 2.2 suggests that stories rarely quote sources criticizing the war as unwinnable or too costly. Such stories are few and far between. In one September 2006 story, Democratic senator Robert Menendez was quoted arguing that the Iraq war had become a "massive failure." In another instance, the paper quoted Eric Massa of the United States Naval Academy, who claimed: "We will never be successful in creating a Jeffersonian democracy in Iraq at the tip of a bayonet . . . that's a fool's errand. The longer we try it, the more dire the consequences."

A last example is seen in November 2006, when the *New York Times* cited Leslie H. Gelb, president of the Council on Foreign Relations, arguing that "the [American] public realizes we can't afford to win and probably can't win, but it doesn't want to lose [the war]."[85]

Though pragmatic criticisms are sparse in stories on withdrawal, they are not completely lacking in media coverage more generally. Other studies show that procedural challenges are quite common in the editorials and op-ed sections of the *New York Times*.[86] However, prominence in editorial sections notwithstanding, the question still

TABLE 2.2: Procedural and Ambiguous Arguments for Withdrawal
New York Times (1/1/2005–5/31/2007) No. Articles = 139

Procedural	% of Articles Appearing	Ambiguous	% of Articles Appearing
Cost of War (too high)	2%	American Public Favors Withdrawal	14%
War as a Quagmire/ Unwinnable	3.6%	Iraqi Public Favors Withdrawal	<1%

Source: Lexis Nexis

remains of why there are so few pragmatic criticisms in *New York Times* reporting. The answer becomes clearer after undertaking a closer analysis. Although reporters are willing to print criticisms of the war from Democratic political sources, most stories convey an impression of the party as concerned more with strategy than with specific criticisms of the war. A brief review of major comments from prominent Democrats places this point into better perspective. One story from May 2007 titled "Democrats Regroup after Veto, Seeking Unity on Iraq Plan" elaborated on the Democrats' mind-set after the defeat of a bill demanding a timetable for the reduction of troops. Democratic presidential candidates were described as walking a "narrow line between satisfying liberals who will be active primary voters and not alienating centrists by taking steps that could be portrayed as threatening the safety of American troops."[87]

After reviewing the statements of many Democrats reported in the *New York Times*, it is clear that most are interested in appealing to centrist and swing voters, without leveling tangible criticisms of the war. As one of the most prominent Democratic senators receiving exposure, Harry Reid explained his electoral approach in strategic terms with the following statements:

> If the president thinks by vetoing this bill [on withdrawal] he will stop us from working to change the direction of the war in Iraq, he is mistaken. . . . Now he has an obligation to explain his plan to responsibly end this war.[88]
>
> We are legislators. . . . We understand legislation is the art of compromise, consensus building. We are willing to sit down and talk with the president [about Iraq], but we have certain things we believe to be important to the country. I'm sure he does too.[89]

Other senators echoed Reid's approach. Democratic senator Charles Schumer explained his position as follows: "We are going to keep at it, and we are going to continue this discussion for the good of the country. And we believe the more it is debated and discussed, the more the difference between the parties is apparent to the American people, the less flexibility the president will have in maintaining the course."[90] Senator Carl Levin explained in March of 2007 that he "looked toward another *procedural* fight next week over Iraq."[91]

During the period analyzed, the *New York Times* reported that Democrats were usually hesitant to take concrete stances aimed at encouraging political opposition to the war. In calling for a drawdown of troops in Iraq, Democratic presidential front-runner Hillary Clinton refused to set a specific timetable for withdrawal.[92] In a mid-2007 proposal, Senate Democrats presented a "non-binding resolution" that intentionally failed to mention withdrawal, while stressing the importance of "success" in Iraq.[93] Finally, Democrats running for the presidency stated in a 2007 presidential debate that they would not pursue a full withdrawal from Iraq until 2013 at earliest.[94]

Aside from substantive and procedural critiques, another type of criticism is addressed in Table 2.2. Ambiguous criticisms may be either substantive *or* procedural, depending on how they are reported. From Table 2.2, one can see that the first ambiguous criticism, American public opposition to the occupation, can be framed based on pragmatic or substantive assessments of the war, or neither. Of the nineteen stories that contained information on public opinion polls, seven were based on parochial criticisms of the Bush administration for poor "handling" of the war and eroded public confidence in the executive branch, or criticisms of the war as "going badly," and "a mistake." One story, for example, printed information on a CNN-*USA Today* poll, "found that fifty-three percent of respondents said it had been a mistake to send troops to Iraq and that sixty-one percent said Mr. Bush did not have a clear plan for handling the situation there."[95] Another ten of the polls contained neither procedural nor substantive attacks on the administration, merely addressing policy questions related to the war's funding and general public support for a withdrawal timetable.

Only two of the stories published any polling information that was substantively critical of the war. One faulted Bush for a lack of honesty in his motivations for going to war; the other similarly stated that over half of Americans felt "the Bush administration intentionally misled the public when its officials made the case for war."[96] In and of themselves, these two polls (over a period of eighteen months) are insufficient evidence of strong moral dissent in the *New York Times*. Similarly, the *New York Times* failed to cite Iraqi opposition to the war in any significant way. In short, Iraqi moral opposition to the occupation is of little interest.

PRO-WAR ARGUMENTS AS A MAINSTAY OF REPORTING

This analysis supports Herman and Chomsky's claims that pro-war sources often dominate the news, even during periods when "antiwar" Democrats gain control of Congress. Table 2.3 demonstrates the high frequency with which pro-war sources are quoted in *New York Times* stories on withdrawal. Pro-war Republicans vehemently support the occupation, and that support is evident in the elite print media. Sources stressing the importance of defeating "insurgents" and "terrorists" are quoted in 9 percent and 24 percent of *New York Times* stories, respectively.

Leaders such as former president Bush argue, for example, that "insurgents" in Iraq "know that as democracy takes root, their hateful ideology will suffer a devastating blow. So we can expect the violence to continue."[97] Withdrawal, Bush claims, will only "embolden terrorists," as "our defeat in Iraq would constitute a defeat in the war against terror and extremism and would make the world a much more dangerous place." Drawing a parallel with the September 11 terrorist attacks, Bush claimed that "the enemies we face [in Iraq] harbor the same depraved indifference to human life as those who killed 3,000 innocent Americans on a September morning in 2001."[98]

TABLE 2.3: Arguments against Withdrawal
New York Times (1/1/2005–5/31/2007); No. Articles = 139

Reason Against Withdrawal	% of Articles Appearing
Support the Troops	41%
Fight Terror	24%
Promote Stability/Prevent Civil War	18%
Defeat Insurgents	9%

Source: Lexis Nexis

Reporters pride themselves in "objectively" reporting official statements and actions. When these leaders warn of the "chaos and confusion" that will result from withdrawal, reporters stress those claims.[99] These warnings are prevalent in reporting, as 18 percent of *New York Times* stories contained quotes from those emphasizing the need to stay in Iraq to limit the violence. Competing political leaders often appropriate the same symbols when attempting to convince the public of the veracity of their claims. This is certainly the case when it comes to the fourth pro-war claim—that Americans need to "support the troops." Though references to the progress of the troops or the importance of supporting the troops are the most common justifications made by those who favor war, these leaders certainly enjoy no monopoly on rhetorical support for those in uniform. As former president Bush repeatedly invoked images of the troops in statements justifying war, he also admitted, "I think you can be against my decision [not to set a timetable for withdrawal] and support the troops, absolutely."[100]

In a political climate where Democrats, Republicans, and even many antiwar protestors claim they are allies of America's soldiers, the "support the troops" claim fails to add much substance to the debate over war. But this is precisely what one would expect under a propaganda system where media is heavily dominated by government misinformation. Chomsky argues that one of the most vital functions of media propaganda is to divert attention away from issues of substance.[101] Public immersion in a debate over "who supports the troops more" serves such a diversionary function, considering the vacuous nature of this debate.

ASSESSING MEDIA PERFORMANCE IN TIMES OF WAR

Tuchman argues that media should fulfill the function of a facilitator in debates on policy issues: "According to the Enlightenment model of rational discourse, the public must be exposed to competing ideas if truth is to prevail. Unless the public can determine the truth by assessing diverse opinions, it cannot wisely decide how it will be governed. To protect the public's right to know, the various branches of government must guarantee free speech."[102] In studying media and social movements, Rojecki stresses the question of "whether the news media provide a durable space for opposition politics."[103] If one adopts the facilitator standard when examining media debate, then it is easy to conclude that media coverage of Iraq is heavily propagandistic. Rojecki asserts that "the two most important dimensions of the problem all political movements face" are "finding a place on the media agenda and filling it with a credible and persuasive message."[104] On both counts, antiwar activists are denied access to national media.

Doris Graber argues persuasively that television news is a potentially valuable medium for facilitating social learning, since audiovisual content is helpful in increasing audience retention of information.[105] Graber notes that a large majority of adults gravitate toward television and audio-visual learning when following the news.[106] Most are "satisfied that they receive enough or even more than enough information about their political world" through these sources.[107] The question of whether news audiences are content with media coverage, however, is quite different from the question of whether coverage actually incorporates the vital information audiences need to assess the world around them.

The case study from this chapter finds strong evidence that protest-related visual content is highly propagandistic, providing readers and viewers with a distorted view of the withdrawal issue. Unless news audiences have venues for interpreting protests outside of mainstream media, it will be difficult for them to interpret news in ways that challenge prowar narratives. Whereas audiences may be content with the news they consume, the omission of critical points of view ensures that many do not even know what they are missing. To the extent that the public retains any knowledge of protestors, that information is likely based on false consciousness. Herman echoes this conclusion, challenging claims that media are deserving of praise:

> Of course the media defend their heavy and largely uncritical dependence on the primary definers for news on the ground that they make the news and define the reality, so that giving them the floor is justified on grounds of inherent relevance. What this ignores is that the media may be helping these primary sources accomplish their goals by serving as conduits of assertions and claims that may be false, misleading, and designed to manipulate the public, effectively by allowing themselves to be managed.

Shanto Iyengar and Donald Kinder conclude that "thematic coverage of related background material [for news stories] require[s] in-depth, interpretive analysis, take[s] longer to prepare and is more susceptible to charges of journalistic bias." Although this explanation may explain in part how reporters operate on an individual level, it does little to explain the macroeconomic and political forces determining why news takes the form it does.[108]

A theory of media propaganda, as laid out by Herman and Chomsky, provides valuable insights into the structural factors influencing media coverage of antiwar activism. Though Gitlin's cultural approach to media coverage of social movements provides some insights, it fails to adequately describe the extraordinary extent to which propaganda messages are *consistently* embedded in reporting, or why substantive antiwar views are excluded from reporting on withdrawal. The extraordinary consistency of media propaganda raises serious doubts about Gitlin's claims regarding the vulnerability of hegemonic routines.

CHAPTER THREE

Worthy and Unworthy Victims: The Politicization of Genocide and Human Rights in U.S. Foreign Policy

In November of 2006, the editors of the *New York Times* delivered a stinging rebuke to the Turkish government in response to its historic repression of the Armenian people: "Turkey's self-destructive obsession with denying the Armenian genocide seems to have no limits," in light of its denial of responsibility for the deaths of up to 1.5 million Armenians during the First World War. One Turkish novelist was charged with the "crime" of "insulting Turkish identity" by discussing the genocide. The editors attacked the Turkish government, claiming "it is absurd to treat any reference to the issue within Turkey as a crime and to scream 'lie!' every time someone mentions genocide.... It is time for the Turks to realize that the greater danger to them is denying history."[1]

The *New York Times*'s anger at the Turkish government did not last, however. Though the paper initially employed tough language in addressing Ottoman and Turkish human rights abuses, it was silent when it came to officially recognizing the genocide. After Democrats in Congress introduced a resolution recognizing the Armenian genocide in October of 2007, the *New York Times* failed to run an editorial in support of the resolution. Coverage of the resolution throughout the entire mainstream press allowed for a limited range of opinions. Newspapers either refused to run editorials in favor of the congressional resolution or vociferously attacked the resolution as counterproductive and ill-advised. No newspaper supported the official recognition of genocide, which is precisely what one would expect in a propagandistic media system that distinguishes between worthy and unworthy victims based on strategic rather than humanitarian concerns.

The Armenian genocide, which is explored at greater length later in this chapter, receives attention because it is representative of a larger trend in the mainstream press, whereby reporters and editors prioritize U.S. strategic objectives at the expense of human rights concerns. Evidence of the media's politicization of human rights is not restricted to the Armenian case, as a number of other cases examined below also confirm this general trend.

This chapter examines media coverage of the questions of genocide and government repression in relation to four separate humanitarian issues: 1. the repression of Kurds by the Turkish government; 2. the repression of Kurds by the Iraqi government under Saddam Hussein; 3. the genocide committed against the Armenian people by the Ottoman government; and 4. the mass killing of Iraqi civilians under U.S. occupation. Under the expectations of the propaganda model, civilian deaths caused by the United States and its allies should receive little to no media attention, and coverage of the violence of "enemy" states should be extensively highlighted. A propaganda model predicts that coverage of Kurdish civilian deaths will be prominent when the violence is undertaken by the enemy government of Saddam Hussein, and the violence of the Turkish military against Kurds will be downplayed, ignored, or framed as a relatively minor problem when compared to Hussein's killings.

A number of other expectations follow. A propaganda model predicts that media coverage of Saddam Hussein's repression of the Kurds increases dramatically only *after* the United States designated the Iraqi regime an enemy state. One also expects that the media's reaction to the congressional resolution condemning Armenian genocide will be critical, due to the strategic value of the U.S.–Turkish alliance. Finally, a propaganda model would expect that attention to Iraqi deaths under the U.S. occupation will focus primarily on Iraqi rather than American responsibility for these deaths.

Some scholars disagree with Edward Herman and Noam Chomsky's assumptions about worthy versus unworthy victims and uneven media attention to each group. Contrary to the propaganda model's predictions, Todd Gitlin argues that media is potentially open to dissident views challenging U.S. foreign policy on humanitarian grounds. Gitlin examines the case of U.S. involvement in the Vietnam War in making his argument. By 1970, Gitlin maintains, "the argument that the [Vietnam] war was one consequence of U.S. imperialism gained more and more repute, more and more credence. . . . The Vietnamese were no longer represented as napalmed *victims* [emphasis added]; now they were heroic fighters, women bearing rifles on their backs, a patient Ho Chi Minh. Underground papers as well as the mass media relayed these images."[2]

Gitlin's claim about media attention to victims of American violence stands in contrast to the assumptions of the propaganda model, which distinguishes between those killed who are designated as worthy and unworthy victims. According to Herman and Chomsky, those who are "abused in [communist or other] enemy states" receive substantial attention in the news, as their oppressors are subject to the "high moral and self-righteous tone" of reporters, columnists, and editors.[3] They analyze news coverage in the *New York Times*, CBS, *Newsweek*, and *Time* of religious leaders killed in Soviet-dominated countries such as Poland and religious figures killed in U.S.-allied capitalist states in Latin America. The murder of Polish priest Jerzy Popieluszko by the Polish secret police received more coverage in these news outlets than dozens of religious figures killed throughout Latin American countries by capitalist, U.S.-allied forces from the 1960s through 1980s.[4] Herman and Chomsky explain that "the act of violence and its effects on Popieluszko were presented in such a way as to generate the maximum emotional impact on readers. The act was vicious and deserved the presentation it received. The acts against the unworthy victims [in Latin American countries] were also vicious, but they were treated differently."[5] Competing claims about media openness to U.S. and allied human rights violations are examined below.

WORTHY AND UNWORTHY VICTIMS OF HISTORY: THE ARMENIAN AND SREBRENICA CASES AS GENOCIDE?

Media commentators commonly describe the murder by Serbian forces of thousands of Bosnians in Bosnia-Herzegovina as genocide. In the case of the Bosnian war, 8,000 civilians in the Srebrenica region were killed by Serbian forces in the mid-1990s. Those killings were designated as genocide by international legal authorities, including the International

Criminal Tribunal for the Former Yugoslavia (ICTY) and the International Court of Justice. Though some charged the United States with implicitly supporting or at least tolerating the Srebrenica massacre at the time it occurred, U.S. leaders were not shy in framing the massacre as genocide.[6] Under the auspices of NATO authority, the United States participated in the 1995 bombing of Bosnia-Herzegovina, allegedly to prevent further human rights atrocities committed by Serbian military forces. This set the stage for later media and political celebrations of U.S. altruism in response to its actions in the Balkan peninsula.

The question of genocide is also relevant when reviewing Turkey's history. Discussions of genocide committed against Armenians by the Ottoman Empire retain a special significance today, since the Turkish state is located in what was once the heart of the Ottoman Empire. Although most historians agree that genocide did indeed take place, Turkish leaders refuse to acknowledge it, punishing those who dare to speak up against government denials. Turkish leaders reacted harshly to a French law making it illegal to deny the existence of the Armenian genocide, and threatened intellectual, diplomatic, and trade relations. Turkey also removed its ambassador to the United States in anticipation of congressional consideration of recognizing the genocide.

The Armenian genocide is *not* a historical artifact. It is illegal to speak of the genocide in Turkey today, and those who violate this law are subject to criminal prosecution. Most important, the genocide remains significant in light of two major developments. First, Turkey continues the repression of civilians within and outside its borders and refuses to allow dissenting perspectives that question government denial of the genocide. Second, government violence has resulted in the death of thousands of Kurd civilians. Omission of these crimes in the U.S. media allows for Turkey's continued immunity and enables its future human rights abuses.

The Armenian and Srebrenica cases represent two examples of the politicization of genocide. Although U.S. political leaders were extremely critical of a 2007 congressional bill that designated the Armenian killings as genocide, they enthusiastically supported Congress's designation of the Srebrenica massacre as genocide a few years earlier in 2005. The 2005 genocide bill was introduced to coincide with the tenth anniversary of the Srebrenica massacre, whereas the Armenian bill sought to address atrocities committed over eighty years ago. According to the expectations of the propaganda model, one would expect to see enthusiastic media support for the Srebrenica bill (and condemnation of mass killing in an enemy state), followed by contempt for the Armenian initiative (and downplaying of mass killing in a friendly state). Media frames are expected to portray the deaths of 8,000 civilians in the non-allied country of Bosnia-Herzegovina as a major tragedy, and downplay the significance of the slaughter of an estimated 1–1.5 million people in the political predecessor of the allied state of Turkey.

The predictions of the propaganda model are validated in the case of media reactions to the Armenian genocide bill. Print media responded negatively to congressional efforts to introduce the bill, with some outlets refusing to address the issue editorially. The U.S. press sent a clear message that humanitarian concerns are not on a par with geopolitical interests when strategic U.S.-Turkish relations are threatened. The *New York Times* did not print a single editorial or op-ed highlighting the congressional resolution for the entire month of October 2007, when Democrats such as Nancy Pelosi indicated strong initial support for the genocide bill. Regional papers such as the *San Francisco Chronicle*, *Los Angeles Times*, and *Houston Chronicle* did not run editorials addressing the congressional resolution either.

Most media coverage overwhelmingly emphasized that the resolution should be abandoned, due to the strategic value of Turkey to the United States. The editors of the *Boston Globe*, *Chicago Sun-Times*, *Chicago Tribune*, and *Washington Post* all rejected the legitimacy of the genocide resolution. None of the editors of these papers denied that the genocide occurred; they simply concluded that the proposed bill constituted an unwarranted threat to U.S.-Turkish relations. The editors at the *Boston Globe* claimed that "a resolution before Congress has provoked an upsurge of nationalism that threatens U.S. interests and would do nothing to lift Turkey's willful amnesia. It should not be pursued at this time."[7] The *Chicago Tribune* attacked the resolution on pragmatic grounds as well: "All it does is antagonize the people and government of Turkey, who have been of crucial help to our efforts in Iraq and Afghanistan. . . . [Members of Congress are] putting a valuable ally in a very sore spot."[8] The *Chicago Sun Times* decried the resolution because Turkey might respond by "[closing] crucial air and land supply lines into Iraq to U.S. troops and stop cooperating in other ways with the United States' war effort."[9]

Some outlets assumed that the genocide resolution was not only counterproductive but morally reprehensible. In an editorial titled "Worse than Irrelevant," the *Washington Post* claimed that the bill posed a "high risk to vital United States security interests," and that "its passage would be dangerous and grossly irresponsible." The editors warned that the bill "could destabilize the only region of Iraq [the Kurdish north] that is currently peaceful."[10] The *Chicago Sun-Times* echoed the claim: "The last thing the United States needs as it struggles to stabilize Iraq is for Turkey to turn the only calm area in that country into a battleground—a scenario that could play out if it loses diplomatic influence because of resentment over the ill-timed genocide accusation."[11] Warnings against Iraq's "destabilization" were reported heavily in the media at the time, when the Turkish government planned to bomb areas of northern Iraq containing Kurdish separatists fighting Turkey for independence. However, the mass media's alleged concern with destabilization seems questionable at best, considering that U.S. editors and journalists refused to strongly condemn Turkey when it did actually bomb parts of northern Iraq a few months later. In short, it was Congress's alleged provocation of a Turkish bombing and destabilization of northern Iraq, rather than Turkey's actual bombing and the destabilization of northern Iraq, that received the strongest condemnations in the U.S. press.

Editors and pundits claimed to empathize with the Armenian people, though they stressed that U.S. sympathy must be limited to informal, unofficial statements of recognition that genocide occurred. Such acknowledgments were preferred by those who did not want to insult the Turkish government at a time when it was performing the strategic role of supporting the U.S. occupation of Iraq. The editors at the *Chicago Sun Times*, for example, argued: "The United States can and should acknowledge that the killing and torture of up to 1.5 million Armenians was genocide, as an expression of sympathy and understanding to Armenians. Such a statement would be emblematic of our vigorous support for human rights. But formalizing that stance serves no purpose." Similarly, columnists such as Charles Krauthammer, Richard Cohen, David Ignatius, and Victor Davis Hanson agreed in the *Washington Post* and *Chicago Tribune* that the genocide took place, while also challenging the congressional resolution as ill-timed or inappropriate. The reasons they provided for such a course of inaction were again based on a strategic concern about maintaining strong U.S.-Turkish relations.[12]

Media outlets were not entirely skeptical of the congressional resolution. Columnists such as Andrew Greeley and Georgie Anne Geyer of the *Chicago Sun-Times* and *Chicago Tribune* expressed moral opposition to Congress's retreat on the resolution, and supported its passage as an official expression of Western recognition of the Armenian genocide.[13] Such exceptions are not entirely unexpected. Even the most effective propaganda systems do not completely exclude dissident views. Greeley and Geyer's op-eds, however, were but a few examples of deviations from the norm, and they are not representative of the dominant editorial trend.

The analysis of the eight newspapers discussed above reveals that not a single news organization supported the genocide resolution in its editorials; four were actively opposed, and another four did not even bother to discuss the topic. News reporting from media outlets was no less biased. Stories were heavily reliant on the Turkish government's perspective. A review of headlines from the *New York Times*, *Washington Post*, and *Boston Globe* in the first few days following the congressional committee's passage of the bill puts this pattern into perspective. Headlines from the three papers included: "Inside the Turkish Psyche: Traumatic Issues Trouble a Nation's Sense of Identity," "Turkey Seethes at the United States Over House Genocide Vote," "Vote by House Panel Raises Furor on Armenian Genocide," "White House and Turkey Fight Bill on Armenia," "Turkey Swift to Admonish United States Over Vote," and "Tensions Rise in Turkey on Two Fronts." News sources were heavily tilted toward U.S. and Turkish political leaders who opposed the resolution. In the first three days following the House committee's passage of the genocide bill, sources that were critical of the initiative were quoted twice as often in the *New York Times*, *Washington Post*, and *Boston Globe* than were supportive sources. President Bush, prominent executive-branch spokespersons, congressional Republicans, and Turkish political leaders effectively dominated coverage, heavily outweighing supporters of the bill.[14]

The U.S. political reaction to the tenth anniversary of the Srebrenica massacre was very different from its treatment of Armenian genocide bill. President Bush directed attention to Serbian forces responsible for the killing—to the "evil people who kill the innocent without conscience or mercy."[15] Congress introduced a resolution commemorating the massacre, although this time it enjoyed widespread bipartisan support. While the Armenian bill was cast into the dustbin of history by Democrats and Republicans alike, passage of the Srebrenica bill was not in doubt. The bill passed the House of Representatives and the Senate in June and July of 2005 respectively, with full support in both chambers. The resolution was quite blunt in its language, stating that:

> the massacre at Srebrenica was among the worst of many horrible atrocities to occur in the conflict in Bosnia and Herzegovina from April 1992 to November

> 1995, during which the policies of aggression and ethnic cleansing as implemented by Serb forces in Bosnia-Herzegovina from 1992 and 1995 with the direct support of the Serbian regime of Slobodan Milosevic and its followers ultimately led to the displacement of more than 2,000,000 people, an estimated 200,000 killed, tens of thousands raped or otherwise tortured and abused.

The acts of Serbian forces, Congress determined, "meet the terms defining the crime of genocide in Article 2 of the Convention on the Prevention and Punishment of the Crime of Genocide." Congress faulted the United Nations and all its member states for failing to prevent the atrocities, stating that they "should accept their share of responsibility for allowing the Srebrenica massacre and genocide to occur in Bosnia and Herzegovina from 1992 to 1995 by failing to take sufficient, decisive, and timely action, and the United Nations and its member states should constantly seek to ensure that this failure is not repeated in future crises and conflicts."[16]

Media reactions to the tenth anniversary of Srebrenica paralleled political reactions. The thousands of civilians killed were designated the most worthy of victims, as media outlets covered them in great detail. An op-ed writer at the *New York Times* remembered those civilians who were "slaughtered. . . . Despite the efforts of a dedicated few in Serbia, and despite the war crimes prosecutions at The Hague, Serbia is no closer today than it was a decade ago to reckoning with its war guilt."[17] An editorial in the *Chicago Sun-Times* and an op-ed in the *St. Louis Dispatch* labeled the massacre "the most barbaric mass murder" and the "worst atrocity" in Europe since the Holocaust.[18] The *Chicago Tribune* editors extensively described new evidence implicating Serbian forces in the execution of civilians: "A decade-old video . . . was shown in The Hague at the war crimes trial of ex-Yugoslav President Slobodan Milosevic and then replayed on television in Serbia. The video amounted to a grisly travelogue of the Scorpions, a bloodthirsty Serbian paramilitary unit that reputedly operated under the command of Serbian police in Belgrade and allegedly participated in some of the Srebrenica murders. . . . The video showed the paramilitaries taking six unarmed Bosnian Muslim prisoners to their deaths. Four of the young men were shot at close range, gunfire providing a soundtrack of death."[19]

Current political leaders in Serbia, and even the general citizenry, were attacked for the actions of past officials. The *Chicago Tribune* wondered whether the Serbian execution video would "finally shatter the wall of denial [of the Srebrenica atrocities] that continues to envelope Serbia."[20] In the *New York Times*, Courtney Angela Brkic drew an analogy between the Nazi Holocaust and the Bosnian atrocity: "At the end of the Second World War, Allied troops forced German citizens to walk through Nazi death camps. They were confronted by crimes committed in their name, in order to ensure that those crimes could not be denied or minimized later. The people of Serbia and Montenegro, by contrast, have never been forced to acknowledge the crimes committed in their name." Serbia's intransigent behavior, Brkic concluded, was "befitting a psychopath." The Serbian parliament continued to "deny complicity in war crimes," and "undercut any hope of justice" as they continue to "cheat their country out of any decent future."[21] Whereas the equation of the Srebrenica murders with the Holocaust was acceptable to pundits, a comparison between the Ottoman Empire's killing of over a million Armenians and the Holocaust was unthinkable in the U.S. media, which emphasizes the importance of strategic relations over human rights.

Media pundits were not shy about issuing ultimatums to the Serbian government, although similar stipulations were never placed on Turkish leaders. Louise Branson of *USA Today* announced: "Serbia is at a crossroads. It has a choice: Face up to the past . . . or continue on its present slide with an economy in shambles and no happy future."[22] Media outlets chastised the United States and its allies in their response to the massacre. Whereas editors and op-ed writers attacked political leaders for going too far in trying to pressure the Turkish government to recognize the Armenian genocide, merely acknowledging that genocide took place in Bosnia-Herzegovina was considered inadequate and irresponsible. A LexisNexis review of U.S. newspaper coverage from June and July 2005 (when the House and Senate were deliberating on the Srebrenica genocide initiative) indicates that at least fifteen different papers ran editorials or op-eds denouncing the events at Srebrenica as genocide.[23] Of those fifteen papers, fourteen faulted the United States, United Nations, or NATO for either not preventing the massacre or for failing to adequately punish those involved in the ten years afterward.

The editorial content in the Armenian and Bosnian cases could not be more different. All of the newspapers reviewed in the Armenian genocide case either ran editorials that were opposed to the congressional resolution or refused to run articles addressing the topic at all. Conversely, there was not a single editorial or op-ed in the Srebrenica case that attacked or criticized Congress for denouncing the massacre. Though editorials in the Armenian case focused overwhelmingly on whether Congress would alienate Turkish allies, not a single one of the Srebrenica editorials or op-eds emphasized the congressional resolution. None challenged the resolution on the grounds that it would threaten U.S.-Serbian relations. No editorial criticized U.S. leaders for pushing the Serbian government too hard on human rights issues; such criticisms were beyond the pale of legitimate criticism.

Media reflections on the Srebrenica massacre ranged from celebrations of the U.S. role in promoting human rights in Bosnia-Herzegovina to attacks on the United States, NATO, and the United Nations for incompetence, inability, or unwillingness to prevent genocide. On the celebratory end, an op-ed from Richard Holbrooke (a participant in the Dayton Peace Agreement that ended the war in Bosnia) was printed in the *Washington Post*, *New York Sun*, and *Pittsburgh Post-Gazette*. Holbrooke attempted to create a causal chain, connecting the allied bombing campaign with an end to human rights abuses and the onset of a peace agreement. While denigrating the United States and other parties for failing to act soon enough, he maintained that "sending 20,000 U.S. troops to Bosnia as part of a NATO-led peacekeeping contingent . . . took real political courage. . . . Without those 20,000 troops, Bosnia would not have survived, two million refugees would still be wandering the face of Western Europe, [and] a criminal state would be in power in Bosnia itself."[24] No op-eds or editorials examined disputed Holbrooke's claim that the United States and its allies served as a force for protecting human rights, as the United States was not presented as exacerbating humanitarian disasters through its own bombing campaigns and support for repressive dictators and autocrats abroad.

Pundits and editors faulted the United States for not holding Serbs accountable enough for their abuses, but no one was willing to entertain the notion that the United States should rescind its demands that Serbs acknowledge that genocide took place. High expectations in the Srebrenica case were not replicated in the Armenian case, where Turkey was not seriously pushed to acknowledge genocide. In the example of Srebrenica, editorials and op-eds in the *New York Times*, *Washington Post*, *St. Louis Dispatch*, and *Providence Journal* took aim at the United States and its allies for not taking sufficient steps to capture the two figures—Radovan Karadzic and Ratko Mladic—who were most responsible for the Srebrenica massacre.[25] In one example, the *St. Louis Dispatch* claimed in no uncertain terms that the failure to capture and punish both men "is an insult to humanity. The nations of the world, which allowed genocide in Rwanda in 1994 and in Bosnia in 1995, can pledge 'Never again.' This time, we can mean it."[26] An op-ed in the *St. Louis Dispatch* condemned "a world that looked [to Srebrenica] mostly with indifference to their suffering," while an op-ed writer at the *Washington Times* approvingly quoted U.S. Undersecretary of State for Political Affairs Nick Burns, who argued that atrocities in the Balkans have "been put on the backburner for years. We have to go back and complete the job" of punishing those involved in the massacres on the peninsula.[27]

The Srebrenica massacre was also explained as a function of bureaucratic and organizational incapacity. In the *San Antonio Express News*, Gary Martin reflected that "Srebrenica remains a horrible memory and a case study in the ineffectiveness of the United Nations, NATO, and the international community to follow its instincts and stop genocide."[28] In the *Washington Post*, Edward Joseph spoke bitterly of the United Nations declaration of Srebrenica as a "safe area" prior to the massacre, despite the ensuing Serbian crimes that took place. There was "no will" on the part of the United Nations and NATO "to act to prevent the tragedy." Officials at the United Nations "put protecting the organization above protecting civilians," while "United Nations mission staff were based in the Croatian capital of Zagreb—physically and emotionally distanced from the suffering of the Bosnian people."[29]

Few would dispute that the attacks at Srebrenica constitute major war crimes, and few outside Turkey challenge the belief that genocide was conducted against the Armenian people. However, there is a clear difference between media reactions to efforts to recognize both historical injustices. The murder of 8,000 at Srebrenica, as far as media editors were concerned, could not be highlighted enough, and political leaders could not do enough to rectify the tragedy. In the case of the Armenian genocide, however, where the death toll eclipsed Srebrenica by an estimated 125 to 180 times, editors spoke with great disdain about the irresponsibility of political leaders' recognition of genocide. Recognizing the atrocity was not considered a legitimate responsibility of government. The Armenian dead may be acknowledged occasionally in the rhetoric of media outlets, but certainly not in official circles—at least not in the form of serious political initiatives.

Some critics might contend that the analogy between the Srebrenica and Armenian cases is inappropriate considering the long amount of time that has elapsed since the Armenian genocide, and the relatively short time since the massacre in Bosnia. Any claim that the Srebrenica massacre retains greater salience because of its relative "freshness" compared to older atrocities is highly suspect. U.S. citizens are saturated in media coverage of the Nazi Holocaust, which took place over sixty years ago. In light of such attention, one can safely conclude that time, in and of itself, does not sufficiently explain why older massacres or genocides fail to receive extensive coverage. The Nazi Holocaust is discussed endlessly in U.S. classrooms and in books and other media precisely because it was carried out by an enemy state, whereas the Armenian genocide, as the legacy of an allied Turkish state, is either neglected or forgotten by the U.S. public. In addition, both the Serbian and Armenian atrocities were fresh stories in the news, considering political attention to both issues. Finally, the Armenian case remains relevant because of sustained coverage of Turkey's repression against those who recognize the genocide today. The Armenian genocide, then, is far from ancient history. It relates directly to recent news stories and to Turkey's continued political repression in modern times.

The primary determinant of unequal coverage of government atrocities is the strategic value, or lack thereof, of the repressor state. The implications of the distinction between worthy Bosnian and unworthy Armenian victims are tremendous. Those who suffer far larger atrocities in allied countries are marginalized, since insulting strategic partners simply will not do. Victims of repression in non-allied states are highlighted and mourned endlessly, although such attention is at best insincere among those who distinguish between victims based upon strategic, rather than moral, considerations.

THE USES OF THE KURDS IN MEDIA COVERAGE OF TURKEY AND IRAQ

The dichotomy between worthy and unworthy victims also applies in other cases involving the United States and enemy states. In their 2002 update to *Manufacturing Consent*, Chomsky and Herman show precisely this, as they highlight the politicization of genocide in relation to U.S. policy. In their updated case studies, the authors demonstrate that the word *genocide* is commonly used by media in the conflict in Kosovo (in reporting from the mid-1990s) and in reference to Saddam's repression of the Kurds (from 1991 to 1999, after he was designated an enemy of the

United States). Conversely, the term is used far less often in the case of mass deaths resulting from sanctions in Iraq (in reporting from 1991 to 1999), from the Indonesian occupation of East Timor (from 1990 to 1999), and from Turkey's repression of the Kurds (from 1990 to 1999).[30]

Although Herman and Chomsky's review of news coverage of Iraqi and Turkish repression spans only the ten-year period of the 1990s, an updated analysis reveals much the same pattern of politicization of human rights issues during the 1980s and in the post-2000 period. In reviewing recent events in the Middle East, one sees that media coverage neglects Turkey's attacks on Kurdish civilians, instead heavily emphasizing the deaths of Turkish soldiers and civilians at the hands of Kurds themselves. Extensive attention was devoted to the conflict between Kurdish guerilla groups (framed as aggressors) and the Turkish government (framed as a victim) from October to December 2007. The Turkish parliament voted in October of 2007 to authorize a military attack on Iraq, and Turkey amassed 60,000 troops near the border after Kurdish rebels killed at least a dozen Turkish soldiers. Due to pressure from the United States and its allies, the Turkish government eventually backed away from its proposed invasion, announcing it would first pursue a diplomatic solution to the conflict.[31] The Turkish government did eventually attack Kurds based in northern Iraq, bombing targets on three separate occasions in ten days, and with U.S. logistical support.[32] In February of 2008 Turkey attacked Iraq, bombing areas in which Kurdish rebels allegedly resided. Villagers were reportedly "unable to flee the bombing . . . because heavy snow had closed many roads."[33] Kurdish members of the secessionist Kurdistan Workers Party (PKK) also reportedly conducted attacks against the Turkish government, attempting to establish an independent Kurdish state in part of Turkey.[34]

Kurdish nationalists have been condemned by U.S. and Turkish leaders for targeting civilians and government forces. Estimates suggest that over 37,000 people have been killed since the onset of the PKK's independence effort in southeast Turkey in 1984.[35] As the founder of the PKK, Kurdish nationalist figure Abdullah Ocalan received much of the negative attention. Ocalan and other PKK members have been attacked for targeting not only Turkish civilians and government, but also Kurdish civilians who are seen as allied with the Turkish state.[36] However, if tens of thousands have been killed in the conflict—many as a result of Kurdish terrorist violence—the Turkish government can hardly be divorced from those deaths. This reality is acknowledged by human rights groups.[37] The

Turkish government has a long record of engaging in violence against Kurdish civilians and has engaged in such violence with only minor objections, and even the active support of Western leaders. The vast majority of weapons supplied to the Turkish military during the peak of its repression of the Kurds in the 1990s, for example, were provided by the Clinton administration.[38]

Turkey is accused of sponsoring "mystery killings" of thousands of Kurdish civilians via support for government-associated death squads.[39] The government bombed Kurdish towns with napalm, "wiped off the map" over 3,000 Kurdish villages, and "violently and illegally displaced upwards of 380,000 Kurds throughout the 1990s."[40] Amnesty International also suggested that the government may be executing civilians with impunity.[41] Human rights groups, U.S. media outlets (at times), and U.S. political leaders quietly acknowledge that the Turkish government is complicit in the torture, kidnapping, and unlawful detention by Turkish security forces and government sponsored militias.[42] Turkey is recognized as a world leader in the area of "cultural repression." The Turkish state has completely prohibited the use of the Kurdish language, despite the fact that 20 percent of the country's population (over 13 million people) is Kurdish. Until the early 1990s, the government refused even to acknowledge that the Kurds existed as a people, instead insisting that they were merely "Mountain Turks" who denied their Turkish heritage.[43]

Those who speak out against Turkey's repression are censored and punished. One Kurdish student and publisher was prosecuted by the government for engaging in "terrorism" after he published a lecture from U.S. scholar Noam Chomsky. The lecture, which contained some brief criticisms of Turkish human rights abuses, was deemed a threat to "the indivisible unity" of the country. Turkey's "anti-terrorism" laws ban any books, movies, and television and radio programs that discuss Kurdish nationalism. Government police arrested thousands who signed petitions supporting the teaching of Kurdish in public schools. The government even shut down a television station in one major city in the southeast of the country for playing Kurdish songs.[44]

Despite extensive documentation of Turkish repression, only Kurdish actions are designated as terrorist in U.S. reporting. The PKK is attacked by Turkish and U.S. officials as a terrorist entity, and these attacks are uncritically transmitted in media coverage. A review of *Washington Post* stories from January 1990 through December of 2007 (a period marked by increased violence between Kurdish nationalists and the Turkish government) finds that the terrorist label is systematically applied *only* to the actions of rebels, and not to Turkey's government itself. Of the over 115 news articles focusing on the topic of Turkish-Kurdish violence and terrorism, not a single story referenced Turkey's actions against Kurdish civilians as terrorism, whereas *all* of the stories uncritically repeated either Turkish or U.S. official claims that Kurds were engaging in terrorism.[45] A closer analysis of U.S. reporting provides a better understanding of this politicization.

U.S. media reports have at times acknowledged Turkish human rights abuses. However, Turkish repression is never framed as terrorism. Turkish violence against the Kurds is presented as a relatively minor setback in the grand scheme of U.S. and European relations with Turkey, as opposed to Saddam Hussein's repression of Iraqi Kurds, which is presented as a major human rights tragedy. Kurds killed by Saddam Hussein are "honored" as "victims" of a major "atrocity" by the *New York Times*. Hussein's gassing of Iraqi Kurds is commonly referred to as a "tragedy," a "massacre," or as "genocide" in the press.[46]

Iraqi Kurds, however, were not always seen as worthy of this attention. The mass media's focus on the victims of Saddam Hussein exploded only after Iraq invaded Kuwait in August of 1990. It was at this point that the first Bush administration officially labeled the regime of Saddam Hussein, which had previously been an ally, as an enemy of the United States. Media coverage responded accordingly. A review of the *Washington Post*'s coverage of Kurdish suffering shows that attention was meager when Saddam Hussein's crimes were at their peak. Hussein ordered the gassing of the Kurdish town of Halabja in March of 1988, resulting in the deaths of between several hundred to thousands of civilians. However, as Table 3.1 shows, coverage identifying Hussein's actions as an "atrocity," a "massacre," or as "genocide" was three to four times more common in the twenty-nine months after Iraq's invasion of Kuwait than it was in the twenty-nine months following Halabja, but prior to the Kuwait invasion.

Media coverage of Iraq's repression of the Kurds represents a classic example of the politicization of human rights. Iraqi Kurds were designated three to four times more worthy of media attention following Iraq's designation as an enemy state. Conversely, allies who continue to direct violence against the Kurds of Iraq are viewed positively in the U.S. press. Editors portray the United States and Europe as "sympathetic to" Turkey as it suffers under the Kurdish "terrorist threat,"

TABLE 3.1: Framing of Iraq's Repression of the Kurds in the *Washington Post* News Stories, Op-Eds, and Editorials, 1988–1993

Description of Crimes	No. of Articles w/Description: Pre-Invasion of Kuwait (3/1/1988–8/2/1990)	No. of Articles w/Description: Post-Invasion of Kuwait (8/2/1990–1/2/1993)
Genocide	7	23
Massacre	7	25
Atrocity	6	26

Source: Lexis Nexis

instead of sympathizing with Kurds suffering under Turkish terror. Although the United States and its allies "have hesitated to accept Turkey as a political equal as long as it was committing terrible human rights abuses against Kurds," such abuses are not considered enough to dampen U.S.-Turkish relations (as they were in the case of Saddam Hussein). The editors at the *Washington Post* grant Turkey a "second chance" to pursue a "breakthrough with its Kurds," even as human rights groups continue to release reports lambasting the government for widespread human rights violations and terrorism.[47]

Application of the term *genocide* has become so politicized that it is used more often to refer to predicted genocides than to cases where critics claim genocide is actually occurring. Though the *Washington Post* referred to Turkey's treatment of the Kurds as genocide in only four instances over seventeen years, stories in the same paper have discussed the possibility of genocide occurring in Iraq (in the case of a U.S. withdrawal) a total of twenty-one times during only two years of coverage from January 2006 through January 2008. The warning of Republican senator John McCain that Iraq withdrawal could lead to mass killing is taken far more seriously than human rights violations already taking place in countries deemed to be strategically valuable.[48]

The violent repression of Kurdish civilians is the subject of righteous condemnation when those actors responsible are officially designated enemies of state, as in the case of Saddam Hussein. Turkish leaders successfully target Kurds for torture and assassination, benefiting from strong U.S. political and military support, and accompanied by only minor objections in media. Such violations, as far as U.S. media and political elites are concerned, are far less worthy of being described as a tragedy, atrocity, or genocide. These violations are certainly not described as terrorism or considered worth compromising U.S.-Turkish relations. Concurrently, Iraqi terror directed against the very same Kurds is morally reprehensible, and to be condemned with the bluntest language, so long as the victims are on the Iraqi rather than the Turkish side of the border. An analysis of the *Washington Post*'s coverage of Iraq and Turkey shows that genocide is again heavily politicized when contrasting the cases of Turkish and Iraqi government violence against Kurds. Iraqi government responsibility for the deaths of an estimated 100,000 Kurds was described as genocide in seventy-nine stories reviewed in the seventeen-year period from January 1993 through January of 2005. In contrast, Turkey's responsibility for the deaths of tens of thousands of Kurds in the seventeen-year period from January 1990 to January 2007 is described as genocide in only four stories. In other words, Iraqi actions were more than twenty times as likely to be classified as genocide than those of Turkey, despite the claims of human rights groups, political leaders and Kurdish protestors that the term applied to both cases.[49]

Efforts to distinguish between worthy victims (Iraqi Kurds) and unworthy ones (Turkish Kurds) have been somewhat altered, however, in recent years. By 2007, attacks on Iraqi Kurds became acceptable in media reporting, so long as the aggressor was the Turkish government, rather than Saddam Hussein. The United States granted tactical and diplomatic support to the government of Turkey as it bombed various Kurdish areas in northern Iraq, allegedly aimed at PKK rebel targets.[50] Despite reports of civilian deaths, U.S. editorials lent moral support to the Turkish government.[51] Most media outlets opposed a military incursion, but continued to sympathize with Turkey. The editors at the *New York Times* postured that "Turkey's anger is understandable. Guerillas from the PKK have been striking from bases in Iraqi Kurdistan with growing impunity and effect. . . . The death toll for Turkish military forces is mounting."[52]

Editors at the *New York Times* placed responsibility for the violence primarily upon the shoulders of the Kurds, rather than Turkish leaders, as they argued, "The Kurds will find it much easier to prosper if they can live in peace with Turkey." How such cooperation was possible in light of Turkey's systematic human rights violations and its assault on the Kurdish civilian population was not addressed. The paper's editors also portrayed the United States as an honest broker between the two sides, rather than a consistent supporter of Turkish repression of the Kurds: "Washington must now try to walk both sides back from this brink. It then should make a serious and sustained effort to broker a long-overdue political agreement between Turkey and Iraqi Kurdistan."[53] The editors at the *Washington Post* presented the conflict through a pro-Turkish lens. Significant attention was directed to pragmatic assessments of the effectiveness of a Turkish political victory over Kurdish rebels: "The reality is that the PKK threat cannot be quickly eliminated by military means. . . . Neutralizing it will require closer cooperation between Turkish and Iraqi Kurdish authorities, more effective Turkish military operations inside Turkey, and more political reforms in both countries."[54]

This case study is instructive in one important respect: it suggests that U.S. media attention to the repression and terror of foreign countries is not driven by humanitarian concerns, but by the strength of the alliance between the United States and the country in question. Little else can explain why the *very same* Kurds who are regarded as worthy victims when killed by U.S. enemies such as Saddam Hussein are not worthy when killed by an allied government like Turkey. Strategic rather than humanitarian concerns explain why Iraqi Kurds killed by Hussein when he was an ally are three to four times less worthy than the same Kurds killed by Saddam Hussein once he became an opponent of the United States. The consequences of such propagandistic news coverage are stark for those who take human rights seriously. A genuine concern with social justice requires a consistent condemnation of terror, regardless of whether it is pursued by U.S. enemies or allies.

WORTHY AND UNWORTHY VICTIMS: THE CASE OF MILITARY AND CIVILIAN CASUALTIES IN THE IRAQ WAR

While media coverage of civilian deaths in allied and enemy states closely follows Herman and Chomsky's predictions, it is unclear whether reporting distinguishes between worthy and unworthy victims in cases where the United States is directly involved in military conflict. Gitlin's claim, reviewed at the introduction of this chapter, that media outlets may focus extensive attention on U.S. responsibility for civilian deaths is tested extensively here. U.S. military and Iraqi civilian casualties in Iraq are addressed below. Three categories of analysis are pursued, focusing on coverage of the following: U.S. soldiers killed by Iraqi "insurgents"; Iraqi civilians killed by other Iraqis, and; Iraqi civilians killed by U.S. forces. Those Iraqis killed by the United States are separated into two categories:

those depicted as murdered by individual rogue soldiers and those killed as a consequence of U.S. foreign policy.

With only a brief survey of U.S. media coverage of Iraq, one begins to discern a general pattern whereby the United States is depicted as a benevolent force, rather than as exacerbating a humanitarian crisis. Verbal emphasis is directed at U.S. deaths, although photos of the dead receive little if any attention.[55] The focus on U.S. humanitarianism and concern over casualties is evident in a *Time* magazine story that emphasizes the consequences of withdrawal:

> A reduction in the United States combat presence would probably produce one clear benefit: a lower United States casualty rate. But a chilling truth is that as the United States death toll declined, the Iraqi one would almost surely soar. Just how many Iraqis would die if the United States withdrew is anyone's guess, but almost everyone who has studied it believes the current rate of more than a thousand a month would spike dramatically. It might not resemble Rwanda, where more than half a million people were slaughtered in six months in 1994. But Iraq could bleed like the former Yugoslavia did from 1992 to 1995, when 250,000 perished.[56]

Time's predictions were particularly propagandistic at a time when statistical studies suggested that over one million Iraqis were already killed under the U.S. occupation, and in light of estimates that over half of Iraqi deaths were the result of U.S. military operations.[57] The notion that a U.S. withdrawal will result in a dramatic increase in civilian casualties is a construct of the U.S. press, not an empirical fact. Reporters, columnists, and editors take for granted the claims of political leaders that a departure would enable more violence, as the United States is seen as the only force keeping Iraq from full-blown civil war or genocide. Iraqi public opinion, on the contrary, overwhelmingly subscribes to the opposite view, that the U.S. occupation itself is exacerbating violence in Iraq. One poll from 2005 found that less than 1 percent of Iraqis questioned felt the United States and its allies were successful in decreasing Iraqi violence. Surveys from 2006 showed that two-thirds of those questioned felt nationwide security would improve and sectarian violence would decrease if the United States withdrew. Studies from 2007 found the same results.[58]

Reporting on the U.S. occupation ranges from praise of the United States for fighting sectarian violence to criticisms of the occupation for failing to prevent sectarian war. This range of expressible views necessarily omits the view of most Iraqis that it is the United States, rather than warring Iraqi factions, that is responsible for creating instability. On the optimistic side of this debate, the editors at the *Washington Post* claim that U.S. forces are "performing noble work in trying to protect Iraqi civilians" from sectarian violence and foreign incursions from neighboring states.[59] The United States is presented as paying a heavy price in its efforts to save Iraqis from themselves and from external threats.

Op-ed writers in the *Washington Post* express the more pessimistic side of mainstream opinion, asserting that the United States failed to achieve its humanitarian goals. In one example, John Podesta, Lawrence Korb, and Brian Katulis claim that although the United States "contributes to regional instability" this consequence of the occupation is not beyond correction. Despite an increase in "sectarian cleansing" throughout Iraq, the Bush administration has had "success" in the "reduction of casualties in certain areas" as a result of its "surge."[60] Michael Gerson contends that the U.S. response to sectarian violence has "improved from dismal to minimal," but warns against withdrawal. "The fragile sectarian balance of several Middle Eastern countries would be upset, causing serious destabilization. A precipitous U.S. withdrawal from Iraq could make a miserable problem significantly worse."[61]

WHAT DO WE KNOW ABOUT CASUALTIES IN IRAQ?

U.S. military deaths in Iraq are meticulously documented in the U.S. press. Soldiers are deemed heroes preventing the emergence of civil war. As of the end of 2008, 4,221 U.S. troops had lost their lives in Iraq, according to the Iraq Coalition Casualty Count project. The thousands of U.S. deaths, however, pale in comparison to the number of Iraqis who have been killed since the 2003 United States invasion. Even the most conservative statistical estimates of death rates in Iraq heavily implicate the United States as a guilty party. The Iraq Body Count project, using only casualties reported in newspapers, estimated that over 24,000 civilians were killed between 2003 and 2005. Of those killed 37 percent were the result of U.S. military actions, as opposed to 9 percent from "insurgents."[62] Iraq Body Count unquestioningly demonstrates a consistent pattern of U.S. attacks on civilians. In mid- to late- 2007, "the civilian death toll by US fire was 96 in October, with 23 children among them, while in September U.S. forces and contractors killed 108 Iraqi civilians, including 7 children. In August U.S. troops killed 103 civilians, 16 of them children, and in July they killed 196. During the last five months of 2007, U.S. forces in Iraq killed over 600 Iraqi civilians."[63]

Scientific surveys of Iraqi neighborhoods implicate the United States in even larger death tolls. One survey from 2004 published in the British medical journal *The Lancet* estimated that 100,000 Iraqis were killed in the first eighteen months of the occupation. Most of those deaths were said to be a result of air strikes by the United States and its allies. Under the U.S. occupation, risk of violent death was fifty-eight times more likely than before the 2003 invasion.[64] Another *Lancet* study from 2006 found that 655,000 were killed, over half as a result of U.S. actions.[65] A 2007 study estimated that over 1.2 million civilians were killed by the height of the civil war.[66] Previous studies have shown that the *Lancet* reports received marginal coverage in the U.S. media.[67] When news stories did recognize the reports, they were downplayed to reduce their potential for damaging the image of the United States in the eyes of the U.S. public. In one example, Tony Karon of *Time* magazine conceded that an "uncomfortable aspect for the United States of the *Lancet* study is the conclusion that the majority of the violent deaths had been caused not by terror attacks, but by United States air strikes." Karon countered that U.S. bombings of civilians were actually the fault of the "insurgents":

> Civilian casualties are pretty much inevitable when air power is used in cities, despite the best intentions and technological capabilities of those dropping the bombs. That's precisely why the rebels hide out among the civilian population: They know better than to isolate themselves as a target for their enemy's superior firepower, instead forcing them to inflict casualties on the civilian population in order to kill enemy combatants, thereby creating a force multiplier for the insurgency.[68]

Karon's comments demonstrate that, even when Iraqis are characterized as worthy victims, and U.S. forces are admitted to be responsible for those killings, they must be absolved from any responsibility. "Insurgents," it seems, make easy scapegoats.

Perhaps most disturbing of all estimates of Iraqi deaths was released in early 2009. At this time, the *New York Times* quietly conceded in one back-page story that over 740,000 husbands were killed in Iraq since the 2003 invasion. Factoring in women and children killed, that number of dead may reach as high as 1 to 1.5 million or more. Sadly, the *New York Times* story failed to spur serious attention in the rest of the U.S. press.

NEW MEDIA, IRAQ, AND THE POLITICS OF CASUALTY COVERAGE

If journalists see the United States as committed to humanitarian interventions, then its actions cannot possibly be framed as repressive. In light of this assumption, one would expect that civilians killed by the United States will receive meager attention in reporting on Iraq, and certainly not be portrayed as a consequence of a militaristic foreign policy. A lack of coverage of civilian casualties is not due to a lack of actual deaths at the hands of the United States; the previous section documented U.S. responsibility for the deaths of a minimum of hundreds of thousands of civilians, perhaps more than one million.

The next section examines media attention to three groups: U.S. military casualties, Iraqis killed by other Iraqis, and Iraqis killed by the United States.

1. U.S. Casualties as Major News

A review of CNN's reporting on Iraq in 2006 and 2007 shows that the question of U.S. deaths is of utmost concern. Of all the stories reviewed from the program *This Week at War* (originally covered in chapter 2), an overwhelming 86 percent referenced U.S. soldiers killed in Iraq. Casualty coverage of U.S. deaths is highly ritualized, with regular updates on the individual soldiers killed each week and discussions with the friends and families of the dead. There is no such focus on interviewing the families of those killed in Iraq by U.S. forces. Comprehensive estimates of the U.S. dead are common. There is a strong concern with documenting each and every U.S. soldier killed. A brief report from *This Week at War* host John Roberts demonstrates this pattern quite well. By early November of 2006, Roberts reported, "More than 2,800 United States troops died in that frustrating mission to establish peace here. Soldiers like Sergeant Will Mock, 23 years old from Harper, Kansas. CNN's Arwa Damon met him two years ago on his first tour of duty here. Mock was a confident leader who genuinely believed in the idea he could help make Iraq a better place."[69]

Media attention to military casualties is accompanied by reminders of the nobility of the mission in Iraq. Even when reporters criticize the administration for failing to effectively fight the "War on Terror," the good intentions of U.S. leaders are never in question. CNN correspondent

Michael Holmes reinforces this position when he reports that the United States is fighting terror in Iraq so that it does not have to fight them at home: "Over the last couple of days, I've spent a lot of time with many ordinary Iraqi student engineers, women's activists . . . and they say why do you want to fight them over here and take our lives. Our lives are being lost so that U.S. lives are more secure."[70] Criticisms are directed against the campaign in Iraq by those who feel that U.S. lives are being sacrificed by leaders who have no realistic plans for victory. CNN correspondent Jamie McIntyre, for example, discussed the conclusions of the Iraq Study Group report that "the United States doesn't have enough troops to really do it [the surge] effectively."[71] Network anchor John Roberts repeated this concern over the "fundamental question of strategy . . . the violence keeps increasing in Baghdad. What's the problem? Are the troops effective? Is there just something fundamentally wrong with the plan? If you've got all those Iraqi forces [trained for security operations], what is happening? Why can't you bring some of the U.S. troops home?"[72]

2. The Spectacle of Iraqi-on-Iraqi Violence

Iraqis killed as a result of sectarian violence receive an enormous amount of coverage on CNN. This is not surprising, considering that those responsible for these deaths—"insurgents" and foreign fighters—are officially designated as enemies by U.S. political leaders. Consistent focus on these victims has the added benefit for U.S. propagandists of reminding U.S. viewers of the "humanitarian" nature of the mission.

Victims of sectarian violence are referenced in 91 percent of all the *This Week at War* programs. Attention directed at these victims, however, is less specific and more abstract than that allotted to U.S. soldiers killed in Iraq. General references to death tolls from sectarian violence are common, although reports of specific individuals killed, and reactions from family and friends, are rare. Still, comprehensive figures are regularly provided of thousands of civilians killed due to "insurgent" and militia violence. A few examples demonstrate this practice in detail:

- "Monday [November 20], police in Baghdad find 60 bullet-riddled bodies. Government officials are targeted. Even a television comedian is killed. Thursday [November 23], coordinated car bombs in the space of 30 minutes kill more than 200 people and injure hundreds more in Baghdad's Shiite stronghold of Sadr City."[73]

- In August of 2006, *This Week at War* reports "558 violence incidents" for July. All of them are attributed to enemies of the United States in Iraq: "The attacks caused 2,100 deaths and 77 percent of casualties resulted from sectarian violence."[74]

- In September of 2006, a U.N. report is discussed, concluding that 6,600 civilians were killed in the previous two months. None of those deaths are attributed to U.S. military operations.[75]

- In October of 2006, *This Week at War* reports on approximately 1,500 people executed in Baghdad alone. These deaths are deemed "a stunning admission that there is a real security problem here on the ground."[76]

- In November of 2006, reports surface that over half a million Iraqi refugees have been relocated in Jordan. Refugee numbers are expected to be exacerbated in light of the "mass kidnapping" of Iraqi intellectuals, teachers, and doctors by militia groups and death squads.[77]

Heavy emphasis on the victims of sectarian violence fulfills an important political objective, directing attention away from Iraqi civilians killed by the United States.

No harsh words are spared in condemning those responsible for such attacks. In one example, a reporter from *This Week at War* reviews a U.N. report claiming that by mid-2006 "an average of 100 Iraqi civilians [were] losing their lives every day. . . . It really is a very devastating state and it's only escalating. The violence is only increasing, especially in the capital of Baghdad."[78] Iraq's suffering under civil war and "insurgent" attacks is depicted as "devastating" and "staggering"—as a "crisis" that the United States "seems powerless" to stop.[79] Iraqis struggle "to hold on to normal lives in the face of disruption, uncertainty, torture and death."[80] The message of this reporting is clear: a U.S. withdrawal will hurt the worthy, unfortunate victims of civil war. Sectarian violence has created a climate of "fear and intimidation," reporter Arwa Damon explains: "What we're seeing right now is various militias, belonging to both the Sunni and the Shia factions, carrying out acts of violence against people of the other sect. . . . Sectarian violence and fear of being the next victim . . . is actually ripping apart the fabric of society here, tearing apart neighborhoods."[81]

No similar portrayal of Iraqis as desperate due to U.S. bombing or destruction is apparent anywhere in *This Week at War*'s reporting.

3. U.S. Violence Against Iraqis: No Cause for Condemnation

CNN pays some attention to Iraqis killed by the United States. However that attention is far less than that directed at U.S. soldiers or those killed by "insurgents" or militias. Of all the CNN programs analyzed, only 25 percent discussed Iraqi civilians who were killed by U.S. forces. Iraqis killed by other Iraqis receive over 3.5 times the coverage of Iraqis killed by the United States. Similarly, U.S. soldiers killed in Iraq receive more than three times as much attention than do Iraqis killed by the United States. Such statistics, however, do not fully convey the nature of media coverage of Iraqi casualties caused by the United States. While U.S. killing of Iraqis received attention in one quarter of all stories, much of that coverage was devoted to *exonerating* U.S. troops for responsibility in the deaths.

The Haditha killings are a prime example of U.S. downplaying of civilian casualties. In November of 2005, U.S. marines allegedly murdered twenty-four Iraqis in cold blood, including women and children, in the western Iraqi town of Haditha. A number of marines were subsequently put on trial by the U.S. military for their alleged role in the executions. The charges of murder in Haditha inevitably received attention in the U.S. press, as their incendiary nature made them difficult to ignore, especially at a time when most Americans opposed the occupation of Iraq, and when the military itself was prosecuting those involved in the incident. Sustained coverage, however, does not necessarily translate into critical coverage. CNN anchors and guests consistently approached the Haditha question from a defensive position, questioning the legitimacy of the charges at every turn. The events at Haditha were not described as a "massacre," and certainly not an example of U.S. "terror"; rather, reporters and guests referred more passively to the "deaths" and to those who had been "killed" in the incident, only occasionally appropriating the more blunt term "murder."[82] Use of the murder description, however, is hardly evidence of media independence from government, considering that the marines involved in Haditha were charged with the crime of murder by military authorities.

The dominant reaction to the Haditha murders was one of denial. When asked "how shocked" she was after hearing the charges against the marines, correspondent Jennifer Eccleston offered a noble depiction of the troops. "It's very hard to imagine that the men we were with would actually take part in this, would have knowledge of this and not do anything about it or being complicit in some sort of cover-up. They were nothing but exemplary when we were with them. They acted professionally. They were doing their job." Correspondent Aneesh Raman framed the behavior of troops he was embedded with as "exemplary"; they were simply "trying to do their job" in Iraq.[83] Reporter Jamie McIntyre suggested the acts may have been self-defense—a rather controversial claim considering the news media had little access to definitive evidence regarding the case. McIntyre cited one of the attorneys from the case, claiming "they have a good defense of either justifiable homicide or self-defense," and "no evidence of a cover-up. . . . It looks like the prosecution may have a tougher time proving what they think happened."

As discussed in chapter 1, *This Week at War* guest lists are dominated by military sources. Framing of the Haditha killings also took on a pro-military slant. General George Joulwan, one guest on the program, argued that the charges against the marines would hurt the war effort. They would have "an effect on the troops. We come from a culture that this—we don't permit this. It doesn't go on."[84] Retired General James Marks, a regular guest on the show, reacted to charges against Army Private Steven Green, who allegedly raped and murdered an Iraqi woman and her family. When asked whether U.S. soldiers' legal immunity from Iraqi courts enabled incidents such as Haditha and other executions, Marks responded, "I've got to challenge that. The United States very specifically holds its soldiers and its Marines and its service members to an extremely high standard. It is not fertile ground for the commission of crimes and in fact the United States military will very aggressively pursue any allegation." The claim was repeated by CNN reporter Arwa Damon: "Even though this [the charge against Green] is the fifth incident that is being investigated, I think there's a certain amount of recognition that this [U.S. executions] is not happening all across the country. . . . The United States military is taking [the charges] very seriously. These types of incidents consume senior commanders, consume their senior leadership. They have to right this type of wrong."[85]

Part of the reason for the moderate coverage of U.S. soldiers charged with murder has to do with the nature of the crimes in question. The deaths at Haditha, though clearly not reinforcing the frame of the United States as a humanitarian power, do not fundamentally challenge the overarching goal of humanitarian intervention espoused by political and media elites. The Haditha killings can, and indeed have been, counter-framed as an example of the role the United States government and military play as the distributor of justice, as the "righter of wrongs," in the words of one CNN reporter. Media coverage of Iraqis killed by individual "rogue" soldiers represents a partial exception to the expectations of the propaganda model. Iraqis killed by U.S. troops can be categorized as "partially worthy" victims in media coverage, in that they are represented as the victims of individual soldiers, but not of American foreign policy more generally. Reporting on "partially worthy" victims, however, should not be taken as an example of media independence from political officials. The Haditha trials were an initiative of the government, not the mass media. Additionally, even when CNN did cover Haditha, it was heavily reliant on military sources denying that the Iraqis killed were victims of U.S. violence.

Revelations that U.S. troops may murder Iraqi civilians, though incongruent with images of the troops as "heroes," can at least be tolerated in reporting. So long as civilians killed are repositioned within a framework portraying the government as the party responsible for correcting the "rogue" behavior of individual soldiers, the government's professed goals of democratizing Iraq, fighting terrorism, and preventing civil war may survive intact. What cannot be tolerated in media reports and editorials, however, are portrayals of American foreign policy itself as fundamentally repressive, and systematically leading to the deaths of thousands of innocent civilians. Although such a criticism could easily be made in light of the detailed studies showing hundreds of thousands killed due to U.S. operations in Iraq, this challenge is certainly not seen in CNN's war reporting.

A review of the episodes of *This Week at War* finds that not a single report suggests that mass killing in Iraq is a consequence of U.S. foreign policy. On the single occasion when *This Week at War* did mention the *Lancet* report, the estimated deaths of hundreds of thousands of Iraqis were not even attributed to U.S. actions. This exoneration of the United States is all the more revealing, considering that the *Lancet* report charged the United States with responsibility for Iraqi deaths. Rather than concede that the United States bears responsibility for causing humanitarian disaster, reporters simply repeated the claims of former president Bush that the report was not "credible."[86] Iraqi majority sentiment that the United States, rather than any other group, is most responsible for exacerbating humanitarian disaster is predictably ignored in CNN reporting.

One caveat should be noted regarding unworthy victims of U.S. state violence. It is not true that criticisms of U.S. state violence are never reported in *This Week at War*. On one occasion, such a criticism did appear on the program, from a shadowy figure nicknamed "Azzam the American." Azzam, who is thought to be a U.S. citizen who converted to Islam, appeared in an alleged al-Qaeda video threatening attacks on the United States.[87] Azzam condemned the United States and Britain for "atrocities in the two Iraq wars."[88] He argued: "After decades of American tyranny and oppression, now it's your turn to die. Allah willing, the streets of America will run red with blood matching drop for drop of America's victims."[89] Criticisms of U.S. policy as repressive do not have to be reserved only to religious fundamentalists or terrorist groups. Reporters and editors can easily find critics of U.S. policy as imperialist or driven by selfish material motives among antiwar activists, scholars, and members of the general public. The equation of moral condemnations of the war with extremist groups, then, reveals a great deal about the limits of "legitimate" dissent in the press. "Responsible" critics question the war because it takes too many U.S. lives, or because it is too costly or unwinnable, but criticisms of U.S. repression and imperialism are associated only with fanatical enemies of the state—people who are hardly taken seriously by U.S. news.

LESSONS FROM MEDIA COVERAGE OF THE MIDDLE EAST

This chapter does not seek to answer the question of what specifically constitutes genocide. That question is bound to incite much controversy among those who engage it, and it is beyond the scope of this study. Rather, the goal here is merely to describe how the concept of genocide is politicized by media and political leaders to reinforce official agendas. Of the eight categories of people killed that are examined in this chapter, almost all fall within the worthy and unworthy victims categories. One can include as worthy victims: Iraqi Kurds killed by Saddam Hussein (after he became an official enemy), those killed in the Srebrenica massacre, and Iraqis killed due to sectarian violence and "insurgent" activity. Unworthy victims include Armenians killed during Ottoman rule, Iraqi Kurds killed by Saddam Hussein (before he became an official enemy), Iraqis killed by the Turkish government, and Turkish Kurds killed by the Turkish government. Only one category—Iraqis killed by U.S. soldiers—fails to fit completely within the worthy-unworthy victims dichotomy. For these partially worthy victims, however, media reporting does not constitute an example of media independence from officialdom. Coverage of these victims is devoted to denying claims that they were executed by U.S. forces, and to omitting claims that they are victims of U.S. foreign policy. To the extent that Iraqi civilians are seen as victims, critical coverage comes about *only* because the United States military chooses to acknowledge them as potential victims.

There is no consistent humanitarian standard for ensuring that victims of state and non-state violence receive balanced coverage. U.S. media coverage is highly propagandistic, creating a polarization between various groups depending on the specific political context in which the repression takes place. If the goal of media coverage is to ensure that all victims of terror and violence are treated equally, then the U.S. press abysmally fails in providing fair coverage. On the other hand, if the goal of coverage is simply to reflect and justify elite values that favor specific types of victims over others, then the coverage is impressive in its consistent transmission of those values.

CHAPTER FOUR

Journalistic Norms and Propaganda: Iraq and the War on Terror

The study of the media as a political institution is prevalent in the social sciences.[1] This approach explores how national and international institutions influence politics at the individual level. As individuals, reporters retain strong "incentive[s] to adapt to prevailing conditions [within institutions] than seek to change the institutional order."[2] Scholar David Michael Ryfe explains that reporters are consigned to a sort of "path dependency." They tend to conform to an informal system, reinforcing specific "taken for granted assumptions and behaviors" that are adopted reflexively after years of socialization and positive reinforcement.[3] Journalists see themselves in many different ways—as interpreters of social reality, instruments of government, representatives and critics of government, and as aiding in the policymaking process.[4] They claim values of "objectivity," "impartial" reporting, "neutrality," "fair and balanced" coverage, and professional "detachment."[5] However, scholars are increasingly challenging the claim that reporters serve as unbiased actors, and there is much ambiguity about precisely what "objectivity" means.[6]

Professional journalists rely heavily on official sources, and they usually refrain from citing sources outside of the bipartisan spectrum of opinion. Bartholomew Sparrow discusses media dependency on government sources as influenced by business constraints. Media outlets are "homogenous," serving a "functional" role by reinforcing the "political and economic status quo."[7] Journalists ritualistically rely on centralized sources such as executive branch officials, members of Congress, and party leaders in order to provide "timely information" since reporters operate under market constraints to produce large amounts of news with fewer and fewer resources.[8] While journalistic catering to official perspectives is ensured through the "routinization" of the media-government partnership, political leaders may also withhold information or publicly chastise media when they feel coverage is not sufficiently sycophantic.[9] Advertiser pressure also plays a crucial role in disciplining reporters, editors, and owners to refrain from criticizing business interests and behaviors. Numerous studies demonstrate that journalists, editors and owners are conservative in their economic beliefs, and heavily influenced by advertiser pressures to curtail programming considered critical of business.[10]

PRESS-STATE RELATIONS AND THE PRODUCTION OF NEWS

National media organize the production of news around various "news beats." Observational studies of journalists at the state, national, and local levels identify a historical pattern of media solicitation of political elites. News beats (whether it be the White House press room, local city halls, or other locations) are deemed "the appropriate sites at which information should be gathered."[11] Though news workers are largely unsupervised when working in the field, their affiliation and preoccupation with these central sites ensures their emphasis of official sources.[12] As journalists work together, reporting from various centralized sites of production, their shared experiences contribute to a socialization process that legitimizes the status quo.[13]

It is worth reflecting upon what type of reality journalistic socialization produces. Herbert Gans's classic study of news routines identifies a number of common assumptions under which journalists operate. These assumptions include an ethnocentric preoccupation with politics in the United States (to the neglect of the rest of the world), a commitment to "altruistic democracy" as it is understood by U.S. elites, a preference for the "moderate" center of the political spectrum, and a faith in capitalism as a form of social organization.[14] Reporters' "objective," unquestioning transmission of official statements makes them partners in the promulgation of government propaganda. Official sources serve as the major foundation for stories, with one classic study indicating they reach as high as 78 percent of all sources quoted in papers like the *New York Times* and *Washington Post*.[15]

Not all scholars agree that the press is a lapdog of the state, or that journalistic norms and routines ensure government dominance of mass media. Timothy Cook argues that media play an instrumental and partially independent role in the governing process. He describes the relationship between reporters and officials through the "negotiation of newsworthiness," whereby "a bargain of sorts is struck at newsbeats." Journalists wield power, Cook contends, by retaining "final say about the ultimate product." Serving as more than "mere extensions of the government," media outlets are allegedly critical in their pragmatic questioning of elected leaders.[16] Cook cites the example of media coverage of the 1991 Gulf war, when reporters pursued tactical criticisms of the "means" by which the conflict was pursued, "thereby raising doubts about President Bush's ability to accomplish the goals he set forth." This conflict "enables journalists to include tension and conflict that would otherwise be absent from their stories, and it also provides a way for reporters to perform a political ritual that distances them from their sources."[17]

There is good reason to question Cook's claims about media sovereignty. Criticisms of how presidents pursue policy, rather than the legitimacy of those policies, hardly qualify as independence (or even semi-independence) from government. If anything, such critiques represent a form of active support, as reporters voice their agreement with the government's foreign policy goals and principles, and seek to assist officials in pursuing them. Even when wars are opposed, criticisms do not question official motives—only whether they can be achieved. Cook maintains that "news from the White House newsbeat is not always from the White House's chosen perspective . . . presidents never get quite the coverage they want."[18] However, this is an authoritarian standard for evaluating media. According to this claim, journalists' submission to government occurs only when officials receive fawning coverage, with reporters refusing to level even procedural criticisms of policy. Such official worship, however, is literally impossible to achieve when conservative officials viciously attack reporters as un-American simply for reporting that attacks in Iraq take place.[19] Such criticisms never include evidence that reporting fluctuates out of proportion with changes in Iraqi violence. Typically, Republican claims are taken as evidence, in and of themselves, of media bias.[20] Such unsubstantiated polemics place reporters in a difficult position. Reporting that violence does occur under the United States occupation by itself certainly does not constitute evidence of antiwar bias. However, reporters may still feel pressured to curtail their reporting of "bad news" in Iraq by right-wing pundits and conservative political leaders. Though journalists could placate Republicans by refusing to report on violence in Iraq, few in the general public would take such reports very seriously.

Cook is correct that "merely calling attention to an issue does not ensure that one's preferred alternative will be pursued, let alone enacted."[21] But this claim makes little more than a straw man out of progressive critiques of media propaganda. Media critics on the left do not argue that reporters can *ensure* policy victories for political elites, since policy outcomes are always uncertain. The most important question is not whether media can ensure victories for officials, but whether reporters and editors produce news stories and editorials that *challenge* the bipartisan range of consensus and debate on important issues. If reporters fail in the basic task of incorporating dissident views in their stories, they cannot be classified as independent or even partially independent from government.

EVIDENCE OF JOURNALISTIC CENSORSHIP: THE STORY OF GARY WEBB

There is significant evidence that journalists are not interested in challenging bipartisan dominance of the news. Journalists who step outside this spectrum are in danger of being castigated. No case demonstrates this better than that of former *San Jose Mercury News* journalist Gary Webb. Prior to his ostracism from the mass media, Webb had built a successful career as an award-winning investigative reporter. In recounting his early success, Webb explained the freedom he enjoyed in selecting stories as one

> my editors wholeheartedly encouraged since it relieved them of the burden of coming up with story ideas. I wrote my stories the way I wanted to write them, without anyone looking over my shoulder or steering me in a certain direction. . . . In the seventeen years of doing this, nothing bad happened to me. I was never fired or threatened with dismissal if I kept looking under rocks. . . . And then I wrote some stories that made me realize how sadly displaced my bliss had been. The reason I'd enjoyed such smooth sailing for so long hadn't been, as I'd

> assumed, because I was careful and diligent and good at my job. It turned out to have nothing to do with it. The truth was that, in all those years, I hadn't written anything important enough to suppress.[22]

This all changed with the publication of Webb's controversial investigative series, "Dark Alliance."

In 1996, Webb published his bombshell stories, alleging CIA complicity in the international trafficking of cocaine. Webb's reporting never suggested that the agency was directly dealing in the drug, but merely that it turned a blind eye to the activities of Nicaraguan Contras (with which the CIA was working) that were smuggling drugs into the Los Angeles area. The story quickly became "the most talked-about piece of journalism" in 1996, and was unsurprisingly subject to harsh criticism in the mainstream press.[23] Stories in national papers criticized Webb for using unnamed sources, ironically at the same time that they employed anonymous sources to discredit him. The attack on Webb and the *San Jose Mercury News* became so vicious that the *Los Angeles Times* assembled what was described as the "Get Gary Webb Team" by one of the two dozen reporters involved.[24] The *Washington Post*, aside from relying on unnamed sources to debunk Webb's series, refused to print a letter from *Mercury News* editor Jerry Ceppos highlighting the nuanced nature of the "Dark Alliance" series' claims. The *Washington Post* often transmitted CIA denials of the series through an uncritical lens. Reporter Walter Pincus (who had written critically of Webb) was also shown to have collaborated with the CIA, engaging in spying operations in foreign countries for U.S. Army Counterintelligence.[25]

Close ties between journalists and the CIA exist in many different media outlets. As the CIA admits, it enjoys "relationships with reporters from every major wire service, newspaper, news weekly and TV network. . . . In many instances we have persuaded reporters to postpone, change, hold, or even scrap stories that could have adversely affected national security interests or jeopardized sources or methods."[26] Such relationships raise serious questions about whether journalists have climbed "on board" with official sources, and to what extent critics of American foreign policy retain credibility with reporters.

The close, largely *consensual* relationship between reporters and officials helps explain why the mass media continued to ignore overwhelming evidence of American complicity in the cocaine drug trade. Evidence of Lieutenant Colonel Oliver North's complicity in the cocaine trade and

Department of Defense intelligence agents' claims of CIA complicity are well documented.[27] The U.S. Senate Subcommittee on Narcotics and Terrorism found that CIA cargo planes were used by Contra forces as they transferred weapons from the United States to Central America, and then returned with shipments of cocaine. Frederick Hitz, inspector general for the CIA, also documented the tendency of the U.S.-allied Contras to traffic in cocaine.[28] Most of this information, however, was overlooked by the press.

Media censorship in the face of government propaganda is not confined to Gary Webb. However, his experiences do shed light upon the limits of journalistic autonomy. Despite evidence of CIA toleration of cocaine trafficking, Webb was excommunicated from the journalism profession, primarily for making minor mistakes in reporting a series that was, by and large, accurate. Accuracy, however, is of little value when a reporter moves against the political grain. "Objectivity" requires that journalists defer to official sources, no matter how ill-founded their claims. Only sustained attention from an antagonistic political party enables mainstream journalists to cover challenges to the party in office. In the case of the CIA-cocaine trafficking incident, antagonistic views were sorely lacking from an adversarial party.

PROPAGANDA AND NEWS MANAGEMENT IN THE IRAQ WAR

CIA cultivation of sources is not the only way that government manages the news. Presidents employ sophisticated image-management techniques in order to foster positive images of the executive branch. Journalist Mark Hertsgaard chronicled the Reagan administration's many successes in this area, in his classic work *On Bended Knee: The Press and the Reagan Presidency*. Reagan's staff essentially undertook a sustained campaign to "sell" the president to the American public.[29]

Utilizing its "extensive public relations apparatus," the Reagan White House utilized the press as a "positive instrument of governance," and as a "reliable and essentially non-intrusive transmitter" of White House propaganda.[30] This was accomplished by a number of methods, including regular phone conversations with television network reporters and editors, limiting direct access to Reagan himself, inviting reporters to White House lunch meetings in order to develop positive relationships, and finally "manipulation by inundation" of information in the form of constant press releases and official statements.[31] Hertsgaard explains that this strong relationship with reporters was not built upon mutual respect. Although reporters might have bought into the Reagan administration's spin, White House officials harbored a deep, paternalistic contempt for reporters and the general public's right to be informed on major issues.[32]

Paternalistic views of the press were also evident in the Bill Clinton and George W. Bush administration's news management methods. Bill Clinton famously announced the beginning of the 1998 U.S. bombing campaign against Iraq on the night before the Monica Lewinsky impeachment hearings began in Congress. Clinton also began a bombing campaign against Sudan three days after he testified to a grand jury regarding the Lewinsky scandal. The suspicious timing of the bombings raised serious questions about Clinton's use of media to divert attention away from charges of sexual indiscretion.

Bush administration officials appropriated a "postmodern" approach in dealing with reporters. Political reality was not seen so much as fixed and empirically observable, but as an object to be manipulated and socially constructed by the White House. One senior Bush advisor elaborated on the administration's mindset to *Wall Street Journal* reporter Ron Suskind after he wrote a story critical of a presidential ally:

> In the summer of 2002, after I had written an article in *Esquire* that the White House didn't like about Bush's former communications director, Karen Hughes, I had a meeting with a senior adviser to Bush. He expressed the White House's displeasure, and then he told me something that at the time I didn't fully comprehend—but which I now believe gets to the very heart of the Bush presidency. The aide said that guys like me were "in what we call the reality-based community," which he defined as people who "believe that solutions emerge from your judicious study of discernible reality." I nodded and murmured something about enlightenment principles and empiricism. He cut me off. "That's not the way the world really works anymore," he continued. "We're an empire now, and when we act, we create our own reality. And while you're studying that reality—judiciously, as you will—we'll act again, creating other new realities, which you can study too, and that's how things will sort out. We're history's actors . . . and you, all of you, will be left to just study what we do."[33]

The administration's heavy-handed news management tactics were witnessed on numerous occasions. Officials such as former secretary of defense Donald Rumsfeld attacked journalists for "exaggerating" the violence in Iraq and downplaying the "good" news accompanying the occupation.[34] Such attacks are contrary to the findings in chapters 3 and 7, which demonstrate that media reporting on Iraqi violence is heavily dependent on official propaganda, not independent of it.

In their dealings with the Iraqi press, the Coalition Provisional Authority (headed by United States administrator Paul Bremer) announced that it would shut down newspapers that publish "wild stories" if material was deemed provocative in inflaming ethnic violence.[35] Such behavior reflects the administration's commitment to censoring stories that do not comport with its preferred narrative. In part of an "information offensive" in Iraq, the American military also paid Iraqi newspapers to covertly plant stories that were authored by American troops.[36] These stories were aimed at promoting a positive image of the occupation at a time of mass Iraqi opposition to the U.S. military presence. The administration's manufacture of the news also occurred in the United States, where it aired dozens of "fake news segments" across a number of television stations, some of which promoted an image of the United States' success in Iraq.[37]

Reporters admit from time to time that they suffer from nationalistic pressures that censor their reporting. Administration pressure appears to encourage positive coverage of government policies. Former CBS reporter Dan Rather openly discusses the "climate of patriotism" that surrounded the September 11 attacks, the pressures to engage in "self-censorship," and the "reluctan[ce] to ask the tough questions for fear of being seen as unpatriotic."[38] Similarly, White House Press Corps and United Press International reporter Helen Thomas speaks of her censorship by former president George W. Bush and his press secretaries. Thomas was designated persona non grata and ignored at press conferences for her criticisms of government politicization of WMD intelligence, the United States' violations of the Geneva Conventions, and the large-scale loss of Iraqi and American lives as a result of the invasion.[39] Thomas discusses a number of methods employed by the administration to discipline unwieldy reporters. These include the threat of taking away press access to the president, and attempts to pressure newspapers to punish their reporters for stories with which the administration disagrees.[40]

Reporters also suffer great physical dangers when reporting from war zones. In the case of Iraq, dozens of journalists lose their lives every year. Editors are certainly aware of the increasing threat suffered by those whose "every path is strewn with danger, every checkpoint, every question a direct threat."[41] These deaths provide an increased incentive to "embed" with the United States military, considering that the number of non-embedded journalists killed in Iraq were over seventeen times higher (from 2003 to 2007) than the number killed who worked under the protection of American troops.[42]

But reporters are also forced to deal with other problems such as military censorship. Soldiers attempt to prevent reporters from covering events on the ground in Iraq, confiscating and destroying film, tapes, and electronic files that cover attacks on American troops.[43] In this case, reporting is designated as "biased" against the troops.

The discussion of overt government censorship only scratches the surface of the much larger issue of journalistic propaganda. Though reporters are occasionally the subject of attack from political leaders, such censorship is far from the norm. Media organizations would not be very effective in reinforcing the status quo if they had to censor every journalist they employ. Instead, conformity is achieved primarily through a long-term process of socialization and indoctrination. Indoctrination takes place in U.S. primary and secondary educational institutions (particularly journalism schools), and through positive reinforcement while working in the classroom and in the field. It is the lack of overt censorship, then, that makes U.S. media so effective in disseminating propaganda.

A review of journalists' historical accounts of the Iraq war demonstrates the extent to which they internalize official dogmas. In his reporting during the run-up to the Iraq war, former MSNBC host Phil Donahue explained: "Access is everything. . . . If you're the executive producer at one of the big news shows and you piss off Karl Rove, you're not going to get Condi or Rummy or any of those guests who would legitimize your

TABLE 4.1: Journalists Killed in Iraq (2003–2007) Total = 125

Year	Total Foreign Journalists Killed
2003	14
2004	24
2005	23
2006	32
2007	32

Source: The Committee to Protect Journalists, http://www.cpj.org/Briefings/Iraq/Iraq_danger.html

show as a serious, important program."[44] Donahue's statement reveals much about journalists' worship of access to officialdom. Reporters are more concerned with gaining access to officials than with questioning the legitimacy of their statements. Gaining access to high-level officials, rather than holding their feet to the fire, is deemed the primary means of legitimizing one's news organization.

Reporting on Iraq provides one of the best recent examples of the media's voluntary domesticity. Reporters were overwhelmingly content to accept the Bush administration's statements about Iraq's alleged weapons of mass destruction. Tom Yellin, executive producer of documentaries for ABC, explains the phenomenon:

> Colin Powell went in front of the United Nations and said, "The weapons of mass destruction exist." When you have Secretary of State Colin Powell, Secretary of Defense Donald Rumsfeld, the president of the United States, all kinds of people inside the United States government and the British government making the same point. . . . I think it would have been bad journalism, frankly, to go out on a limb and say, before knowing what we know now, that weapons of mass destruction did not exist in Iraq. I don't think you could have said that then in any convincing way, and it would have been bad reporting. It turns out that there weren't. But I don't think that it would have been appropriate to report at the time.[45]

Barton Gellman, a reporter for the *Washington Post*, echoes Yellin's claims:

> We now know in retrospect that much of what was said about WMDs was not true. So you would want the press to have turned that up before the war. . . . It was a very, very, very, very hard thing to do . . . we couldn't get the smoking gun. . . . We had some pretty good stories in my paper and elsewhere that had unnamed analysts saying the case was weaker than was being made publicly. . . . So you could neither name the person speaking nor adduce any evidence. Now critics of our performance say what we should have done was to give those officials equal billing with the president of the United States, who was saying, "I know, and here's the evidence, and here's the secretary of state, and here are the slides." We couldn't do that. We shouldn't do that.[46]

At the heart of Yellin's and Gellman's statements lies a deep trust in prominent official sources over less prominent ones. Yellin's and Gellman's comments, however, are as propagandistic as the stories they produce. I am aware of no critics on the left who were asking prior to the

Iraq war that media outlets uniformly report that Iraq did *not* possess weapons of mass destruction. Rather, the expectation was simply that intelligence assessments questioning whether Iraq possessed WMD or posed a threat to the United States should be seriously discussed *alongside* official claims that a threat existed. Contrary to the claims of Yellin and Gellman, there was extensive evidence prior to the invasion of Iraq that questioned a WMD threat. These challenges came from official sources that were in the best position to know: weapons inspectors who served in Iraq. United Nations weapons inspector Hans Blix, for example, continually reiterated his inability to locate WMDs in Iraq shortly prior to the 2003 invasion.[47] Similarly, former inspector Scott Ritter wrote extensively claiming that Iraq had disarmed after years of inspections in the 1990s.[48] Rolf Ekéus, former director of the United Nations Special Commission on Iraq, and Mohammed ElBaradei, the director general of the International Atomic Energy Agency, also challenged the notion that Iraq posed a chemical, biological, or nuclear threat.[49] Such sources were hardly of any significance to reporters. As David Martin, a reporter at CBS, explains: "The fact that the inspectors couldn't find them [WMDs] . . . that just made the case, 'He [Saddam Hussein] is hiding something, he is hiding something.'" Working from this mindset, reporters saw what they wanted to see: a serious threat to U.S. national security, even when no evidence could be found.[50] Trusting the Bush administration's propaganda, reporters interpreted the lack of evidence of an Iraqi threat as proof of Hussein's effectiveness in hiding that "threat."

Journalists' marginalization of critical intelligence speaks volumes about their bias in favor of high-level official sources. When journalists claim there were no sources questioning WMD intelligence, what they really mean is that there were no sources they considered *worthwhile* to quote. For media outlets operating on the margins of the mainstream press, however, there was far more willingness to question official dogmas. Secondary market news providers such as Knight Ridder, operating outside Washington, D.C., consistently cited lower-level government intelligence experts who were disputing the administration's claims.[51] John MacArthur of *Harper's* magazine lambasted the mainstream press for their complicity in disseminating propaganda:

> They didn't bother to find alternative sources. These people were all over the place. Any reporter knows that if there's one weapons inspector speaking publicly, there are others who aren't. . . . You have to go find them. But if there's one

> Scott Ritter saying this, that means there are ten or twenty Scott Ritters quietly saying it. You just have to go find them. It doesn't take much work.

Mainstream journalists did not fail to criticize the Bush administration due to lack of evidence or a scarcity of dissident views, but rather because they are socialized to be dependent on prestigious official sources. As MacArthur elaborates: "Journalists . . . they see their role as following the party line and repeating or accurately reporting what the government is saying. . . . That's the way journalism works in an official journalism town like Washington . . . with reporters who are largely dependent on official sources. . . . They can't operate without being part of the system."[52] In the few instances when reporters did actually question WMD claims, the reports were often buried on the back pages of major newspapers.[53]

American reporters were also timid in their criticisms because they ideologically supported the invasion. Serious challenges to the reasons for war were unwelcome in most commentary. Thomas Ricks, the Pentagon correspondent for the *Washington Post*, for example, described the media prior to the invasion as follows: "There was an attitude among editors: 'Look, we're going to war, why do we even worry about all this contrary stuff?'"[54] Larry Johnson, former U.S. deputy director of Counterterrorism, reflected: "The media are supposed to be the fourth estate but they decided to completely climb in bed with the administration on this [WMD]. . . . Early on [before the invasion] I felt there were some real dangers going into the war and I tried to get an op-ed into various major newspapers and the word kept coming back that no one wants to hear this because we're going to war."[55] Most operating in the press felt that questioning the administration carried with it major risks. Journalists did not want to be accused of defending Saddam Hussein, promoting their own agenda, or being unpatriotic.

Active cooperation among reporters, the Bush administration, and military planners was the norm during the 2003 invasion of Iraq. A systematic review of prewar reporting found that media outlets closely followed the Bush administration's rapid changeover in deemphasizing Osama bin Laden and focusing on Saddam Hussein.[56] A review of the testimony of reporters who were "embedded" with the U.S. military demonstrates the extent to which reporters subscribed to the war fever. Gordon Dillow of the *Orange County Register* spoke of limits on reporting casualties, based upon what "editors were going to find sufficiently tasteful or acceptable for a newspaper reading public." Dillow "refrained from describing dead Iraqis. It's the same way that TV news won't air certain images that are too graphic, even if there's a certain news value to them."[57] When journalists' reports are judged insufficiently sanitized, editors always reserve the power to censor coverage. A survey of two hundred journalists by the American University's School of Communications found that editors heavily censored news reports for reasons "other than basic style and length." Forty-two percent of journalists surveyed indicated that editors discouraged them from reporting images of dead Americans, while 36 percent were discouraged from showing pictures of hostages. Fifteen percent of reporters felt that "on one or more occasions" their news outlet edited material so that the final cut did not accurately depict the story.[58]

Concern for civilian casualties was neglected as media emphasized the tactical success of the march toward Baghdad. Media executives were overwhelmingly supportive of the military program whereby reporters were embedded with military units. CNN executive vice president Eason Jordan celebrated the program as a victory for all: "On the whole, I think the media won in the process; the military won in the process; and most importantly, news consumers in the United States and around the world won in the process. It was a win, win, win from my perspective. . . . think it went far better than 99 percent of people on the news team ever anticipated." On the domestic front, Jordan explained that CNN went to great lengths to secure military approval of the retired generals it used as guests: "I went to the Pentagon myself several times before the war started and met with important people there and said, for instance, at CNN, here are the generals we're thinking of retaining to advise us on the air and off about the war. And we got a big thumbs up on all of them. That was important."[59]

Though critics draw attention to the dangers of potential military censorship, there appears to be little evidence of such a trend. Reporters cited their tremendous amount of freedom to cover stories how they liked. Richard Ray of Fox News recounted his experiences as an embedded reporter:

> There were not a lot of rules. We were asked never to give out locations. Other than that, they trusted us to know that we should report and what we should not. I made it clear to my commanding officer that if I had a question about anything controversial, I would discuss it with him first. They gave us access to everything . . . they trusted us, and I think we were trustworthy. . . . They looked out for us

> and were protective in every way they could be. We tried to earn their trust, and I think we did.[60]

This anecdotal evidence is reinforced by systematic research. One study of 111 embedded reporters found widespread support for the program as providing them with "access to information they could not otherwise get."[61] Other studies found that journalists were content with embedding, and that reporting was more likely to be sympathetic to the military.[62] In general, reporters had tremendous freedom in the embedding process—so long as they refused to challenge official doctrines.

Even after a number of media outlets began to editorially oppose the Iraq war in 2007 and 2008, reporting was still heavily tailored to the administration's strategies and initiatives. One study following the 2007 "surge" of troops into Iraq found that total coverage of the conflict fell dramatically after congressional debate decreased in relation to the issue of a phased withdrawal.[63] As Mark Jurkowitz from the Project for Excellence in Journalism explained:

> In 2006, we had a new Democratic Congress that got elected. They thought they had a mandate to end this war. The president comes in with a surge in January. . . . Somewhere in the middle of [2007], it became evident, as the president continued to win legislative battles and get funding for the war without timetables for withdrawals or deadlines, that that battle had effectively been won. And that kind of coverage began to drop off fairly dramatically.[64]

This development demonstrates the limits of journalistic independence: even when editors openly oppose war, they are still limited in the attention they draw to critical issues such as withdrawal from Iraq.

BRITISH AND AMERICAN JOURNALISTIC NORMS IN COMPARISON AND CONTRAST

The U.S. media are often castigated for their ethnocentrism, parochialism, and inattention to the rest of the world. Communication scholars Howard Tumbler and Frank Webster characterize coverage of Iraq as "highly partisan, American-centric throughout, and framed by a conviction that the United States military forces were fighting a just war. . . . All the American news organizations backed the United States' mission in Iraq, from editorial line to report content."[65] However, many of the studies of British media provide contrasting pictures of whether the national media serves as an apparatus for state propaganda. Although propaganda is clearly practiced in British media, the extent and consistency to which those messages are conveyed is open to debate when compared to U.S. reporting.

British reporting is often more cosmopolitan in orientation than that of the U.S. press. This is reflected in the rhetoric and actions of Britain's flagship public news service: the BBC. Unlike public television outlets like PBS, the BBC regularly collects newscasts from around the world, making them available to the British public. Thousands of news stories are gathered from many regions of the world, including Asian-Pacific, European, Middle Eastern, African, and North and South American sources. As Richard Sambrook, the director of the BBC's global news division, explains, "The BBC's brand is internationalist—we bring you the world with a global perspective."[66] Newspapers such as the *Telegraph* and *Independent* are also world leaders in reporting of foreign news. The *Independent*'s commitment to unembedded reporting in Iraq was discussed at length in chapter 1, but the more conservative *Telegraph* is also designated a national leader in reporting global conflicts.[67]

There are significant differences between both the United States and United Kingdom regarding the notion of objectivity. The commitment to objectivity as a fair and unbiased mirroring of real world events is contested on many levels in the United Kingdom. Peter Foster of the *Telegraph* proclaims that "the belief in 'objective reporting' always was absurd—nothing more than a style of prose which created the illusion of fairness. Selection of facts, as any journalist knows, is everything." This does not mean that "objectivity" is shunned in the United Kingdom. Far from it. As the BBC's Richard Sambrook celebrates: "Comment is free but facts are sacred. . . . Accurate, objective news and information, which all sides can trust, provides a foundation stone of rational debate. . . . Objectivity is crucial to providing news people can trust."[68] Even in criticizing objectivity, Peter Foster admits to the desirability of news reporting as a form of truth. Though "there are no crystal balls" and "no definitive account," he still feels reporters should promote "a conversation by which we arrive at some collective notion of truth."[69]

A majority of journalists surveyed in both the United States and United Kingdom adhere to principles of objective journalism.[70] However, "objectivity" does not always mean the same thing in both countries. The reporting of the antiwar *Independent* demonstrates the weaker hold of objectivity in parts of the British press. The paper's reporting on Iraq is far less parochial and much more internationalist than that of the liberal *New York Times*. A brief survey of other media outlets also demonstrates that British media coverage of Iraq is less propagandistic than that of the American press. British media were less likely to refer to the invasion of Iraq by the U.S. government's propaganda term "Operation Iraqi Freedom." One study from the University of Maryland's Center for International and Security Studies found that the British media "gave greater attention to the ramifications of United States policy for other nations and to the work of international agencies such as the United Nations and the International Atomic Energy Agency [responsible for inspecting Iraqi WMD]."[71] Other studies established that though the British media were less likely to challenge "official narratives" and humanitarian claims for war, it also granted significant and positive coverage to antiwar activists.[72]

At least some room exists in British media for dissident perspectives. Journalist and documentary filmmaker John Pilger, for example, discusses his experiences with the left-leaning tabloid the *Daily Mirror* over the last four decades:

> I wrote for the *Mirror* for twenty years. I joined it back in the 1960s when I arrived from Australia. You don't really have anything like the *Mirror*—as it was, and as it is trying to be again—in the United States. . . . During the time I was there, it was very adventurous politically. It reported many parts of the world from the point of view of victims of wars. I reported Vietnam for many years for the *Mirror*. In those days, it played a central role in the political life of this country. . . . Since September 11, the *Mirror* has reached back to its roots, and decided, it seems, to be something of its old self again. I received a call asking if I would write for it again, which I've done. It's a pleasure to be able to do that. It's become an important antidote to a media that is, most of it, supportive of the establishment, some of it quite rabidly right-wing.[73]

Other left-of-center papers in the United Kingdom—including the *Guardian* and the *Independent*—provide forums for opinions that only appear in the non-mainstream media in the United States. News stories and op-eds from mainstream British journalists like Robert Fisk, John Pilger, Jonathan Steele, and Patrick Cockburn appear regularly only in progressive American magazines such as *Z Magazine* and *Counterpunch*. These stories are ignored by the U.S. mainstream media, which views them as beyond the pale.

Significant differences are also evident when reviewing the ideological biases of prominent books marketed by British and U.S. journalists. U.S. reporters such as Rajiv Chandrasekaran (*Washington Post*), Thomas Ricks (*Washington Post*), and James Fallows (*The Atlantic*) provide criticisms of the Iraq war on "practical grounds"—for failing in its "planning and execution," as misguided in its attempt to promote democracy, and as a "strategic failure."[74] Conversely, many British books marketed are far more critical of U.S. and British legitimacy in the Middle East. Jonathan Steele, Patrick Cockburn, and Robert Fisk have released numerous books condemning the war in Iraq as imperialistic, militarily repressive, and designed to secure control of the region's oil supplies. Other prominent themes in these books include a strong emphasis on Iraq's long history of distrust of Western colonial and neocolonial actions, widespread Iraqi opposition to the occupation, and emphasis on the growth of Iraqi nationalism.[75]

Despite the increased openness of the British press, other studies convincingly show that its coverage of Iraq is heavily propagandistic. A study by the Cardiff University School of Journalism found that 60 percent of newspaper stories and 34 percent of broadcast stories examined used either news agency copy or public relations information as a basis for their reporting.[76] In the foreign policy area, news is often strikingly one-sided. In *Guardians of Power: The Myth of the Liberal Media*, David Edwards and David Cromwell highlight a pattern of media commentary whereby reporters and editors reject criticisms of United States–United Kingdom supported sanctions against Iraq (which were responsible for the deaths of hundreds of thousands of civilians). Edwards and Cromwell found that British media outlets neglected reports of civilian casualties in Iraq as a result of the American-British invasion, and downplayed reports of civilian casualties in Afghanistan.[77] BBC correspondents are heavily partial to humanitarian war claims and U.S. promises "to bring good, to bring American values to the rest of the world," through the use of military force.[78] Support for the Iraq invasion extends beyond this anecdote. Analysis of British television news found that BBC1, ITV, Channel 4, and Sky News heavily stressed Iraq's alleged possession of WMD prior to the war, and these outlets were also much more likely to describe the Iraqi people as in favor of the invasion.[79] British television refrained from showing graphic images of the war, with content that was "full of action, but without the grisly consequences."[80]

Similarly to U.S. journalists, British reporters celebrated the embedding process. Nearly two dozen interviews conducted with British journalists found that they were highly satisfied with reporting alongside U.S. military units, although those who were embedded with British troops were less content. James Mates from ITV News celebrated the media-military alliance as "a very, very satisfactory journalistic experience." Colin Brazier of Sky News was "astonished by how much information we were given, how little interference or attempted interference there was. It was the most information I've ever had the *privilege* of dealing with" (emphasis added). British television was more reliant on embedded reporting than it was on non-embedded sources.[81] American military commanders' openness to British reporters was likely due to the highly favorable coverage that the invasion received in the British press. As Brazier explained, reporters saw embedding as a privilege rather than a threat to their autonomy.

JOURNALISTIC CENSORSHIP VS. CO-OPTATION

This chapter demonstrates that, in the overwhelming majority of cases, media propaganda is not the result of overt editorial or government censorship. Such methods serve more as an auxiliary protection from moral dissent against war, not as the first line of defense. Omission of antiwar views is most often the result of journalists' own contempt for progressive views. From their early days in elementary and secondary schools, later on in journalism programs, and throughout their years reporting, journalists learn to be "team players" by not stepping too far out of line from the conventional values expressed within the party systems of the United States and United Kingdom. A slew of positive incentives are granted to journalists who fall in line behind received truths. Reporters are allowed to retain their positions in two of the most powerful, wealthiest, and best-paying media systems in the world, and progress through these systems in ways they never could if they questioned bipartisan propaganda. Gramsci's notion of "hegemony," discussed in the introduction to this book, is *not* the equivalent of conspiracy. Reporters take it as objective truth that the United States is a benevolent superpower, committed to promoting human rights, reducing poverty, and protecting global democracy. Debate may be pursued over how best to pursue these goals, but not over whether the United States is committed to them. Mainstream scholars should keep this reality in mind when they misrepresent the central tenets of hegemony theory and the criticisms made by progressive media critics.

CHAPTER FIVE

Iran, Nuclear Weapons, and the Politics of Fear

with Paul Fasse

In late 2007, *Time* magazine printed a feature on the issue of human rights and Iran. The story, "Intimidation in Tehran," described the situation in the country's capitol as marked by paranoia. The political "obsession with security" and "intimidation" against government critics had become unbearable. Azadeh Moaveni spoke of her "family's long-planned departure" from the country, which took place in the summer of 2007. Expressing concern about Iran's "enormous annual brain drain," Moaveni still enjoyed a "profound sense of relief, as though we were rowing away from a sinking ship. . . . Watching from afar, I will be eager to see how a hard-line government will woo back the middle class, alienated by the imposition of a more Islamic social order."[1]

This story raises important questions about U.S. reporting on Iran. Does *Time*'s critical tone appear systematically in media reporting? If so, are topics such as Iran's assault on human rights and alleged nuclear weapons development of primary concern? What role do journalistic norms play in influencing the tone of reporting and editorializing on United States-Iranian relations? All of these questions are addressed in this chapter, co-written with Paul Fasse.

POLITICAL FRAMING OF IRAN: THE THREAT OF NUCLEAR WEAPONS PROLIFERATION

Before examining British and U.S. media coverage of Iran, it is necessary to understand how officials construct the political context of United States-Iranian relations. Iran has long been portrayed as a threat to U.S. security. Attention to Iran's nuclear power program increased following the Bush administration's declaration of the "War on Terror." Former president Bush claimed that the country was in "active pursuit of technology that could lead to nuclear weapons." That pursuit "threatens to put a region already known for instability and violence under the shadow of a nuclear holocaust."[2] Aside from its bluntness, the president's attack was rather simplistic. Bush's claim that Iran wants nuclear weapons to "destroy people" is a far cry from the assessments of international weapons inspection agencies like the International Atomic Energy Agency (IAEA), which takes a less cavalier and more nuanced approach.[3] Prominent Democrats such as Secretary of State Hillary Clinton and President Barack Obama, though somewhat less incendiary in their comments than Bush, also portray Iran as a threat in light of its enrichment of uranium in the city of Natanz and planned enrichment in the city of Qum.[4]

The Bush administration approached relations with Iran by unilaterally threatening a military attack. Former vice president Dick Cheney announced that "all options are on the table" and pushed the former president to remain open to a military strike.[5] When the United States deployed a second aircraft carrier to the Gulf region during the 2007 British-Iran "hostage crisis," Cheney announced that the action "sends a very strong signal to everybody in the region that the United States is here to stay, that we clearly have significant capabilities, and that we are working with friends . . . to deal with the Iranian threat."[6] The United States and United Kingdom have engaged in war games to prepare for a potential invasion of Iran, although such a possibility seems remote.[7] More likely is the possibility of a coordinated tactical air strike, possibly with Israel playing a lead role.[8] The Pentagon and CIA have elaborated upon a number of plans to attack Iran. Military planners admit to possible strikes against an Iranian uranium enrichment plant and conversion facility, and even the possible use of tactical nuclear weapons for penetrating deeper targets.[9] Pentagon plans elaborate upon possible airstrikes against as many as 1,200 to 2,000 targets, supposedly "to annihilate the Iranians' military capability."[10] Plans for an attack at times include the use of U.S. Air Force bases in Bulgaria and Romania in Eastern Europe.[11]

Despite the stark portrayals of Iran, domestic and international intelligence does not characterize the country as a national security danger. Iranian leaders explain that their enrichment of uranium is only intended for peaceful energy purposes.[12] The country retains the right to enrich uranium as a signatory to the Non-Proliferation Treaty.[13] Furthermore, Iran has generally maintained a strong record of cooperating with IAEA inspectors, who insist on examining their program since Iran was found to be pursuing uranium enrichment in secret.[14] This does not mean that the relationship between Iran and the IAEA is without its problems, as the agency long pushed for a resolution of various "outstanding issues" regarding the inspections. The IAEA also criticized Iran for its failure to meet all of the agency's demands, admitting that Iranian cooperation has not been "as full, timely and proactive as it should have been."[15] Nonetheless, the IAEA admits, following its pursuit of numerous unannounced inspections, that Iran "provided sufficient access to individuals and has responded in a timely manner to questions and provided clarifications and amplifications on issues raised in the context of the work plan."[16] The late September 2009 dispute with the U.S. over Iran's second nuclear facility in the city of Qum does not represent a violation of the NPT, since Iran is only required to notify the group of completion of uranium enrichment facilities 180 days prior to the their first day of operation.[17] Furthermore, the "secret" Qum facility was openly declared to the IAEA by Iran prior to its completion and before the Obama administration offered its public denunciations.

Some of the earlier and most skeptical estimates from U.S. intelligence claimed that Iran was ten years away from developing a nuclear bomb.[18] In 2003, the IAEA concluded that there was "no evidence" of a nuclear weapons program in Iran, and this conclusion was reaffirmed in 2005, after three years of investigating Iran.[19] Later analyses in 2006 and 2007 uncovered similar findings.[20] The CIA estimated in late 2006 that there was "no firm evidence of a secret drive by Iran to develop nuclear weapons," whereas a 2007 comprehensive examination from over a dozen U.S. intelligence agencies (the National Intelligence Estimate) concluded that there was a high probability that Iran stopped work on its suspected nuclear weapons program more than four years earlier. The estimate concluded that Iran's approach to nuclear power was pragmatic, "guided by a cost-benefit approach rather than a rush to a weapon irrespective of the political, economic, and military costs."[21]

None of the findings above are meant to suggest that Iran is *not* developing nuclear weapons. It is theoretically possible that Iran may be developing such weapons. Iran's construction of nuclear weapons would not be surprising in light of the belligerent rhetoric directed by American and Israeli leaders against the Iranian regime. Military threats to Iran's national security could very possibly incite Iran to intensify its development of nuclear weapons. However, it must be pointed out that, as of late 2009, there was no physical evidence suggesting that Iran was developing nuclear power for military purposes. Whether Iran will become a nuclear power in the future cannot be known, just as one cannot "prove" with 100 percent certainty that Iran has no nuclear ambitions. The most important conclusion to draw from this ambiguous situation, then, is that mass media outlets and political leaders *currently* have nothing of substance to empirically demonstrate that Iran is or will constitute an imminent threat in the future.

Despite the lack of evidence of an Iranian nuclear threat, U.S. political leaders continue to demonize Iran as a danger to U.S. national security. Congress passed a bill designating Iran's Revolutionary Guard a terrorist organization, due to its alleged support for anti-occupation combatants in Iraq.[22] The Bush administration illegally authorized the kidnapping and assassination of Iranian officials who were formally invited into Iraq by its government.[23] Claims of Iranian involvement in attacks on U.S. troops are highly uncertain according to United States government sources. General Peter Pace, Chairman of the Joint Chiefs of Staff, announced "no firm proof" exists that "Tehran is arming Iraqis." "The discovery that roadside bombs in Iraq contained material made in Iran does not necessarily mean that the Iranian government is involved in supplying insurgents."[24] The charge that Iran is "meddling" in Iraq is also not substantiated by Iraqi leaders, who support Iran as playing a "positive and constructive role in improving security in Iraq."[25] Iraqi leaders deplore U.S. efforts to demonize Iran, as well as efforts to capture and assassinate Iranian diplomats.[26]

The United States remained committed to a unilateral approach in "negotiating" with Iran.[27] The range of policy options pursued by the Bush administration vacillated between blanket demands for Iran to stop its enrichment (without offering any concessions in return) and overt military threats.[28] The administration's disinterest in negotiations was expressed best in 2003, when it flatly rejected an offer from Iranian leaders to discuss alleged nuclear weapons development. Iranian Foreign Ministry spokesman Hamid Reza Asefi announced the push for negotiations, conditional upon U.S. abandonment of its threats of regime change, the removal of the "Axis of Evil" designation, a removal of Iran from the United States' list of terrorist states, and an end to the United Nations sanctions regime. In return, Iran offered to accept tighter restrictions from the IAEA on uranium enrichment in exchange for "full access to peaceful nuclear technology." Iran also offered support for the Arab League Beirut declaration proposing a two-state solution to the Israeli-Palestinian conflict based upon the pre-1967 border lines and increased pressure on Hezbollah to convert solely into a political rather than a military organization.[29] The Bush administration continued its rejectionist stance toward negotiations through mid-2006, when it became open to unilateral "negotiations," with minimal U.S. commitments. Administration officials insisted that Iran concede on the major issues prior to the beginning of negotiations.[30] The Obama administration, though supposedly supporting negotiations, announced that the United States would impose further sanctions and possibly attack Iran if it continues to develop nuclear weapons.[31] Inspectors' long-standing conclusions that Iran is not developing such weapons are consistently ignored.

While the Bush administration attacked Iran and rejected negotiations, the question remained, to what extent did the media echo this approach? What role do journalistic norms, values, and behavior play in influencing coverage of Iran? Is there sufficient room for criticisms of the Bush administration's approach? Does coverage conform to administration deception and propaganda by allowing only procedural criticisms? Are there any significant differences in U.S. and British coverage, despite the Tony Blair and Gordon Brown governments' close ties with former president Bush? All of these questions are discussed in this chapter.

REPORTING ON IRAN: HUMANITARIAN ISSUES AND WEAPONS OF MASS DESTRUCTION

In *The United States Press and Iran: Foreign Policy and the Journalism of Deference*, William Dorman and Mansour Farhang discuss the simplistic themes that dominated U.S. reporting of Iran during the Cold War. Former Iranian prime minister Mohammed Mossadegh, for example, was demonized as a "lunatic" and a "communist dupe." Mossadegh was seen as "highly irrational and discredited" following his nationalization of Iranian oil, despite his tremendous popularity and his democratic election by the Iranian people.[32] In contrast, Shah Mohammad Reza Pahlavi—who overthrew Mosaddegh in a coup organized by the United States and Great Britain—was presented in a favorable light despite his responsibility for the bloody repression of thousands of Iranians. Opposition to the Shah was ignored by the media in the decades following Mossadegh's overthrow, while those who revolted against him in the 1979 revolution were portrayed as religious fanatics, rather than nationalists leading a mass-based revolution. The negative coverage of Iranian dissidents was greatly distinguished from the sympathetic media coverage of the Solidarity movement in Poland. As Dorman and Farhang explain: "Where Poland is concerned, the Solidarity movement, its leaders, its tactics, and its achievements are well known to the attentive U.S. public, and sympathy and admiration for their cause and conduct among Americans cannot be in doubt. In the case of Iran in revolt, the opposite was true."[33]

While Iran's humanitarian issues are a common concern of U.S. reporters today, they are far eclipsed by interest in Iran's nuclear power program. Table 5.1 shows that, in a sample period analyzed for MSNBC online news, stories on Iran's nuclear program and alleged nuclear weapons development appeared most frequently in 2007—twice as often as stories on human rights issues. Human rights issues increased dramatically, however, during 2009, when U.S. reporters charged the Iranian government with defrauding the June presidential election. Coverage of Iran and nuclear issues, however, also remained strong in this period.

TABLE 5.1: Most Common Themes in MSNBC Stories on Iran June–August 2007

Theme	%
Nuclear Power and Weapons of Mass Destruction	30%
Iraq-Related	23%
Iranian Human Rights Violations	15%
Military Conflict with United States and Allies	12%
Iranian Media	5%
Other	15%

Source: MSNBC website

Even in the few months after the beginning of the May 2007 negotiations between Iran and the United States, the issue of nuclear weapons remained most salient.[34] A comprehensive review of national network news from early 2003 to mid-2007 finds that attention to Iran's nuclear program and nuclear weapons appeared in 41 percent of ABC stories, 43 percent of NBC stories, and 46 percent of CBS stories mentioning Iran.[35]

Long-term patterns in coverage of the nuclear issue are closely tailored to presidential foreign policy agendas. News reports surfaced as early as the mid-1970s that Iranian Shah Muhammad Reza Pahlavi openly planned to develop nuclear technologies and nuclear power.[36] Reports from the mid-1980s also suggested that Iran might be pursuing nuclear weapons under Ayatollah Khomeini.[37] Iranian interest in nuclear weapons, however, was of little concern when the allied Shah openly pursued them.

It was only after the Bush administration began attacking Iran's alleged weapons development that coverage significantly increased. Figure 5.1 reflects this stark trend, with the largest increases from 2003 onward, when the Bush administration began its rhetorical attacks against the Iranian regime and invaded Iraq. Coverage hit a peak in 2006, however, and declined by 2007, as the surge in Iraq dominated news of the Middle East, and the National Intelligence Estimate pronounced that Iran was not developing nuclear weapons.

Major national newspapers issued formal apologies for their reporting on Iraq and the weapons of mass destruction issue. In August of 2004, *Washington Post* journalist Howard Kurtz printed a systematic, critical review of the paper's coverage. Kurtz quoted *Washington Post* editor Bob

FIGURE 5.1: Network News Coverage on Iran, Nuclear Power & Nuclear Weapons

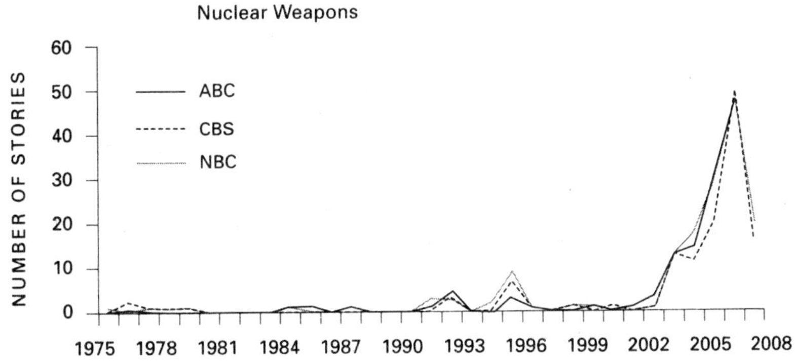

Source: Vanderbilt News Archive

Woodward, who claimed, "We should have warned readers we had information that the basis for this [war based on the weapons of mass Destruction claims] was shakier" than commonly thought. Challenges to the Bush administration's weapons of mass destruction narrative "are exactly the kind of statements that should be published on the front page," rather than buried in the back of the *Washington Post*. Editor Leonard Downie agreed, remembering one critical story by Walter Pincus: "In retrospect, that [story] probably should have been on page one instead of A17, even though it wasn't a definitive story and had to rely on unnamed sources. It was a very prescient story."[38] The editors of the *New York Times* printed a similar recantation. Employing the "bright light of hindsight," they found "a number of instances of coverage that was not as rigorous as it should have been." Administration claims were "allowed to stand unchallenged. Looking back, we wish we had been more aggressive in reexamining the claims as new evidence emerged—or failed to emerge."[39] Editors' claims that there were merely "a number of instances" of coverage that was not skeptical enough are a serious understatement. Reviews of the *New York Times* reporting on Iraq's alleged weapons of mass destruction found that the paper *systematically* marginalized critical claims in most all of the stories that were published prior to the 2003 invasion.[40]

Editors' critical reflections on Iraq are relevant when examining coverage of Iran. The editors at the *New York Times* and *Washington Post* framed their reporting of Iraq as a question of agency—that they merely needed to exercise more independence from government sources. Such claims should not be accepted outright. Rather, a comprehensive examination of U.S. and British reporting is required.

Reporting throughout the Muslim world has set the standard for what a critical approach to the Iranian weapons question looks like. A few examples provided below are enlightening. In the pro-United States *Kabul Times of Afghanistan*, Sayed Salahuddin criticizes the United States "show of force" in the Gulf (in an attempt to intimidate Iran) as "greatly alarming."[41] Similarly, Qatar's *Al-Rayah* discusses the perceived hypocrisy of U.S. actions: "The strange thing is that the attack on Iran over its nuclear programme is not met with any Western position towards Israel which possesses more than 200 nuclear warheads, a position which, in addition to being characterized by double standards, contains unacceptable favouritism." Turkey's *Milliyet* characterized "the possible effects of [an attack on Iran] as worrying. . . . Ankara thinks returning to diplomacy is essential to end this crisis." The pan-Arab *Al-Hayat* promoted "an agreement with all the countries concerned with the non-proliferation of nuclear arms. An agreement may encourage the international community to exert pressure on Israel to open its nuclear plants to inspection." Syria's *Al-Thawrah* questioned whether Iran's possession of nuclear weapons "constitute[s] a danger to international peace," and Egypt's *Al-Akhbar* complained: "What worries the U.S. president about the Iranian nuclear file is the security of Israel and the safety of its people if Tehran possess the nuclear weapon. As for the danger which the Israeli nuclear weapons arsenal poses to the people of the Arab countries, this is the last thing to arouse concern to the United States and its allies in Europe."[42]

REGIONAL NEWS COVERAGE: THE *CHICAGO TRIBUNE* AND *CHICAGO SUN-TIMES*

Arab newspapers are not subject to the same kinds of nationalistic pressures felt by reporters and editors in the United States. Newspapers, television news, and magazines in the United States are more belligerent in their rhetoric. They are more likely to reinforce the United States' dominant military position in the world rather than to question it. In the case of regional papers, the conservative-leaning *Chicago Tribune* and the centrist *Chicago Sun-Times* generally vacillate between conservative hard-line and liberal positions in covering Iran. The *Chicago Tribune*'s editors chastise Democratic president Barack Obama for claiming "he'd be happy to sit and talk with America's worst enemies without preconditions."[43] The *Tribune*'s contempt for discussions "without preconditions" is, in reality, a contempt for negotiations themselves, as the details of the specific concessions from each party to a negotiation are always to be resolved through discussion, rather than in advance of discussion.

The *Chicago Tribune* depicts Iran as a "grave threat" that is "secretly developing nuclear capabilities. . . . Iranian negotiators have essentially stonewalled the IAEA." Iran has pursued little more than "empty promises. . . . [It] is still on the path to being capable of building a bomb. It shows no signs of stopping."[44] The *Chicago Tribune* is not beyond the use of flamboyant imagery in constructing images of an Iranian threat. One editorial, for example, included a cartoon of an Iranian cleric embodied as an octopus, with its many tentacles menacingly stretching out across the countries of Iraq, Afghanistan, Lebanon, and Palestine. The accompanying story warned: "Imagine a Tehran with nuclear weapons—and the ability to spread nuclear expertise to its terrorist clients throughout the region. That is what the world faces. Tehran has proclaimed its progress in enriching uranium, a sure path to an atomic bomb. . . . Iran has tromped through deadline after United Nations–imposed deadline to freeze its outlaw nuclear program."[45]

The *Chicago Sun-Times* represented the mainstream-liberal perspective, highlighting the tactical dangers of a U.S. attack on Iran. Richard Williamson posited that the "United States can't just talk while Iran builds [a] nuclear weapon," but that "military action, while able to degrade Iran's nuclear program and set it back many years, would not be conclusive."[46] Ali Akbar Dareini maintains that despite Iran's continued uranium enrichment, the "United States can't afford another war" in the region.[47] Both of these criticisms represent pragmatic assessments of the ability of the United States to fight a war against Iran, rather than a serious questioning of whether the United States retains the *right* to do so.

The *Chicago Tribune*'s columns, in contrast, take a hawkish tone. Clarence Page portrays Iranian president Mahmoud Ahmadinejad as "a man positioning himself for power in the Middle East."[48] Victor Davis Hanson proclaims that "most [world] players don't care enough to stop Iran from getting the bomb, or apparently don't think it's worth the effort and cost. . . . Most in Europe . . . feel it's a U.S. problem to organize global containment of Iran."[49] Hanson's claim is fiercely propagandistic, in that it falsely complains that the global community prefers to abdicate responsibility for "containing" Iran to the United States. In reality, it was the European community that first took the initiative in pursuing negotiations over Iran's nuclear program, with the United States only begrudgingly joining at a later point, and refusing to engage in substantive negotiations. As will be discussed in chapter 9, global opinion polls have also shown that the majority of people throughout the world look at the United States and its activities with great anxiety, rather than seeing the United States as world policeman.

The *Chicago Tribune*'s editorial position clearly reinforced the former Bush administration's approach toward Iran. Following the December 2007 National Intelligence Estimate, the Bush administration continued to portray Iran as a growing threat. As Bush summarized: "I view this report as a warning signal that they [Iran] had the [weapons] program, they halted the program. The reason why it's a warning signal is that they could restart it." The *Chicago Tribune* followed this same approach. It claimed that "Iran may not have an active nuclear weapons program now" but "without answers on all its clandestine nuclear activities, the IAEA can't—and shouldn't—let Iran off the hook. Nor should the rest of the world. . . . Mohammed ElBaradei [of the IAEA] has long tolerated Iran's stonewalling—and allowed Tehran the benefit of the doubt."[50]

The *Chicago Tribune*'s dependence on the administration did not mean there was no room for dissent in the paper. Columnist Georgie Anne Geyer, for example, criticized the U.S. designation of Iran's Revolutionary Guard as terrorist: "One might think that we are having enough problems in Iraq not to add more."[51] Similarly, former president Jimmy Carter editorialized in the paper that "the United States has not set a good example, having already abandoned the Anti-Ballistic Missile Treaty, binding limitations on testing nuclear weapons and developing new ones, and a long-standing policy of forgoing threats of 'first use' of nuclear weapons against non-nuclear states." Geyer's comment, however, contains little more than a strategic warning about U.S. overextension. Although Carter's comments were strongly critical of the former administration's approach, his single column in one of the nation's most prominent newspapers did not disprove the general rule of media belligerence toward Iran.[52]

COMPARING COVERAGE ACROSS BRITISH AND U.S. NEWSMAGAZINES

Comparing newsmagazine framing of Iran in the United States and United Kingdom demonstrates the significant differences between the two countries' reporting. In the British press, there exists a relatively larger range of views, with progressive-left sources like the *New Statesman* expressing radically different perspectives than the conservative *Economist*. The *Economist*'s views are more closely associated with those in the U.S. press. The magazine frames Iran as a "headache," speculating over Iran's "alleged efforts to develop a missile cone that could carry a nuclear warhead." Iran's leaders "distrust Western intentions, sense that offence may be Iran's best defence, and feel that Iran is poised to regain its natural place as the region's strongman."[53]

The *Economist* continued on its bellicose path after the December 2007 National Intelligence Estimate announcement. The magazine maintained that Iran's "mischief" could manifest itself in the development of a nuclear weapon within a year.[54] "The basic diplomatic strategy for the

United States," the *Economist* claimed, was to "get Iran to halt enrichment and negotiate inducements, including co-operation on other advanced, but less dangerous, nuclear technologies to make the suspension permanent. Mr. Ahmadinejad firmly rules this out. Ironically, this week's National Intelligence Estimate will make it harder to muster the diplomatic wherewithal to press him to change his merry tune."[55]

Significant differences exist between individual British news outlets. The *New Statesman* allows room for progressive critics of the United States and United Kingdom. As with the Arab press, strong attention is directed toward the United States and Israel's continued possession of nuclear weapons in the face of their demands that other countries unilaterally disarm.[56] Andrew Stephen warned against a war that could be started by the Bush administration's "sheer incompetence," in light of its claims that Iran is supplying explosive devices to attack U.S. troops in Iraq, and General Peter Pace's admission that the evidence is lacking. Katharine Gun worries about the "dreadful possibility of action against Iran" and warns against "any act of aggression towards that country."[57] Perhaps most critically, John Pilger's writings in the *New Statesman* suggest that United States policy is driven by the desire to exercise control over Iran's oil.[58] United States policy, Pilger contends, cannot possibly be driven by perceptions of a nuclear danger: "Iran is incapable of building a nuclear weapon before 2017. . . . The 'threat' from Iran is entirely manufactured, aided and abetted by familiar, compliant media language that refers to Iran's 'nuclear ambitions.' The one piece of 'solid evidence' is the threat posed by the United States." Pilger was referring to *U.S. National Security Presidential Directive 35: Nuclear Weapons Deployment Authorization*. "It is classified, of course, but the presumption has long been that *NSPD 35* authorized the stockpiling and deployment of 'tactical' nuclear weapons in the Middle East."[59]

The *New Statesman* criticisms do not apply only to the United States but to the United Kingdom as well. It is true that former prime minister Tony Blair was involved in multi-party talks with Iran over its nuclear program, and former foreign secretary Jack Straw did dismiss a military attack as "inconceivable."[60] However, British-Iranian relations have been marked by a high level of conflict, considering the Iranian government's detainment of seven British marines and eight sailors in March 2007. Blair publicly attacked Iran as a leading "state sponsor of terrorism" and declared that military action against Iran was "not off [the] table."[61] Prime Minister Gordon Brown announced that he would "back airstrikes on Iran" if it is shown that Iran is responsible for attacks on U.S. and British troops.[62] Condemnations of a possible attack on Iran, then, apply to British officials as much as they do to U.S. officials.

Political leaders in both countries have taken the lead in targeting Iran, but their respective media behave quite differently in their reporting of the conflict. Unlike the British press, U.S. newsmagazines are not open to dissident views. Most alarmist is the *Reader's Digest*, which ran a story highlighting the "World's Most Dangerous Leaders," including Iranian president Mahmoud Ahmadinejad. The magazine warned that "a nuclear Iran could be emboldened to step up terrorism . . . could threaten to block the flow of Persian Gulf oil . . . could encourage strikes on American forces," and "could welcome conflict" with the West in an "apocalyptic" Islamist fashion.[63] *Newsweek*, *Time*, and *U.S. News and World Report* reinforce this position. *Newsweek* blames Iran for "the juvenile games they're playing with the international community," which "make[s] them look more like dangerous delinquents every day."[64] *U.S News and World Report* dismisses negotiations as enabling Iran to continue its uranium enrichment process.[65] *Newsweek* congratulated former president Bush for his "patience" in dealing with Iran, but announced that "there is no reasonable argument for taking military action off the table. If the Iranians refuse to negotiate seriously . . . the military option needs to be on the table and in plain view."[66]

It is inaccurate to claim that U.S. newsmagazines have not been critical of United States policy toward Iran. They have often been fiercely adversarial within bipartisan boundaries. *Newsweek* concludes that "bombing dispersed and deeply buried nuclear sites" is "impractical"; "Realistically, the United States has no military option. Iran has dispersed many nuclear facilities and hardened others. Even if U.S. forces could find and destroy those targets . . . they could be rebuilt relatively quickly."[67] *Time* warns against the likely destabilizing consequences of an attack for Iraq, and *Newsweek* worries about the lack of allied support in the event of an attack.[68] These criticisms are not intended to question the right of the United States to attack sovereign nations, but merely the feasibility of such attacks.

NEWS NORMS, IRAN, AND U.S. NEWS MEDIA AND TELEVISION

An extensive review of U.S. television and Internet news demonstrates the limits to journalistic autonomy and independence from government.

If critical reporting were simply a matter of reporters *choosing* to take a more critical stance toward government, one would expect to discover increasingly critical coverage after the failure to find weapons of mass destruction in Iraq. In reality, media reporting on Iran is extraordinarily similar to that of reporting on Iraq—thoroughly reliant on official propaganda. An analysis of MSNBC online news stories on Iran (drawn from various wire services such as the AP and Reuters) confirms this practice without question.

The sample of MSNBC stories from the summer of 2007 is plagued by assumptions that Iran is developing nuclear weapons. In all the stories examined, claims that Iran is, or may be developing, nuclear weapons appeared over twice as often as claims that Iran is not, or may not be developing them.[69] References were often blunt, suggesting "Iran's nuclear ambitions," and at times blurring the lines between the nation's civilian nuclear program and the alleged weapons program with headlines such as "Ahmadinejad: West Can't Stop Iran's Nukes."[70] Although Iranian president Ahmadinejad never publicly claimed Iran was developing nuclear weapons, this headline creates the misleading impression that he actually admits to such a program. At other times, MSNBC reports indirectly suggest that Iran is pursuing a weapons program, stating that "IAEA officials have informally identified an Iranian enrichment operation running 3,000 centrifuges as the start of a large-scale program, while experts say that the number could produce enough material for several warheads a year. Tehran says it wants to operate 54,000 centrifuges—*enough for a full-scale nuclear weapons program.*" Although this report never explicitly declares that Iran is pursuing a weapons program, the poor and vague wording leaves readers with the impression that Iranian leaders have admitted to pursuing nuclear weapons.[71]

MSNBC also repeats official mantras regarding Iran's "opposition" to negotiations and supposed U.S. openness to them. Though the historical review earlier in this chapter demonstrated that it was the United States, rather than Iran, that opposed negotiations, this inconvenient reality does not comport with administration propaganda—and hence it must be discarded. MSNBC accomplished this by quoting officials such as State Department spokesman Tom Casey, who contended that "I don't think Iran's track record is particularly noteworthy or particularly likely to give me or anyone else confidence that anything will come of [the summer 2007] discussions."[72] Associated Press reporters quoted in MSNBC stories also appropriate this approach, highlighting only

U.S. attempts to initiate talks.[73] Though these reports may contain a small grain of truth in that the United States did attempt to "negotiate" (although rarely and under the most limited of circumstances), these statements also misrepresent the historical context of the talks. The United States is depicted as taking great strides to reach out to Iran while Iran's long-standing support for talks is erased from existence. Importantly, in all the MSNBC stories examined, none bothered to mention that Iran was the first party to reach out in 2003, with the United States rejecting any possibility of talks. The media's framing of the United States as supportive of negotiations is thoroughly Orwellian. If official demands that Iran must fulfill all U.S. demands *prior* to talks count as "negotiation," then the term truly is vacuous.

A wider study of television news outlets reveals a journalistic commitment to the most egregious types of distortion. Analyzing *NBC Nightly News* programs from March of 2003 through July of 2007, one sees a serious imbalance in coverage of the Iranian nuclear program. NBC programs contained four times as many suggestions that Iran is, or may be, developing nuclear weapons than suggestions that it is not or may not be developing weapons. Table 5.2 summarizes the reliance of U.S. television on official sources. U.S. officials and experts (who were overwhelmingly likely to frame Iran as a threat) constituted 72 percent of all quoted sources. U.S. sources appeared three times as often as foreign sources, keeping with the pattern of parochialism documented in chapter 1. Former administration officials, including George W. Bush, Condoleezza Rice, Colin Powell, Donald Rumsfeld, and John Bolton appeared most often as quoted sources. This dependence allows for an extreme reliance on official spin.

TABLE 5.2: Source Breakdown for NBC Stories on Iran and Nuclear Power/Weapons of Mass Destruction (March 2003–July 2007)

U.S. Officials	50.5%
U.S. Experts	21.5 %
Iranian Officials	10.5%
Foreign Experts	4%
U.S. Military	4%
British Officials	4%
Person on the Street (Iranian)	3%
Other	3%

Source: Lexis Nexis

For example, though the IAEA is mentioned in over one-quarter of all stories examined, the agency's actual intelligence conclusions appear in just 7 percent of stories, and only one of those stories (or 1.5 percent of all stories) admitted to the agency's conclusion that it found no evidence of a weapons program.

NBC Nightly News reporting on Iran represents one of the most obvious examples of fear-mongering. In the early stages of the Iraq war, the outlet referred unequivocally to the conflict between the United States and Iran as a "nuclear crisis," rather than to critical intelligence assessments that there was no crisis. Iran was assumed to be complicit in the "development of nuclear weapons," despite the lack of tangible evidence of a weapons program.[74] It seems that reporters learned little from the Iraq debacle, in which a similar deference to official misinformation greatly harmed journalists' credibility. The failure to learn lessons from Iraq was most obvious when NBC reporters alarmingly reflected in 2004: "Before President Bush went to war against Iraq, the administration raised the threat of Saddam Hussein and nuclear weapons. Well, it turns out Iraq didn't have any nuclear weapons or capacity for producing them any time soon, but now there's more and more evidence that Iraq's neighbor is determined to develop nuclear weapons and the capacity to deliver them."[75]

Media speculation moves beyond weapons of mass destruction allegations, encompassing scenarios involving global Armageddon. For example, when *NBC Nightly News* anchor Brian Williams interviewed Lt. Col. Rick Francona, the Colonel postulated, "The mere thought that the Iranians would provide a nuclear weapon to a terrorist group like Hezbollah or Islamic Jihad, is—is—it's just frightening."[76] No evidence need be provided with such scare tactics, as was the case with reporter John Seigenthaler's interview with the *Washington Post*'s Dana Priest, in which they discussed "Iran and the potential threat of terrorism." In Orwellian style, Priest speculates, "If the United States were to strike Iran's nuclear sites, intelligence officials believe Iran would unleash its own terrorist groups, mainly the Ministry of Intelligence agents all over the world and the terrorist arm of Hezbollah based in Lebanon. These groups are likely to try to strike across the border into Iraq, but they are also likely to try to target civilian targets in the United States, Europe, and elsewhere." Seigenthaler provoked even more alarm by questioning whether that "mean[s] there are Iranian terrorist groups in the United States? And if so, what can the United States do about it?" Again, no evidence was deemed necessary for establishing a fifth column threat inside the United States.[77]

As with MSNBC, *NBC Nightly News* reporting depicted the United States as unconditionally favoring negotiations and Iran as opposed. Administration officials such as Condoleezza Rice were uncritically cited, arguing "Iran needs to make a choice now to return to negotiations" and needs to "take the path to negotiation offered them" in mid-2006. Long-standing U.S. contempt for negotiations is ignored due to its lack of propaganda value.[78] The United States is seen, rather, as offering generous "incentive[s]" to the regime in order to persuade it to end its nuclear enrichment.[79] Media celebrations of U.S. "multilateralism" are followed by some criticisms of the former administration's policy. These criticisms are overwhelmingly tactical. Plans to go to war with Iran are denigrated as "counterproductive" and attacked for failing to take into account the "dispersed" nature of Iran's nuclear program.[80]

This section evaluates the nature of media reporting in the five months prior to, and the five months following, the introduction of the National Intelligence Estimate (NIE). Skeptics may wonder whether media coverage of Iran changed significantly following the issuance of the December 2007 NIE. The release of the document represents a potential milestone in U.S.–Iranian relations, in that it highlights the full extent of the administration's exaggerations and deceptions.

Sustained media attention to administration misinformation has the potential to transform political debate in the United States. As with NBC, however, ABC and CBS news reports prior to December 2007 conformed to administration propaganda. Journalistic norms may prevent reporters from questioning the foundation of Bush's rationale for war, but they do not prevent the demonization of officially designated enemies. A striking example of this double standard is the holding of foreign officials' feet to the fire while fawning over domestic officials. One example is the interview between Iranian President Mahmoud Ahmadinejad and CBS *60 Minutes* reporter Scott Pelley. Pelley's questioning of Ahmadinejad is hostile indeed, as this excerpt demonstrates:

Pelley: The issue that threatens war between Iran and the United States is Iran's determination to keep enriching uranium. You have said in the past that you have 3,000 centrifuges in a line producing highly enriched uranium. Do you have more now?

Ahmadinejad: No. Our plan and program is very transparent. We are under the supervision of the [IAEA] agency. Everything is on the table. We have nothing to hide.

Pelley: Transparent? Sir, it's been hidden for more than fifteen years. You've been operating a secret nuclear program. It's nothing if it's not secret.

Ahmadinejad: Who is saying that?

Pelley: Well, the IAEA. You, in fact, agreed with the IAEA to confess what you've done in secret over the past years. It is not transparent, sir.

Ahmadinejad: The agency is supposed to supervise and ask questions, and we'll respond. Our activities are very peaceful.

Pelley: But when I asked you a question as direct as, "Will you pledge not to test a nuclear weapon?" You act— you dance all around the question. You never say yes, you never say no.[81]

Pelley's interrogation of Ahmadinejad is precisely what one would expect of a reporter responding to the propagandistic pressures of American officials. Strong criticism from journalists, however, is never applied to U.S. officials. The example of a CBS interview between Charles Gibson and President Bush is useful in demonstrating this point:

Gibson: Admiral Fallon, the head of CENTCOM, said in a recent newspaper interview, he said the military strike against Iran is not in the offing. It would be a strategic mistake. Do you agree?

Bush: I think it's very important for us to pursue our objectives diplomatically. I also know it's important for all options to remain on the table, and they are on the table.

Gibson: Including military?

Bush: Yes, sir.

Gibson: So he's wrong?

Bush: As the commander in chief, all options are on the table. And—

Gibson: When he says it's a strategic mistake?

Bush: My, my objective is to solve this issue diplomatically. And I fully intend to and I believe we can. But diplomacy is effective when all options are available to a president and all options are available.[82]

Gibson's exchange with the former president is what one would expect to find in a media system intent only on pragmatically assessing U.S. foreign policy. At no point did Gibson verbally denigrate the president for his militaristic stance toward Iran. Gibson never referred to the intelligence community's conclusion that Iran is not developing nuclear weapons, or to U.S. official deception in manufacturing a false notion of an Iranian threat. In contrast, Pelley attacked Ahmadinejad for refusing to answer questions about Iran's problems with nuclear transparency. Gibson's strategic questioning of Bush allows CBS to appear strongly adversarial in dealing with the president, while in reality refraining from saying anything of substance. Had Gibson criticized Bush in the same fashion as Pelley did Ahmadinejad, questions would have emerged regarding the Bush administration's contempt for the intelligence record on Iran, and Bush's lack of transparency in honestly addressing Iran's nuclear program. Questions would be posed exposing the administration's material interests in the Middle East and preoccupation with Gulf oil. None of those questions were asked in Gibson's exchange.

It is *not* the case that U.S. reporters always fail to offer substantive criticisms of their political leaders. At times, attacks on officials are quite harsh, so long as those officials are challenging received truths rather than promoting them. A case in point is CBS reporter Bob Schieffer's lament against Republican presidential candidate Ron Paul:

Schieffer:	What do you feel about Iran? Do you see that as a threat to this country?
Paul:	No. I think . . .
Schieffer:	You don't?
Paul:	No. I think Iran—I think our policy towards Iran is a threat. That's what I fear. You know, I fear that tomorrow we might bomb Iran. That really scares me. But Iran doesn't have a nuclear weapon. Our CIA says they might, and they're thinking about it. But they've committed no crimes. As a matter of fact, the United Nations inspectors say that they have no evidence that they're working on a nuclear weapon. So the fact that we might bomb them, that our other candidates say that they won't take anything off the table, even a nuclear first strike, that's what really scares me.
Schieffer:	So we just leave them there and let them go about their business, and if they get a nuclear weapon?[83]

It is difficult to interpret Schieffer's hostile questioning as anything less than fear-mongering. Despite Paul's efforts to explain that Iran is developing nuclear weapons, Schieffer responds with speculation (backed by no evidence) that Iran is an imminent threat. The implications of such an attack are clear enough. Schieffer's insinuation that Paul is ignoring dangers to the United States is blatant evidence of media propaganda.

Reporting after the December 2007 National Intelligence Estimate changed somewhat, although not substantively. The refutation by U.S. and world intelligence communities of the former Bush administration's nuclear claims caused a serious decline in coverage in the following months. Total news coverage of the Iranian nuclear issue in the five months following the introduction of the National Intelligence Estimate was approximately 79 percent lower for CBS, and 38 percent lower for ABC than in the five months prior to the National Intelligence Estimate's introduction. However, a review of coverage following the National Intelligence Estimate suggests that reporters continued to frame Iran as intent on developing nuclear weapons.[84] It is difficult to distinguish much of the reporting in the post-December 2007 period from that in the earlier period. On the *CBS Evening News*, for example, reporter David Martin referred to "new pictures of Iran's uranium enrichment plant" that "show the country's defense minister in the background, as if deliberately mocking a recent finding by United States intelligence that Iran had ceased work on a nuclear weapon."[85]

Other reports also insinuated that Iran was still working on nuclear weapons. On ABC's *This Week*, George Stephanopoulos questioned Vice President Joe Biden's rejection of former speaker of the House Newt Gingrich's claims that Iran is developing nuclear weapons. "On the broader point," Stephanopoulos argued, "if Iran is continuing to enrich uranium, if they continue to have a reactor to develop materials that could only really be used for a nuclear weapons program, isn't that the same thing? And don't we have to take it seriously?"[86] CBS even framed Israel's illegal 1982 attack on Iraq's Osirak nuclear power plant as vital to the survival of Western nations.[87] Reporter Bob Simon labeled the Israeli pilots who violated international law by attacking Iraq as "superheroes." Simon cited the Israeli government's claims that Iran may be two years from developing nuclear weapons, rather than international and U.S. estimates that Iran is not a nuclear threat. Simon provided U.S. viewers with "a rare look inside the organization that may well be called upon to do something about it [Iran's alleged nuclear program]: the Israeli air force. Drawing an analogy between the 1982 Israeli bombing of Iraq and an attack on Iran, Simon claimed that "Israel's decision makers are faced with a similar choice [today as in 1982]. Will they take out Iran's nuclear facilities? The Israelis hope they won't have to, but can they do it?"[88]

COVERAGE IN ELITE PRINT MEDIA

In February of 2009, the *Los Angeles Times* reported: "Iran has enough fuel for a nuclear bomb if it decides to take drastic steps of violating its international treaty obligations, kicking out inspectors and further refining its supply."[89] Of course, such assessments were not the least bit grounded in the reality of Iran's nuclear power program, which for years, intelligence agencies concluded, was not developing nuclear weapons. The basis for a flurry of Iran stories in February arose from the finding that Iran had increased its low-enriched uranium, which is suitable only for nuclear power use and not for nuclear weapons development. This fact did not stop U.S. media outlets from following the *Los Angeles Times*'s lead in offering unsubstantiated worst-case nightmare scenarios. An editorial in the *New York Times* similarly postulated that Iran possessed the needed uranium to develop a small bomb, obscuring the fact that low-enriched uranium is insufficient for weapons production.[90] A *Boston Globe* editorial in the same month ominously warned that Iran's launching of a new satellite "foreshadow[ed] the capability one day to deliver warheads on intercontinental ballistic missiles."[91] Again, the state of existing intelligence was deemed irrelevant when predicting possible Armageddon. Reporting of Iran's construction of a second nuclear power site at Qum in late 2009 also framed Iran as a nuclear threat, as discussed in this book's postscript.

Despite significant differences between both U.S. and British media in reporting Iraq withdrawal, little evidence is found of such a difference in reporting on Iran. In examining reporting in the United Kingdom's *Guardian* of Manchester and the United States' *Washington Post*, one finds many similarities. An analysis of 235 news articles in the *Post* on Iran and the nuclear issue from mid-2003 to mid-2007 finds that the paper's reports are over twice as likely to contain phrases suggesting Iran is or may be developing nuclear weapons, as opposed to statements suggesting that it is not, or may not be developing them.[92] The repetition of claims of an Iranian threat is not due solely to reporters transmitting official dogma; in fact, over 85 percent of all the assertions came from reporters' own words or reporters' paraphrasing of other sources, rather than from official sources themselves. It is not that the *Post* ignored the IAEA in its reporting. The IAEA is cited in 73 percent of all the paper's stories on Iran's nuclear program despite the fact that the paper tilts by a two-to-one ratio in favor of suggestions that Iran is developing nuclear weapons. It appears that the IAEA itself, rather than its critical conclusions, has propaganda value for United States media. Little else explains why the organization is regularly cited, while its actual conclusions are consistently marginalized.

Belligerent rhetoric is used far more often in discussing the Iranian "threat," as opposed to the United States and Israeli military threat to Iran. Belligerent terms are applied approximately twice as often to Iran's alleged weapons development. Such terms, portraying Iran as a "threat" and discussing the "fear" invoked by a potentially nuclear armed Iran, and the "danger" of such a development, are contrasted with similar references to a U.S. "threat," to the "fear" of a United States or Israeli attack, or the "danger" both countries pose to Iran.

As with other U.S. newspapers, the *Washington Post*'s coverage is laced with alarmist language. Stories warn of Iran's power to "Hit Europe" and Israel in light of its "testing of long-range, surface-to-surface missile[s]."[93] The paper's reporters uncritically discuss administration efforts to "curb [Iranian] nuclear arms," with U.S. leaders paternalistically pondering "what to do about Iran."[94] Iran's defiance of U.S. efforts to demonize Iran is described as "narrow[ing] U.S. options" in dealing with this menace.[95] United States' hypocrisy in nuclear weapons proliferation is swept aside in stories. The Bush administration's long-standing attacks on Iran for weapons development are accompanied by the United States' own *open* admission that it is seeking to expand its nuclear weapons arsenal through the Reliable Replacement Warhead (RRW) program. Though the Reliable Replacement Warhead program received over $70 million in funding from 2005 through 2007 (and over $150 million was projected through 2008), the program has not been placed into its proper context in regard to the U.S. double standard in encouraging nuclear proliferation.[96] Despite the hundreds of features the *Washington Post* ran on Iran in recent years, only three of those stories (from 2005 and 2007) also mentioned the Reliable Replacement Warhead program and the United States' own nuclear weapons development program. This meager coverage amounts to less than one story on average per year. As discussed in the postscript, coverage of the Obama administration's revival of the

RRW program in late 2009 was also ignored in major newspapers. As a result of the censorship of critical reporting on the U.S., readers are left with de-contextualized coverage of the United States' imposition of a nuclear development ban on countries in the developing world, simultaneously pursued alongside the United States' own illegal commitment to nuclear weapons development (the Non-Proliferation Treaty requires the United States to take steps toward nuclear disarmament, *not* rearmament). To the extent that the Reliable Replacement Warhead program received much media coverage at all, it was largely the result of Congress's decision to impose major cuts in the program, although such attention was rarely related back to Iran.[97]

Similar to the *Washington Post*, the *Guardian*'s news coverage of Iran is also heavily propagandistic. The *Guardian* resorted to broad speculation over Iran's alleged power to initiate war against the United States and its allies. One such example is a highly publicized May 2007 story by reporter Simon Tisdall, titled "Iran's Secret Plan for Summer Offensive to Force U.S. Out of Iraq." The article maintained that Iran was attempting to ally with al-Qaeda to expel the United States from Iraq, although it relied on only a single anonymous U.S. official source and no citation of expert sources who might challenge this claim.[98] The backlash against the piece was immediate. David Edwards of the British media monitoring group Medialens degraded the story as the "single worst piece of journalism I can recall reading." His comments were reinforced by numerous *Guardian* readers who were appalled with the report.[99] Middle East professor and expert Juan Cole described Tisdall's story as "silly," and Tisdall himself as being used "to push a sinister agenda . . . U.S. military spokesmen have been trying to push implausible articles about Shiite Iran supporting Sunni insurgents for a couple of years now, and with virtually the sole exception of the *New York Times*, no one in the journalistic community has taken these wild charges seriously. But the *Guardian*?"[100]

The *Guardian*'s reporting on Iran parallels that of the *Washington Post*, as an analysis of stories from the two-year period of January 2005 through December 2006 demonstrates. Examination of over two hundred stories on Iran and nuclear issues finds that the paper was approximately 2.3 times more likely to report suggestions that Iran is, or may be, developing nuclear weapons, as opposed to suggestions that it is not or may not be developing them. Use of bellicose rhetoric casting Iran as a "threat" or "danger" to the United States and its allies, or references to Western "fear" of Iran appeared 44 percent more often than language criticizing the "danger" or "threats" of the United States and its allies, or "fear" of an allied attack on Iran.[101]

Upon closer inspection, the *Guardian*'s framing is extraordinarily similar to U.S. accounts. Iranian leaders are stigmatized for "play[ing] cat and mouse with the IAEA for 18 years" and "evading full disclosure" on their nuclear program.[102] A parallel can be drawn in the case of British and U.S. reporting of weapons proliferation. As with the Reliable Replacement Warhead program in the United States, the modernization of the British Trident nuclear submarine program has been subject to intense debate among members of Parliament. However, little critical self-reflection is seen in the debate over Britain's proliferation of nuclear weapons in the *Guardian*.

Despite the *Guardian* running hundreds of stories on Iran and its nuclear program, only fifteen of those stories (from 2005 through 2007) mention the British Trident program and British weapons proliferation. This constitutes an average of five stories per year, or less than one every two months.[103] Of those fifteen stories, most spoke approvingly of the need to promote renewal of the Trident program as a "deterrent" against Iranian nuclear weapons. The program is deemed vital for "self-defense" and protection of the greater good. Of the fifteen *Guardian* stories, only four speak critically of British hypocrisy in opposing Iranian nuclear development while supporting such development at home.[104] Essentially, this translates into an average of just over one critical story every year. Even these stories, it should be noted, are not evidence of media independence from government, considering that they rely on British officials who are themselves criticizing the United Kingdom's double standard on nuclear proliferation.

Although there are many similarities between *Guardian* and *Washington Post* reporting, it should be noted that there are significant differences as well. The *Post* is more likely to reference the Non-Proliferation Treaty—which prohibits member states from developing nuclear weapons—in reference to Iran's activities. Such references appeared in 38 percent of stories examined. In contrast, the *Guardian* referenced the Non-Proliferation Treaty in relation to Iran in only 16 percent of its stories—less than half as often as the *Post*. The *Post* was also less likely to stress the restrictions of the Non-Proliferation Treaty in regard to its own or its allies' violations of the agreement. Such concerns were not mentioned in a single story. The *Guardian* rarely referenced the Non-Proliferation Treaty in regard to its own or its allies' behavior, but such concerns did at least appear in four percent of stories.

The *Guardian* is somewhat more multilateral in its approach than the *Washington Post*. In the case of the *Post*, reporters speak of the U.S.-European "offer" to Iran aimed at preventing nuclear weapons development, while also reporting statements from Iranian president Ahmadinejad, who complains "of the double standard implicit in Iran being denied a nuclear program by countries with large stockpiles of atomic weapons." Although such an excerpt appears critical of the United States and its allies, it nevertheless fails to reference the *specific political context* in which the United States ignores its legally binding Non-Proliferation Treaty requirement to move toward disarmament rather than redevelop its weapons supply. In the case of the *Guardian*, writers explicitly refer to United States–United Kingdom violations of the Non-Proliferation Treaty. The *Guardian* implicates the United States in undermining the Non-Proliferation Treaty, *in addition to* the more general critique of Western double standards over nuclear weapons development.[105] In one example, *Guardian* security editor Richard-Norton Taylor condemns the United States and United Kingdom for turning against

> the logic of the Non-Proliferation Treaty. Britain cannot disarm, it suggests, precisely because such weapons will inevitably spread. As the Ministry of Defense put it in its December 2003 defence white paper, the "continuing risk from the proliferation of nuclear weapons, and the certainty that a number of other countries will retain substantial nuclear arsenals, mean that our minimum nuclear deterrent capability, currently represented by Trident, is likely to remain a necessary element of our security. . . . " The lesson non-nuclear states seem to be learning is that nuclear weapons earn you respect and deter foreign countries from attacking you. That is a very dangerous message, one that can't be allowed to go unanswered.[106]

Although the *Guardian* and the *Washington Post* are very similar in their reporting, their editorials, op-eds, and commentaries are significantly different. An analysis of thirty editorials and fifty-eight op-eds in the *Post* and thirty-one commentaries from the *Guardian* demonstrate that substantive challenges to United States–United Kingdom foreign policy arise in the British press, but not in the U.S. media. Table 5.3 summarizes the differences between the two papers across seven major issues.[107] In nearly all of these areas, the *Guardian*'s commentaries distinguish themselves as less parochial, less propagandistic, and more open to critical points of view.

TABLE 5.3: Editorial Framing of Iran and Nuclear Power/Weapons in the *Washington Post* and *Guardian* 1/1/2005–12/31/2006 (*Guardian*); 6/1/2003–6/1/2007 (*Washington Post*)

Editorial Categories	*W. Post* (Editorials)	*W. Post* (Op-Eds)	*Guardian* (Commentary)
1. Iran Is Developing Nuclear Weapons	90%	93%	74%
Iran Is Not Developing Weapons	0%	16%	29%
2. IAEA Is Referenced	61%	29%	45%
IAEA Conclusions Are Referenced	3%	2%	10%
3. Belligerent Language (Against United States/Allies)	23%	16%	48%
Belligerent Language (Against Iran)	42%	40%	32%
4. United States/Allies Nuclear Hypocrisy	0%	0%	58%
5. United States/Allies and the Non-Proliferation Treaty	3%	2%	35%
6. Iran and the Non-Proliferation Treaty	39%	14%	42%
7. United States Support for Iran's Enrichment	0%	3%	16%
8. 1953 United States-Allied Overthrow	0%	5%	16%

Source: Lexis Nexis

In terms of the nuclear weapons question, the majority of articles in both papers propagandistically suggest that Iran is, or may be developing, a weapons program. These suggestions appear in 90 percent of *Washington Post* editorials, 93 percent of *Post* op-eds, and 74 percent of *Guardian* commentaries. However, as these numbers indicate, *Guardian* commentaries are significantly less likely to stress this point. *Guardian* commentaries are also more likely to stress that Iran may not be developing nuclear weapons, as such claims appear in nearly 30 percent of all the paper's articles, contrasted with none of *Post* editorials and 16 percent of *Post* op-eds.

A closer examination demonstrates the differences between the papers. Prior to the 2007 National Intelligence Estimate release, the *Washington Post*'s editors implicated Iran in "stalling the IAEA and its inspectors," concluding that "unless Iran's rulers are confronted with a broad and coherent international coalition that is prepared to apply painful sanctions—through the United Nations or, if necessary, independently—they will not stop pursuing a bomb." This interpretation left little room for dissent, as the editors assessed that claims that Iran was not developing weapons were "ludicrous."[108] By April 2008, the *Post* continued to expound upon the importance of "diplomatic and economic pressure aimed at stopping Tehran's nuclear program," despite the fact that civilian nuclear power operations are protected under the Non-Proliferation Treaty.[109] This approach is very much in line with the Bush administration's response to the December 2007 National Intelligence Estimate, as the president continued to claim that Iran was a serious threat and needed to be contained.

Absolutist claims were also reinforced in the *Washington Post*'s op-eds. One article by Robert Kimmitt (former deputy secretary of the department of Treasury) claimed that "there is no debate about the fact that Iran is embarked on a path toward obtaining nuclear weapons."[110] Even if Iran were secretly developing nuclear weapons, the *Post* marginalizes those who claim that the motivation may be self-defense from a U.S. attack. Rather, pundits frame Iran as fanatically committed to world annihilation. *Post* op-ed contributor Charles Krauthammer pontificates that "ultimately, human survival" is "at stake in the dispute over Iranian nukes. Iran is the most dangerous political entity on the planet . . . if we fail to prevent an Iranian regime run by apocalyptic fanatics from going nuclear, we will have reached a point of no return."[111] Another contributor, Robert Samuelson, writes as if the long-standing principle of mutually assured destruction that drove deterrence theory in the Cold War is no longer relevant in the post–Cold War world. Samuelson argues, "If North Korea and Iran gain nuclear weapons, other countries . . . would ultimately go nuclear. Then, every nuclear danger would rise dramatically: miscalculation, *preemptive attacks*, theft, a global market in weapons technology, and use by terrorist groups other than nuclear powers. If North Korea and Iran go nuclear . . . residual self-restraint of 'mutual assured destruction' might evaporate."[112] Samuelson provides no evidence for why countries like Iran and North Korea are more likely to transfer weapons to terrorist groups, or why they are more likely to undertake preemptive attacks. Such claims are merely assumed as objective fact—uncritically repeated by pundits committed to transmitting government propaganda.[113]

Editorializing in the *Guardian* is often diametrically opposed to that in the *Washington Post*. In keeping with the British media's more cosmopolitan tradition, the *Guardian* allots serious attention to Iranians themselves (specifically representatives of Iran based in London), who take a decidedly non–U.S. perspective on the nuclear issue. Iranian ambassador to London Rasoul Movahedian argues forcefully that "again and again the 'Iranian threat' is invoked as part of a neocon agenda to deepen U.S. military involvement in the area. But its goal—to downgrade Iran's role in the region—is both implausible and ill founded. . . . Instead of demonising, the United States must accept that we have every right to a civil nuclear programme."[114] Hamid Babaei, Secretary of the Iranian Embassy in London, takes issue with the United States' and the United Kingdom's targeting of Iran's

> peaceful nuclear programme. . . . Instead of resorting to exaggeration about the issue and relying on unfounded stories . . . it would be much more useful to review impartially the existing facts and figures. . . . Iran has signed the [Non-Proliferation Treaty] treaty and has time and again renounced the pursuit of any nuclear weapons programme. . . . The International Atomic Energy Agency [inspectors] haven't hesitated to monitor any movement, whether animate or inanimate, in Iranian nuclear sites. In addition, there are 1,400 persons [and] hours of inspection of the sites by the authority. This evidence rules out any baseless accusations about Iran's "intentions."[115]

A serious discrepancy between the papers is also evident in the politicization of the IAEA's findings. While Table 5.3 suggests that both the *Washington Post* and *Guardian* refer to the IAEA in articles about Iran, the long-standing conclusions of the organization (that Iran does not possess a weapons program) are more likely to appear in the *Guardian*. References to the critical conclusions of the IAEA appear in 10 percent of *Guardian* commentaries, contrasted with 3 percent of *Post* editorials and 2 percent of its op-eds. The editors at the *Post* are not hesitant to display their open contempt for head IAEA inspectors such as Mohammed ElBaradei. Editorials express disdain for ElBaradei's efforts to ease tensions between the United States, Europe, and Iran through brokering a nuclear accord directly with Iranian leaders. The *Post*'s editors balk at "the nerve of Mr. ElBaradei, an unelected international civil servant" who "considers himself above his position." They condemn ElBaradei's alleged effort "to excuse the Iranian [nuclear] activity" and for his bypassing of the United Nations Security Council in negotiating with Iran. ElBaradei is seen as "a diplomat who apparently believes he need not represent anyone other than himself."[116]

The U.S. media's contempt for the IAEA is not replicated in the *Guardian*. Commentaries in the paper often confirm the IAEA's conclusion that "it has found no evidence of a nuclear weapons programme."[117] When given the choice, *Guardian* writers are happy to side with the IAEA over the United States. In one commentary, for example, Ian Williams chastises the United States for

> smearing IAEA chief Mohammed ElBaradei. . . . When it comes to Iran's nuclear capabilities, whose word would you rather take: that of a Nobel prize-winning head of an international agency specializing in nuclear issues who was proved triumphantly right about Iraq, or that of a bunch of belligerent neocons who make no secret of their desire to whack Iran at the earliest opportunity and who made such a pig's ear of Iraq? That is the stark choice facing the sane people of the world, given the smearing of IAEA chief Mohamed ElBaradei for not joining the hysterical lynch mob building up against Iran.[118]

The data in Table 5.3 suggests that *Guardian* commentaries are less likely to use belligerent language in framing Iranian actions. U.S. op-eds, in contrast, glorify hawkish posturing against Iran. George Will discusses the importance of a "credible threat of force" in deterring foreign powers from developing nuclear weapons, while David Ignatius ethnocentrically assumes that "Iranians are counting on the West's prudence [in confronting Iran] to save them from their own actions."[119] In an Orwellian style, negotiations are portrayed as contingent upon U.S. unilateralism and military threats. Jim Hoagland argues, "Europeans will get nowhere if there is not in the background a credible United States threat of force to block Iran's nefarious ambitions."[120] Robert Kagan contends that "fear of United States military action is probably the only reason Iran even pretended to negotiate with the Europeans."[121] The bizarre portrayals of U.S. contempt for negotiations as vital to the success of negotiations contrast with *Guardian* commentaries. U.S. threats are framed negatively as a threat to world peace. Jonathan Freedland argues that if Iran is pursuing nuclear weapons, this "doesn't necessarily make Iran a threat . . . a threat can be described mathematically—as the sum of capability plus intention. Iran may be on its way to having the capability, but what of its intentions?" Freedland portrays any Iranian interest in acquiring nuclear weapons as defensive in intent: "Recent events have confirmed the value of a nuclear arsenal: after all, Iraq, which had no Weapons of Mass Destruction, was attacked by the United States, while North Korea, which has nukes, was left alone. The message is clear: stay safe, go nuclear."[122] Tariq Ali condemns U.S. leaders for having "manufactured this crisis" and attacks the United States and its allies for threatening Iran: "The country [Iran] is not only ringed by atomic states (India, Pakistan, China, Russia, Israel), it also faces a string of U.S. bases with potential or actual nuclear stockpiles in Qatar, Iraq, Turkey, Uzbekistan and Afghanistan. Nuclear-armed U.S. aircraft carriers and submarines patrol the waters off its southern coast."[123] Other authors also attack the United States for its belligerence and intransigence, or refer to Iranian actions as primarily defensive in approach.[124]

U.S. arrogance and parochialism is perhaps best seen in the complete refusal of the *Washington Post* to identify U.S. double standards. As reflected in Table 5.3, not a single editorial or op-ed in the *Post* criticizes the United States for hypocritically dealing with Iran, whereas nearly six in ten commentaries in the *Guardian* criticize either the United States, United Kingdom, or their allies for hypocrisy. George Monbiot's commentaries are instructive in this regard. Monbiot takes aim at current nuclear states:

> The permanent members of the United Nations Security Council draw a distinction between their "responsible" ownership of nuclear weapons and that of the aspirant powers. But over the past six years, the United Kingdom, United States, France and Russia have all announced that they are prepared to use their nukes preemptively against a presumed threat, even from states that do not possess nuclear weapons. In some ways the current nuclear stand-off is more dangerous than the tetchy detente of the cold war.[125]

Unlike the *Guardian*'s reporting, which largely exonerates the United Kingdom for renewal of its Trident nuclear submarine program, the paper's commentaries often disapprove of Trident as hypocritical and dangerous.[126]

There are also similarities and differences in British and U.S. reporting on international non-proliferation agreements. Both the *Guardian* and *Washington Post* heavily cite the relevance of the Non-Proliferation Treaty in relation to Iran. However, as seen in Table 5.3, whereas the *Washington Post* almost completely ignores the Non-Proliferation Treaty application to the United States, such a focus on the United States and its allies is common in the *Guardian*, appearing in more than one-third of all commentaries. George Monbiot, for example, denigrates the United States and United Kingdom for having "junked the non-proliferation treaty," while non-nuclear states continue "using it to develop their own [civilian nuclear] programmes."[127]

Although the United States treats Iran's nuclear program today as part of a major international crisis, U.S. leaders historically supported Iran's procurement of nuclear technology. U.S. readers may not know about the history of U.S. complicity, however, from reading the *Washington Post*. As Table 5.3 demonstrates, references to this history appear in none of the paper's editorials and in only 3 percent of its op-eds. These few references typically did not criticize the United States for its support of authoritarian allies, but merely generically reference that support in brief passing.[128]

The 1952 coup, in which the United States and United Kingdom overthrew Iran's democratically elected prime minister Mohammed Mossadegh, also reflects poorly on both countries. Mossadegh angered U.S. and British oil companies by nationalizing Iran's oil, the benefits of which had long been monopolized by the United States and United Kingdom.[129] His overthrow set the stage for a new era of Iranian history, in which the Shah and his CIA-supported secret service, the SAVAK, became notorious for the torture and murder of dissidents. It is not that this inconvenient history is completely ignored by the *Washington Post*, just *nearly* completely ignored. References to Western responsibility for the coup appear in none of the *Post*'s editorials and in just 5 percent of its op-eds, as opposed to 16 percent of *Guardian* commentaries. Clearly, the *Guardian* allows at least some room for views deemed "inexpressible" by political elites, but such is not the case in the U.S. press.

MAJOR LESSONS FROM THE IRAN CASE STUDY

The alleged independence of U.S. reporters from government is strongly exaggerated. Although media elites claim independence from political spin, there is little evidence of such independence in reporting. In highlighting this fact, I do not mean to suggest that there is some "conspiracy" among media professionals, who are consciously committed to manipulating the U.S. public. As Noam Chomsky states: "Journalists generally have professional integrity. Typically, they are honest, serious professionals who want to do their job properly. None of that changes the fact that most of them reflexively perceive the world through a particular prism that happens to be supportive of concentrated power."[130]

Journalists may see themselves as excluding "conscious values" from their reporting, but this study demonstrates that this is clearly not the case.[131] Rather than serving as "objective" observers, mirroring events in the real world, reporters reflect the dominant values of political elites. These values are taken for granted as simply "the way that things work," with little or no critical thought or reflection. Despite delusions about journalistic neutrality, many institutional constraints continue to shape the views expressed in mainstream discourse. These constraints include overreliance on official sources, nationalistic pressures limiting dissent during times of war, and long-standing processes of socialization, which convince journalists of the benevolence of U.S. military power. These entrenched processes succeed in "normalizing" U.S. views that are often considered extreme throughout the rest of the globe, but as self-evident truths at home.

In addition, U.S. pundits are significantly closer to the foreign policy establishment than pundits in the British press. This is not to suggest that the U.S. media practices propaganda and the British media does not. This is far from the case. However, in drawing across the examples of British magazine and print media coverage, one sees significantly more room for dissent against government policy in the U.K., whereas there is little to no room in U.S. television, Internet, magazine, and regional and print outlets. Some argue that the left-leaning *Guardian* and *New Statesman* should be even more open in their criticisms of the government. This point is well taken, although this study merely intends to show that, *relative* to the United States, British media coverage reflects a less propagandistic approach, although the deck is still heavily stacked in favor of officialdom. The main lesson to draw from this study, then, is that there is nothing inevitable about the coverage observed in the U.S. and British press. Reporting in the Muslim world, and in the U.S. and British press, demonstrate that there are a number of different ways in which the conflict with Iran may be framed.

CHAPTER SIX

Media, Globalization, and Violence: Views from around the World

Opposition to the United States is common in the Muslim world. People throughout the region consistently challenge the legitimacy of U.S. foreign policy. Media in these countries are often unequivocal in their distrust of U.S. power. The *Nation* of Pakistan is one example. The paper attacked former President Bush for making numerous "false statements justifying the Iraq war." The *Nation* condemned the United States for "lying" hundreds of times about weapons of mass destruction, and it called "into question the repeated assertions of Bush administration officials that they were merely the unwitting victims of bad intelligence."[1] It assailed Bush's "muscle flexing" over Iran, which "is unlikely to win support" from neighboring Arab states. These states "are increasingly wary of the United States' intentions," as they blame the United States for "destroying a prosperous and stable country."[2]

The *Nation*'s status as a newspaper in the Muslim world does not preclude it from criticizing Islamic political leaders. The paper is not one-dimensionally "anti-American" or pro-Islamic; it criticizes Iranian president Mahmoud Ahmadinejad, for example, for his "hard-line" positions in dealing with the United States and United Nations.[3] The *Nation*'s attacks on the Bush administration's "overt aggression against Iran" and its "paranoiac prejudice" are not driven by a fanatical contempt for Western culture or values, but rather by fear and apprehension of aggressive actions by the United States. As the *Nation* warns, "The collapse of the Soviet Union in the last decade of the 20th century resulted in a power vacuum that Washington was trying to fill up. The invasions and destruction of Afghanistan and Iraq were just the beginning, while Iran and Syria were next. Controlling Iran is the top priority because of its huge oil reserves and large uranium deposits, which if mined and refined could make Iran, much against U.S.-Israeli interests, a super regional power."[4] The paper's strident opposition to U.S. power is not entirely unique in the Middle East. The *Nation*'s attacks, however, are considered alien in an American press that reflexively embraces U.S. neocolonial power.

How does the *Nation*'s hostility, in addition to reporting on Iraq by other countries, fit within a broader framework of global politics? Addressing these questions is the main focus of this chapter. As readers will see, the *Nation*'s attention to Iraq, though worth studying in its own right, is also representative of a larger "world system" in which countries' attention to, and support for the conflict depends on their level of political, economic, and military investment.

This chapter examines how media throughout the world report the Iraq war. Media outlets' coverage is shown to be a function of corporate ownership and national origin. In short, the most powerful challenges to U.S. and allied policy in Iraq arise from media in poorer countries that reside outside the core of the capitalist order, and from countries that are not involved in the occupation. Conversely, less room exists for moral criticisms of the war in countries that are heavily involved in the Iraq war and countries that are at the heart of the capitalist world economic system.

A REVIEW OF GLOBAL MEDIA STUDIES

Comparison across national boundaries is of major importance in furthering our understanding of global media. Frank Esser and Barbara Pfetsch stress "the lack of comparative research [on media]," while reminding us that we "cannot understand the fundamental principles of media operation without studying various media systems across national boundaries."[5] Unfortunately, the field of media studies focuses too heavily on the United States and Europe.[6] Most studies emphasize reporting in the developed world, at the expense of less developed countries. Studies of media by U.S. intellectuals are "parochial" and "self-absorbed."[7] U.S. academic studies are "highly ethnocentric, because they refer to the experience of a single country [the United States], yet . . . are written in general terms, as though the model that prevailed in that country were universal." Even prominent studies that transcend the study of a single country tend to focus narrowly on areas of affluence such as Western Europe, as well as areas in the democratizing or democratic world.[8]

Progressive critics of the U.S. media are usually met with hostility in mainstream academia. Most intellectuals are uneasy with the claim that capitalist ownership of media is harmful to democratic development. The much-cited media study *Four Theories of the Press* is one of the most important examples of a historical analysis that is tailored to a global pro-capitalist perspective. In this work, authors Fred Siebert, Theodore Peterson, and Wilbur Schramm established four different frameworks for explaining global media: the Authoritarian, Libertarian, Social Responsibility, and Communist models. The authors associated media propaganda with authoritarian and communist countries, rather than with Western capitalist states.[9] Only the media in dictatorial countries were thought to be concerned with opportunistically promoting self-interested, materially driven politics.[10]

In contrast to communist and authoritarian countries, the United States and United Kingdom are described benevolently as the "chief custodians" of the "Libertarian Press Model," and later the "Social Responsibility Model."[11] "Libertarian" media are defined by "freedom from government controls or domination," "insistence on the importance of the individual, the reliance on his power of reasoning, and the concepts of natural rights, of which freedom of religion, speech, and press became a part."[12] Media that operate within these countries are described as informing and entertaining audiences, and advertising products in a capitalist marketplace.[13] The authors of *Four Theories of the Press* provide an update to the Libertarian model, applying it to the United States in the post–Second World War period (renaming it the Social Responsibility model). In the "gradual shift away from 'pure libertarianism,'" the U.S. press is described as "carrying out certain essential functions of mass communication" such as "providing information, discussion and debate on public affairs . . . enlightening the public so as to make it capable of self-government . . . [and] safeguarding the rights of the individual by serving as a watchdog against government."[14]

Siebert, Peterson, and Schramm's unqualified support for Western capitalist media did not escape criticism in the decades following the publication of their book. Some criticized the work as a valuable ideological tool for Western leaders during the height of the Cold War. In assessing the work, critics highlighted the tendency of "prominent scholars [during the Cold War]" to "uncritically accept the very ideological mystification in the media [that] owners propound to explain their own existence: the myth of the free press in the service of society."[15] James Curran and Myung-Jin Park fault *Four Theories of the Press* for seeking to get around the authors' "evident lack of comparative expertise by advancing a convenient, idealist argument."[16] They denigrate the work for viewing "the universe only through Western eyes, [since the book] was followed in the 1960s by a theory which assumed the developed world should imitate the West." This theory, heavily associated with "developmentalism" and "modernization," is discussed below.

The ideological biases of *Four Theories of the Press* are readily apparent. Capitalist media are not criticized for primarily and selfishly pursuing profit motives or reinforcing U.S. and European global power, but rather are framed as innocently reporting stories to inform audiences. Profit motives are never characterized as contradictory to, or competing with the goal of informing a democratically empowered public. The effects of these biases are still apparent today in the area of media studies. Intellectuals commonly assume that corporate ownership of media is vital in the promotion of democracy, or at least not contrary to democracy. The belief that capitalism is synonymous with democracy is not always expressed explicitly by scholars; usually it is tacitly accepted or left unchallenged.

Rejecting beliefs that corporate media ownership is inherently democratic, many leftist critics study the mass media within the "Dependency" paradigm. Dependency is rooted in the works of theorists such as Andre Gunder Frank and Fernando Henrique Cardoso, with Frank describing underdevelopment throughout the Third World as "in large part the historical product of past and continuing economic relations between the satellite underdeveloped and the now developed [core] countries." This intentional underdevelopment of the Third World is considered "an essential part of the structure and development of the capitalist system on a world scale as a whole."[17] The dependency framework situates individual countries between two major poles: wealthy countries that exploit the rules of the international capitalist system to their own advantage and poorer countries that are taken advantage of by this system.

Immanuel Wallerstein dissects the global economy through a "World Systems" analysis, which describes countries as residing in the core (center), periphery (outside), and semi-periphery of the capitalist system.[18] In periphery poor nations, members of repressive and dictatorial regimes often ally themselves with wealthy political and business leaders in core countries, ensuring a transnational alliance promoting capitalist interests. Poor periphery countries are characterized by weak protections for workers, and an abundance of cheap labor to be exploited by multinational corporations based in core countries. Core countries retain a parasitic relationship with less developed countries, in that they disproportionately consume the raw materials and resources of poor countries. Semi-periphery countries, on the other hand, are situated somewhere in between the two poles of the system; some countries are former wealthy countries that have entered economic decline and others are former periphery countries that have benefited from rapid development and upward mobility.

Wallerstein depicts intellectual defenses of the capitalist system as a "useful intellectual tool for the United States" and its allies.[19] Developmentalist and modernization theories—advocated by prominent U.S. intellectuals such as Walt W. Rostow, Seymour Martin Lipset, and David Apter—promote a universalistic approach in which Western capitalism is commonly valued as the appropriate economic development model. The modernization approach promotes the secularization of national politics, capitalist industrialization, and the replacement of non-Western indigenous cultures and values with Western consumer values as means of attaining national "progress." According to modernization and capitalist development theories, the "free market" approach is the only legitimate form of economic organization—one that countries must emulate or face dire consequences.

Developmentalism, Wallerstein contends, is little more than a means of rationalizing capitalist exploitation, undertaken by those living in the neocolonial states of Western Europe, North America, and elsewhere. Rostow's predicted "stages of economic growth"—in which poorer countries experience the "preconditions for take-off [development]," "take-off," the "drive to maturity," and an "age of high mass consumption"—are little more than propaganda and deception in the eyes of Wallerstein and other critics.[20] Poorer states, he argues, exist primarily to enhance the wealth of core states, not to develop into major challenges to the power of those states. Though media reports on Iraq in wealthy countries seldom openly celebrate the virtues of capitalist development, the implicit assumption in reporting is that the U.S. occupation and privatization of Iraq is pursued for the good of the Iraqi people.

World Systems and Dependency theories were further developed in recent years with the introduction of cultural and media imperialism theories. In attempting to "dethrone modernization theory," cultural imperialism frames societal "homogenization as [the] result of cultural domination" by Western media corporations operating throughout the world.[21] Media and cultural imperialism gained traction during the 1970s as a result of initiatives of the Non-Aligned Movement—a loose affiliation of states that attempted to remain independent of U.S. and Soviet dominance during the Cold War. The Non-Aligned Movement (NAM) was instrumental in pursuing a New World Information and Communication Order (NWICO), which sought to break Western dominance of global and national communication networks. NAM members criticized Western states for their "monopoly control over the flow of news and information from developing countries, and exercising it from a limited perspective reflecting the economic and cultural interests of the industrialized nations."[22] They formed the NWICO and coordinated the International Program for the Development of Communication (IPDC)—despite strong Western opposition—to pursue various communication projects in developing countries that were supposed to be free of manipulation by wealthy countries. These programs, though attempting to empower national media in less developed countries, were generally ignored in prestigious media in the wealthy countries.[23]

Some contemporary critics stress the negative consequences of corporate monopolization of media.[24] William Hachten and James Scotten discuss "the expanded international news system"—including major newswire agencies—as "largely an outgrowth of Western news media, especially those of Britain, the United States, and to a lesser degree, France and Germany."[25] The fall of the Soviet Union and the end of the Cold War, the authors explain, ushered in a new era marked by the "triumph of Western journalism." Critics warn that major media conglomerates such as Sony, Vivendi, Viacom, News Corporation, Time Warner, Disney, and Bertelsmann have become wealthier and more powerful as a result of "megamergers" that result in the "loss of diverse opinions and less competition among competing news media."[26] In their much cited work, *The Global Media: The New Missionaries of Corporate Capitalism*, Robert McChesney and Edward Herman discuss the "dramatic restructuring of national media industries [since the early 1980s], along with the emergence of a genuinely global commercial media market."[27] This restructuring, the authors maintain, contributes to the "centralization of media control" and "erode[s] the public sphere."[28] Private media corporations tailor the transmission of information to the needs of corporate advertisers and owners rather than the general public and endangers "citizens' participation in public affairs" and "understanding of public issues."[29]

A backlash has emerged in recent years, with many attacking media and cultural imperialist claims. Some scholars reject the notion that Western corporations are assaulting the cultural autonomy of poor states. Others challenge the notion that the nation-state is no longer relevant in the study of international relations. Nancy Morris and Silvio Waisbord argue that the state matters in an era of corporate domination of the world economy. States are relevant as major "power centers" in the global economic system. They "remain fundamental political units in a world that continues to be divided along Westphalian principles of sovereignty."[30] Others emphasize the continued role of the state in restricting the flow of information within and outside national borders.[31] Daniel Hallin and Paolo Mancini argue that media deliberation and reporting of political issues cannot be understood *without* looking at the state. They depict media systems as "historically rooted in the institutions of the nation-state," with states being distinguished by higher or lower levels of parallelism between media and political institutions.[32]

Skeptics attack World Systems analysis and media imperialism on numerous grounds. These approaches are cast aside as "dated" and "a relic of the past," despite continued scholarly contributions in recent years.[33] Colin Sparks takes issue with media imperialism, which "downgrade[s] the importance of internal conflicts within a developing society, while stressing the conflict between the periphery and core." Sparks directs attention to "a broad spectrum of different social settings in which television consumption [takes] place," countering those who argue that consumption of Western media has universally negative effects on audiences.[34] Media imperialism, Sparks claims, is "increasingly inappropriate" as a field of inquiry:

> The imperialist paradigm accepted the official definition of there being homogeneous national cultures that were in one sense or another "authentic" and which could be identified and defended by the appropriate cultural institutions.... It no longer makes any sense to conceive of the world as made up of closed, self-contained communication spaces that are commensurate with the boundaries of the state system. The flows of communication in the contemporary world are much

> messier than that: media no longer respect political geography and audiences have access to information originating from a range of sources. As a consequence, it no longer makes sense to think of the media system of one state dominating or influencing those of another state.[35]

Terry Flew disagrees with the claim that national cultures are simply taken over by the media conglomerates of wealthy Western states. Instead, Flew posits that cultures often become fused together through a "hybridity," or mixing, in which values and norms from one state are intermingled and mixed with those of others. Media landscapes become "de-territorialized" as media bring the experiences of people from foreign states into the living rooms of media consumers in countries the world over.[36] Flew questions media imperialism claims, suggesting that concern over corporate consolidation may be "exaggerate[d]" by critics.[37] He cites the example of Pan-Arab news outlet Al Jazeera, which transcends national boundaries in its news transmissions, while challenging corporate ownership of mass media (Al Jazeera is not owned by a multinational corporation, but by the emir of Qatar, Sheikh Hamid Bin Khalifa Al-Thani).[38]

Kai Hafez argues, "the mass media are not in the least oriented toward a 'world system' but in fact concentrate upon national markets, whose interests and stereotypes they largely reproduce."[39] Hafez reviews news coverage throughout the Middle East, Asia, Africa, North and Latin America, and Eastern and Western Europe, finding that countries from every region of the world are more likely to focus on events or issues directly related to their own political concerns, as opposed to those of other regions. The "rankings of attention paid to world regions" in the reporting of each country analyzed are closely related to each country's political status as a member of the geographic region in which it resides.[40] In other words, countries pay more attention to political issues that are relevant to the region in which they are located. Hafez's conclusions are echoed elsewhere by those arguing that the U.S. media's global dominance receded in light of the ascendancy of regional and national media concerns.[41]

Although critics of World Systems and media imperialism level many relevant criticisms, they neglect the insights that the approaches provide to the study of media. It is true that many intellectuals overestimate the decline of the state in international relations today. Similarly, across-the-board warnings about the dangers of a Western culture being imposed on unwilling nations may also be exaggerated. Many elites throughout the less developed world, for example, are enthusiastic in their consumption of Western products, and their openness to Western-led capitalist development. However, conceding these points does not mean that media throughout the world are not being increasingly privatized under a world system characterized by the "free market." Lee Artz and Yahya Kamalipour discuss a global pattern of "media deregulation, privatization, and commercialization," highlighting "recent decisions by the International Monetary Fund and a score of national governments to privatize and deregulate their media—a distinct form of globalization that brings together capitalist classes and their media in joint projects that have no national loyalty or identity in ownership, structure, or interest."[42]

Pradip Thomas and Zaharom Nain voice concern about the effects of the rise of "free market" economic reform on media throughout the globe. The fall of the Soviet Union and the end of the Cold War were followed by the consolidation of American-led military and economic dominance, and the rise of a global capitalist media. As Thomas and Nain argue, the rise of the power of the market is increasingly characterized by the "relentless pace of media privatization and the steady retreat of the state from its public media commitments."[43] These claims reinforce the continued importance of World Systems analysis. Although fears of the imposition of a singular U.S. or European global media culture may be exaggerated, concerns over increased privatization of media remain extremely relevant.[44]

World Systems analysis remains relevant, though marginalized in mainstream academic studies. International media conferences continue to focus on the tremendous "digital divide" in access to information, heavily distinguished across class lines and between wealthier and poorer countries.[45] Corporate monopolization continues as Western companies gain influence in foreign media markets because they often adopt "localization of content" rather than imposing their own content.[46]

National media in poorer countries are increasingly affected by the status of their home states in the World System. Peter Wilkin concludes that media corporations tailor their operations to correspond with their country's standing within the core, periphery, and semi-periphery. Wilkin's study of Brazil chronicles how the country "has become more integrated into the world system and is subject to both pressures from global capital." Media corporations such as Globo (based in Brazil) seek to strengthen their ties with Western multinational media corporations such as Sky (based in Britain) and Microsoft (based in the United States), and attempt to "restructure its debts through banks in the core." Within this context, Globo and other corporations are limited in their "ability to transcend [their] location in the semi-periphery."[47] Brazil's Globo Corporation is merely one example of the application of capitalist pressure on media in the developing world. The pressure of the capitalist system on media is discussed in the next section.

NEOCOLONIAL PLANNING AND U.S. POLICY IN THE MIDDLE EAST

World Systems theory is heavily concerned with colonial and neocolonial relationships between countries in the developed and less developed world. Though mainstream scholars today are not hesitant to admit that European countries pursued selfish material goals during the height of colonialism, similar assessments of U.S. or European foreign policy are rare today. Acknowledging the material interests of the United States throughout the world, however, is essential if one is to understand the nature of U.S. foreign policy, and if one wants to understand how mass media throughout the world report that policy.

Traditional colonial powers were more brazen in their extravagant claims that they were "civilizing" the peoples residing in their colonies, and in celebrating the "white man's burden" in promoting stability and prosperity around the globe. U.S. foreign policymakers are less blunt in their neocolonial declarations, often expressing these claims in secret and behind closed doors. Expansionist claims are sometimes declared in publicly released government documents, although they are drowned out by loud rhetoric proclaiming U.S. support for human rights and democracy. Still, there remains a long record of post–Second World War neocolonial planning that is either neglected or completely ignored in academic studies. U.S. neocolonial planning transcends individual historical periods. One of the boldest enunciations of this planning is seen in the works of George Kennan, a major architect of the Cold War and the anti-communist policy of containment. Kennan directed the Policy Planning Staff (PPS), which was created in 1947 to provide strategic advice for the State Department as it formulated foreign policy objectives and planned the postwar reconstruction of Europe. Kennan is well known for authoring article "X," which appeared in the establishment journal *Foreign Policy*, but he is less well known for his then-classified work with the PPS.

Article "X" more innocently referred to the need of the United States to protect itself from Soviet aggression and the importance of a "patient but firm and vigilant containment of Russian expansive tendencies." Kennan's classified Policy Planning Study 23, however, cast U.S. policy in more blunt terms.

Kennan's writings at the State Department admitted that U.S. foreign policy was committed not only to curtailing Soviet power, but also to exploiting resources in non-core countries. Regarding Africa, Kennan advocated that:

> a union of Western European nations would undertake jointly the economic development and exploitation of the colonial and dependent areas of the African Continent. . . . The African Continent is little exposed to communist pressures: and most of it is not today a subject of great power rivalries. It lies easily accessible to the maritime nations of Western Europe, and politically they control or influence most of it. Its resources are still relatively undeveloped.

Kennan also described the Middle East as vital to United States national "security," considering its tremendous oil resources, which at the time were largely undeveloped by the West.[48] Concern with oil was reiterated by the State Department immediately following the Second World War. The Middle East was described as "a stupendous source of strategic power" and "probably the richest economic prize in the world in the field of foreign investment."[49] In reference to Saudi Arabia, the State Department assessed that oil resources needed to "remain under U.S. control for the dual purposes of supplementing and replacing our dwindling reserves, and of preventing this power potential from falling into unfriendly hands."[50]

Other political elites in post–Second World War history also spoke of the need to prevent Soviet or indigenous dominance of national oil reserves in poor countries. Oil-rich theocracies in the Middle East enjoyed strong U.S. support. Democratic president Harry Truman, for example, promised Saudi leaders that "no threat to your kingdom could occur which would not be a matter of immediate concern to the United States."[51] Dwight Eisenhower remarked that the Middle East remained the most "strategically important area in the world." In its National Security Council memorandums, Eisenhower's administration summarized America's problems with "radical and nationalistic regimes" in poorer countries that were responsible to public pressure for "the immediate improvement in the low living standards of the masses." Interested in promoting "a political and economic climate conducive to private investment," Eisenhower opposed regimes that responded to the demands of the masses for a more egalitarian distribution of natural resources. In speaking of Middle Eastern oil, Eisenhower's government explored U.S. options for "combating radical Arab nationalism" and "hold[ing] Persian Gulf oil by force if necessary." Support for Israel was deemed "logical" in ensuring control of this oil.[52]

The Carter administration also committed to using force to ensure control of oil. Carter's national security advisor Zbigniew Brzezinski stressed the need to maintain "critical leverage" over Europe and Asia by retaining control over their oil supplies.[53] Kennan spoke of U.S. control over Japan's sources of oil as representing a sort of "veto power" for preventing Japanese leaders from pursuing developmental paths that were too independent of the United States.[54] Control over oil lines was deemed vital by Nixon administration National Security Advisor and Secretary of State Henry Kissinger, who remarked that access to "cheap and plentiful oil" was the "basic premise" upon which postwar Western capitalism was built.[55] Kissinger was intent on ensuring U.S. control over "plentiful oil," as he supported the use of military force as "the only feasible countervailing power to OPEC's control of oil." To combat OPEC "extortion" and high oil prices, Kissinger claimed, the United States should rely upon Israeli military power for defeating its Arab neighbors and consider the use of U.S. military forces to secure Saudi oil fields for U.S. consumption.[56] Regional Middle Eastern allies—including Iran, Israel, and Saudi Arabia—were expected to serve as local "cops on the beat" promoting U.S. strategic interests, in the words of Nixon's Secretary of Defense Melvin Laird.[57]

Despite idealistic rhetoric, liberal presidencies also reinforced the U.S. commitment to power politics. The Carter administration voiced concern with protecting the U.S. supply of oil from the Middle East. In *National Security Directive 63*, the administration reacted to the Soviet invasion of Afghanistan by promising that an "attempt by any outside force to gain control of the Persian Gulf region will be regarded as an assault on the vital interests of the United States. It will be repelled by the use of any means necessary, including military force."[58]

The Carter administration created a Rapid Development Task Force to protect against just such an incursion. Serving as a military command structure (later transforming into Centcom), the task force was stationed in the Middle East and allowed for rapid action against forces hostile to

U.S. economic interests. Under the "Carter Doctrine," the United States announced its commitment to protecting oil rich Saudi Arabia from external threats. The Reagan administration further committed the United States to protecting the Saudi regime from internal threats to its authoritarian power structure.[59] In his 1982 National Security Strategy (NSS), Reagan also targeted "inefficient economies" (interpreted as socialist or communist-leaning) and "the growing scarcity of resources" as major factors that emboldened Soviet expansionism. In accord with the Carter administration's aggressive approach, Reagan's strategy recommended that the United States "strive to increase its influence worldwide through the maintenance and improvement of forward deployed forces and rapidly deployable United States-based forces, together with periodic exercises, security assistance, and special operations."[60]

Although the end of the Cold War was heralded as a major turning point in global politics, the United States' policy planning indicates otherwise. The George H. W. Bush administration's pronouncement of a "New World Order" was followed by a fixation on Middle Eastern oil as vital to U.S. "national security." This concern was announced publicly in George H. W. Bush's 1991 National Security Strategy, which emphasized "threats to the oil supplies that flow through the Persian Gulf" in the absence of competition with the Soviet Union. Concern was also directed at political threats to U.S. dominance, not only oil-rich countries but in countries adjacent to these countries. U.S. operations in Lebanon from 1983 to 1984 and in Libya in 1986 were deemed vital to promoting U.S. power in the Middle East and North Africa. As the 1991 NSS explained, the United States would continue to respond "to threats to United States interests that could not be laid at the Kremlin's door. Therefore, we will maintain a naval presence . . . in the Persian Gulf. . . . We will conduct periodic exercises and pursue improved host nation support and prepositioning of equipment throughout the region."[61]

Material interest in oil was also voiced in a Defense Policy Guidance report written in 1992. Such guidance reports are disseminated to military officials and to the head of the Defense Department and provide an overarching framework for directing U.S. foreign policy. The draft was authored by Undersecretary of Defense Paul Wolfowitz, who at the time served under President George H. W. Bush. Wolfowitz—who later became the architect for the 2003 Iraq invasion—announced that "the number one objective of U.S. post–Cold War political and military strategy should be preventing the emergence of a rival superpower," and the prevention of "any hostile power from dominating of a region [the Middle East] whose resources would, under consolidated control, be sufficient to generate global power."[62] The draft was later rewritten after it was leaked to the *New York Times* and *Washington Post*. Once made available to the general public, its embarrassing contents served as a catalyst to pressure the Bush administration to order revisions to the report.

U.S. leaders express conflicting stances on foreign policy—quietly articulating neocolonial designs while loudly promising to promote democracy and human rights. However, it is important to acknowledge that selfish motives typically trump humanitarian rhetoric. Nowhere is this more apparent than in the case of the 1991 Gulf war, when humanitarian rhetoric came into direct conflict with power-politics objectives. Now-declassified policy documents issued by the Bush administration demonstrated the conflict between humanitarian rhetoric and neocolonial action. Although compromise with Saddam Hussein was universally condemned in the run-up to the 2003 Iraq war, historically the United States was a major supporter of Hussein's regime prior to the 1990 invasion of Kuwait. U.S. support for Hussein's pre-1990 atrocities was voiced in high-level classified documents from the George H. W. Bush administration at the time. In *National Security Directive 26* (published on October 2, 1989), President Bush established an official justification for retaining a foothold in the Middle East, and for U.S. support of Hussein. Titled "United States Policy toward the Persian Gulf," *NSD 26* explained:

> Access to Persian Gulf oil and the security of key friendly states in the area are vital to United States national security. The United States remains committed to its vital interests in the region, if necessary and appropriate through the use of military force, against the Soviet Union or any other force with interests inimical to our own. ... The United States will continue to sell United States military equipment to help friendly regional states meet their legitimate self-defense requirements. ... Normal relations between the United States and Iraq would serve our longer-term interests and promote stability in both the Gulf and the Middle East. The United States should propose political and economic incentives for Iraq to moderate its behavior and to increase our influence with Iraq. ... We should pursue, and seek to facilitate, opportunities for United States firms to participate in the reconstruction of the Iraqi economy, particularly in the energy area.[63]

U.S. foreign policy toward Iraq officially reversed following the invasion of Kuwait, due to material considerations, rather than human rights concerns. Iraq possesses an estimated 10 percent of the world's oil. Its occupation of Kuwait and suspected plans for invading Saudi Arabia would have given it control of approximately 45 percent of the global oil supply. This was seen as unacceptable to officials in Washington. In reacting to this nightmare scenario, the Bush administration released *National Security Directive 54* on January 15, 1991, identifying a new enemy in the region now that the Soviet Union had collapsed. The document, titled "Responding to Iraqi Aggression in the Gulf," again equated U.S. national security with control over Iraqi oil, and restated the government's willingness to use force to ensure its dominance of that oil. Iraq, "by virtue of its unprovoked invasion of Kuwait . . . and its subsequent brutal occupation" became "a power with interests inimical to our own."[64] Though ensuring Middle Eastern "stability" previously required support for the Iraqi terrorist state and demands that the "Butcher of Baghdad" moderate his human rights abuses, regional stability now required a major war with Iraq. Perhaps most cynically, anyone who claimed (following Iraq's 1990 invasion *and* prior to the 2003 invasion) that Saddam Hussein should be persuaded to "moderate" his human rights behavior would have been demonized in the U.S. media as an apologist for human rights atrocities. Critics of the 2003 Iraq war were derided, perversely, by the very same political leaders who supported Saddam Hussein's regime in the past. The disjuncture between U.S. support for Saddam Hussein and later vilification of the "Butcher of Baghdad" proceeded unquestioned in the U.S. press (discussed in chapter 3).

Following the 1991 Gulf war, both the Clinton and George W. Bush administrations reaffirmed America's long-standing concern with Middle Eastern oil. The interests of the Clinton presidency strongly overlapped those of George W. Bush's administration. Clinton's 1996 National Security Strategy focused on the threats of global terrorism and weapons of mass destruction developed by rogue regimes. The document recommended keeping "U.S. forces forward developed" throughout the globe during "peacetime," and the "use of our armed forces" to ensure "our economic well being." The document specifically cited the 1991 Gulf War as a case where the United States ensured its material interests in oil. The NSS emphasized the need for the "free flow of oil" as a "vital [U.S.] interest," and the importance of retaining "naval vessels in and near the Persian Gulf," in addition to "combat equipment," "aviation bases," and "ground forces."[65]

Although the Clinton administration did not commit military forces to a long-term occupation of Iraq, its oil interests remained the same as those of the Bush regime. During the planning stages of the 2003 Iraq invasion, Bush's Deputy Secretary of Defense and Iraq war architect Paul Wolfowitz explained to diplomats at an Asian security summit that the military focus on Iraq superseded threats from North Korea: "The most important difference between North Korea and Iraq is that economically, we just had no choice in Iraq. The country swims on a sea of oil."[66] Similarly, Vice President Dick Cheney summarized: "With two-thirds of the world's oil and the lowest costs [the Middle East] is still where the prize ultimately lies."[67]

By May of 2003, Wolfowitz explicitly recognized that the Bush administration's emphasis on Iraq's alleged weapons of mass destruction was chosen for "bureaucratic reasons," as it represented "the one reason everyone [in the administration] could agree on." Wolfowitz also conceded a "huge" reason for the attack: it would allow for an end to the unpopular stationing of U.S. troops in Muslim holy lands in Saudi Arabia, and it would permit forces to be relocated in Iraq.[68] Vice President Dick Cheney conceded the strategic importance of oil when his Energy Task Force announced plans to make the Middle East "a primary focus of U.S. international energy policy" and "open up areas of their [oil-rich Middle Eastern countries] energy sectors to foreign investment."[69] Finally, President Bush cautioned against a withdrawal of troops from Iraq, promising that such an action would "let Iraq radicals use oil as a weapon" against the United States.[70]

The Bush administration's concern with control of vital oil resources was formally articulated in its early policy declarations. The 2002 National Security Strategy described U.S. plans to "further strengthen market incentives and market institutions" and focus on "emerging markets and the developing world." The 2002 NSS promised to act "preemptive[ly] against terrorists," "strengthen our own energy security," and "expand the sources and types of global energy supplied"—all while "dissuad[ing] future military competition" from foreign powers. Senior aides to the president announced the administration's grand plan immediately after the invasion of Iraq. The invasion was seen as a "first step . . . a first test, but not the last," in demonstrating three major points, including the United States' commitment to promoting democracy abroad; sending a "clear warning" to governments "that support for terror will not be tolerated"; and initiating a "demonstration effect" whereby the United States would "never allow American military supremacy to be challenged in the way it was during the Cold War." Unsurprisingly, coverage of the 2003 announcement did not receive much attention in the media. When it did garner coverage, reporting failed to cite critics who highlighted the contradictions between promoting democracy and ensuring neocolonial dominance in the Middle East.[71]

THE IRAQ INVASION AS A CAPITALIST EXPERIMENT

Support for capitalist investment is characterized through a number of key public policy requirements, especially for the world's poorer countries. For example, countries that accept loans from the International Monetary Fund (IMF) and World Bank (key global financial institutions) are required to undergo "structural adjustment" of their economies in accord with market principles. Requirements include the privatization of public enterprises, mandatory cuts in state pension and wages for government employees, the opening of markets to increased import of foreign products, mandatory deregulation of private industries, increased openness to foreign investment, and a renewed focus on exporting raw goods and products to core capitalist states. These requirements remain relevant when studying the U.S. attempt to promote privatization of public resources in Iraq.

The occupation of Iraq represents a critical component of capitalist intervention. The twin blows of U.S. military power and economic coercion were applied to Iraq to demonstrate the full commitment to a world economic system in which the United States remains at the center. Though many deny the claim that U.S. policy in Iraq is coercive, it is important to remember that most Iraqis have long opposed the occupation, as well as privatization schemes, viewing both as attempts to impose the will of a foreign power on domestic politics.

Within a capitalist framework, long-standing U.S. policy goals were put into action in Iraq, with attempts to privatize Iraqi oil and open up investment to U.S. corporations. The commitment to privatization of Iraq's oil and to foreign dominance of this resource is a major characteristic of the neocolonial order. Attempts to privatize Iraq's oil gained prominence over the last few years following the 2003 invasion. By 2005, reports arose of a State Department plan to appropriate at least 64 percent of Iraq's oil reserves for development by foreign corporations. In promoting the use of "production sharing agreements," the Iraqi government was encouraged to support extended twenty to thirty year contracts with these foreign companies, which by some estimates would cost the country billions of dollars.[72]

Informal pressures against Iraq's nascent democratic government continue following the handover of Iraqi "sovereignty." The Bush administration solicited the assistance of a private consultant group to recommend passage of a new national oil bill. The oil law recommended increased openness to foreign investment in Iraq's oil industry, while the bipartisan 2006 Iraq Study Group report recommended that "the United States should assist Iraqi leaders to reorganize the national oil industry as a commercial enterprise."[73] Private control was planned for sixty-three of Iraq's eighty oil fields, with only seventeen left in the hands of Iraq's national oil company. U.S. leaders dealt with possible resistance bluntly and paternalistically, threatening to cut off funds for reconstruction if Iraqi leaders refused to move forward with privatization plans.[74] Meanwhile, U.S. and British oil companies were left free to push privatization agreements with Iraqi officials. Four major companies—Exxon Mobil, Shell, British Petroleum, and Chevron—entered final stages in negotiations with Iraqi officials in mid-2008 regarding the securing of no-bid contracts to begin extraction from Iraq's largest oil fields.[75]

Market reform was promoted for Iraq's entire economy. The Bush administration's plan for post-invasion Iraq was always to rebuild the entire society, from the top down in line with the Washington consensus. Coalition Provisional Authority officials disbanded Iraq's army, government, and police, planning to re-create them as they saw fit. Aside from oil privatization plans, U.S. leaders support the privatization of the rest of Iraq's economy. As with most countries throughout the global periphery, U.S. officials support tying debt reduction to "free marketization" in Iraq. Plans for reducing Iraq's foreign debt were linked to the achievement of capitalist reforms, with promises to relieve as much as 80 percent of the country's debt upon full economic transformation. These plans, announced by the U.S. Department of State and Treasury, are conditionally based on Iraqi willingness "to provide foreign investors greater access to Iraqi natural resources, and increase investment opportunities for multinational corporations." The three-stage plan—developed by the United States, Japan, Russia, and other European countries—was set to eliminate $40 billion in Iraqi debt immediately, with no conditions required. However, another 30 percent of the country's debt would only be approved once Iraqi officials arranged a "structural adjustment" plan with the International Monetary Fund. A final 20 percent of the country's debt would be granted after Iraq implements structural adjustment.[76]

Aside from structural adjustment, the Bush administration forced through a number of reforms during the rule of the Coalition Provisional Authority. CPA head Paul Bremer issued one hundred public orders, many of which were designed to move Iraq's economy away from a nationalized, central-planning structure, and toward a market-based system. Order 39, for example, required that 200 Iraqi national companies be privatized, and applied to business operations in the areas of manufacturing, banking, and mining, among others. This privatization set the stage for the mass transfer of profits from these industries back to investors in the developed world, in contrast to nationalized industries that would have kept the money within state boundaries and for reconstruction purposes. Order 39 allows for full foreign ownership of Iraqi businesses, no restrictions on tax-free remittances of profits back to the United States and other countries, and does not require any reinvestment in local businesses or public infrastructure.[77]

The logic behind the privatization of Iraq was expressed lucidly by BearingPoint Inc., which was contracted by the Bush administration to manage the transition:

> It should be clearly understood that the efforts undertaken will be designed to establish the basic legal framework for a functioning market economy; taking appropriate advantage of the unique opportunity for rapid progress in this area presented by the current configuration of political circumstances. . . . Reforms are envisioned in the areas of fiscal reform, financial sector reform, trade, legal and regulatory, and privatization.[78]

Privatization also transcended the two hundred firms addressed in Order 31. The Bush administration's plan for Iraq is an *all-encompassing* capitalist project, attempting to transform Iraq on many levels. Other privatization laws passed under Bremer's government include:

- Order 81, which introduces a patent system granting monopoly rights over seeds as an agricultural commodity, in contradiction to the Iraqi constitution which did not allow for private control over biological resources.[79] One report on Order 81 addresses the initiative in greater detail: "United States plant-breeding companies under this order include the exclusive rights to produce, reproduce, sell, export, import and store the plant varieties covered by intellectual property right for the next 20–25 years. During this extended period nobody can plant or otherwise use plants, trees or vines without compensating the breeder."

- Order 12, which eliminates "all tariffs, customs duties, import taxes, licensing fees and similar surcharges for goods entering or leaving Iraq."

- Order 40, which creates a privately run banking system, allowing foreign banking corporations to enter Iraq's market, and purchase as much as 50 percent of Iraqi banks.

- Order 49, which decreases the taxes on corporations operating in Iraq from a progressive to a flat rate. The order also introduced a cap on income taxes, further limiting any possibility for progressive taxation (in which the wealthy pay a proportionately higher percent of their incomes than the poor or middle class).

- Order 17, which introduces immunity privileges for foreign contractors operating in Iraq. These contractors are not subject to or punishable under Iraqi law. This system is similar to the capitulation system introduced during the era of formal colonialism, in which nationals from the colonizing countries were granted immunity from laws in the colonized country.[80]

The U.S. and allied commitment to capitalist development is not only observed in its policies in Iraq, but also in the policies it opposes. U.S. political leaders reject comprehensive efforts to fund mass reconstruction of Iraq. Minimal funds were allocated to reconstruction, in line with U.S. political leaders' opposition to "social welfare" spending. Many critics of the United States maintain that it has a major responsibility to rebuild Iraq, considering the tremendous amount of destruction that it wrought upon the country. U.S. leaders supported both Iran and Iraq during the catastrophic 1980–88 war, which cost Iraq over one million lives. The United States was also shown to have knowingly targeted Iraq's infrastructure during the 1991 Gulf War. This attack amounts to a war crime under the rules of the Geneva Conventions, which require that warring powers take all possible steps to protect civilians and public infrastructure.[81] The United States was the primary supporter of sanctions against Iraq, which the United States conceded killed as many as 1.5 million Iraqis during the 1990s.[82] Finally, approximately one million people have been killed during the U.S. occupation, with the United States directly responsible for many of these deaths.[83]

Despite its responsibility for mass destabilization and destruction, the U.S. commitment to rebuilding Iraq is rather meager in its allocation of funds, at least when compared to the mayhem for which the United States is responsible. The Bush administration committed less than $20 billion to reconstruction by mid-2008, despite the reality that it would cost hundreds of billions (or more) to rebuild Iraq after decades of war and sanctions. The refusal to commit funds to reconstruction represents a major characteristic of the "free market" plan for Iraq. Government intervention is viewed positively in terms of ensuring corporate profits for private interests, but the same intervention is frowned upon when the beneficiaries are the masses. The United States initially allocated a mere $18.4 billion for rebuilding Iraq after decades of war, and much of that was redirected to military operations and to the construction of permanent military bases which the United States plans to keep in Iraq.[84] Self-reliance—common in free market rhetoric—is touted as the primary means by which the Iraqi people will rebuild their society. As Brig. General William McCoy explained, "The United States never intended to completely rebuild Iraq . . . this [reconstruction] was just supposed to be a jump-start."[85]

Bush administration officials never intended to commit large-scale U.S. funding to reconstruction. One government report issued in 2007 concluded that at the time of the 2003 invasion "the Defense Department had no strategy for restoring either government institutions or infrastructure. And in the years since, other [government] agencies joined the effort without an overall plan and without a structure in place to organize and execute a task of such magnitude."[86] In the early days of the occupation, administration officials promised the U.S. public that Iraq would spend its own oil funds on reconstruction, rather than U.S. funds.[87] The lack of a government reconstruction plan contrasts greatly with the detailed level of planning that went into the privatization of Iraq.

Structural economic adjustment in Iraq became so controversial because the majority of Iraqis strongly oppose it. This opposition raises serious questions about the adequacy of democratic representation in Iraq. U.S. contempt for protests against privatizing Iraq stand in direct contradiction to democratic expectations that political leaders should follow public opinion in forming public policy, or at least seriously consider public opinion. Taking Iraqi opinions seriously would require a rethinking of privatization schemes. Iraqi workers, for one, are vehemently opposed to the privatization of Iraqi oil. Major conferences and protests have been held by thousands of workers who were employed in state-owned industries that opposed the Bush administration's plan.[88] Members of the Iraqi Federation of Oil Unions went on strike against the Iraq parliament's planned privatization.[89] The wider Iraqi public also strongly resists privatization of the country's oil. By a two-to-one ratio, Iraqis indicate that they are opposed to opening their country to foreign investment—a support that transcends ethno-sectarian lines. Regarding government plans for privatization, 63 percent of those surveyed indicated their preference that oil be developed by nationalized companies, with only 10 percent strongly supporting, and 21 percent moderately supporting the use of foreign companies. A mere 4 percent of Iraqis feel they were provided with "totally adequate" information regarding the parliament's proposed oil law. Just 20 percent feel information provided is "somewhat adequate," with 76 percent feeling it is "inadequate." This evidence strongly confirms the existence of a democracy deficit between the people of Iraq, on the one hand, and U.S. and Iraqi political leaders on the other.[90]

GLOBAL MEDIA, IRAQ, AND THE CAPITALIST WORLD SYSTEM

If global reporting really is distinguished according to each country's position in the capitalist world system, these distinctions should be evident in reporting on Iraq. The Iraq war is the defining intervention of the twenty-first century and national media coverage of Iraq should be distinguished by each country's economic and political position in relation to the intervention. Wealthy core countries that are directly involved in the conflict, or closely allied with countries involved, should provide the most media coverage, but be the least open to moral criticisms. Conversely, poorer, non-core countries should provide less coverage (due to their lack of involvement), but be more open to moral criticisms of war. Coverage should also be differentiated based on the level of media consolidation within each country, and the extent to which national media are owned by corporations located within (or outside of) countries at the heart of the capitalist world system.

An analysis of thirteen different countries, representing the core, periphery, and semi-periphery of the world system, reveals a stark pattern in reporting and commentary. The newspapers analyzed in these countries were selected because of their high levels of national prestige and influence. Background information on each newspaper is presented later in this chapter, as each group of countries is examined in greater depth.

Media in the wealthy core countries of the United States, United Kingdom, Spain, and Australia is somewhat distinguished from media in the core countries of New Zealand, Israel, and Canada that are not invested in Iraq's experiment in capitalism. Media coverage in all of these core countries, however, is strongly distinguished from "non-core" periphery and semi-periphery countries (Mexico, Singapore, Pakistan, China, South Africa, and China) that are not invested in the Iraq war.

Table 6.1 provides a summary of the owners of the thirteen media outlets introduced above.

Clearly, the media within wealthy countries such as the United States, United Kingdom, Spain, and Australia enjoy a significant advantage in terms of their high levels of global reach, influence, and profitability. The most important distinction between core and non-core is the intensity of coverage. The period from February 2007 through January 2008, which is examined here, represents a time when major policy deliberation was occurring in the United States and across the globe over a possible withdrawal from Iraq and the success of the "surge" of troops.

As expected, core countries that are either heavily invested in Iraq or closely allied with the United States cover the Iraq conflict with greater frequency. Table 6.2 demonstrates that media in core countries that are involved in the war average between 52 to 160 stories on Iraq per month, depending on the specific country and paper in question.

Taken together, core countries that are or were economically invested in the Iraq war reported on average 93 stories per month, as contrasted with non-invested core countries, averaging only 33 stories per month. Finally, periphery and semi-periphery countries (with the exception of Pakistan, which will be discussed later) average only 18 stories per month. When media attention to Iraq is expressed as a per-

TABLE 6.1: The World System and Concentration of Media Ownership

Newspaper and Country	Owner	Major Countries Where Media Owner Operates
Invested Core Countries		
New York Times (United States)	NY Times Co. (with its subsidiary, International Herald Tribune)	United States, France, Brazil, Dubai, Turkey, India, Israel, etc. (180 countries total worldwide)
Times (United Kingdom)	News Corp.	Australia, United Kingdom, United States, New Zealand, Israel, Brazil, Indonesia, Romania
The Australian (Australia)	News Corp.	Australia, United Kingdom, United States, New Zealand, Israel, Brazil, Indonesia, Romania
El País (Spain)	Grupo Prisa	Portugal, Mexico, Colombia, Argentina, Chile, United States
Non-Invested Core Countries		
Jerusalem Post (Israel)	Mirkaei Tikshoret Ltd.	Israel
Globe and Mail (Canada)	CTV Globemedia	United States, Canada
Herald (New Zealand)	APN News	Australia, New Zealand
Non-Core Countries		
South China Morning Post (China)	SCMP Group	China
Straits Times (Singapore)	Singapore Press Holdings	Singapore
Nation (Pakistan)	Nawai-i-Waqt Group	Pakistan
Nation (Thailand)	Nation Multimedia Group	Thailand
Reforma (Mexico)	Grupo Reforma	Mexico
Star (South Africa)	Independent News and Media	South Africa, Australia, New Zealand, India

Source: Lexis Nexis

TABLE 6.2: Media Coverage of Iraq: A World Systems Approach

Newspaper and Country	Average Number of Iraq Stories Per Month	Iraq Stories as a Percent of all Stories
NY Times (United States)	159.5	2%
El País (Spain)	84.3	1.2%
The Australian (Australia)	76.7	1.5%
Times (United Kingdom)	52.3	1%
Nation (Pakistan)	42.5	2.8%
Globe and Mail (Canada)	41	0.7%
Jerusalem Post (Israel)	30.8	2%
Herald (New Zealand)	28.3	0.9%
Straits Times (Singapore)	24.6	0.8%
Reforma (Mexico)	22.6	0.3%
Nation (Thailand)	16.5	0.1%
South China Morning Post (China)	13.5	0.3%
Star (South Africa)	12.8	0.4%

Source: Lexis Nexis

centage of all stories run in each paper, similar patterns emerge. Core countries, whether invested in Iraq or not, tend to cover the country with greater frequency than non-core countries (again, with the exception of Pakistan).

Media attention to Iraq is radically different in many of the countries in this study. As Table 6.3 shows, the month-to-month fluctuations in reporting on Iraq correspond closely with each country's economic position in the world capitalist system. Those papers that most closely overlap in their fluctuations in monthly coverage are core countries that are invested in Iraq (again, the United States, United Kingdom, Spain, and Australia). The most distinct coverage in the countries sampled is observed between wealthier core countries on the one hand, and poorer periphery and semi-periphery countries on the other.[91] This is not to suggest that every core country will be negatively correlated with every non-core country in their coverage of Iraq. Such a pattern is unlikely to appear. However, these correlations do demonstrate significant relationships between countries military involved in Iraq, as contrasted to countries that remain uninvolved. Such differences should not be that surprising, considering that these non-core countries have little incentive to pay

TABLE 6.3: Overlapping and Diverging Coverage of the Iraq War Throughout the World

Papers w/ the Most Similar Month-by-Month Coverage of Iraq	% Overlap in Each Pair's Month-by-Month Coverage	Papers w/ the Most Different Month-by-Month Coverage of Iraq	% Overlap in Each Pair's Month-by-Month Coverage
El País (Spain) and *The Australian*	87%	*Herald* (New Zealand) and *Nation* (Pakistan)	-28%
NYT (United States) and *The Australian*	85%	*Times* and *Nation* (Thailand)	-21%
El País and *Times* (United Kingdom)	85%	*Jerusalem Post* (Israel) and *South China Morning Post* (China)	-11%
Times and *The Australian*	79%	*Herald* and *South China Morning Post*	-1%
The Australian and *Globe and Mail* (Canada)	68%	*Herald* and *Nation* (Thailand)	-1%

Source: Lexis Nexis

attention to the day-to-day developments of the conflict and have weaker ties (than wealthy, non-invested countries) with core countries that occupy Iraq. An examination of the chasm separating core and non-core countries shows that many of these countries (and their respective newspapers) are not only weakly associated, they are at times diametrically opposed in their coverage.

A closer inspection of the countries above reveals stark patterns. Strong uniformity in coverage is undeniable among many core countries, whereas divergence in coverage between core and non-core countries is also apparent. The two examples in Figures 6.1 and 6.2—*El País* (Spain) and *The Australian* and the *Nation* (Thailand) and *Times* (United Kingdom)—are instructive.

The month-to-month fluctuations in coverage in the *Australian* and *El País* (both invested core countries) is nearly identical, whereas the coverage in the *Nation* and *Times* (one a core, and the other a non-core country) diverge dramatically.

The main reason for these patterns should be clear: countries cover the Iraq war according to their level of political and economic involvement in the conflict and their closeness to countries that are or were heavily involved.

FIGURE 6.1: Parallel Media Reporting of Iraq in the Developed World

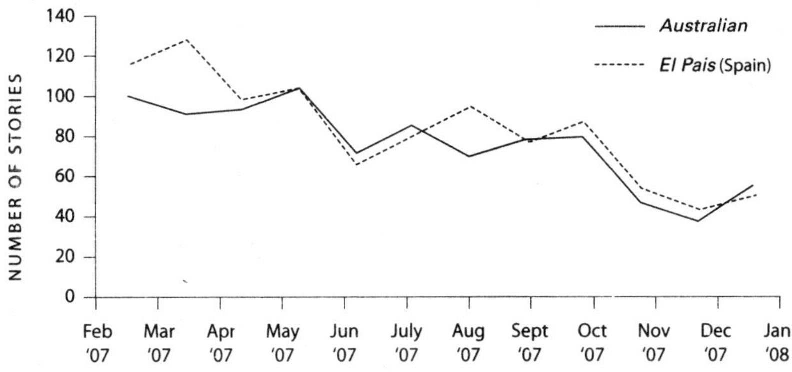

Source: Lexis Nexis

FIGURE 6.2: Divergent Media Reporting of Iraq in the Developed and Less Developed World

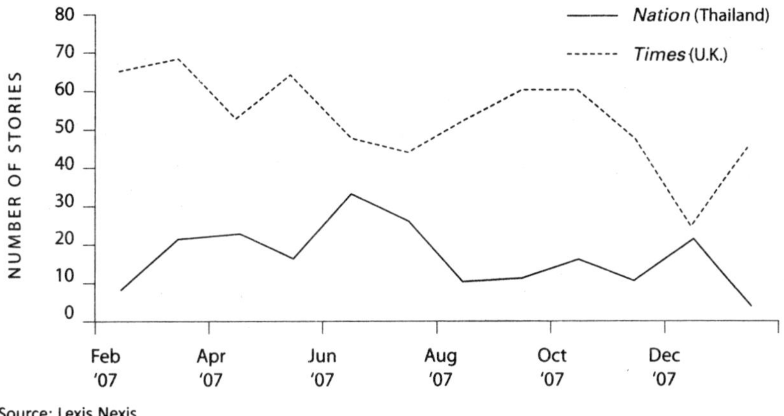

Source: Lexis Nexis

MEDIA SIMILARITIES IN CORE COUNTRIES AT WAR

The major countries involved in the invasion and occupation of Iraq share many similarities in their coverage. They are all home to media that are the most heavily consolidated within the capitalist world system, retaining this dominant position because of the massive assets they hold throughout countries in the developed and underdeveloped world. With parent countries heavily invested in Iraq, these papers heavily tailor their coverage to reflect official policy debates over the war. These media devote, on average, between two to five stories per day to the issue of Iraq. These outlets are very similar in their volume of coverage and in the fluctuations in their coverage (see Figure 6.3).

Previous studies find that U.S. news outlets offer a narrower range of opinions than European counterparts.[92] The U.S. press is seen as more vigilant in its attacks on war protestors.[93] Although British liberal media outlets like the *Guardian* and *Independent* tend to be less restricted in their criticisms of the Iraq war than their liberal U.S. counterparts, more conservative British papers like the *Times* and *Telegraph* more closely approximate the coverage seen in U.S. mainstream media. As the second-largest paper in the United Kingdom, the conservative-leaning, Rupert Murdoch-owned *Times* heavily focuses on official debates in Washington and London. Unlike the *Guardian* and *Independent*, the *Times* is thoroughly situated at the center of the U.S.-led global media empire as well, as an outlet owned by the U.S.-based *News Corporation*. Major stories the paper focused on during 2007 and early 2008 included the planned de-escalation of Britain's military forces in Iraq, former Prime Minister Tony Blair's resignation, the handover of power to Prime Minister Gordon Brown, and the standoff between British and Iranian forces over the detainment of British sailors off the coast of Iran.

Coverage in the *Times* overlaps strongly with U.S. media, which promote the "humanitarian motivations" of the occupation. The surge is celebrated as "little short of a triumph" in reducing U.S. fatalities and Iraqi violence.[94] Blair was heralded for liberating Iraq, with British forces play-

FIGURE 6.3: Media Coverage of Iraq in Developed (Invested) Countries

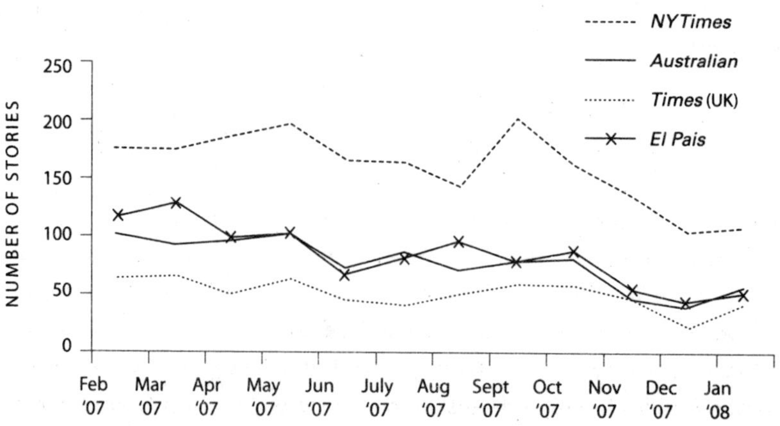

Source: Lexis Nexis

ing a "significantly positive role" in occupying southern Iraq.[95] Studies implicating the United States and United Kingdom for killing hundreds of thousands of Iraqi civilians are thoroughly questioned in the paper as lacking in methodological soundness, despite employing statistical sampling techniques widely accepted in the social science community.[96]

As a mainstream liberal newspaper, the U.S.-based *New York Times* enjoys global reach and influence. It is the leading agenda-setting paper in the United States, and it is the global representative of U.S. power. The paper is similar to the *Times* (United Kingdom) in its reporting in that it refuses to substantively challenge the legitimacy of the Iraq war. The paper does, however, heavily stress critical government reports questioning the *effectiveness* of the occupation. Attention is drawn to the Bush administration's opposition to withdrawal from Iraq, as well as Congress's battle with the president over war funding.[97] Critical reports that receive media attention include findings of "waste and fraud in Iraqi rebuilding projects," predictions of the disintegration of Iraq due to sectarian violence, optimistic accounts of the success of the surge, and occasional reporting of critical findings that Iran is not developing nuclear weapons.[98]

The right-leaning *Australian* offers a similar framing of the Iraq war, focusing closely on developments in British, Australian, and U.S. politics. As a Murdoch-owned, News Corp. asset, it is thoroughly integrated into the U.S.-led global media system. Previous research found that the *Australian* has a history of positively portraying the Iraq conflict.[99] In the early days of the war, it heavily focused on the "progress" of the campaign, refused to refer to the attack as an "invasion," and failed to print images of the human costs of the war.[100] As the largest daily and only national newspaper in Australia, the outlet featured stories in 2007 and early 2008 that included the Bush Senate debate on war funding, the controversy over the surge, administration claims that withdrawal would ensure Al Qaeda's victory in Iraq, Prince Harry's military obligation to serve in Afghanistan, the end of the Blair government and beginning of Gordon Brown's term in office, and updates on the fate of David Hicks, the Australian who was captured training in al-Qaeda camps in Afghanistan. Keeping with its tradition of conservatism, the *Australian* holds much contempt for leftist critics of the Iraq war. Its opinion pieces condemn war critics as "appeasers of hate"—having lost "their moral compass" by criticizing the Iraq war, and displaying "reflexive hatred of the United States"[101] The *Australian* appears similar to U.S. media in terms of its contempt for moral challenges to the war.[102]

Out of all the core countries involved in the Iraq war, *El País* is perhaps the most open to challenges of substance. *El País* is well regarded in Spain as one of the leaders of the democratic revolution in media reform, which has its roots in the political developments of the 1960s. The paper, founded in 1976, became the leading national newspaper by taking advantage of the end of prior censorship and easing of direct government censorship and control, as mandated by law.[103] As the largest circulation paper in Spain with over two million regular viewers, this "paper of record" critically refers to the "poisonous legacy" of the Iraq war, while reporting claims that the war is lacking global support and illegal under international law.[104] *El País* also attacks the Bush administration for its "continuing belligerence" in escalating the conflict with Iran. The United States shows "aggressiveness" in the "chaos [it] unleashed" on Iraq, which has actually "increased the influence of [Islamist] fundamentalism."[105]

Despite the efforts of *El País* to question the Iraq war, it still remains at the core of the U.S.-European capitalist media system, retaining major business assets in the Western Hemisphere. Its month-to-month fluctuations in coverage of Iraq are remarkably similar to those of other core countries. *El País* also heavily emphasizes official policy debates in Washington, and relies on familiar dogmas expressed by the Bush administration and its allies. Major stories covered in the paper include coverage of General Petraeus and the "surge," Bush's focus on Iraq as the vital front in the "war on terror," sustained attention to Iran's detainment of British sailors, and increased violence in Iraq against U.S. troops. The paper's editors uncritically repeat the Bush administration's claims that a vote against increased war spending will unacceptably "paralyze the armed forces, which would be left without funding." Such commentary is rather pedestrian in reinforcing the Bush administration's propaganda messages.

ALLIED CORE COUNTRIES: CONTINUED SUPPORT FOR WAR

Core countries that are allied with the United States but not involved in the Iraq occupation also fall firmly within the capitalist ideological sphere. The mass media in these countries may not retain the vast holdings of media based in the United States, but their affluence and close relations with the United States reinforce their standing in the core of the capitalist world system. These countries represent a middle ground, often

FIGURE 6.4: Media Coverage of Iraq in Developed (Non-Invested) Countries

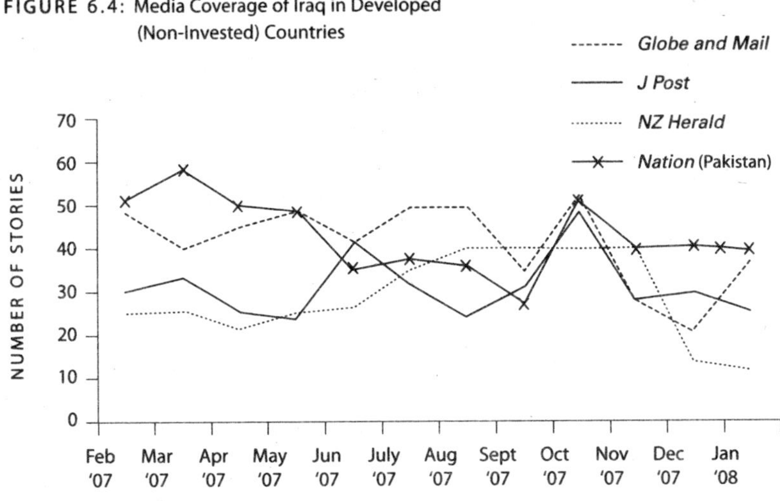

Source: Lexis Nexis

devoting less attention to the Iraq conflict than countries invested in the conflict, but also covering it more than poorer countries and remaining less open than periphery and semi-periphery countries to moral attacks of the war. These news outlets devote, on average, approximately one to one and a half stories per day to the topic of Iraq. Figure 6.4 shows that media in these countries are less uniform in their month-to-month variations in coverage than are media in countries that invaded Iraq. The analysis below also shows that these media are similar, however, in their failure to seriously and consistently challenge U.S. occupation of Iraq. The figure also includes one caveat: the *Nation* of Pakistan. Although Pakistan is not a developed country, the *Nation* is included in Figure 6.4 because it is more similar to core countries in the amount of coverage it devotes to Iraq, and because of its political leaders' long history of military collaboration with the United States in the war on terror.

Canada has little directly invested in the occupation of Iraq, and this reality is reflected in the *Globe and Mail*'s reporting. For one, the paper covers the Iraq war with less frequency than media in countries occupying Iraq, but more often than countries with weaker historical and cultural links with the First World. The *Globe and Mail* is based in a country and a political system that has traditionally taken strong steps to prevent the consolidation of national media outlets. Foreign ownership by multinational media conglomerates in Canada is prevented by law, so the *Globe and Mail* and other media remain in the hands of Canadian corporations.[106] Canada's lack of involvement in Iraq and its relative independence from U.S. multinationals allow it room to refrain from heavily covering the "war on terror." This does not mean that the paper fails to cover the conflict. Major stories in the *Globe and Mail* during the period examined include the Turkish government's military incursions into Iraq, controversies regarding military contractors working under the occupation, and emphasis on the Iraqi government's problems with instability.

The *Globe and Mail* appears noncommittal and somewhat bland in its editorializing on the situation in Iraq, although it remains ideologically committed to the wider "war on terror" in Afghanistan (in which Canada *has* committed troops). In an editorial, "Canada Must Stay the Course," the paper argued: "Canada cannot abandon Afghanistan. We have made a commitment to the Afghan people and to the international community, and if we believe the governing structures there can be stabilized, we are obliged to stay on ethical, humanitarian and practical grounds that relate to our own national security interests and those of our allies."[107] In the case of the Iraq war (where it is not involved), the paper is much less vigilant and more cautious in its rhetoric. A sense of futility characterizes the *Globe and Mail*'s characterization of the surge, as the following excerpt suggests:

> Those hoping for a modicum of clarity on Iraq have again been disappointed. This week's Congressional progress report by General David Petraeus, the commander of United States forces in the country, and United States Ambassador to Iraq Ryan Crocker has only served to fuel the prejudices of either side in the bitter political debate over the direction of the United States adventure. Some predict a bloodbath if United States troops remain. Some predict a bloodbath if they leave. The tragedy of Iraq is that both may be right.

The editorial provides little insight into the question of whether the surge was beneficial for Iraqis, or simply a continuation of an unpopular, repressive occupation. The *Globe and Mail*'s disinterest in the ideological battles surrounding the occupation, however, is not surprising considering the lack of resources that Canada invested in the conflict, and Canadian media's relatively independent position from U.S. multinational media conglomerates.

As a Middle Eastern country with close economic and political ties with the United States, Israel has a major incentive to report closely on the war in Iraq. Previous research shows that Israeli media defended the push for war, stressing that Saddam Hussein possessed weapons of mass destruction, that he was a threat to Israel, and that war was inevitable.[108] A closer examination shows that the conservative-leaning *Jerusalem Post* historically retained close ties with other core countries, as it was previously owned by the Hollinger Group and Canada's conservative business leader Conrad Black.[109] The *Jerusalem Post* was recently sold to the Israeli business firm Mirkaei Tikshoret Ltd., but this sale has done little to decrease the ideological alliance between the United States and Israel in the "war on terror."

As of 2007, Israeli officials were strongly supportive of the occupation of Iraq. However, Israel has *not* devoted troops and funds to the war. Hence, the issue takes up less attention in papers like the *Jerusalem Post* (measured in the number of stories it prints on Iraq), in contrast to media in countries that have occupied or are currently occupying Iraq. Despite the lack of Israel's investment of forces and resources, the "humanitarian" mission is still celebrated in the *Jerusalem Post*. One of the major themes in the paper is that the privatization experiment in Iraq is necessary for the promotion of democracy. Critics framing the occupation as neocolonial, however, are strongly condemned. One commentary in the *Jerusalem Post*, for example, speaks of the controversy regarding "the [United States'] idea of promoting democracy as a strategy in the Middle East. It is pretty funny that this idea of spreading human rights, higher living standards, and the rule of law to Middle Eastern societies was so easily transmuted by many in the West and most in the Middle East into ravenous imperialist aggression."[110]

Aside from assuming benevolent intentions on the part of the United States, the *Jerusalem Post* supports U.S. efforts to attack Iran. Employing a hyper-militarist framework, the paper demonizes Iran for "trying to seize control in Iraq" and speaks of the need "to impose sanctions to limit their acquisition of nuclear capabilities."[111] Though intelligence agencies have long found that there is no evidence of a nuclear weapons program, this does not stop the Israeli and U.S. media from systematically focusing on Iran as a danger.[112] The *Jerusalem Post*'s defense of escalation against Iran stands in contrast to depictions in other papers that are examined below.

As with the *Jerusalem Post* and *Globe and Mail*, the *New Zealand Herald* does not question the moral legitimacy of the Iraq war. A centrist paper with over 190,000 daily readers, the *Herald* retains strong relations with British and Australian media. It is thoroughly reliant on foreign corporate news organizations that are based in core countries, such as the

Associated Press, Reuters, the *Observer* (United Kingdom) and the *Independent* (United Kingdom). This reliance is not surprising considering that New Zealand shares a long history with the United Kingdom, as a onetime colony under the British Empire. As a news outlet that is owned by an Australian corporation (APN News and Media), the *Herald* subsumed much of its attention to Iraq in 2007 and early 2008 within stories about Australian electoral politics. Attention was directed to the 2007 Australian election for prime minister, which was seen as vital in light of the electoral changeover from Prime Minister John Howard to Kevin Rudd and the announcement of Australia's plans for removing some troops from Iraq. The *Herald*'s political ties to Australia account for much of the paper's sustained focus on Iraq.

The close relations between the *Herald* and core country newswires and organizations are accompanied by a commitment to defending the nobility of the Iraq conflict. This defense is limited, however. *Herald* editorials denigrate "Bush's stubborn desire to 'stay the course'" with "policies [that] are not working."[113] The editors criticize the United States for continuing a war that is not "winnable," citing the lack of progress in meeting benchmarks set for ensuring Iraqi political progress.[114] According to the *Herald*, the Iraq war needs to be seen as a noble effort, but a mistake nonetheless. The paper's framing corresponds closely with Australian Prime Minister Kevin Rudd's and New Zealand Prime Minister Helen Clark's claims that the Iraq war has been counterproductive in fighting terrorism and that the invasion was a mistake.[115]

MEDIA COVERAGE IN POORER COUNTRIES: AN UNPOPULAR WAR

While media in wealthy core countries are more limited in their criticisms of the Iraq war, this trend is not observed nearly as consistently in non-core countries. Suspicion of the United States' motives is deeply embedded in the periphery, where many have felt the brunt of U.S. violence. Left out of the dominant position in the capitalist world order, the countries depicted in Figure 6.5 cover the conflict less frequently than those core countries involved in Iraq and non-invested core countries. The fluctuations in coverage from papers in poorer countries have little in common, at least on the month-by-month level. However, these media systems throughout Latin America, Asia, and Africa are very similar in three ways:

FIGURE 6.5: Media Coverage of Iraq in Less Developed Countries

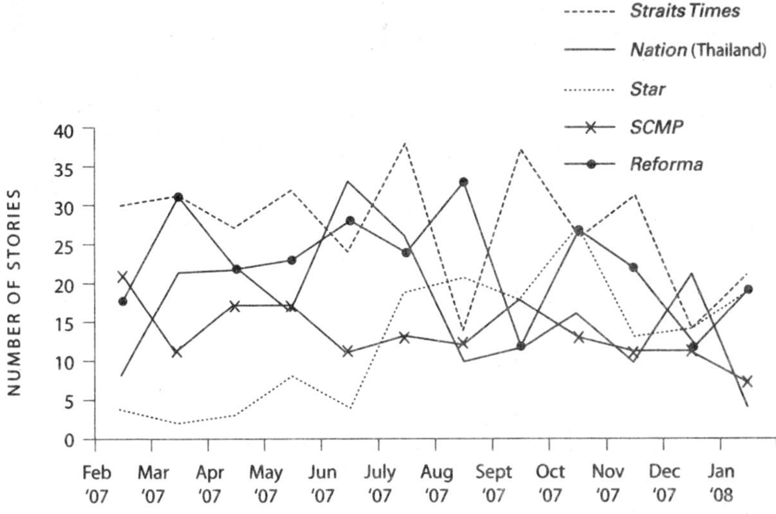

Source: Lexis Nexis

in their relative lack of attention to Iraq compared to core countries; in their freedom (with the exception of South Africa's *Star*) from Western corporate ownership; and in their increased openness (contrasted with core countries) to framing the war as fraudulent and unjust.

In general, the Iraq war is incredibly unpopular among the public and media in most of these non-core countries.

The *Nation* of Pakistan is located in a non-core country, yet unlike other non-core countries it devotes extensive coverage to the Iraq war. Unlike the media in core countries, however, it opposes the occupation of Iraq with a vigor unseen among privileged Western audiences. Similarly to the other non-core countries, the paper's writers reflect the views of the world's poor, who often view the United States as an aggressive, imperial, and even terrorist power.

The *Nation*'s extensive coverage of and opposition to the war is not surprising considering Pakistan's relationship with the United States. Pakistani political leaders such as Pervez Musharraf and Asif Ali Zardari, although known for their authoritarianism and corruption, have been supported by the United States. In contrast, Pakistan's intelligence service enjoys strong ties with the Taliban and Islamist forces. The Pakistani people deeply distrust the United States and the Pakistani leaders it supports. Public animosity stems from long-standing U.S. opposition to democracy in Pakistan. Widespread cultural distrust of the United States is reflected in the *Nation*'s framing of Iraq. Pakistan's status as a Muslim country located at the junction of the Middle East and Asia also puts it in a unique position due to its religious sympathies with the people of Iraq. The *Nation* expresses this sympathy by siding with the Iraqi public against the U.S. occupation.

The dangers of the United States escalating conflict with Pakistan following 9/11 have received little attention in the U.S. press. Cross-border unmanned attacks with Predator drones and U.S. troops' September 2008 cross-border incursion from Afghanistan into Pakistan (allegedly in the name of fighting terrorism) have threatened to throw this nuclear power into chaos and led to the deaths of numerous civilians. Because of the United States' involvement in the region, Pakistan's media retains a strong incentive to follow U.S. actions in the Middle East. Pakistan's security depends upon awareness of U.S. militarism.

As the only Latin American media outlet examined here, Mexico's *Reforma* was subject to much analysis in recent years. *Reforma* became more independent from the government in its reporting after the Mexican media transitioned from an authoritarian system to a more mixed system based upon civic values and market economics. Described as a "civic-oriented" paper, *Reforma* is characterized as the least propagandistic and authoritarian of Mexican print media in its coverage of entrenched political elites. The paper is less positive and passive in its reporting on the Mexican presidency, as its coverage has become less presidentially centered over the years.[116] Much of *Reforma*'s discussion of Iraq is placed within the larger context of U.S.-Mexican relations. Iraq is mentioned in regard to regional concerns about Western Hemisphere trade agreements and conflicts over immigration.

When the issue of Iraq does receive direct attention, *Reforma* is more open than U.S. newspapers to moral criticisms of the war. Columns attack the United States for relying on "half-truths and lies that justified the war," and criticisms of the United States for having gotten into a major "fiasco." There remains "a very high cost in [U.S.] lives," in addition to the cost to Iraqis, which, truth be told, are not so much interested in the views published in the United States."[117] On the issue of Iran, coverage is very different from that seen in core countries. *Reforma* attacks "the president's bellicose intentions" toward Iran: "What is worrying is that U.S. public opinion seems to be buying the same argument for a second time [considering the WMD rationales given in Iraq]." The U.S. public's belief that Iran constitutes a nuclear threat is a problem, the paper argues, because the "threat" is grounded more in "the propaganda machine of Bush" than in reality.[118] Of course, *Reforma* also allots space to defending the Iraq occupation, warning that "a withdrawal of Western troops without the existence of internal Iraqi political agreement, will unleash an unstoppable slaughter of disastrous humanitarian consequences." In general, then, the paper could be best characterized as a venue that is open not only to views that are supportive of the war but also those that fundamentally and morally challenge it.[119]

The *Star* of South Africa has paid the least attention to the situation in Iraq out of any newspaper in this study. The issue does not appear to retain much relevance for the readers of the paper. South African media were historically dominated during the apartheid era by the racist, government-owned South African Broadcasting Co.[120] Privately owned elite newspapers often practiced self-censorship during this era despite the lack of direct government censorship.[121] In accord with the "free market" model, South Africa's government opened up the national media system to private and foreign ownership during the 1990s. For example, Independent News and Media, an Irish multinational corporation, owns the *Star* and over a dozen other South African newspapers.

South African media were described as thoroughly reliant on the reporting of Western newswires in their coverage of the 2003 Iraq invasion. Reporting was also criticized as "superficial" and "shallow" in covering the early war.[122] This shallow reporting has continued today in the form of meager coverage. As with other media in poorer countries, readers of the *Star* do not see much of the Iraq war, and as a result have less of a chance of being indoctrinated by propagandistic media coverage. The *Star*, however, offers a number of pragmatic criticisms of the conflict, questioning the rush to war and the failure of the United States to win multilateral support.[123] It also criticizes the occupation as a "disastrous misadventure," although the "consequences of a precipitate withdrawal are almost as daunting as the cost of persisting with a lost cause."[124]

The *Star* moves beyond such limited criticisms, too, unlike media in the First World. Although it is owned by a media conglomerate based in Ireland, this ownership in and of itself does not seem to be enough to ensure extensive coverage of Iraq, or to ensure that substantive criticisms are censored from commentary. South Africa and Ireland's lack of involvement in Iraq seem to be a major factor in explaining the *Star*'s lack of attention to the issue, as well as its openness to moral challenges of the occupation. Criticisms of the war are sometimes extremely fierce. The

United States' efforts to sell soldiers such as Jessica Lynch and Pat Tillman as heroes are rejected as "nothing but a pack of lies"—a "propaganda" that is seen as an "utter fiction."[125] The paper harshly speaks of the U.S. presence, which is "radicalizing these angry, occupied people" of Iraq. The United States poses a "danger" to the world, in part due to its disregard for the civilians killed in Iraq. The Department of Defense, for example, was criticized on the sixth anniversary of the September 11 terrorist attacks in the paper for tracking U.S. military deaths while neglecting civilian deaths—"a sign of ignorance, or total disinterest in the impact the ongoing war has on Iraqi citizens."[126]

The three Asian media outlets are also characterized by low interest in Iraq. The issue of Iraq appears in less (often much less) than one story per day, on average. With a daily distribution of nearly 400,000 (the highest in Singapore), the *Straits Times* is well known for its low level of freedom and lack of independence from government censorship.[127] Government control over Singapore's media may help explain why mainly limited criticisms of the Iraq war appear in the *Straits Times*. The persistence of more positive views of the occupation is not surprising, considering that Singapore's government provided support to the occupation in the form of military equipment, although it allocated no troops. It should be pointed out, however, that this support is rather meager, and that the issue of Iraq lacks salience for the paper.

Much of the attention to Iraq in the *Straits Times* is subsumed under other stories discussing regional issues, such as China's buildup of military power and the Association of Southeast Asian Nations (ASEAN) meeting. The U.S. preoccupation with the Middle East and Iraq is discussed as the prime reason that U.S. leaders have neglected ASEAN.[128] When the *Straits Times* does focus more directly on Iraq, views expressed range from tactical criticisms to principled support. To "withdraw immediately," the paper's editors warn, is "not viable, militarily or politically . . . the United States cannot withdraw totally from Iraq, leaving the Iraqi government defenseless." Quick withdrawal is not a serious option, as "the real debate in Washington is between the 'long stay' and the 'long goodbye.'"[129] Attention is focused on David Petraeus's report of "the progress of military operations . . . dispatched to defeat the insurgency," while demeaning "neighbouring Iran as one of the chief culprits for the mayhem in Iraq." Some room is left for limited criticism, such as the contention that violence in Iraq has declined due to the emergence of a newly segregated Iraq, which occurred as the result of the ethnic cleansing of Shiite and Sunni death squads.[130] Such a criticism, however, questions the effectiveness of the surge in reducing violence, not the basic presumption that U.S. goals in Iraq are fundamentally humanitarian.

The *South China Morning Post* of Hong Kong is distinguished from the *Straits Times* in its coverage due to its increased openness to criticisms of the war. Based in Hong Kong, the *Morning Post* is capitalist in its orientation, owned by the SCMP Group and backed by Malaysian rather than Western business interests. The *Morning Post* operates within a "semi-democratic territory" under an economy with strong links with Western businesses as well as the "post-socialist" Chinese mainland.[131] The paper is known for its focus on political and economic issues, despite the fact that media consumers in Hong Kong are generally more interested in sensationalism, sex scandals, crime stories, and human interest pieces.[132] The political role of Hong Kong's press, however, has become more relevant in recent years as concern over possible repression by mainland China increased following the United Kingdom's 1997 handover of sovereignty.[133]

Mild criticisms of the Iraq war have been supplemented with major attacks on the legitimacy of the occupation. The *Morning Post* takes issue with the invasion as lacking United Nations support, and the United States as lacking an exit strategy. The paper stresses the need to "avoid dangerous miscalculations" in the future regarding WMD intelligence issues.[134] On the substantive level, the paper lambastes U.S. "military spending [as] vastly disproportionate to the threats it faces."[135] "The United States has brought more destruction to Iraq than anything else." The occupation has "brought more death and destruction than real democracy.... The White House selectively picked intelligence to justify the war," and "the real reason the Bush neo-conservatives invaded Iraq was a loathing for Hussein, their lust for his oil and their fantasy that they could control the Arab world to benefit the West and Israel."[136] Such criticisms are unthinkable in the U.S. press, in the editorials of media outlets owned by News Corp., or in the media owned by other Western corporations dedicated to buttressing U.S.-led capitalism.

The final Asian paper examined, the *Nation* of Thailand, is unrelenting in its characterizations of the United States as a deceptive, imperial power in the Middle East. It attacks the Bush administration's "arrogance of power," framing the United States as a "liar," despite its humanitarian justifications for using force in Iraq and elsewhere.[137] The *Nation*'s critical reporting has at times been drawn from Britain's progressive-left press—outlets such as the *Guardian*. The United States' loss of "moral authority" is highlighted extensively, in light of "massive displacement of the civilian population" in Iraq.[138] "The numbers are staggering: each month, some 40,000 Iraqis flee their homes because of the war. Half of them go to other parts of Iraq; the rest go abroad. Iraq's population, frankly, is bleeding away. This devastation is even more dramatic because, since the invasion . . . only 3,183 Iraqis have been resettled in third countries."[139] As with the other newspapers in poorer countries, the *Nation* devotes little attention to Iraq. Coverage is often subordinated under attention to regional issues such as the ASEAN meeting and the 2007 six-party talks with North Korea.

IMPLICATIONS OF THE CAPITALIST GLOBAL MEDIA SYSTEM

The dissemination of propaganda by media in core countries is more easily understood after examining how these media outlets fit into the larger global media system and the capitalist order. Wealthy countries that benefit the most from global capitalist expansion and are most directly involved in U.S. occupation of Iraq retain a strong incentive to defend these ventures in their media's commentary. In contrast, poorer countries that are more skeptical of privatization and U.S. neocolonial policies express criticism far more frequently and vociferously in their national media.

There are, of course, exceptions within the broader world media system. Some papers owned by multinational conglomerates in poorer countries (such as South Africa's *Star*) are nowhere near as cavalier in their defense of U.S. power and the privatization of Iraq. In short, Western corporate ownership of media in the less developed world is not *always* enough to guarantee sustained or sympathetic coverage for the war, as the exception of South Africa's *Star* shows. Some media outlets in the developed world (such as the *Guardian* and *Independent* of the United Kingdom) are also more open than one would expect. Other factors that influence media coverage are also likely at play, one being the variation in cultural and journalistic norms that persists from country to country (which was specifically addressed in chapters 4 and 5).

CHAPTER SEVEN

Public Rationality, Political Elitism, and Opposition to War

Political leaders are often distrustful of the American public's political competence. Many officials feel that the people lack the basic critical thinking skills and ability to play a direct role in public policy formulation. These feelings were perhaps best expressed in a 1998 Pew Research Center survey, which found that officials commonly felt that the public does not "know enough about issues to form wise opinions about what should be done." Only 31 percent of members of Congress, 13 percent of presidential appointees, and 14 percent of civil servants confirmed their trust in the public to form "wise" decisions on public policy issues. Conversely, 47 percent of congressional representatives, 77 percent of presidential appointees, and 81 percent of civil servants felt that Americans were unable to form informed decisions on policy matters.

A number of reasons are provided by officials for their suspicion of the public. Civil servants and presidential appointees highlight the "information problem" of the average citizen. Members of the public supposedly "do not fully understand what government is and what it does for them." Political elites blame the mass media for conveying negative stereotypes of government to the public. As one presidential appointee from the Department of Defense argues, "Americans' [negative] opinions [of government] are based on anecdotal information received from media, rather than through an understanding of the extent of government and all it provides."[1] Whatever their reasons, political officials are clear about their contempt for public opinion. If there is a problem with American politics, they contend, it lies in both overly critical media and an incapable public, not with unrepresentative or corrupt political leaders.

Although American leaders loudly proclaim their faith in the wisdom of the people, these expressions represent more rhetoric than reality. Officials publicly celebrate the ability of the masses to govern—especially during election years—but quietly express a discomfort with public opinion as a force for determining public policy. These conclusions arise out of the works of major scholars such as Benjamin Page and Marshall Bouton, who speak of a "foreign policy disconnect" between the public and their officials. After examining public opinion on a variety of issues such as the war in Iraq, United States–United Nations relations, and global warming, Page and Bouton remark that the public's views "deserve more respect than they have been getting from decision makers."[2] In *Politicians Don't Pander*, Robert Shapiro and Lawrence Jacobs conclude that "politicians seek to move public opinion to where the parties want to go in terms of policy rather than responding to public opinion."[3]

Is the U.S. public as ignorant or as incompetent as political leaders often assume? Are Americans capable of forming educated opinions about policy issues? Does it even make sense to speak uniformly about *one* public? To what extent can we differentiate between members of the general public, based on major demographic factors such as education, electoral attentiveness, and media consumption? These questions have yet to be addressed in any major detail in many studies, but are explored at length in the next two chapters.

The study of public opinion is vital in a democratic society. Citizens demand that government consider their wishes when setting public policy. Political leaders who ignore the mass public do so at their peril come election time. As the 2006 and 2008 elections demonstrate, large segments of the general public can effectively come together to punish the party of the president during times of domestic economic and foreign military crisis and unrest. Public anger over Iraq served as an effective catalyst for eliminating the Republican majority in Congress in the 2006 midterm election, while public anger at former President Bush during the 2008 economic meltdown aided President Obama in his victory of Republican presidential candidate John McCain.[4]

ELITE THEORIES OF PUBLIC OPINION

Intellectuals disagree over whether the American citizenry is competent enough to influence the political process. Those who take an elitist position on this issue emphasize the volatility of public opinion, and the inability of the public to form coherent opinions. Advocating an "elite theory" of public opinion, Phillip Converse contends that many Americans hold "non-attitudes" on political issues. This claim is based upon evidence that individual survey respondents vary considerably in their opinions of what constitutes the largest national problem from one survey to the next and on claims that many citizens do not hold uniformly conservative or liberal stances on a wide variety of political, economic, and social topics.[5] Through his studies of public opinion, Gabriel Almond emphasizes that "large portions of an electorate do not have meaningful beliefs." Almond contends that "foreign policy attitudes of most Americans lack intellectual structure and factual content."[6]

Great efforts are made to differentiate between informed minorities and the uninformed mass public. James Rosenau distinguishes between the mass of Americans who are allegedly "uninformed about specific foreign policy issues or foreign affairs in general" and the most interested and educated, who play a more active role in foreign policy. Rosenau concludes that 75 to 90 percent of the public hold relatively "superficial, undisciplined feelings" on important policy matters. The mass "response to foreign policy matters" is "less one of intellect and more one of emotion." Conversely, the "attentive public," which constitutes perhaps 10 percent of the citizenry, is "more inclined to participate in the opinion making process." This public, Rosenau claims, holds "structured opinions" that are "highly significant," and these individuals are "more inclined to participate in the opinion making process."[7]

Demographic factors are thought to play a major role in differentiating the political knowledge of citizens from various social groups. Michael Carpini and Scott Keeter discuss significant distinctions between individuals based upon their level of income, race, sex, and age.[8] Formal education is also said to play a vital role in influencing public opinion. In his landmark work *War, Presidents, and Public Opinion*, John Mueller presents evidence that "it is the well-educated segment of the population that most nearly typifies the follower mentality [in line with official positions]. Thus, contrary to a common belief, it has been the well-educated members of the society who have most consistently supported the prosecution of the wars in Korea and Vietnam." More specifically, those who held college degrees were consistently more likely to support both wars, as opposed to those who completed only high school or grade school.[9]

There is strong disagreement about how effective the mass public is in influencing foreign policy decisions. G. William Domhoff frames politicians as "highly responsive to the power of elites' agenda . . . because of the power of the wealthy few to shape foreign, defense, and economic policies to their liking." The mass public, Domhoff concludes, enjoys very little control over major policy areas related to economics, military spending, and international relations.[10] Gladys Lang and Kurt Lang speak of a "bystander public," claiming that "the preferences of the mass public do not translate directly into executive decisions," since the public

> is in no position to make policy, to draft a law, or even to commit a public body to follow through on a decision. . . . The mass public can obstruct or approve, but not directly implement. The "decision" they make when they vote is nothing beyond the expression of a judgment, a judgment on what others have done or are proposing to do.[11]

The Langs cite the example of the Watergate scandal, explaining that the main force driving attention to the issue was not the media or the general public, but rather a political informant—in this case former FBI deputy director W. Mark Felt, also known as "Deep Throat."[12]

Kurt and Gladys Lang's rejection of an active public role in influencing public policy is challenged by a number of recent studies. Andrew McFarland explains that "social movements have a major impact on the American policymaking process." McFarland portrays activists participating in the civil rights movement as "mature and educated" members of society, who utilized and actively worked with sympathetic government institutions such as the Supreme Court and the Eisenhower administration to promote desegregation.[13] Jack Walker concludes that "spontaneous [social] movements that sweep through society . . . represent a form of mobilization from below that government leaders are almost compelled to recognize if they expect to maintain their legitimacy."[14] Margaret Keck and Kathryn Sikkink argue in *Activists Beyond Borders* that social movements are not only successful at the national level but also at the transnational level in proactively influencing political systems. The authors explore a number of successful social movements that promoted the global abolition of slavery, human rights in Latin America, and women's citizenship and environmental protections the world over.[15] All of these studies retain one important similarity—they demonstrate, contrary to the Langs' assumptions, that mass-based citizen movements can play a vital and direct role in formulating policy and influencing lawmaking. These social movements apply pressure on officials *prior* to governmental action, rather than following it.

Average citizens are at times successful in proactively limiting American foreign policy. This point is stressed by William LeoGrande, who examines the Reagan administration's policy in Central America during the 1980s. In the case of Nicaragua, the public prohibited the Reagan administration from committing United States troops to combat the democratically elected leftist Sandinista government.[16] The administration was forced to rely on a surrogate force, utilizing the anti-Sandinista Contra terrorist forces, which were responsible for destroying civilian, military, and political targets in Nicaragua.[17]

Scholars also address the 1991 Gulf war as an example of the public's ability to limit the United States' military power. The public developed a "Vietnam Syndrome" characterized by opposition to long-term wars of occupation. George H. W. Bush best expressed elite opposition to the Vietnam Syndrome when he explained, "I don't think that [public] support [for the 1991 Gulf war] would last if it were a long, drawn-out conflagration. I think support would erode, as it did in Vietnam." As Chairman of the Joint Chiefs of Staff under the George H. W. Bush administration, Colin Powell also factored public opposition to open-ended wars into his planning of the 1991 Gulf War. The Powell Doctrine was developed from this understanding of public resistance to war, with the Bush administration committing to short-term, overwhelming use of force rather than an extended occupation.[18] Political leaders are dissatisfied with the limits placed on them by the public. Resistance to extended war is seen as regretful, with antiwar sentiment interpreted as a sickness or "syndrome."[19] These views speak volumes about elite distrust of a critical, proactive public.

John Zaller's *The Nature and Origins of Public Opinion* remains one of the most influential studies of public opinion. Similarly to Converse and other elite theorists, Zaller contends that the mass public is uninformed on political issues.[20] He cites Americans' poor performance on civics IQ tests as evidence of public ignorance. The public, Zaller argues, is often unaware of the context of political conflicts. For example, Americans remained largely unaware during much of the 1980s of which side the United States supported in the conflict with Nicaragua (it supported the right-wing Contra guerillas against the leftist Sandinista government). Historically, research also shows that less than one-half of eligible voters are able to provide the name of their congressional representative.[21]

Public knowledge of foreign policy issues is based on a variety of sources, some of the most important including consumption of media, involvement and interest in the political process, and formal education.[22] Only a small minority of people, however, heavily consume elite discourse as transmitted through national print media.[23] Such consumption, along with higher levels of education, plays a major role in indoctrinating a select number of Americans in favor of official views.[24] The indoctrinating effects of media and education are increasingly acknowledged in scholarly studies. Richard Sobel finds that political leaders "may encounter great difficulties in persuading a relatively uninformed public. Even though it might seem that the president could be most successful in persuading people who are least educated, informed, interested, or concerned about the issue . . . these individuals are least likely to expose themselves" to the messages of political leaders.[25] As Zaller concludes, "The more citizens know about politics and public affairs, the more firmly they are wedded to elite and media perspectives on foreign policy issues."[26]

The indoctrinating effects of education and media exposure are not uniform across the general public. When officials disagree on public policies, the most educated, most politically attentive, and those with the most exposure to media are more likely to follow and internalize the ideological biases driving debates between political elites.[27] This interested segment of the public becomes polarized, however, between competing views, as examples such as the Vietnam War and 1991 Gulf war demonstrate. In earlier periods of these conflicts when political leaders agreed on the course policy should take, the interested public reflected the consensus among officials; in later periods when political leaders disagreed strongly on the path of policy, the interested public was more likely than others throughout the mass public to reflect this conflict among Democratic and Republican political officials.[28]

THE RATIONAL PUBLIC

It is encouraging for democracy that not all analysts of public opinion view the mass public as incapable, uninformed, or uninterested in politics. An increasing number of critics challenge elite theories of public opinion. These critics frame the American public as generally rational in its formulation of opinions, even if many citizens do not always understand the specific details of many policy disputes. They present extensive evidence of collective public reasoning on complex political topics, and argue convincingly that political leaders should pay more attention to public preferences.[29] James Stimson finds that public support for presidents, Congress, and local political officials fluctuates jointly in positive and negative directions over time.[30] The different political offices in the United States are evaluated collectively, with public approval of each branch of government inextricably linked to the others. Benjamin Page and Robert Shapiro find high levels of stability over a number of years in the answers provided by those who are polled on major policy issues such as crime, education, foreign policy, transportation, and foreign aid.[31] Page and Shapiro conclude that changes in public opinion are not unpredictable, but move in a gradual, stable fashion. The authors argue that "various bits of new information may cumulate and alter the individual's beliefs in a systematic way that produces real long-term change in policy preferences." In short, the public tends to respond when new information on political issues becomes available, and as reality changes over time.[32]

The question remains: How is the public able to form coherent opinions on major issues, often with only meager attention to the specific details of political conflicts? William Gamson concludes that Americans display a considerable complexity in the ways they interact with the news regarding issues such as the Arab-Israeli conflict, among other topics.[33] Samuel Popkin argues in *The Reasoning Voter* that the mass public possesses "low information rationality"; they are able to form stable opinions with relatively little information compared to the voluminous information that is actually available. Low-information rationality is developed by the public's accessing of "information they have learned about the political system in their personal lives, from the media, from political leader's statements, from their demographic backgrounds, and from judging individual candidates' ideologies from their party identification."[34]

Apathetic citizens also display the ability to amass increased knowledge of political issues. Television news viewers with little interest in political issues disproportionately learn more from watching television—the preferred medium of the masses. In contrast, newspapers and news magazines are more popular outlets of learning for those with higher interest in political issues.[35] The average American, Doris Graber argues, "can think effectively and draw sound inferences on many fronts," despite reliance on television news, which is demonized for low-brow programming and superficial news coverage of political questions.[36] As Graber finds through her intensive interviews with dozens of individuals with low incomes and low levels of formal education, people often display high levels of political sophistication. Detailed, thoroughly thought-out responses consistently dominate discussions of political and social issues in groups that Graber surveyed.[37]

Americans are traditionally thought of as depoliticized, preferring entertainment programming and infotainment over traditional political news stories. However, entertainment-oriented audiences are more interested in political issues in recent years. This newfound interest appears to be, in great part, the result of increased consumption of entertainment-based "soft news" programs with a political focus. Soft news programs such as *The Daily Show* with Jon Stewart, *Late Night* with David Letterman, and *The Colbert Report* mix traditional foreign policy stories with comedic editorializing. As consumption of soft news increases, viewers' attention to, and interest in, foreign policy increases.[38] By framing international news stories within an entertainment format, soft news programs reduce the informational costs of becoming better informed about international relations. In short, a major by-product of soft news consumption is the transformation of the traditionally apathetic and politically disinterested into more engaged, civic-minded citizens.

THE RATIONAL PUBLIC'S ASSESSMENT OF IRAQ

This book has focused on documenting the strength and effectiveness of official propaganda and hegemony in influencing messages transmitted in the American press. Although hegemony is clearly a valuable tool for understanding media coverage of war, this theoretical framework is not always useful in explaining the *effects* of media propaganda on the public. In increasingly larger numbers, Americans are often quite effective in rejecting media and political propaganda. In other words, mass opinion is not simply confined to pro-war feelings or to tactical criticisms. Americans subscribe to a number of challenges to the Iraq war that fall outside the bounds of the bipartisan hegemonic framework that operates in Washington.

Contrary to the claims of elitists, the American public does rationally react to changes in information related to military conflicts. Public opinion collectively grew more critical of the occupation of Iraq in light of the war's increasing cost in financial resources, American and Iraqi lives, and the growth of sectarian violence. A comprehensive review of the status on the ground in Iraq reveals a land of increased desperation and destruction. Public infrastructure in Iraq was in worse condition by 2008 than prior to the 2003 invasion. In short, the state of Iraq grew steadily and significantly worse during the U.S. occupation, and Americans responded critically to these developments.

The United States originally allocated a meager $18 billion for reconstruction in Iraq, and half of that money was redirected to the "pacification" of Iraqi resistance to the occupation.[39] Despite media and administration propaganda celebrating the American commitment to democratizing and rebuilding Iraq, such goals are far from a central part of the U.S. agenda. Contrary to their humanitarian rhetoric, American officials announced the end to limited reconstruction in Iraq as early as 2006.[40] Reports from 2006 through 2008 estimated Iraqi unemployment at between 60 to 70 percent, and the lack of jobs is considered a major factor fueling violent resistance to the United States.[41] Iraq's electricity grid, according to government estimates, will not reach its pre-invasion capacity until 2011, and by 2008 it provided for less than half of the demand of the Iraqi people. Baghdad's neighborhoods have access to less than two hours of electricity some days. Estimates suggest that up to $80 billion is required to reconstruct the country's electric network, more than three times the money allocated by the United States for all of Iraq's reconstruction.[42]

Iraq's water treatment facilities suffered under years of neglect due to the American-British sponsored United Nations sanctions, as well as during the occupation. The U.N. sanctions, responsible for the deaths of up to 500,000 Iraqi children, prevented the importing of basic components needed to rebuild Iraq's shattered infrastructure. Problems with reconstruction continued following the end of the sanctions. The construction of the waste treatment plant in the city of Falluja, supposedly "the centerpiece of an effort to rebuild Iraq," is deemed a "failed" project by the *New York Times*. More than half of Iraqis in the years following the U.S. invasion suffered from a lack of access to safe drinking water.[43] Over 20 percent of Iraqi children were chronically malnourished by 2006—a dramatic increase following the onset of the occupation.[44]

The occupation of Iraq, in light of the dire circumstances discussed above, was accompanied by a major human rights crisis, fueled by the increase in internally displaced and refugees fleeing the country as a result of chronic violence. By mid-2007, an estimated four to five million Iraqis were expelled from their homes, half with no access to food.[45] Despite discussions in the American media of the 2007 surge's success, the Iraqi Red Crescent Organization estimated that the number of internally displaced actually increased from 499,000 to over one million after American forces were increased.[46] As mentioned in chapter 3, Iraqi deaths are estimated at over one million in the post-invasion period.[47]

Much was made of the decline in monthly attacks following the "surge" of 30,000 troops that the United States sent to Iraq in 2007. There is significant disagreement, however, over whether the decline in Iraq's violence had anything to do with the expanded American troop presence or whether it was the product of a combination of the Sunni Awakening movement (in which Sunni resistance groups declared a truce with American troops in order to target al-Qaeda), the Sunnis' loss of the Sunni-Shia civil war in Baghdad, or the decision of Shia militiamen to stand down in their attacks on the Iraqi government and American troops.[48] Regardless of this debate, it should be remembered that Iraq remained one of the most dangerous countries in the world following the surge, as average attacks per month decreased from a high of between 5,000 to 6,000 per month in 2006 to about 1,000 to 2,000 per month in late 2007 and 2008. The decline in attacks needs to be evaluated *relative* to the lack of regular violence prior to the invasion. Although total deaths from bombings, shootings, and executions were estimated at between 2,000 to 2,500 deaths in early 2007 during the first stages of the surge, monthly violence remained at high, albeit relatively lower levels by late 2007, of between 900 to 1,100 people per month.[49] Again, this constitutes approximately 1,000 *more* deaths per month than occurred prior to the invasion. Under such circumstances, Americans are correct in assuming that Iraq is still plagued by high levels of violence.

As national public opinion polls demonstrate, American public support for war steadily declined in light of Iraq's deterioration. Public opinion became increasingly critical by late 2004 to early 2005. As the American National Election Study of 2004 found, a majority of Americans viewed the Iraq war as no longer worth it by late 2004, at the time of the presidential election. Information on increased public opposition to the war is provided in detail in Figure 7.1, which is derived from monthly polling data from CNN, the Pew Research Center, ABC News, and the *Washington Post.* As Figure 7.1 demonstrates, public opposition to the war, opposition to Bush's handling of the war, and support for

FIGURE 7.1: Public Opposition to the Iraq War (2003–2007)

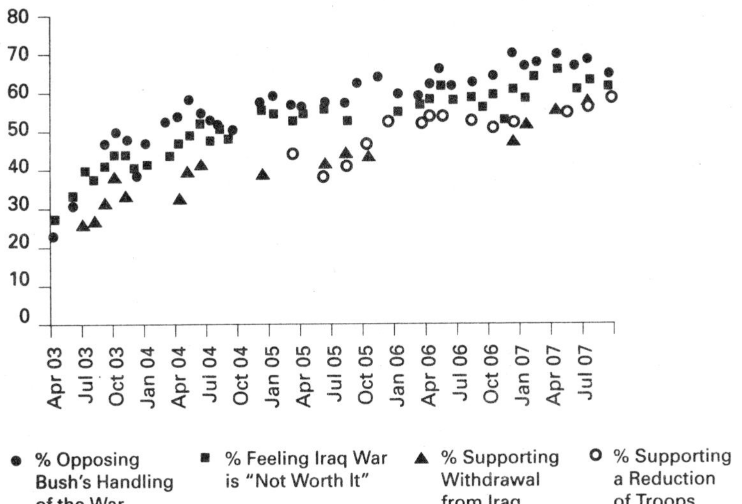

Source: Data from Table 7.1 is pulled from www.pollingreport.com, and is from the following poll series conducted by:CNN, Pew Research Center, ABC News, and the Washington Post.

troop reductions and withdrawal increased steadily from 2003 to 2007.[50] Opinion changed in a rational, predictable way, despite short-term positive and negative fluctuations, as Iraq's security situation deteriorated.

In the four survey questions on Iraq listed in Figure 7.1, the average change in the opinion of all respondents for each individual question fluctuates by between 2.5 to 4 percent from each month to the next. These average fluctuations reinforce the extraordinary amount of stability of public opinion, contrary to elitist claims that the public is unpredictable and fickle.

Furthermore, there is a strong degree of overlap across the responses to the four questions above. The answers to each of the four questions listed in Figure 7.1 are strongly correlated with one another, specifically in the ways public responses to each question change from one month to the next.[51] In other words, support for troop reduction and full withdrawal, opposition to Bush's handling of the war, and views of the war as not worth it all tend to change in a similar direction, increasing over time.

There is much disagreement about the reasons for why the public opposes war. Research finds that increasing American military casualties play a strong role in fostering antiwar sentiment.[52] Americans favor military intervention when the stated goal is defending another democratic country but are less willing to use force to benefit dictatorships. Negative media depictions of enemy countries and portrayals of an "enemy" state as aggressive, as violating international norms, or retaining an alien or hostile political culture, are all helpful in building domestic support for the use of force.[53] American intervention, when characterized as policing a country that is either suffering from civil war or in danger of falling into civil war tends to be extremely unpopular.[54] Former president Bush's justifications for extending the occupation clearly fall under the unpopular rubric of fighting to prevent civil war.

Disagreement exists over whether civilian casualties are a powerful factor in fomenting opposition to war. Political scientist John Mueller concludes that in the wars in Korea, Vietnam, and Iraq, "American public opinion became a key factor . . . in each one there has been a simple association: as casualties mount, support decreases. Broad enthusiasm at the outset invariably erodes." Support for war in Iraq declined even more precipitously than did support in earlier conflicts.[55] Political scientist Christopher Gelpi challenges Mueller's simple casualty narrative, arguing that the "American public regularly makes judgments about the potential costs and benefits of military operation[s]. As the likelihood of obtaining any benefits diminishes, the human cost of war becomes less tolerable, and casualties reduce support for operation[s]. On the other hand, if and when the public is optimistic about a successful outcome, it is far more willing to bear the human cost of war."[56]

Sadly, public opinion polls ignore the most obvious way to answer the question of why Americans turn against wars—simply ask them. Did the American public turn against the war because of the increasing cost in dollars and lives? Is opposition driven by feelings that the war is unwinnable? Or does the public see the war as immoral and repressive? This chapter and chapter 8 address these simple questions by surveying Americans to identify why they oppose war.

In 2009, I surveyed over two hundred Americans living in the Midwest on their feelings about Iraq. These respondents live in a variety of locations, including the city of Chicago, its suburbs, and rural areas in central Illinois. Participants represented a wide range of occupations, ages, and racial backgrounds. Although those surveyed clearly do not constitute a representative sample of the entire population of the United States, they at least provide some basic information on why many Americans oppose the war. Some hard-nosed social scientists may fault this survey as unrepresentative of the entire American public. This study, however, was not designed to generalize to all 300 million Americans. It has a few simple purposes: to allow a small number of respondents to provide *more detailed* answers than are typically allowed in national surveys of larger numbers of people; and to provide a test run for a number of questions that are never or almost never asked by mainstream polling organizations and see whether these questions resonate enough with Americans that they may be asked again in future national polls.

Unfortunately, the vast majority of public opinion surveys never assess whether the public opposes war for moral, as opposed to pragmatic reasons. This study is meant to take the first step in addressing this problem. Respondents were asked to provide detailed reasons why they felt one way or another in questions related to Iraq. Since this is not a national survey, readers are advised to cautiously assess the percentages I provide in this chapter and in chapter 8. These percentages are not to be taken as definitive or irrefutable evidence of how people feel about the Iraq war. They are merely meant to show that a sizable number of Americans agree with one policy opinion over another, and that further examination is needed. Having acknowledged this limitation, however, it should be noted that all other public opinion data cited in this chapter and the next that are not associated with my Midwest survey *are* generalizable to the entire public. This information was gathered by national polling organizations that use survey techniques that allow them to generalize their questions to all 300 million Americans.

Americans began rejecting the pro-war views of the Bush administration claiming "progress" in the occupation within less than two years of the March 2003 invasion.[57] According to the Harris polling group, by 2005 63 percent of Americans supported "bringing most of our troops home in the next year," with only 35 percent supporting extension of the occupation until a stable government is established. In that same year, over six in ten people felt that the Bush administration "generally misleads the American public" on political issues in order "to achieve its own ends."[58] Critical opinions intensified in early 2006 when Iraq fell into civil war. By March of that year, when sectarian violence exploded, 68 percent of Americans supported a draw-down of troops. Two-thirds of the public felt, contrary to the promises of the Bush administration, that the situation in Iraq had and would continue to worsen, and expressed low confidence in the possibility of a successful occupation.[59]

Bush's claims that the Iraq war is a vital part of the "war on terrorism" were rejected by most people as well. By late 2006, 60 percent of Americans felt that the Iraq war actually increased, rather than decreased, the likelihood of a terrorist attack against the United States.[60] Americans deferred to the wishes of the Iraqi public rather than those of the Bush administration when 73 percent expressed their support for American withdrawal if Iraqis desired such an action.[61] Negative public opinion persisted, despite administration rhetoric in 2007 that the United States was succeeding through the surge in stabilizing Iraq. By May of 2007, four months into the surge, 75 percent of those surveyed felt things were going badly in Iraq, and six in ten felt that the United States should have never gotten involved in the occupation. Only 23 percent approved the Bush administration's handling of the conflict.[62] By midyear 2007, most Americans supported the Democratic Party over the Republican Party, hoping they would pursue a major policy change in Iraq. President Bush's approval rating had reached an all-time low, at just 33 percent.[63]

Supplementing the national survey data cited above, my survey of midwesterners provides much insight into the American public's feelings toward Iraq by 2009. Similarly to the American public as a whole, most midwesterners surveyed (68 percent) supported a timetable for withdrawal. The vast majority (81 percent) felt that the conflict was "not worthwhile," with 79 percent agreeing that the occupation was "not succeeding" in reducing violence in Iraq. Many of those surveyed opposed the conflict for failing to produce defensible results. For example, one respondent explained: "Currently no good has come from the war for our side or theirs. [Iraq] is still in disarray, and we are not gaining anything from being there." Another respondent explained, in the midst of the surge, that "there may be a temporary reduction in violence in Iraq related to the United States' presence, but the Iraqi people ultimately need to involve themselves to produce change—however, people in poverty (regular citizens) have much difficulty standing up to force—they're busy trying to feed themselves."

Despite the increase in public discontent, the question remains of why, specifically, did people turn so quickly against the Iraq occupation? The evidence from the Midwest survey suggests that Americans respond, along the lines of the "rational public" thesis, to changes in events on the ground in Iraq. When those surveyed were asked for specific reasons why they opposed the war, the three most common reasons provided were that the occupation was too costly in the midst of economic meltdown and recession; military casualties were unacceptably high; and the conflict was "unwinnable."

TABLE 7.1: The Midwest Survey: Reasons for Public Opposition to War

Reasons for Supporting Withdrawal	Respondents Who Mentioned Reason	Respondents Citing Reason as Most Important Factor
The War Is Costing Too Much Money	27%	42%
American Casualties are Too High	21%	17%
The War Is Unwinnable	16%	23%
Iraqi Casualties Are Too High	16%	10%
The War Is Fundamentally Wrong and Immoral	7%	0%
Violence in Iraq has Increased Under the Occupation	9%	5%
The Surge Succeeded in Reducing Violence	4%	3%

Source: Author research

Table 7.1 depicts the major reasons provided for opposition to war among midwesterners who supported a timetable for withdrawal. Although Gelpi and Mueller debate whether opposition to war is driven by assessments of the conflict as unwinnable or by the cost in American lives, in the Midwest survey both reasons retain major significance in motivating public resistance.

However, in times of economic downturn and recession, the cost of the conflict may trump both assessments of potential victory and military casualties. Other reasons for antiwar sentiment include the increase in Iraqi casualties; the increase in violence in Iraq since 2003; views of the war as immoral; and assessments that the surge opened up a window for withdrawal.

Setting a timetable for ending the Iraq war took on renewed urgency in light of the dire economic situation of many Americans. The conflict retains little significance for people who are unable to pay for basic cost of living expenses, or who are in danger of losing their homes during the subprime mortgage and financial crises. The increasing cost of the war is depicted in Figure 7.2. The Congressional Research Service estimates that the war directly cost American taxpayers more than $600 billion from 2003 to 2008, but others project that it will cost between $1 trillion to $3 trillion in the long term.[64]

FIGURE 7.2: Cost of War in Billions Per Year

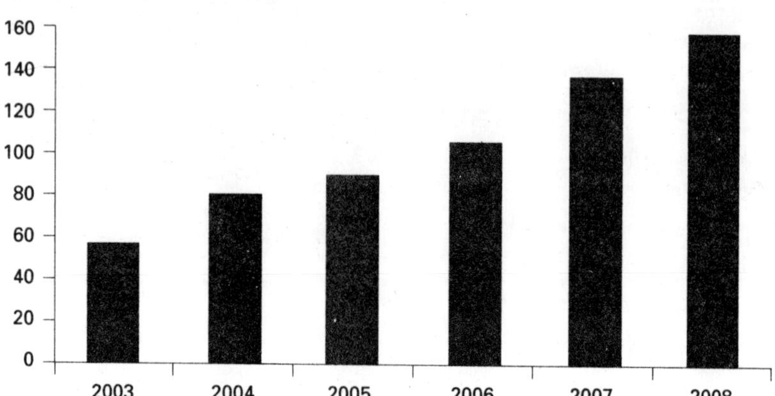

Source: Amy Belasco, "The Cost of Iraq, Afghanistan, and Other Global War on Terror Operations Since 9/11," Congressional Research Service, 15 October 2008, http://www.fas.org/sgp/crs/natsec/RL33110.pdf

My survey of midwesterners reinforces the vital role of the war's cost in inciting antiwar opinions. Many feel the United States should be allocating hundreds of billions of dollars to address problems at home rather than committing funds to open-ended combat operations abroad. The concern with cost is not simply pragmatic but also moral. Many feel that the money spent does not help the Iraqis, but rather makes the security situation in Iraq worse. As one respondent explains, "In my opinion, this war just raises taxes and this seems pointless, there's no winning team. And this war puts a bad reputation on the president and the nation. Families who want the troops to come home are waiting, and we need to worry about ourselves rather than other countries."

Other responses express similar concerns:

- The overall cost in money and lives has been insane. We are spending trillions on benefiting a people that would like to see us leave and money which could be used to fix domestic problems. American men and women are not coming home and Iraq men and women are dying as well.

- I think that a convincing reason to withdraw from Iraq is that it is costing the United States so much money. If you think about it, we're going to war and spending billions of dollars just to commit violence. On the other hand, you see that our economy is weak, the stock market is [negatively] affecting many citizens and employment has become an issue in the United States. Therefore, to benefit our country, we can withdraw from Iraq and instead of using money toward killings and violence we can use the money to get our economy back on track.

High levels of violence in Iraq are considered in large part to be a consequence of the occupation itself. Figure 7.3 depicts the relationship between attacks in Iraq and criticisms of the war. Clearly, increased criticisms of the war are expressed more often when violence increases.[65] Feelings that the war increases instability in Iraq are also expressed in the Midwest survey. Sixty-five percent feel that the war in Iraq is no longer "worthwhile" and is not succeeding in reducing violence in Iraq, as opposed to only 6 percent who feel the conflict is "worthwhile" and is succeeding in reducing violence. One of those surveyed expresses his concern with the harmful effects of the occupation this way: "I agree that it [the war] has generally not been worthwhile. The only way to promote Iraqi stability is if American troops withdraw and let the Iraqis establish their own stability. As long as we Americans are taking sides, violence will never end. The best thing is to remove our troops from Iraq and let the Iraqis establish their own government."

Another respondent feels that the United States' "inability to identify a clear enemy prevents us from warring in the preferred American style—

FIGURE 7.3: Monthly Attacks & Opposition to War

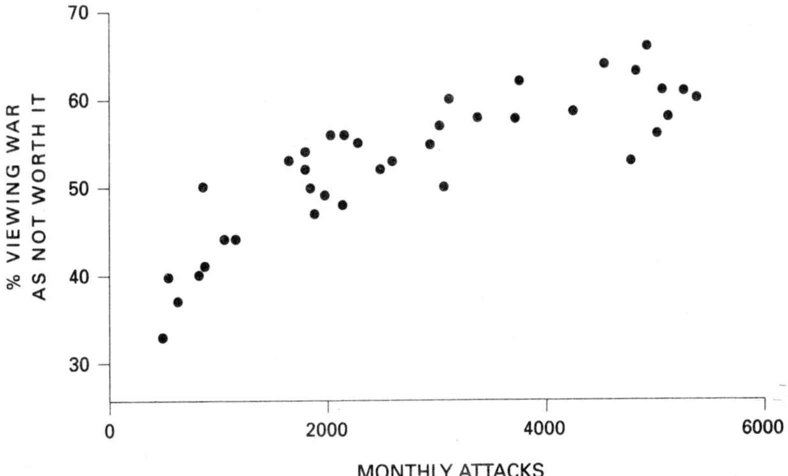

Source: www.pollingreport.com and from an ABC/Washington Post poll series, the data on attacks in Iraq comes from the MIPT Terrorism Knowledge Base.

big battles. The result is violence against the civilian population, oftentimes alienating the very group we are supposed to protect."

By a three-to-one ratio, midwestern respondents feel that the United States is guilty of contributing to Iraq's deterioration rather than reducing it. Similarly to the American public at large, a majority of respondents either somewhat or strongly agree that the United States is "responsible for increasing the violence in Iraq," and less than one-quarter somewhat or strongly disagree with this statement.[66] This opposition to the war is well summarized in these survey comments:

- Iraqis will not cooperate with American troops because they do not want us there. Therefore, it [the occupation] has not helped their community at all. People in Iraq are rejecting American troops there and this has caused an increase in violence in Iraq.

- Just the fact that we have been in Iraq for so many years says that we have not accomplished what we set out to do. By causing so much strife, just from being over there, we seem to be promoting conflict between the groups of Iraqis, as well as sectarian violence. . . . I think that the fact that we are occupying Iraq makes the Iraqi citizens angry and encourages them to engage in acts of violence against the United States. I think that they use suicide bombings and car bombings as a way of protesting our occupation. If we were not there, thousands of innocent civilians would not be killed.

- I don't think we have seen any positive effects from the United States' occupation, and there continues to be violence and instability. The United States is clearly escalating the violence just by occupying Iraq. We are not greeted as heroes but as enemies.

The American public's conclusion that the United States is contributing to Iraq's instability corresponds closely to the views of the Iraqi people (addressed in more detail in chapter 9). The American public appears to possess a remarkable insight in terms of its perceptions of the Iraq conflict, in contrast to the condescending claims made by elite theorists. These insights are very much in line with Iraqis who experience the conflict on the ground.

Antiwar feelings are strongly linked to month-to-month fluctuations in American military deaths. Though casualties do fluctuate more wildly

FIGURE 7.4: Public Opposition to War & Military Casualties

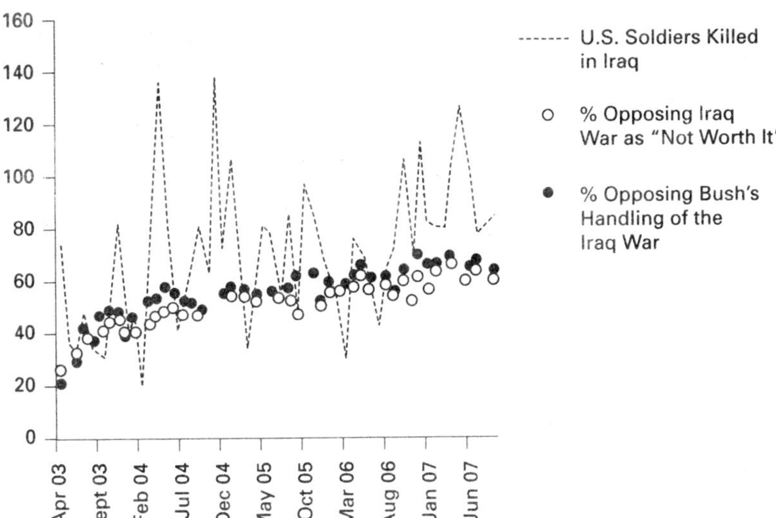

Source: www.pollingreport.com and from an ABC/*Washington Post* poll series.

than public opinion, the positive relationship between casualties and opposition to war is statistically significant.[67] Opposition to Bush's handling of the war and feelings that the war is "not worth it" significantly increase during months when casualties are growing.[68] This relationship is represented in Figure 7.4.

American public opinion reached its tipping point in 2004, when monthly American casualties reached their highest level in the entire five-year period examined (2003 to 2007).[69]

Critical coverage of the war is also related to changes in casualties. As Figure 7.5 indicates, increased *New York Times* attention to American deaths, though fluctuating greatly, is positively and significantly associated with increased monthly casualties.[70] Although the growth and decline of monthly casualty stories is relatively small—often by just a few stories a month—the pattern is clear: elite media outlets' reporting of American casualties generally changes proportionately with rising and falling casualty levels.

Additionally, in the months when casualties—and media attention to those casualties—increases, public opposition to the war grows significantly.[71] Americans seem to respond to aggregate monthly changes in American casualties as reported in media. Reporting of landmark casualty counts—when casualties reached 1,000 and 4,000—seem to gain serious attention from news consumers. As columnist Victor Davis Hansen observes:

FIGURE 7.5: American Deaths & Media Coverage

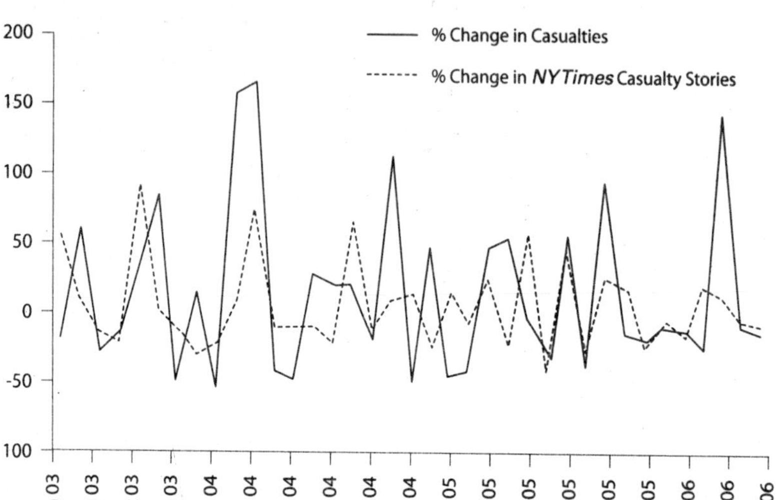

Source: Lexis Nexis and from the Iraq Coalition Casualty Count Project: http://www.icasualties.org/

"Public support for the war [in 2005] commensurately declined" in response to increases in "the aggregate number of American military fatalities," and in light of "the nightly ghoulish news of improved explosives and suicide bombers."[72] American opposition to the war, however, is more likely affected by audiences reading about the total number of deaths at any given time, as reflected in Figure 7.6, rather than as a response to small increases in the number of news stories on casualties per month.

It is no accident that increasing violence in Iraq is accompanied by a growth in American military casualties. Violent attacks in Iraq reached new heights in late 2006 and 2007, when the civil war reached its peak, and as cumulative American casualties steadily increased (see Figure 7.7). The relationship between press attention to casualties and increased public opposition to war, however, appears to be a complex one. On the one hand, we see a positive relationship between increases in monthly casualties and increased public opposition to war, and on the other, there is no statistically significant relationship between monthly increases in the number of *New York Times* stories covering casualties and increased public opposition to war. A number of possible explanations can account for the lack of a relationship. For one, the month-to-month fluctuations in a paper like the *New York Times* may not be replicated in other newspapers

FIGURE 7.6: U.S. Military Deaths (Cumulative)

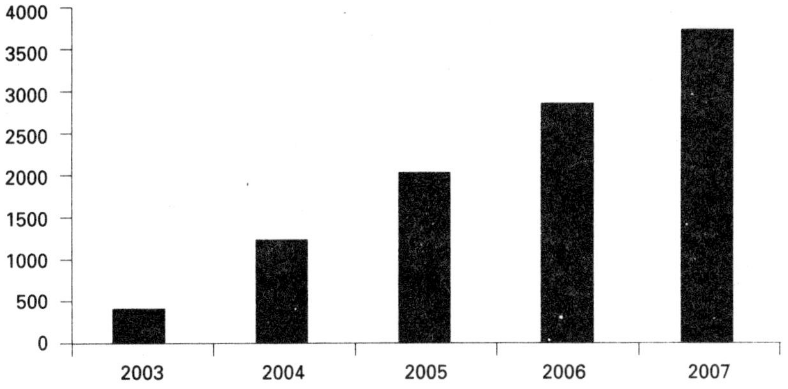

Source: The Iraq Coalition Casualty Count Project: http://www.icasualties.org/

and in television news outlets, although another analysis needs to be undertaken to demonstrate this.

Another possibility is that the public reacts mainly to aggregate numbers of soldiers killed, responding to estimates provided on a monthly basis by media outlets. This possibility seems more likely than the alternative scenario, where the public responds to very small month-by month fluctuations in the number of casualty stories in the news. News readers and viewers are probably reading or watching a relatively small number of stories each month (perhaps as little as one story)—or talking to friends and family who see stories summarizing whether casualties are on the rise or decline, and they are responding accordingly. This seems to make sense, since the fluctuations in the month-by-month coverage of casualties in papers like the *New York Times* are so minuscule, and unlikely to produce much of an effect in and of themselves. To put these minor fluctuations into perspective, the total attention to casualties in the *New York Times* increases, on average, by just 1.5 stories during months when casualties are increasing in Iraq, whereas coverage decreases on average by only two stories per month when monthly casualties are declining. It is extremely doubtful that the general public would notice such small changes in the frequency of casualty stories.

There is strong evidence, however, that Americans pay close attention to U.S. casualties in Iraq on a more general level. Table 7.2 reproduces the findings of polls conducted by the Pew Research Center from 2006 through 2008.[73] The results demonstrate that most Americans did pay close attention to casualties in the news, as over 60 percent of respondents

FIGURE 7.7: Escalating Attacks & Casualties in Iraq

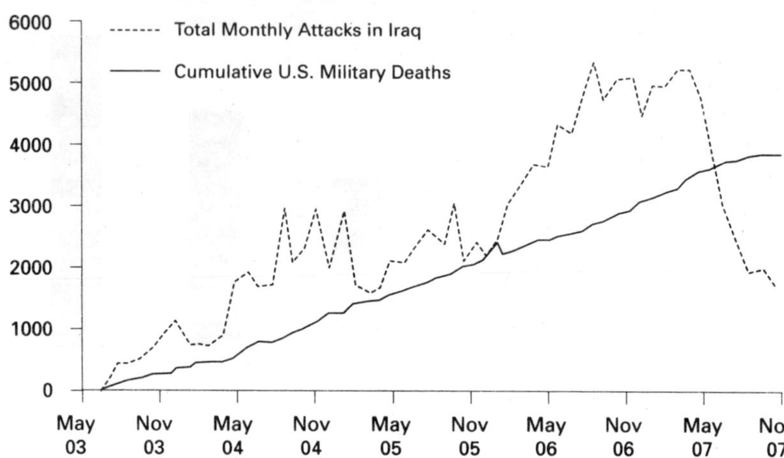

Source: The MIPT Terrorism Knowledge Base and from the Iraq Coalition Casualty Count Project: http://www.icasualties.org/

correctly estimated the number of Americans killed in both 2006 and 2007, although only a plurality were able to do so in 2008. The 2008 decline in casualty awareness can likely be explained by the fact that the issue of Iraq largely fell out of major newspaper headlines and television stories by late 2007 following the surge, and because American casualties had reached an all-time low by this period.[74] Decreased attention to Iraq, then, was followed by increased public ignorance about the number of U.S. military deaths in the country.

Further examination of the Pew polls finds that although knowledge of casualties was high across different demographics, those who followed news on Iraq were statistically more likely to provide an accurate estimate of the number of U.S. soldiers killed. More specifically, consumers of Rush Limbaugh's radio program, NPR listeners, and Fox News Bill O'Reilly viewers were better able to provide the correct number of Americans killed, as compared to those who did not consume these programs.[75] In short, a majority of Americans appear to have followed stories on U.S. casualties in the news on some level, and regular news consumers are particularly effective at providing information on casualty levels.

Much of the limited month-by-month variation in coverage of casualties is explained by the media's reliance on official sources. Officials at the Department of Defense exercise tremendous informal power over reporting, with 75 percent of the stories on casualties in the *New York Times*

TABLE 7.2: Public Knowledge of U.S. Casualties

April 2006	% Providing Each Response	Feb 2007	% Providing Each Response	Dec 2008	% Providing Each Response
500	3%	1,000	4%	2,200	14%
1,500	17%	2,000	17%	3,200	23%
2,500*	**61%***	**3,000***	**62%***	**4,200***	**43%***
3,500	19%	4,000	17%	5,200	20%

*Boldface figures indicate the correct response to questions about how many Americans died, as well as the percent of Americans who correctly estimated casualties.

Source: Pew Research Center, "April 2006 News Interest Index," April 2006, http://people–press.org/dataarchive/; Pew Research Center, "February 2007 Political Survey," 2 February 2007, http://people–press.org/dataarchive/; Pew Research Center, "December Political and Economic Survey," 3 December 2008, http://people–press.org/dataarchive/.

every month based solely on press statements released by the DOD listing the names of the dead.[76] Only one-quarter of the stories in the *New York Times* originate from the actual reporting of events in Iraq that led to the deaths of soldiers. Fluctuation in month-to-month reporting, then, is influenced more directly by the decision of military officials to release casualty reports than it is upon actual changes in the number of attacks and deaths on the ground in the war zone.

The great irony of the findings in this chapter is that elite media never *intended* to foster antiwar dissent in their reporting of casualties and violence in Iraq. The liberal editors of papers such as the *New York Times* and *Los Angeles Times* did not even endorse a withdrawal from Iraq timetable until 2007, almost four years into the conflict. Nonetheless, simply by reporting that Iraqi violence and American casualties were on the rise from 2003 through 2007, it appears that national news outlets played a major role in mobilizing public opposition to war. As Figure 7.8 suggests, the most important period in terms of the media's effect appears to be from mid-2003 through mid-2005.

As violence in Iraq grew rapidly from relative calm to thousands of attacks per month in 2004 and 2005, Americans grew increasingly skeptical of a war that appeared to be spiraling out of control. Figure 7.8 suggests that public opposition grew most strongly during months when coverage of the violence increased dramatically.[77] This rapid growth in violence stood in stark contrast to the promises of the Bush administration that United States forces would be greeted as "liberators" and that the resistance against the occupation was confined to a few "dead enders."

FIGURE 7.8: Coverage of Iraq Violence & Opposition to War

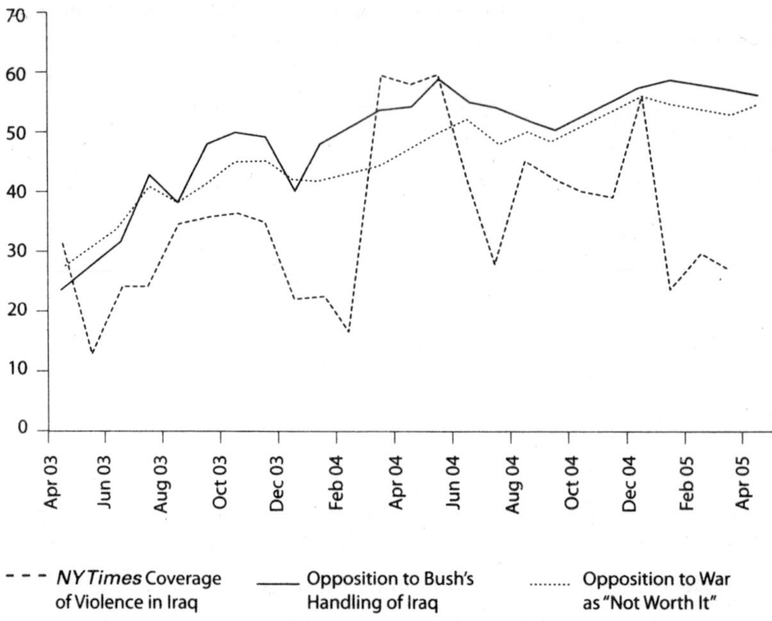

Source: Vanderbilt News Archive, as well as from the ABC/Washington Post poll series drawn from www.pollingreport.com

Although U.S. media were responsible for inciting opposition to the war, this does not mean, as conservative media critics contend, that reporters are consciously or ideologically driven to undermine the war at every turn. There is little evidence that reporters were driven by partisan considerations to promote a Democratic Party "antiwar" agenda at the expense of a Republican president in power.[78] A more likely reality is that reporters felt compelled to cover increasing violent attacks in Iraq, in addition to growing American casualties, because they feared they would lose credibility if they refused. Few Americans, after all, would take media outlets seriously if they refused to acknowledge that Iraqi violence and American casualties were on the rise from 2003 to 2007.

THE MIDWEST SURVEY AND IRAQ

The relationship between increased casualties and opposition to war is also evident in the Midwest survey. Many of those questioned cite both increases in Iraqi violence and increased military casualties as justifications for opposing the occupation. Respondents consistently speak of the dangers faced by American soldiers in the face of growing violence:

> After the September 11th attacks Americans were eager to fight terrorism on all fronts and to explore all the avenues to go about it. When no weapons of mass destruction were found in Iraq they started to have the first doubts about the motives for the war. I think people are generally supportive of all the humanitarian effort but as the occupation drags on, with weekly bombings and casualties, people are afraid it will turn into another Vietnam, another no-win situation.

Similarly, another respondent comments:

> Every single soldier from the United States is put in danger by terrorists, as well as the danger of "friendly fire" that may be hard to prevent, but remains a threat. I'm concerned for needless death of any being on our planet. These people are someone's father, mother, son, daughter . . . and the after-effects [post-traumatic stress disorder] will continue to devastate families for a long to come, even if they do survive.

Midwesterners often expressed anger at sacrificing American lives for a conflict with no foreseeable end and with questionable benefits for American national security. The loss of American lives is considered unacceptable in a civil war that continues to kill thousands of Iraqis and in which the long-term stability of Iraq is in doubt.

Iraqis' mass contempt for the occupation is seen as delegitimizing the occupation, despite the American media's celebrations of the surge and the limitations of criticisms to pragmatic grounds.[79] As one respondent explains:

> It is obvious that the Iraqis do not respect our presence and are still lashing out at our troops. I do not see the reason for us to be there. The longer we are there, the more casualties we are going to have without a main cause. Many critics are saying that this war is Vietnam all over again, and I am starting to believe it.

Another critic of the war comments that the "success" of the surge came at the expense of the military's credibility in future conflicts:

> Our soldiers are dying for private gain and the strain is eroding the United States military. We are severely constrained by these efforts. We are unable to deal with

> a real threat to security. Future threats will meet skepticism from the public because of needless waste built on lies. We will suffer an "Iraq syndrome" as we suffered from the "Vietnam syndrome" in the past.

HOPE FOR THE PUBLIC'S POWER IN DEMOCRATIC POLITICS

A number of key points with regard to public opinion, media, and war were identified in this chapter. Contrary to the conclusions of many intellectuals, the public is quite rational, responding to changes in information when formulating its opinions on Iraq. That the general public is attentive enough to follow major political issues such as Iraq while formulating informed opinions is encouraging for supporters of democracy. Sadly, political contempt for public opinion serves as a major impediment to democratic representation. Political and media elites continue to play a vital role in limiting democratic government. By conceding that the public is able to reject many of the media's hegemonic messages, I do not want to obscure the fact that there are crucial differences between sectors of the public based upon their demographic backgrounds. The effects of education, political attentiveness, and media consumption on public opinion are discussed at length in the next chapter. The role of the media and American educational institutions in indoctrinating the most privileged members of the public also receives significant attention.

CHAPTER EIGHT

Media Effects on Public Opinion: Propaganda, Indoctrination, and Mass Resistance

The last chapter focused on how the American public collectively and rationally responds to changes in information regarding events on the ground in Iraq. It is not always helpful, however, to examine public opinion as a whole, since there are significant differences between sectors of the public based on demographic backgrounds. This chapter examines how education, attention to politics, and consumption of media influence individual opinions of war. Members of the general public with elite backgrounds—those with higher formal education, those paying closer attention to electoral politics, and those consuming media in greater proportions—are more closely wedded to elite ideologies, as expressed by political officials.[1] This should not be surprising despite claims from some elitists that the most educated and privileged Americans are the most independent-minded citizens. Consumption of elite discourse exerts strong indoctrinating effects on those who absorb official communications in large quantities.

I define "elites" as those liberals and conservatives in the general public who consume greater amounts of elite media, pay more attention to electoral politics, and retain higher levels of education. Although these people are not elites in the sense that they fail to hold major positions in government, they *are* elite in the sense that they are closely in tune with the ideological debates that rage among political officials and in media. The information in this chapter employs data from my Midwest survey and relies on public opinion surveys from organizations such as the

TABLE 8.1: Public Trust in Elite Media Based on Levels of Attentiveness (2004 National Election Study)

Respondents with High Trust in Media		Respondents with Low Trust in Media	
% Paying Little Attention to the 2004 Election and Media	18%	% Paying Little Attention to the 2004 Election and Media	12%
% Paying Moderate Attention	32%	% Paying Moderate Attention	6%
% Paying High Attention	42%	% Paying High Attention	7%

Source: University of Michigan's project, Inter-University Consortium for Political and Social Research.

American National Election study as well as other national polling groups. Much of the national public opinion data was accessed through the University of Michigan's survey database—the Inter-University Consortium for Political and Social Research.

There is good reason to suspect that media consumption, higher education, and increased attention to politics influence how people see the world. On the most general level, increased consumption of elite forms of media—particularly national print media—is positively associated with increased trust in media. The relationship between increased media consumption and increased trust in media is both significant and positive.[2] In other words, those who follow print media closest are more trusting of the news they consume, as indicated in Table 8.1.

Conversely, respondents who follow national print media less often retain less trust in that medium. Increased trust in media is also associated with increased consumption of electoral politics. Those who paid more attention to the 2004 election in television news and magazine articles, for example, were more likely to trust in media to report issues fairly.[3]

Confidence in government and media are also significantly related. Those with high trust in media tend to be more trusting of government to "do the right thing" regarding to major policy matters, whereas those with low trust in media are less likely to trust government, as Table 8.2 demonstrates. Importantly, the relationship between trust in government and media is evident for both conservative and liberal respondents.[4]

Although the ties between trust of media and trust of government were established above, the question of the indoctrinating effects of media must also be examined. How *specifically* are increased media consumption, for-

TABLE 8.2: Public Trust in Media and Government

	Low Media Trust	High Media Trust
Low Gov. Trust	61%	40%
High Gov. Trust	39%	60%

Source: University of Michigan's project, Inter-University Consortium for Political and Social Research.

mal education and political attentiveness related to opinions of American foreign policy? This question is answered below.

ELITE INDOCTRINATION IN THE IRAQ WAR

A theory of indoctrination posits that those who consume media more frequently, pay more attention to electoral politics, and achieve higher levels of education are more likely to accept and defend the limits on debate articulated by political officials. The "war on terror" represents a classic case in which political leaders disagree about the prospects for American military success. The war in Iraq—prior to the 2003 invasion—represents an example whereby many Democrats and moderate Republicans challenged the Bush administration's promises of an effective long-term occupation. A review of the policy debate that took place prior to the invasion puts this conflict in perspective.

Democrats in Congress, military officials, and former Republicans in the executive branch challenged the feasibility of the proposed 2003 invasion. Some of their objections are summarized here:

- Democratic Representative Barbara Lee introduced a resolution in the House encouraging President Bush to work with the United Nations to resolve the conflict peacefully rather than through an invasion.

- Republican Representative John Spratt introduced a resolution requiring United Nations Security Council authorization prior to the use of force in Iraq.

- Former national security advisor Brent Scowcroft warned that an invasion of Iraq would "turn the whole region [of the Middle East] into a cauldron and destroy the war on terror."

TABLE 8.3: Congressional Voting on the Invasion of Iraq

House of Representatives			Senate		
	Democrats	Republicans		Democrats	Republicans
Support	81	215	Support	29	48
Oppose	126	6	Oppose	21	1

Source: gov.track.us website.

- Former secretary of state James Baker urged the United States to enlist a broad base of allies prior to going to war.
- Dick Armey, Republican House of Representatives Majority Leader worried that an occupation would lead to a "quagmire that will endanger" the Republican domestic agenda.
- Former secretary of state Henry Kissinger urged against invasion without support from American allies.
- Former national security advisor Zbigniew Brzezinski condemned a war "undertaken because of a personal peeve, demagogically articulated fears or vague factual assertions."
- Retired General Anthony Zinni stressed the dangers of an invasion when American forces were "stretched too tight all over the world."

Opposition to the war went beyond the skepticism of a few prominent officials. As Table 8.3 indicates, a majority of Democrats (57 percent) in Congress opposed a bill authorizing the president to go to war, despite a sizable minority in the party (43 percent) supporting it.

It is possible to observe differences in opinion between demographic groups based upon statistical testing.[5] The relationships between education, political attentiveness, and media consumption is clear: those benefiting from higher levels of formal education tend to follow politics most closely—accepting or rejecting various partisan messages from Democratic and Republican political actors with greater frequency than those with lower levels of education and those who follow politics less closely. The venue through which highly educated, politically attentive

FIGURE 8.1: Public Support for Invading Iraq (2002)

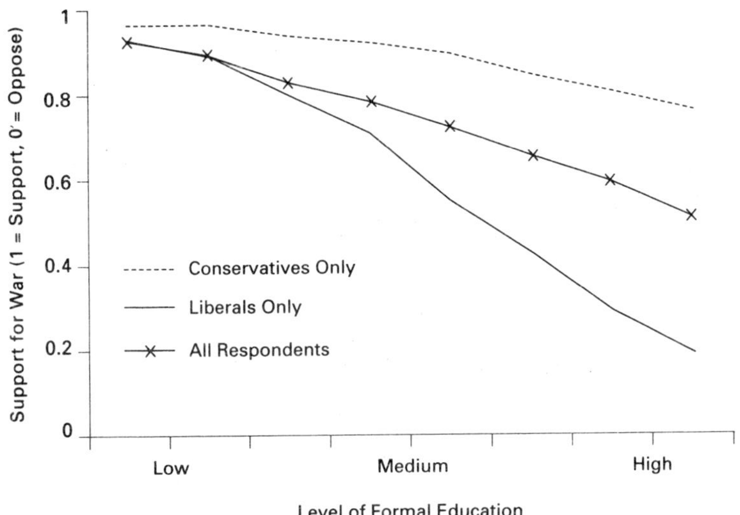

Source: University of Michigan's project, Inter-University Consortium for Political and Social Research.

citizens absorb messages from officials is the mass media, most specifically national newspapers and television networks.

Public opinion of the Iraq invasion was strongly supportive in early 2003. As American soldiers were put in harm's way, a "rally around the flag" effect emerged in support of the administration's war motives. Overall, 70 percent of Americans felt the war was worth fighting in March 2003, and President Bush's job approval rating increased by 16 percentage points during the February to April 2003 period.[6] However, not all Americans supported the war equally. Support for the invasion was significantly lower for those with higher levels of formal education, whether they described themselves as liberals, conservatives, or moderates (see Figure 8.1). Furthermore, highly educated citizens were more likely to reflect the strong level of debate in Washington regarding the merits and drawbacks of the invasion. Warnings that the war represented a strategic mistake and that the United States needed to secure greater support from its allies were well received by highly educated liberals, while liberals with lower levels of education were less likely to oppose the president.

Liberal media outlets such as the *New York Times* and *Boston Globe* offered plenty of procedural criticisms of the rush to war. The editors of the *New York Times*, for example, warned in January of 2003 that "the political, economic, and military implications of combat . . . demand every effort by the United States to resolve this confrontation short of war. That may involve extending the period of inspections, and certainly requires Washington to return to the Security Council for further deliberation before turning to the use of force."[7] *Boston Globe* editors argued that "more detail is needed to convince a skeptical world that Saddam cannot be contained and that even a successful military attack would not have harmful after-effects." They worried that "with a possible invasion of Iraq just weeks away, the country is woefully unprepared if, as the Central Intelligence Agency has warned, Saddam Hussein responds with a smallpox attack on this country."[8]

The most educated Americans closely followed the debates in the elite media over the timing of an attack and the merits of using force without allied support. This group expressed more apprehension about an attack, at least compared to those Americans with lower levels of formal education. Support for war among highly educated conservatives still remained high, however. As Figure 8.1 demonstrates, there is little distinction between liberal and conservative respondents with low levels of education, as they both were equally likely to support the conflict.[9]

Elite criticism of the Iraq war increased as the occupation wore on. By 2004, Democratic political leaders and major national newspapers were publicly arguing for a change in management of the Iraq war, as they supported Democratic senator John Kerry over George W. Bush for president. The most politically attentive Americans followed this debate closely, and they were considerably more likely to conclude that the war actually increased the threat of terrorism rather than reducing it. This conclusion should not be surprising for those who followed media coverage of the Iraq conflict, since the occupation served as a lightning rod for Islamist groups wishing to travel to Iraq to target U.S. troops. Of course, not all politically attentive Americans agreed that the Iraq war had increased the terrorism threat. Liberals who paid attention to the 2004 election were more likely than less attentive liberals to conclude that the war failed in fighting terrorism. In contrast, conservatives who followed the 2004 election more closely were no more likely to declare the war a failure in fighting terrorism. More generally, conservatives across the board were more likely to accept administration claims that war is needed to fight terrorism.[10]

It is inaccurate to claim that politically attentive and highly educated Americans are always more critical of the government on issues of war. Concerning withdrawal from Iraq, highly attentive and highly educated

FIGURE 8.2: Public Opinion & Support for Iraq Withdrawal

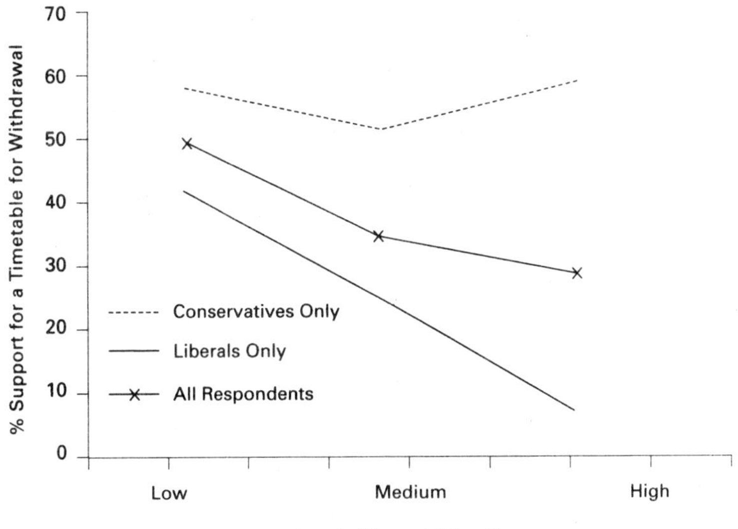

Source: University of Michigan's project, Inter-University Consortium for Political and Social Research.

members of the public are often less open to criticisms of the United States. When asked about the proper length of the Iraq occupation, most Americans by mid- to late- 2005 supported establishing some sort of timetable for withdrawal. Highly educated Americans, however, were *more likely* to oppose setting a timetable, as demonstrated in Figure 8.2, while those with lower education were stronger supporters of a timetable. Liberals and conservatives with higher education were more likely to be divided on the issue in 2005 than were those with less education (see Figure 8.2).[11] The highly educated seemed more in tune with debate in Washington, where leaders from both parties had only just begun to disagree over the merits of withdrawal.[12] Revealingly, highly educated liberals and conservatives were two and a half times more likely to disagree over the merits of withdrawal than were liberals and conservatives at the lowest educational level. In other words, these elites were heavily invested in the newly emerging conflict over withdrawal between Democratic and Republican officials.

The first political disagreement over withdrawal emerged in Washington during late 2005. The battle in Washington occurred amidst increasing disagreement over withdrawal amongst conservative and liberal elites in the general public. During 2005, a small minority of Democrats in Congress began to entertain possibilities of withdrawal.

FIGURE 8.3: Public Opinion, Radio News, & Iraq

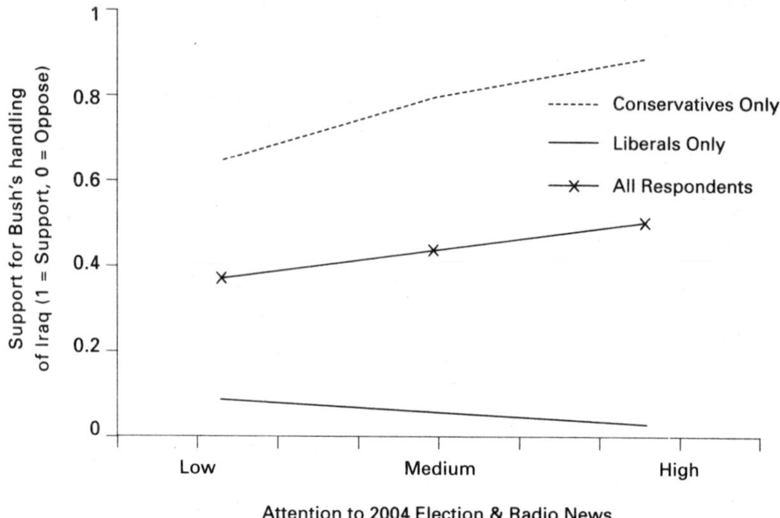

Source: University of Michigan's project, Inter-University Consortium for Political and Social Research.

Democratic representative John Murtha, for example, publicly called for a withdrawal from Iraq based on assumptions that the war was a failure. House Democrats entered into the preliminary stages of a debate regarding the possibility of withdrawal by November 2005. Republicans, on the other hand, consistently opposed plans for withdrawal from 2005 onward. As evidence in this chapter demonstrates, the general public's opposition to the war is heavily based on criticisms of the legitimacy of U.S. power itself. This stands in great contrast to political officials, who oppose the war based on pragmatic concerns.

Public opinion on Iraq is also influenced by citizens' consumption of media. Figure 8.3 reveals significant differences between liberal and conservatives who consumed greater media coverage of the 2004 election—when compared to those consuming less coverage. Respondents who consumed greater amounts of election news on the radio in 2004 were more likely to conclude the war was "worth it." Differences in support for war were more pronounced for liberals and conservatives who paid more attention to the election and consumed more media.

The strong relationship between increased consumption of radio news and increased support for war among conservatives is easily explained by the ideological biases of radio, since the medium is overwhelmingly dominated by right-wing hosts and audiences.[13] The radio punditry, monopolized by conservatives such as Michael Medved, Rush Limbaugh, Sean Hannity, and Michael Savage, was vigilant in defending the Republican-led war effort. It attacked even strategic criticisms of the occupation as unpatriotic.

INDOCTRINATION AND THE "WAR ON TERROR"

The influences of media consumption, electoral attentiveness, and education are also apparent when considering broader questions relating to the "war on terror." Elites in the general public appear to be very different from non-elites in their political views. Those who pay more attention to election politics better understand the motivations of Islamist forces that attacked the United States on 9/11. Those who followed recent national elections closely were consistently more likely, in the year following the 9/11 attacks, to describe Islamists' choice to target the United States as driven by three factors: anger over U.S. support for Israel, perceptions that the United States is an immoral superpower, and a general desire to engage in religious war with the United States. This finding is significant for the most politically attentive audiences across the board, regardless of whether they identify themselves as liberal, conservative, or moderate.[14]

A better understanding of the motivations of the 9/11 attackers, however, does not mean that these elites are sympathetic to their motivations. American officials in both the Democratic and Republican parties refuse to accept claims that U.S. foreign policy is immoral or that its support for Israel is detrimental to the stability of the Middle East. Highly educated Americans are extraordinarily similar across liberal and conservative lines on the issue of the U.S. role in the world. Support for an active role in world affairs is widespread in the United States, as 80 percent of those surveyed disagree with the claim that the United States "would be better off if we just stayed home." Despite widespread popularity for a strong global role for the United States, differences also exist among members of the public based upon key demographic factors. Increased education, for example, is positively associated with support for a strong U.S. presence throughout the world, as shown in Figure 8.4.

This relationship is evident for both liberal and conservative elites, despite the disagreements these individuals express over how effectively U.S. power is exercised across the world.[15]

FIGURE 8.4: Public Opinion & Support for U.S. Power Abroad Based on Education

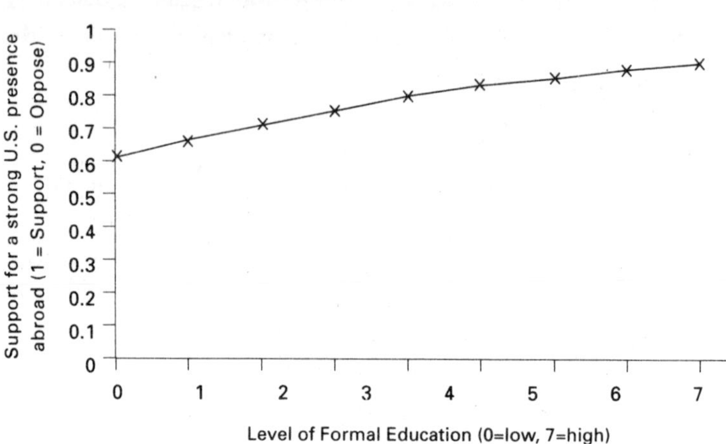

Source: University of Michigan's project, Inter-University Consortium for Political and Social Research.

Public approval of former president Bush, approval of his handling of the "war on terror," support for his handling of relations with foreign countries, and support for the war in Afghanistan are all positively related to higher levels of education, increased electoral attentiveness, and media consumption. On the issue of presidential approval, the public was divided about Bush's job performance for many years. By the 2004 election, many political officials and news editors concluded that Bush could no longer effectively manage the "war on terror" or the occupation of Iraq and shifted support to John Kerry for president.[16] Even when public support for Bush was high in late 2002, at 70 percent, differences among citizens were evident. Increased news consumption, greater electoral attentiveness, and higher education were all significantly related to disapproval of President Bush, especially among self-identified liberals. The role of increased political attention to the 2002 election is depicted in Figure 8.5.[17]

Even in instances where public opinion seems to be overwhelmingly supportive of the president, differences are still apparent among elite segments of the public. A few examples drive this point home in greater detail:

- Approval of Bush's handling of relations with foreign countries was high in 2002, with 62 percent of the public supporting the president, and 38 percent opposing him. Despite strong support, elite disagreement persisted. Liberals with higher electoral interest were more critical of the president than liberals with lower interest.

FIGURE 8.5: Support for the President (2002)

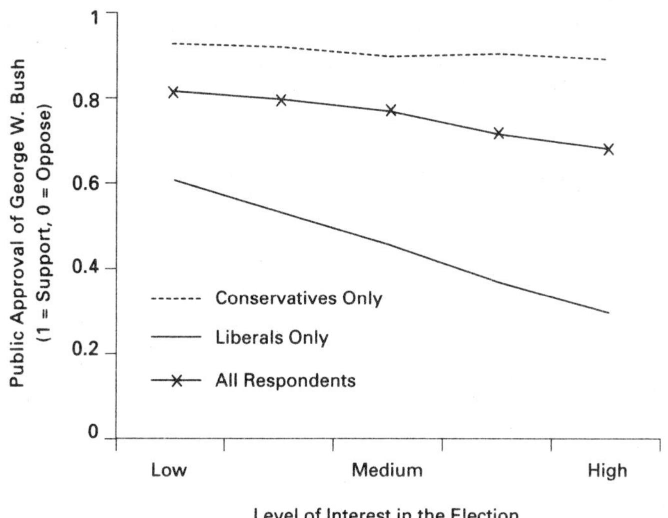

Source: University of Michigan's project, Inter-University Consortium for Political and Social Research.

Conservatives with higher electoral interest were more supportive of the president than conservatives with lower interest.[18]

- Support for Operation Enduring Freedom in Afghanistan was strong among the general public in 2002, with 70 percent supporting the conflict as "worth it" and only 30 percent opposed. In the face of strong approval for the war, differences among the public materialized. Highly educated Americans were more likely to support the war. Conservatives with higher education were significantly more supportive than conservatives with lower education.[19] Those who paid greater attention to the 2002 midterm election in the media were also more likely to support the war, as compared to those who did not follow media coverage of the election. Conservatives who more closely followed election coverage were more supportive than conservatives who less closely followed the midterm election.[20]

- Bush benefited from high levels of support for his handling of the "war on terror" in 2002, with supporters outnumbering opponents by a margin of three to one. Despite this widespread popularity, liberals consuming more news and more closely following

> the 2002 election were more likely to oppose Bush's performance than liberals who consumed less news and followed the election less closely. Similarly, conservatives who consumed more news and with higher electoral attention were stronger supporters of Bush than conservatives who consumed less news and paid less attention to the election.[21] As one can see in Figure 8.6, elite liberals and elite conservatives are once again more likely to be more strongly divided than non-elite liberals and conservatives on the question of Bush's effectiveness in fighting foreign wars. Clearly, there are significant differences in approval of Bush between both elite and non-elite liberals and conservatives, although all elites were more likely to reflect the debate in Washington over the president's effectiveness and competence in fighting terrorism.

Up until this point, this chapter has focused on how the values of elites in the general public closely correspond with those of officials in Washington. However, this is only part of the picture when examining public opinion and the "war on terror." Many aspects of antiwar dissent are downplayed and ignored in contemporary public opinion polling. The next section systematically explores a number of ways in which the general public expresses moral dissent, challenging the legitimacy of U.S. foreign policy at its foundations.

THE SOCIAL CONSTRUCTION OF PUBLIC OPINION: MEDIA EFFECTS ON THE "WAR ON TERROR"

Scholars have focused for decades on how the media influences public opinion on political matters. Media play a vital role in constructing the world that people see, and in influencing which issues the public focuses upon. Academics focus on the media's power to control *what* people think about or *how* they think about it, but little attention is spent exploring how media affects what people actually think of government policies.[22] As media scholar Maxwell McCombs explains, studies focused for more than forty years on how media "set the agenda" for public discussion of policy issues. "Strong causal effects" are observed, McCombs concludes, when the "issues emphasized in the news come to be regarded over time as important by the public."[23] The agenda-setting hypothesis

FIGURE 8.6: Public Opinion on Bush's Handling of the "War on Terror" (2004)

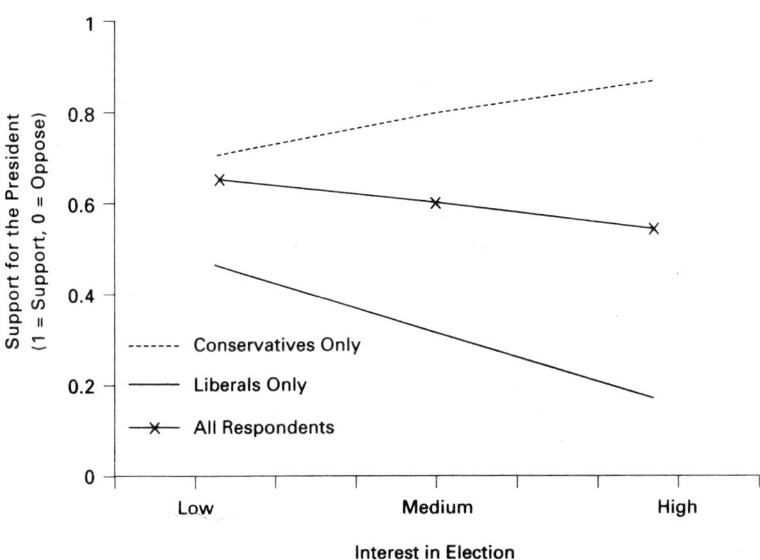

Source: University of Michigan's project, Inter-University Consortium for Political and Social Research.

was long considered path breaking because it challenged earlier beliefs that media exert only "minimal effects" on the public.[24]

Different areas of scholarship focus on the extensive effects of media on public opinion. A number of studies under the "agenda-setting" school emphasize how television media "prime" audiences by influencing which factors "spring to the citizen's mind and which do not."[25] Media stories that focus on specific "episodes" or political events tend to encourage viewers to place responsibility for events with the specific individuals involved, whereas reporting of events in a "thematic" way tends to encourage viewers to see political issues in terms of broader societal trends. The main difference between the two types of framing is that a viewer may think of an issue like poverty as the problem of a certain deficient individual if stories are reported episodically, but see poverty as a social problem if stories focus more generally on the issue of poverty.[26] Other scholars find that news stories portraying the strategic motives of political leaders that are accompanied by personal attacks on other leaders tend to increase public cynicism about politics.[27] Media commentators and the "experts" they invite on their programs are found to exert a strong positive influence over public evaluations of government policies.[28]

There are many other types of media effects as well. In "information processing" studies, Doris Graber, Russell Neuman, Marion Just, and Anne Crigler find that people with low interest in politics tend to learn significantly from audio-visual news.[29] Election studies find that the growth of negative news stories on presidential candidates are accompanied by an increase in viewers' negative images of the candidates. Campaign interest among the general public also rises and falls with increases in media coverage of campaigns, and positive and negative campaign ads positively and negatively influence individual assessments of the election process.[30] Sociologists find that increased viewing of television leads to a "cultivation" of audiences, where heavy television viewers adopt the views widely expressed in television programming. Studies of product advertising suggest that increased viewing of ads is accompanied by increased consumption of promoted products.[31]

The effects of media on public opinion receive extensive attention in many studies. News reports that are critical of antiwar protestors decrease the public's sympathy for demonstrators and increase support for law enforcement.[32] During the 1991 Gulf War, those who consumed television news that prioritized military planning over diplomatic solutions were more likely to support the war.[33] Heavy news consumers in the run-up to the Gulf War were generally more likely to accept the rhetorical arguments for war made by the George H. W. Bush administration, and they expressed stronger commitments to patriotic sentiments.[34] The 2003 Iraq war saw similar associations between media framing and the effect on public opinion. Preliminary tests suggest that the tone of media coverage—whether more favorable or critical of the war—may positively or negatively influence public opinion on the war.[35] Other scholars challenge this possibility, claiming that, over the long term, pre-war media coverage of issues such as weapons of mass destruction and Al Qaeda had little effect on public opinion.[36]

With very few exceptions, media scholars are not willing to concede that media influence more than what issues people think about or how they think about them.[37] Many studies probably fail to find stronger effects due to the superficial nature of their design. These studies are undertaken in laboratory, experimental-style settings. They suffer from "external validity" problems, meaning that the artificial laboratory environment where they are conducted fails to approximate the conditions confronting media consumers in the real world.[38] Social science experiments expose viewers and readers to news stories for an extremely short time; as a result, it is amazing that any effects are found at all for media coverage. Exposure to media, in these experiments, represents little more than a "snapshot in time," as it fails to approximate the day-in, day-out nature of media consumption in the real world. On issues such as Iraq, Iran, and the "war on terror," it may be that media outlets exercise tremendous control over what the public thinks, not simply through the consumption of a few stories in a single day but through long-term exposure to pro-government rhetoric and propaganda.

What is needed, then, is a simpler and more innovative approach, rooted in the regular media consumption patterns of people in the real world. Media content must be analyzed regarding specific policy issues and systematically compared to public opinion surveys in order to evaluate in which cases the media succeeds and fails in influencing what the public thinks. The symbiotic relationship between media reporting and official propaganda makes it difficult, if not impossible, to separate the effects of media and government propaganda. Evidence from the cases of Iraq and Iran demonstrate the tremendous ability of political leaders—utilizing the media as a sympathetic venue—to dominate public opinion. However, such power must be qualified, as there are strong limits to the effectiveness of propaganda over the long term. These realities are explored in detail in the next section.

PROPAGANDA EFFECTS AND REPORTING ON IRAQ AND IRAN

Media coverage of the Iraqi weapons of mass destruction fiasco was startling in its uniformity and propaganda during the run-up to the war. Previous studies found that coverage on CNN, Fox News, ABC, NBC, and CBS was systematically tilted in favor of the Bush administration's arguments during late 2002 and early 2003. National television networks included very little debate regarding the legitimacy of going to war, little coverage of the inspections process, and a strong emphasis on military planning.[39] Analysis of print coverage reveals a similar pattern. *USA Today* and the *New York Times* were heavily biased in favor of official claims that Iraq posed a national security threat, and visual images in the *New York Times* heavily emphasized military planning in the months prior to war.[40] As the most prominent national newspaper, the *New York Times*'s uncritical coverage was troublesome, with nearly 75 percent of the reports on Iraqi weapons of mass destruction containing claims that Iraq was developing or possessed weapons of mass destruction, 9 percent containing claims that Iraq did not possess such weapons, and only 14 percent balancing both positive and negative claims about weapons of mass destruction.[41]

Media and government propaganda are often one and the same. One of the best examples is the media's uncritical transmission of post-9/11 statements from the Bush administration. Consider Bush's January 2003 State of the Union speech, which represents the culmination of the administration's pre-war propaganda campaign. The public strongly reacted to the administration's pro-war statements, as many people uncritically accepted claims of an Iraq threat. An ABC-*Washington Post* poll found that 57 percent of those questioned watched Bush's 2003 State of the Union address. Three-quarters of those who saw the speech approved of Bush's pro-war messages, with 61 percent claiming that the administration effectively made the case for war. Majorities also felt that Iraq retained ties with al-Qaeda, approved of Bush's handling of the Iraq issue, favored military action against Iraq, and opposed more time for inspectors to search for weapons of mass destruction. Presidential rhetoric—as uncritically reported in the media—appears to have had a strong effect on public opinion on Iraq. Figure 8.7 demonstrates that, across the six policy questions examined, those who were exposed to the media's broadcast of the president's State of the Union address were over twice as likely to support the administration's positions, as compared to those who were not exposed to administration rhetoric.[42]

Public misperceptions of the Iraq conflict are closely related to media consumption. According to one 2003 University of Maryland study, majorities of viewers of CBS, ABC, NBC, Fox News, and CNN held at least one of three misperceptions regarding justifications for war: that Iraq possessed weapons of mass destruction, that it retained ties to al-Qaeda, or that the international community supported war. Most disturbingly, Fox News viewers who paid more attention to news on Iraq were consistently more likely to hold larger numbers of misperceptions.[43] Media outlets were eventually effective in educating viewers about the fact that Iraq had no weapons of mass destruction program and did not constitute a threat, although it was not until years after the onset of the invasion of Iraq. Those who followed media reporting on the hunt for Iraqi weapons of mass destruction, in addition to the administration's 2005 decision to stop searching for weapons in Iraq, were more likely to think that Iraq did not possess weapons prior to the 2003 invasion (see Figure 8.8). The

FIGURE 8.7: Support for War & Consumption of Presidential Propaganda

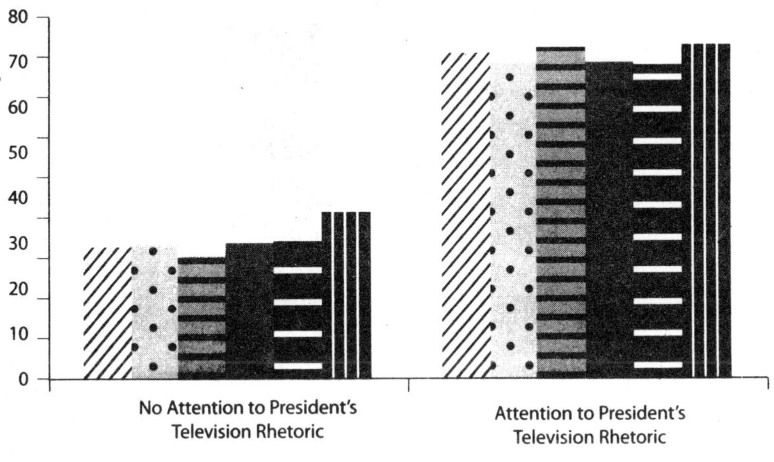

Beliefs that Iraq is tied to Al Qaeda

Support for Bush's handling of Iraq

Support for taking action against Iraq

Belief that Iraq poses a WMD threat

Support for use of ground troops

Opposition to further time for inspections

Source: University of Michigan's project, Inter-University Consortium for Political and Social Research.

media's influence in this case remains relevant in light of the fact that by 2006, 40 percent of Americans still mistakenly believed that Iraq retained weapons or a weapons program shortly before the 2003 war.[44] Such a large number of Americans would never have been so ignorant about Iraq if it were not for the propagandistic coverage seen in pre-war reporting.

Media outlets were successful in educating news audiences about the obvious following the invasion of Iraq—Iraq no longer possessed weapons of mass destruction. This assessment was evident in the "paper of record" by mid-2005, when the *New York Times* concluded that the "justifications for invading Iraq have turned out to be wrong."[45] Critical reassessments continued in following years; by December of 2008, the editors at the *Times* argued that "Mr. Bush and Vice President Dick Cheney manipulated Congress, public opinion, and anyone else they could bully or lie to" while "still acting as though [they] decided to invade Iraq after suddenly being handed life and death information on Saddam Hussein's arsenal. The truth is that Mr. Bush, Mr. Cheney, and

FIGURE 8.8: Percent of Public That Felt Iraq Possessed No WMD Prior to the Invasion

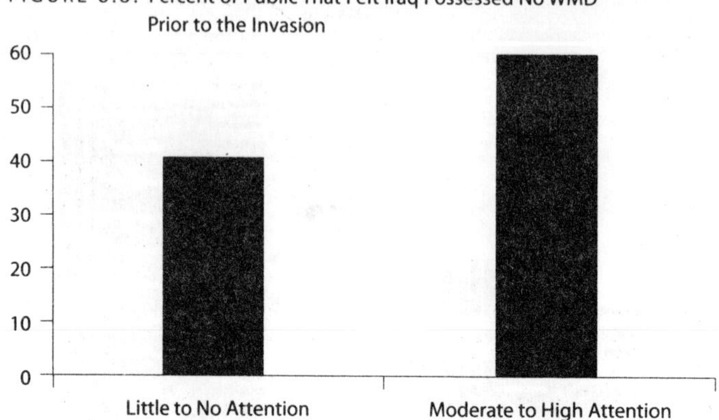

Source: University of Michigan's project, Inter-University Consortium for Political and Social Research.

Defense Secretary Donald Rumsfeld had been chafing to attack Iraq before September 11, 2001. They justified that unnecessary war using intelligence reports that they knew or should have known to be faulty."[46] Similar assessments were absent from the paper in 2002 and early 2003. Critical reporting on the questionable nature of the administration's intelligence claims would have reinforced journalistic independence from government if it appeared regularly before the war began. Instead, this after-the-fact reporting symbolized a failure to adequately inform the people at the time when it mattered most—prior to the invasion.

Similarly to the Iraq case, media exerted a powerful influence on public perceptions of an Iranian nuclear threat. As this book has demonstrated—across a wide variety of media outlets—the U.S. media uncritically report stories portraying Iran as a threat. News editors long considered it axiomatic that Iran has "no other plausible intent" other than "to produce nuclear weapons."[47]

In general, public opinion overlaps that of journalists, editors, and political leaders on the issue of Iran's "threat." By mid- to late- 2007, between 77 and 82 percent of those surveyed by CNN felt that Iran was an unfriendly, enemy state. Polls by Fox News found that from 2003 to 2006 between 57 to 68 percent of Americans felt that Iran actively maintained a nuclear weapons program.[48] CNN polls found that, from 2007 to 2009, between 68 to 78 percent thought Iran was a threat to U.S. national security.[49] Like U.S. political leaders and journalists, a majority of the public supports sanctions against Iran in order to prevent it from developing nuclear weapons.[50] Public opinion appears to be sensitive to the way U.S.-Iranian relations are framed in polling questions. When asked in CBS and Reuters polls how they feel about use of diplomacy and military attacks on Iran, between 54 and 68 percent support a diplomatic solution over a military one, while a military solution is favored by a mere 10 to 21 percent, depending on the month the question is asked. Similarly, between 70 and 76 percent oppose regime change in Iran.[51] However, support for war dramatically increases when respondents are asked if they support an attack if Iran is "close to developing a nuclear weapon" or if Iran is responsible for arming "insurgents" in Iraq to attack U.S. troops. When such belligerent language is applied to Iran, support for war jumps from between 10 and 21 percent to between 43 and 55 percent, according to NBC and CBS surveys.[52]

In February of 2006, the Pew Research Center released a report chronicling the relationship between reporting and public opinion on Iran. Iran was listed as the "greatest danger" to the United States by respondents, in front of Iraq, North Korea, China, and Russia. Furthermore, perceptions of Iran's threat increased by double digits from late 2005 through early 2007. Large numbers of Americans feel that, if Iran is allowed to develop nuclear weapons, it will undertake military attacks against Israel, the United States, and Europe. What forces were responsible for such a dramatic increase in public perceptions of Iran as a threat? What role, if any, did media outlets play in this development? The Pew study provided an answer, finding that respondents who "heard a lot" about Iran's nuclear power program in the news were more likely to view Iran as a threat than those who "heard a little" or heard "nothing at all." In addition, those who followed news coverage of Iran most closely were more likely to feel Iran would undertake a nuclear attack on Israel or give nuclear weapons to terrorists.[53]

Increased exposure to news stories about Iran and its alleged support for international terrorism are positively associated with negative feelings toward Iran. The power of media to inspire fear is represented clearly in Figure 8.9, which shows that those individuals who consume stories about Iran's nuclear program are more likely to perceive Iran as developing nuclear weapons and as a nuclear threat, when compared to those who do not follow Iran in the news.[54]

Most Americans follow the U.S. conflict with Iran to some degree. Studies by *Newsweek* and the *New York Times* suggest that approximately two-thirds of the public follow the Iranian nuclear issue "some" or "a lot" of the

FIGURE 8.9: Consumption of News on Iran

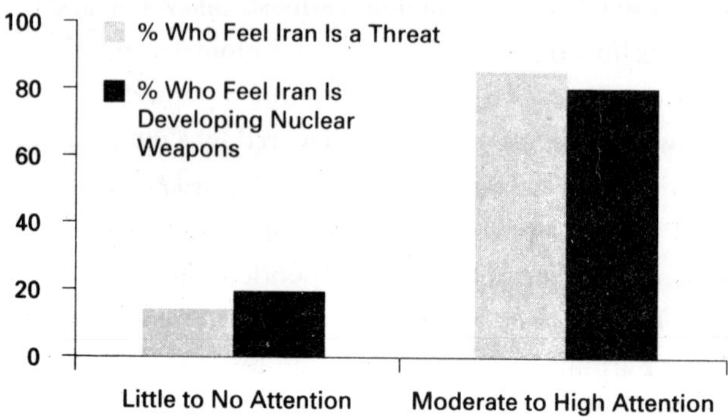

Source: University of Michigan's project, Inter-University Consortium for Political and Social Research.

time, as opposed to about one-third that pays little to no attention.[55] As Figure 8.10 indicates, viewers of MSNBC, Fox News, and CNN are all strong proponents of the belief that Iran poses a threat that requires U.S. action.

Few Americans have any experience with the issue of Iran's nuclear program excluding what they see in major newspapers and television stations. Furthermore, Fox News viewers should be no more likely than MSNBC or CNN viewers to perceive Iran as a threat. There is little evidence that any of these outlets seriously challenged the notion that Iran is building toward nuclear weapons. As earlier analysis showed, no mainstream media outlets sided with U.S. and international intelligence experts who questioned propaganda claims that Iran is developing nuclear weapons. The media's uncritical and uniform repetition of official propaganda is quite disturbing, considering that past Bush administration rhetoric on Iraq's alleged threat turned out to be flagrantly inaccurate and politicized, and international and national intelligence agencies concluded that Iran is not seeking to develop nuclear weapons and does not retain a nuclear weapons program. Journalistic manipulation of audience fears of Iran reflects poorly on a media system that is supposed to inform the public on major political issues, rather than spread misinformation.

PUBLIC INDEPENDENCE FROM THE PROPAGANDA SYSTEM

It is inaccurate to claim that the U.S. public, as a whole, is always duped by hegemonic forces and government propaganda. It is certainly the case

FIGURE 8.10: T.V. Viewers & Opinions on Iran

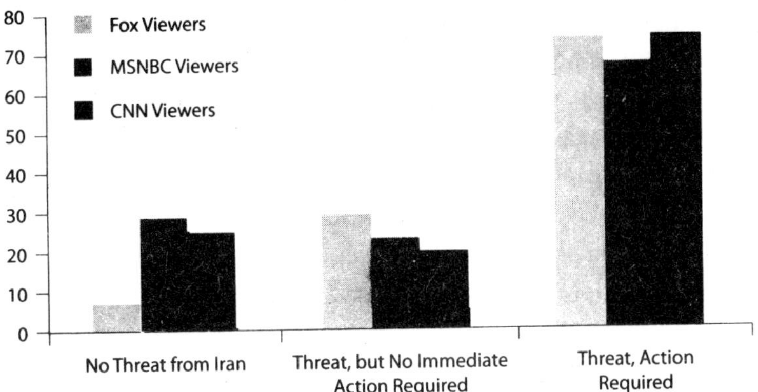

Source: University of Michigan's project, Inter-University Consortium for Political and Social Research.

that government elites manipulate media messages and the public, but the long-term effects of propaganda are more uncertain. Past scholarly attention focused on the ability of the public to formulate opinions, at least partially independently of government spin. Robert Entman speaks of "a circular process in which government officials respond to [public] polling opinions" and in which the public reacts to government actions and media reporting. Entman argues that the flow of information in society "cascades" downward from political officials to the media, and finally to the public, and that information may also flow in the reverse direction from public to media and government.[56] Other scholars argue that the public retains an important role in the policy process. They stress the limitations that elites face when they attempt to manipulate public opinion with hegemonic prowar messages.[57]

While the war against Iraq was extraordinarily popular in early to mid-2003, this soon changed as the occupation wore on. Even during the height of the war's popularity, public support was very limited in nature, only consenting to a war based upon the alleged weapons of mass destruction threat. No matter how much rhetoric about "democracy promotion" appeared in the press, the public never supported an open-ended occupation of Iraq based upon humanitarian rhetoric. Although the Iraq war was supported by approximately three-quarters of the public in early 2003, that support was based on the belief that Saddam Hussein was hiding weapons of mass destruction, not upon the need for the United States to "save" the people of Iraq. Support for war in early

2003 dropped to just 30 percent if it was shown that Iraq only retained a weapons of mass destruction program and not actual weapons. Support dropped to less than 30 percent if no weapons were found through the inspection process.[58]

Opposition to the war took shape among the general public prior to its emergence in mainstream news outlets. By 2004, three in four Americans concluded that "if Iraq did not have weapons of mass destruction or support al-Qaeda, [the] United States should not have gone to war."[59] A majority of the public opposed the war by late 2004, and active support for a withdrawal timeline exceeded the 50 percent mark by mid-2005. A statistical analysis of the withdrawal information (Figure 8.11) shows that there is little evidence that the growth in withdrawal coverage in the *New York Times* increased public opposition to the war.[60]

There is an obvious reason for the lack of a causational link between elite media reporting and antiwar sentiment. Public opposition emerged years prior to media opposition. The public pressured political officials to take the issue of withdrawal seriously, with media only later responding once political elites addressed the subject. In short, an increasingly critical public set the conditions for eventual media opposition to war, rather than the other way around.

Critical coverage of the Iraq war—defined by the number of stories on withdrawal reported in the "paper of record"—did not see its first major spike until 2005. Only after the House of Representatives first began to discuss the issue of withdrawal (see Figure 8.11) did coverage of withdrawal become more regular. After dramatically falling during the last few months of 2005, the *New York Times*'s attention to withdrawal did not significantly rise again until late 2006, when the midterm congressional election resulted in narrow majorities for the Democrats in the House and Senate. It was only by late 2006 that media attention began to seriously consider withdrawal—as reflected in the dramatic increase in monthly stories on the topic. In contrast, majority public opposition to the war as "not worth it" and public opposition to Bush's handling of the war (first appearing in 2004) materialized a full three years prior to editorial support in the *New York Times* and *Los Angeles Times* for withdrawal. [61] Using early to mid-2007 as the crucial turning point, one can conclude that the liberal media's opposition to the war drastically lagged behind public opposition.

A closer examination of media editorials finds that liberal media editors wholeheartedly supported the Iraq conflict during much of 2004 and 2005, when the general public was growing skeptical. When initial public

FIGURE 8.11: Media Coverage & Public Support for Withdrawal

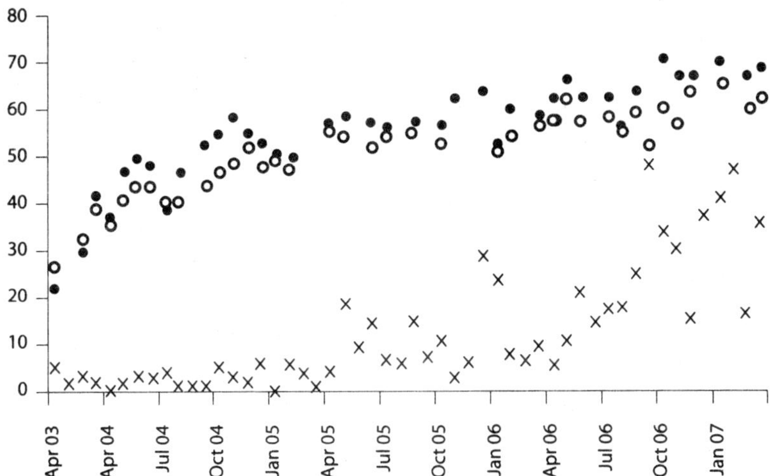

Source: Lexis Nexis, as well as from the ABC/*Washington Post* poll series from www.pollingreport.com

opposition to the war emerged in late 2004, the editors of the *New York Times* supported a change in management of the conflict in favor of Democratic presidential candidate John Kerry. Kerry, they argued, needed to "assure the public that Iraq can be stabilized and moved toward a semblance of democratic government, and that American troops will stay until that happens. That job will be tougher, bloodier, and more expensive than either candidate has been willing to admit."[62] When public support for a timetable materialized in mid-2005, the editors at the *New York Times* framed the conflict as "difficult but winnable," while again criticizing Bush for his refusal "to seize the moment to tell the nation how he will define victory, and to give Americans a specific sense of how he intends to reach that goal." The *Times* explicitly warned against a timetable at this point, postulating that "if American forces were withdrawn, Iraq would probably sink into a civil war."[63]

Public independence from elite media discourse is also evident in the case of propaganda celebrations of the death of al-Qaeda's Abu Musab al-Zarqawi in Iraq. Media outlets were cautiously optimistic in reporting Zarqawi's death from a U.S. bombing raid. Prominent magazines including *Time* and *Newsweek* spoke of Zarqawi's death as possibly setting the stage for "reconciliation" in Iraq (considering al-Qaeda's key role in encouraging civil war between Iraq's Shia and Sunni Muslims), and also warning that continued patience would be required before the occupation could be fully successful.[64] The editors of the *New York Times* and *Washington Post* framed Zarqawi's death as "good news for Washington" and "a big gain for the United States mission in Iraq," while anchors at CNN and Fox News speculated that although Zarqawi's fall may not end all the violence in Iraq, it could mark a major turning point in the decline of the "insurgency."[65]

Most Americans were not taking the media's restrained celebrations seriously. Whereas 82 percent of Americans admitted to paying "some" or "a lot" of attention to Zarqawi's death, less than a third felt his death would make Iraq more stable, and over twice as many felt the violence would continue at similar levels or even increase. Only 16 percent felt his death would be followed by a decrease in sectarian killings; 79 percent felt the killings would continue at the same levels or increase. Of course, celebratory media coverage of Zarqawi's death was not an entire waste: the small minority of the public that followed the story was statistically more likely to accept government promises that Iraqi violence would decrease and to accept the notion that the United States is stabilizing Iraq.[66]

In a third and final example, public independence from media and government propaganda is seen in the 2007 troop surge, which was celebrated in both the liberal and conservative parts of the mainstream press for effectively reducing violence in Iraq.[67] Again, most of the American public rejected this celebration. When questioned in early 2007, 67 percent of Americans opposed the troop surge, and only 29 percent lent their support. Only 24 percent supported an increase in troops; 14 percent supported a continuation of pre-surge troop levels; and 55 percent favored a reduction or full withdrawal. By May 2007 (four months into the surge), 75 percent of those surveyed concluded that the surge did not improve Iraqi security and possibly even worsened it, with only 25 percent claiming that security improved. Only a small minority of the public accepted the Bush administration's promises that the surge would reduce Iraq's violence. Although nearly half of Americans reported viewing Bush's January 2007 troop surge speech, those who were exposed to the speech were statistically no more likely to lend their support to the surge and to an increase in troops, when compared to those who were not exposed to the speech.[68] Although presidential rhetoric was extremely effective in 2001 through 2003 in convincing Americans of the need for war in Afghanistan and Iraq, from 2004 through 2007 the public grew tired of the administration's rhetoric and promises. The president's speeches were no longer very effective in convincing Americans of the need to "stay the course" in Iraq.

The evidence in this section indicates that the effects of media and government propaganda are potentially powerful in the short term but limited over longer periods of time. Members of the mass public reject official spin when it conflicts with their own experiences. The media play an important role in fostering opposition to the war in the sense that the public follows negative developments in Iraq as read or seen in news reports. However, this media effect is not intentional. Editors and journalists never explicitly encouraged mass opposition to the war from 2003 through 2006, when news organizations overwhelmingly supported the conflict, and the public turned against it.

PUBLIC OPINION POLLING AS PROPAGANDA

Up until this point, the focus of this chapter has been on the role of the government and media in influencing and manipulating public opinion. But some crucial actors have been left out—specifically public opinion analysts and polling organizations themselves. Scholars and pollsters—often working for media outlets—play an enormously important role in constructing public opinion in ways that fit with journalists' and academics' ideological predispositions. Polling organizations do not simply "objectively" measure public attitudes; they also mold our understandings of them. Extensive attention in some academic works is devoted to discussing how prominent social actors "construct" public opinion.[69] Justin Lewis speaks of polls as "ideological instruments," warning that it is "the questioner who establishes the framework [for surveys] and sets the parameters for each question. . . . The discourse of public opinion is thus constructed from a particular set of perspectives, while the process of polling is hidden behind the data it produces."[70] Elite domination of polling tends to favor accepted doctrines over nontraditional ones. As Benjamin Ginsberg argues:

> Polls generally raise questions that are of interest to clients and purchasers of poll data—newspapers, political candidates, governmental agencies, business corpo-

> rations. . . . . Questions of no immediate relevance to government, business, or politicians will not easily find their way into the surveys. This is particularly true of issues such as the validity of the capitalist economic system, or the legitimacy of governmental authority, issues that business and government prefer not to see raised at all, much less at their own expense.[71]

Most public opinion polls conducted by professional firms and media outlets question how the public thinks the Iraq war is progressing and whether the public feels the war is a "mistake," "not worth it," or "unwinnable." Many questions only generally ask whether audiences favor or oppose the war, whether going to war was the "right thing," whether the public supports withdrawal, or whether the public approves of presidential performance.[72] Rarely are critical questions, such as whether the administration "intentionally misled" the public about Iraqi weapons of mass destruction, asked in surveys.[73] Questions probing whether the public thinks the war was undertaken for domination of oil, whether Americans are concerned with Iraqi civilian casualties resulting from American attacks, or whether the public sees the conflict as fundamentally wrong and immoral, rather than just a mistake or unwinnable, are overwhelmingly ignored in surveys.[74]

In accord with the expectations of the propaganda model, scholars are generally concerned with assessing pragmatic criticisms of the war that fall within the bipartisan range of views, and not with addressing moral challenges to American foreign policy. The prevailing approach in scholarship is to discuss opposition to war as a function of perceptions that the United States has failed to achieve strategic objectives. Essentially, public hostility to war is seen *primarily* as a result of the U.S. failure to "win."[75] Scholarship is strongly centered on how elite values and actions influence mass opinion, rather than on how and when the general public rejects elite propaganda.[76]

There is ample evidence that the public rejects many of the foundations of U.S. foreign policy. Although both liberal and conservative wings of the mainstream press assume that it is the United States' right to intervene in any country, at any time, for any reason, most Americans reject this imperial role. As one of the few polling organizations concerned with issues of substantive public dissent, the Program on International Policy Attitudes (PIPA) of the University of Maryland finds that most Americans oppose the United States' militaristic dominance of the world. "Americans express surprisingly modest concern for preserving the

United States' role as the [world's] sole superpower."[77] Contrary to the view that the public is consumed with "winning" in Iraq, one study suggests that as little as one-third of Americans are bothered "a great deal" if the United States was to "lose" in Iraq, with majorities not being bothered by this prospect.[78] Furthermore, a majority of Americans reject the continued projection of U.S. power in Iraq over the long term. In contrast to the Democratic and Republican parties, which support keeping permanent military bases in Iraq, most Americans reject permanent bases by a ratio of more than two to one.[79]

Perhaps the most powerful challenge to American power is witnessed in public opposition to using military power to "promote democracy." Most Americans reject this premise for using force, although it receives bipartisan support from political leaders and from liberal and conservative media. When asked in 2005 and 2006, between 64 and 66 percent of Americans explained that "the goal of overthrowing Iraq's authoritarian government and establishing democracy was not a good enough reason to go to war." Furthermore, the Bush administration's use of deception regarding weapons of mass destruction further turned off the public to "democratic" pretexts for war. Seventy-two percent of Americans indicated that "the [American] experience [in Iraq] has made them feel worse about the possibility of using military force to bring about democracy in the future."[80] Though the questions in this survey failed to distinguish between whether force *should* be used to promote democracy and whether force *can* be used to impose democracy, the findings remain a serious challenge to U.S. officials because they demonstrate that most Americans are not swayed by high-minded rhetoric of American altruism and benefaction.

My Midwest survey provides additional insights into public rejection of academic, media, and government propaganda. The critical perspectives expressed in this survey demonstrate that antiwar opposition extends beyond parochial concerns with victory and defeat. When respondents were asked to rank the explanations for war in Iraq, they were provided with four possible explanations for the continued occupation: the need to fight terrorism, the need to prevent civil war, the need to promote democracy, and the need to ensure American control over oil. Although the odds were stacked against the selfish reasons for war by a three-to-one ratio, the most common response provided for the war was interest in Iraqi oil. Fifty-five percent of those surveyed indicated that oil was the "most important reason" for the Iraq war, as compared to 22 percent who cited democracy promotion, 16 percent who claimed fighting terrorism, and only 8 percent who cited preventing civil war. These findings are of extraordinary importance, considering the media's refusal to seriously discuss oil interests in any significant way in stories on Iraq. As discussed in chapter 2, stories in the *New York Times* on withdrawal from 2005 to 2007 failed to cite U.S. interest in oil even a single time as a reason to oppose the war, whereas claims that the United States needs to fight terrorism and prevent civil war appeared in 24 percent and 18 percent of stories respectively.

In the Midwest survey, many respondents reject arguments that the United States is in Iraq simply to fight terrorism. A common conclusion is that al-Qaeda did not operate in Saddam Hussein's Iraq in the pre-war period, and that it was only after the United States occupation began that the group became active in the country. Promises that the United States is preventing civil war are often rejected, as long-term occupations are seen as contributing to rather than reducing violence. Promises to "promote democracy" are also questioned, often because democracy is seen as emerging from within countries themselves, rather than as something that is imposed from the outside. Interest in oil is accepted by many of those surveyed as the main reason for the conflict. This is quite an insightful reflection on the part of the public, in light of the long policy planning record—discussed in chapter 6—of U.S. officials' concern with controlling Middle Eastern oil through military force.

A brief sample of the midwesterners' thoughts on the motivations for war:

- I think American [desire for] oil in Iraq is the best explanation [for war] because: 1. The reasons given before the invasion (weapons of mass destruction, connections to al-Qaeda) were proven false; 2. Many oil companies have profited from the war; and 3. Historically, the United States government has involved itself in the Middle East because of oil and has admitted so.

- The reason the United States remains in Iraq is to keep their hands near the goods. To keep those in charge wealthy with their "friendly" contracts. If the United States truly wanted out, Iraqi civil war would concern our leaders relatively little.

- The need to ensure American access to oil is the most honest factor for our motives in Iraq. Although most Americans wouldn't agree with this reason as a means to go to war, this was the greatest

> factor for policymakers. As a country, we have selfish motivations which overpower any humanitarian efforts of need for action.

Public views of the war's illegitimacy extend beyond critiques of oil politics. By a margin of three and a half to one, midwestern respondents feel the Iraq war is "fundamentally wrong and immoral" rather than "humanitarian in its goal and mission."[81] Media outlets and polling groups systematically fail to examine the public's opinion on the war's immorality. These organizations are more interested in tracking whether the war is "going badly," if it is "bringing stability" to Iraq, if the invasion was a "mistake" or "worth fighting," and how well presidents are "handling" the conflict.[82] If these organizations bothered to explore public perceptions of the war's immorality, they would likely discover many insights. Some of these insights are reflected in the comments of midwestern respondents:

- Iraq was invaded because of oil and to establish a base in the Middle East. This is because America is the only superpower and using the same tactic the British used to construct colonies in other countries who do not consent to their policy.

- We should not intervene in other countries' problems unless they pose a direct threat to the United States' civilian lives and our government. Many other countries around the world hate America for what we have already done.

- The war in Iraq is fundamentally wrong and immoral because the United States is over there for the wrong reasons. The United States doesn't care about Iraq's problems but only about getting what they want, which is Iraqi oil. I feel that the United States is creating more harm the longer they are over in Iraq.

- Although the rhetoric from the media and government seems to favor [war in] Iraq as both humanitarian and heroic, there is no ounce of humanitarianism coming from this war. Many people seek to justify immoral and selfish actions through glorification and positive rhetoric, but those who actually stop to look at what's coming out of the United States' occupation of Iraq know that there are more dire situations in the world to "promote democracy" and expand humanitarianism (in Darfur, and most of the developing world).

In challenging the hegemonic system, the public also opposes war due to concern for the victims of the occupation. This sustained interest runs directly contrary to media reporting, which fails to make the victims of the occupation a serious concern. Media disdain for those killed by the United States was analyzed at length in chapter 3. Further evidence reinforces the findings from that chapter. For example, in the case of Iraq, U.S. casualties receive three times the attention of Iraqi civilian casualties in the headlines of the *New York Times*.[83] The American public, however, appears to harbor no such prejudice for privileging U.S. over Iraqi casualties. When asked about their level of concern for casualties, 78 percent and 87 percent of midwesterners surveyed indicated that they were either somewhat or strongly concerned with Iraqi and American casualties respectively. Similarly, 84 percent of respondents indicated interest in learning more about both U.S. and Iraqi casualties.

Many midwestern respondents, however, admitted their ignorance of Iraqi casualties. They conceded the following: 1) Until they were informed (in the survey) that perhaps over one million Iraqis died during the occupation, they knew very little about the extent of Iraqi deaths; 2) They knew very little about who was responsible (the United States, "insurgents," or sectarian militias) for these deaths; and 3) They felt that the media did a poor job of educating them about this topic of great concern. Some of the responses from those surveyed are instructive:

- I feel that the media does not report on Iraqi casualties as much as they should. Perhaps more Americans would feel differently about the war, and more important, about invading other countries in the future, if they saw the effects of it.

- They [the Iraqis] have already lost over 1 million lives. They are on the verge of a civil war and our occupation has only caused more confusion, hardship, and promoted terrorism against us.... [Casualty estimates of 4,000 Americans killed and over 1 million Iraqis killed] show Americans back at home why so many countries hate us. We act brutally and harshly. There is over a 1:250 kill-death ratio. It isn't the liberation of a country needing help, it is a slaughter.

- This is sad [Iraqi casualty estimates] because the whole world looks at the United States as warmongers. The American people are paying a heavy price for the policy of this administration. This government doesn't seem to care about our soldiers getting killed, how are they going to care about others?

- It makes no sense that we went in to overthrow a hostile dictator and to promote democracy and as a result have killed over a million of the people we were supposedly trying to help. How much democracy can be promoted when we are dropping cluster bombs that are killing innocent men, women, and children?

- I find [Iraqi deaths] very concerning because this large number wouldn't happen if we were not there in the first place. Many innocent civilians have been killed from battles between us and the Iraqis. Also, the number [of deaths] includes the number of people getting killed at their work from car bombs and suicide bombers. That state of unrest got terrible once the United States began to occupy Iraq. . . . I am interested to know which of the Iraqi casualties were at the hands of American attacks and which were caused by civil war between Iraqis. I also would like to learn about the number of Iraqi casualties that happened in civil war strife before the American occupation of Iraq.

The final respondent's comments are particularly revealing. They demonstrate the lack of knowledge of many Americans regarding Iraqi deaths from civil war. Mass death through sectarian violence was not a significant part of Iraqi life prior to the invasion, but this basic point is obscured in a media system that is disinterested in accurately reporting on Iraqi casualties. As a result, many Americans are left without any broader, overarching framework to help them assess American responsibility for the onset of civil war.

LESSONS FROM THE STUDY OF PUBLIC OPINION AND WAR

Political attentiveness, formal education, and news consumption play a vital role in strengthening ties between elites in the general public and political officials. Although media play an instrumental role in influencing public opinion, their effects are not always long-lasting. The public often rejects much of the propaganda disseminated by political and media elites in the long run. Humanitarian justifications for war are dismissed, as are reasons provided for why the United States should remain in Iraq. In the end, the public does not appear to be as incompetent or as incapable as is commonly assumed by academics and political officials. The mass public is capable of forming views independently of elites, and this reality offers hope for democracy at a time when the control of political information is so thoroughly dominated by official sources.

Americans are strongly influenced by mass media and political propaganda during times of war. Depictions of dire threats to national security, coupled with nationalistic pressures to "fall in line" in support of war, effectively create an environment that is supportive of military intervention. These factors, however, are far more effective in the shortterm and much weaker over the longterm. As conflicts wear on, calls to patriotism become a less effective tool for justifying extended involvement. In the case of Iraq, Americans look with suspicious eyes at the failure to find weapons of mass destruction, the manufactured ties between Saddam Hussein and al-Qaeda, the escalating cost of the conflict in monetary resources and human lives, and at scandals such as Abu Ghraib. They remember political leaders' past deceptions, tracing back to the Vietnam War and Watergate era.

Many Americans feel disillusioned and apathetic due to their inability to trust political representatives. Their response, unfortunately, is often to withdraw from the larger political system. Voting is increasingly viewed as the ideal form of political participation (if people vote at all), rather than a bare minimum requirement for the active, civic-minded citizen. Increased cynicism is a double-edged sword. On the one hand, distrust of officials is seen as a basic prerequisite of grassroots democracy for social movements that emerge to demand better representation from unaccountable political leaders. On the other hand, suspicion of one's elected officials also turns off citizens from participating. The goal of activists is always to ensure that skeptical Americans follow the active path, rather than falling into complacency and ignorance.

CHAPTER NINE

Propaganda, Celebrity Gossip, and the Decline of News

This book has examined the prominence of propaganda in the reporting of the United States' conflicts with Afghanistan, Iraq, and Iran. The media systematically marginalizes oppositional voices that reside outside the bipartisan range of opinions. A major component of media propaganda is the neglect of dissent. Intellectuals in the United States often serve the purpose of ideologically justifying the media's continued reliance on official sources. Their defense of government spin is justified through lofty rhetoric proclaiming the U.S. commitment to democracy and human rights abroad. The allegedly superior wisdom of political leaders, in addition to their "need" to mold public opinion through propaganda, is reinforced in media discourse. Such paternalistic assumptions are not loudly proclaimed by journalists and intellectuals, but they are quietly accepted without second thought.

Academic disciplines typically serve concentrated power—either by refusing to challenge the status quo or by explicitly defending the bipartisan spectrum of opinions that drive U.S. politics. The promotion of state propaganda by intellectuals received early support from the nascent public relations (PR) industry. Journalist Edward Bernays played an instrumental role in the use of applied propaganda in convincing the public of the need to enter into the First World War. Bernays worked as an advisor for the Committee on Public Information, a government agency created by executive order from President Woodrow Wilson. The committee, in coordination with the Wilson administration, suppressed the antiwar movement, monitored any groups questioning the war, and condemned them as unpatriotic traitors.

Bernays played an instrumental role in the emergence of public relations. He applied "scientific" data of dubious quality in his efforts to sell the consumption of tobacco to the public, working for the firm Liggett and Myers selling Chesterfield cigarettes. The company, with the help of PR strategies, successfully strengthened its female consumer base with market slogans such as "Cigarettes Are Kind to Your Throat" and "Cigarettes Keep You Thin." Bernays articulated his contempt for the public during his years in the PR industry. His pro-business propaganda relied on the arousal of popular emotional responses, despite the harm to the public by the products advertised. In the case of the cigarette public relations campaign, he recruited young upper-class women to appear in New York's Easter Parade, enthusiastically displaying their cigarettes as "torch[es] of liberty" for public onlookers.[1] Cigarette consumption, then, was equated with women's freedom specifically, and American freedom more generally.

Bernays had much to say about the role of elite manipulation of media and public opinion in a democratic society. In his classic work *Propaganda*, Bernays argued that "the conscious and intelligent manipulation of the organized habits and opinions of the masses is an important element in democratic society. Those who manipulate this unseen mechanism of society constitute an invisible government which is the true ruling power of our country." Intellectuals, Bernays claimed, should reject "the dogma that the voice of the people is the voice of God." Rather, political and economic leaders best "understand the mental processes and social patterns of the masses. It is they who pull the wires which control the public mind." There remains a special role for media, Bernays admitted, in efforts to "mold the minds of the masses." The "manipulation of news" by powerful political and business elites is enabled by corporate ownership of media. Corporate ownership translates into tremendous business power over the major means of societal communication. "Business realize[s] that its relationship to the public is not confined to the manufacture and sale of a given product, but includes the same selling of itself and of all those things for which it stands in the public mind."

Unlike many academics and reporters, Bernays did not try to create an artificial distinction between business ownership of media on the one hand and "objective" reporting of the news on the other. He understood that "the growth of newspapers and magazines" was inherently tied to media content through "the art of the modern advertising expert in making the printed message attractive and persuasive." "Big business"—of which the corporate media is an integral part—"is increasingly availing itself of the services of the specialist in public relations . . . as big business becomes bigger the need for expert manipulation of its innumerable contacts with the public will become greater."[2]

Bernays's contempt for public opinion was shared by many others. Working for the Committee on Public Information alongside Bernays, respected journalist and intellectual Walter Lippmann also spoke with hostility about citizen-based, grassroots democracy: "The common interests [of the country] very largely elude public opinion entirely," with "a fairly large percentage" of the people "bound to agree [on policy issues] without having taken the time, or without possessing the background for appreciating the choices which the leader presents to them." As a result, the public is dependent on elites to "manufacture" the consent of the people. Political and business elites can be trusted to promote the common good and to resist erratic popular impulses of a public that often acts as a "bewildered herd."[3]

By the 1940s, influential political scientist Harold Lasswell spoke specifically of the prominence of the "propagandists of plutocracy"—those wealthy elites who exercise disproportionate control of communication in democratic societies. Any social elite "defends and asserts itself" by relying on manipulation; "when elites resort to propaganda, the tactical problem is to select symbols and channels capable of eliciting the desired concerted acts."[4] Elite manipulation is essential for the good of the masses, Lasswell concluded, since "men are often poor judges of their own interests, flirting from one alternative to the next without solid reason."[5]

Distrust of democracy was never restricted to the early years of the twentieth century. Major political figures and academics echoed this distrust in the post–Second World War period as well. Cold War founder and State Department policymaker George F. Kennan spoke at length about the "the good deal of trouble [that] seems to have stemmed from the extent to which the executive [branch] has felt itself beholden to short-term trends of public opinion in the country." Kennan condemned "the erratic and subjective nature of public reaction to foreign policy questions. . . . I think the record indicates that in the short term our public opinion. . . . can be easily led astray into areas of emotionalism and subjectivity which make it a poor and inadequate guide for national action."[6]

Former National Security Council planner, presidential advisor, and political scientist Samuel Huntington defines legitimate citizen participation in a democracy as limited to formal activities such as voting. Huntington disavows mass mobilization as harmful to democratic modernization, viewing it as a threat that needs to be "moderated."[7] Distrust of mass mobilization is reflected in Huntington's writings on U.S. social movements of the 1960s. He warned against a public that became "ungovernable," due to its protests and direct challenges to government authority. In an age of public distrust of officials, "doubts about the political and economic solvency" of government are accompanied by a "decay of [the] American party system." The "excess" of direct democratic participation in the streets needs to be limited, since "the effective operation of a democratic political system usually requires some measure of apathy and noninvolvement on the part of some individuals and groups." Apathy and noninvolvement "allow democracy to function efficiently," since excess participation produces a "danger of overloading the political system with demands."[8] As discussed in chapter 7, most U.S. officials express a strong distrust of the public's ability to make wise decisions regarding public policy.

Political contempt is not restrained to the public. This book explored at length the Bush administration's contempt for media independence from government (chapter 4). The administration long viewed the public and journalists as passive mediums to be manipulated at will by America's enlightened and benevolent Republican leadership structure. For the most part, modern-day academics, intellectuals, and political leaders do not express their distrust of the public openly, or for that matter their lack of concern with the public's moral challenges to the Iraq war. An effective propaganda system could never be effective if it so recklessly conceded legitimacy to the thoughts and feelings of the mass public. Rather, government, media, and academic propaganda function most efficiently, as Herman and Chomsky conclude, by assuming the moral righteousness of the ruling parties' views without ever questioning their moral foundations. Academics, journalists, and political leaders express their contempt for the public every time they refuse to consider the public's reasons for morally opposing war. When the media ignore public challenges to official war rhetoric, they express a *tacit* commitment to propaganda. When the media refuses to acknowledge criticisms of U.S. imperialism, its coverage deserves to be labeled propagandistic.

Fortunately, the general public is resilient in resisting elite efforts to "manufacture consent" and marginalize dissidents. Although propaganda retains tremendous power in the short term, its effects are often skin deep in the long term (chapters 7 and 8). The public rejects the reasons for continuing the Iraq war given by the two major parties, and it also transcends the Democrats' parochial "antiwar" criticisms. We should be careful, however, not to underestimate the power of the media in "engineering consent"—in the words of Bernays—by diversion of public attention from political issues.[9]

MANUFACTURING CONSENT THROUGH ENTERTAINMENT MEDIA

In relying heavily on celebrity news, corporate media effectively divert attention from critical political issues. Edward Herman and Noam Chomsky maintain that "the mass media are interested in attracting audiences with buying power. . . . It is affluent audiences that spark advertiser interest today." "Large corporate advertisers," they claim, "will rarely sponsor programs that engage in serious criticisms of corporate activities, such as the problem of environmental degradation, the workings of the military-industrial complex, or corporate support of and benefits from Third World [pro-capitalist] tyrannies."[10] Many studies demonstrate that advertisers exert strong pressure over journalists and editors in their reporting of economic issues.[11] The influence of corporate ownership on foreign policy reporting is strong. As chapter 6 demonstrated, papers owned by multinational media corporations report the occupation of Iraq more sympathetically than non-conglomerated papers.

Chomsky argues that corporate ownership of the mass media carries with it dire implications for a democracy that is based on citizen participation and consent. Aside from the elite media, Chomsky describes other media:

> whose basic social role is quite different. It's diversion. There's the real mass media, the kinds that are aimed at Joe Six-Pack. The purpose of those media is to dull people's brains. . . . The goal for corporations is to maximize profit and market share, and they also have a goal for the population. They have to be turned

> into completely mindless consumers of goods. . . . You have to develop what are called "created wants." . . . You have to focus them on the insignificant things of life like fashionable consumption. The ideal is to have individuals who are totally disassociated from one another, whose conception of themselves, their sense of value is just, "how many created wants can I satisfy?"[12]

Much of the public is expected to fulfill the role of uncritical consumers, rather than active participants in the political process. This role is fulfilled in great part through the dramatic decline in reporting on foreign policy issues, motivated by media corporations that are interested in increasing their profit margins. The public is also pacified through the media's top-down transmission of celebrity news and gossip, at the expense of traditional news stories that focus on politics, economics, and other issues of importance.

Changing macroeconomic conditions make it more difficult for the public to critically educate itself on political issues. Income levels for the average worker have declined in an era of outsourcing and downsizing. The majority of workers are forced to work longer hours simply to make ends meet, with middle-class families increasingly reliant on two income earners.[13] Student loan debt has increased, as workers find themselves in need of college degrees to make incomes similar to those of high school graduates decades ago. Workers endure increased job insecurity and decreased pay due to the corporate assault on labor unions. Union membership has declined, as a result of outsourcing, de-industrialization, and business attacks on unions from a high of over 30 percent of the workforce in the 1950s to less than 15 percent by the beginning of the twenty-first century.[14] An increasing disparity in occupational earnings characterizes the post-industrial economy, where workers are polarized between high-paying, high-skilled occupations needed to service global cities and lower-paying, lower-skilled service jobs.[15] As a result of declining wages, many are forced to take on second jobs, while families send both parents into the workforce to get by. At the same time, corporate advertisers and public relations specialists convince many consumers that they need bigger cars and homes, and more consumer products, to live the "good life." Unsurprisingly, credit card debt has grown dramatically, in light of increased wants, economic recession, and declining wages.[16]

In this increasingly unstable environment, many people feel there is little time to understand complex political issues. The mass media do little to assist them in becoming politically informed. One respondent from my

Midwest survey explains her difficulty in following foreign policy in terms of increased pressures from major shifts in the economy: "I am interested in the issue [of Iraq]. It's just that the problem is so massive that I can't even begin to wrap my head around it. With a daughter to take care of, working full-time, and while trying to go to school, I just don't have the time to read about this problem." This respondent is just one of the millions of Americans who are forced to work full-time, along with their spouses, to earn enough money to maintain a decent standard of living. In a country where worker insecurity is growing and corporations convince the public of the need to run up greater consumer debt to purchase "necessary" products, it is no wonder that many have little time to consistently follow political issues. Increased worker insecurity is a vital precondition for the marginalization of the public. Media attempts to divert the public from considering matters of public policy are also vital to this process.

The rise of celebrity news is enabled by a corresponding decline in coverage of news with substance. Estimates from within the mainstream media itself find that coverage of foreign news declined by between 70 to 80 percent in the fifteen to twenty years prior to 2001. The *Los Angeles Times* reflects:

> The amount of time that network television devotes to international news shrank from 45 percent of total coverage in the 1970s to 13.5 percent in 1995—a decline of more than 70 percent—according to a 1997 study by Harvard University. The *Tyndall Report*, which monitors the content of network news shows, says ABC, CBS and NBC combined carried only 1,382 minutes of news from their foreign bureaus last year, a plunge of more than 65 percent from 1989.[17]

The decline in foreign news continues following the turn of the millennium. By early 2007, the *Boston Globe* announced plans to close its remaining three foreign news bureaus, located in Europe, Latin America, and the Middle East, after three decades of service. Similarly, the *Baltimore Sun* declared plans to eliminate its South African and Russian bureaus, following the closure of its other bureaus in China and the United Kingdom. *Washington Post* editor Fred Hiatt decries the closure of bureaus and the "vanishing foreign correspondent" at a time when the total number of U.S. foreign correspondents dropped by 25 percent from 188 in 2002 to 141 in 2006.[18]

The decline of foreign news is protested at times by journalists. Richard Leibner of CBS News highlights the negative effects of this decline as follows:

> The less people know about the things they need to know, the less they will make informed choices when it comes to what they want to know. Before 9/11, for example, how many people would have said that they wanted to know more about places like Afghanistan or Iraq? And you find yourself asking whether we would have approached things differently in either or both of those countries if the American public had known more about them.[19]

Some scholars defend the marginalization of foreign news by arguing that this trend is preferred by the public. Doris Graber argues, "When asked, Americans themselves profess modest interest in foreign news, but when given a choice, they do not seek it out. . . . In a fifteen-year survey of attention to major news stories, reports about international events ranked dead last among stories that people claimed to follow 'very closely.'"[20]

Recent evidence suggests that the public retains strong, rather than moderate interest in many foreign issues, including immigration, trade negotiations, environmental issues, drug-trafficking, and transnational crime issues, among other areas.[21] Evidence following 9/11 suggests that the U.S. public recognizes that it can no longer be ignorant on matters of foreign policy. Newspaper readership grew significantly following the terrorist attacks, and 46 percent of those surveyed indicated that the attacks "made them more interested in politics and political news"—an increase of 7 percent from November 2001 to February 2002. Following 9/11, nearly 70 percent of Americans followed news about terrorism in the United States "very closely."[22] By 2004, over 40 percent also listed foreign policy issues such as the Iraq war and terrorism as very important, as compared to domestic issues such as the economy and unemployment, which less than 26 percent viewed as very important. Public attention to foreign news remained at relatively high levels in 2002 and 2003 during the run-up to, and occupation of Iraq. Half of Americans reported following the conflict "very closely" in this period, with 40 percent paying very close attention by 2004.[23] Even when public attention to foreign news is relatively low, such consumption must be compared to attention to other types of news, rather than simply examined by itself. Studies from the Pew Research Center find that, relative to other stories, coverage of Iraq tops the list of issues to which the public pays attention in any given week or month. The Iraq war, for example, is regularly followed more closely than stories on celebrity gossip and stories on domestic political issues such as the 2008 election, school shootings, immigration policies, the stock market, and environmental disasters.[24]

To claim that Americans are not interested in foreign policy issues or that they do not follow them in the news is misleading. It is more accurate to argue that Americans are de-politicized when it comes to *both* domestic and foreign policy issues, considering that those who closely follow specific events in both issue areas often do not amount to more than 20 percent of the entire public. Only about one in four people, for example, report following national news closely, suggesting that the lack of attention to news extends beyond foreign policy issues.[25] The de-politicization of the public can be explained, in part, by the growth of celebrity news and the decline of reporting on political issues. Though there are limits to how much celebrity news the public will consume, the growth of such stories no doubt directs societal attention away from pressing political issues. Celebrity news, oftentimes referred to as "junk food" or "fluff" news, is relatively inexpensive to produce compared to more costly foreign news stories. Media corporations looking to increase their profits view these stories enthusiastically—especially cable news outlets that are required to fit 24-hour time slots. Although declining, the audience for cable news programs remains significant, with an estimated 2.5 million viewers tuning in for prime time programming as of 2007, and nearly 40 percent of Americans claiming they regularly watch cable news.[26]

Americans are often critical about the growth of celebrity junk food news. When asked what type of story media give "too much attention to," celebrity news and "Hollywood gossip" top the list, ahead of the Iraq war, coverage of political issues and politicians, the presidential campaign, crime and violence, health care, and sports.[27] It is easy to see why the public is concerned with the dangers of celebrity news, considering its growing prominence. Table 9.1 demonstrates that, on any given week, junk food news stories receive significant attention and compete with political news stories. Stories such as the death of starlet Anna Nicole Smith, the Eliot Spitzer (former New York governor) prostitute scandal, the arrest of O. J. Simpson, and the death of Michael Jackson receive strong coverage from news outlets that are happy to fill large time slots with low-cost programming.

Anna Nicole Smith's death was one of the top ten most covered stories from February 4 to March 2, 2007, and it became a top-ten story again during the week of March 25. Despite continued United States conflicts with Iran, Iraq, Afghanistan, and Pakistan, and important political issues at home during the 2008 election, the Anna Nicole Smith story ranked as the eighth most covered story in the first quarter of 2007. Six

TABLE 9.1: Media Coverage of Celebrity News & Traditional News Stories (% of Total News Coverage Allocated to Each Story)

Story (Feb '07)	%	Story (Mar '08)	%	Story (Sept '07)	%	Story (Jul '09)	%
Iraq	22%	2008 Election	27%	O.J. Simpson's Arrest	13%	Michael Jackson's Death	17%
Anna N. Smith	9%	Eliot Spitzer Scandal	23%	Iraq Conflict	10%	Economy	11%
2008 Election	8%	Stock Market Problems	6%	2008 Election	9%	Obama in Russia/Italy	11%
Astronaut Murderer	6%	Iraq	4%	Jena Six Conflict	5%	Sarah Palin's Resignation	7%
Winter Weather	3%	Bottled Water Scandal	3%	Iraq Policy Debate	5%	Health Care Reform	6%
Superbowl	3%	UNC Student Shooting	1%	Mukasey's Nomination	4%	Riots in China	4%

Source: Pew Research Center

percent of all coverage in newspapers, network TV, cable TV, radio, and Internet was devoted to Anna Nicole in the week following her death, and 20 percent of cable news focused on the death. Smith's death accounted for an astounding 50 percent of cable news coverage in the two days (February 8 and 9) following her death.[28]

Serious repercussions follow from the media's reliance on celebrity fluff. Consumers think much more about celebrities, and less about political issues, when they are saturated with such coverage. In the case of Anna Nicole Smith, 38 percent of Americans listed her as the person they "heard the most about in the news lately" when asked in the week of February 12, 2007. This represents a dramatic contrast with recognition of political leaders during the same week, as a combined 35 percent of respondents listed George Bush, Hillary Clinton, Barack Obama, and Nancy Pelosi as the people they "heard the most about in the news."[29] Similarly, during the third week of September 2007 O. J. Simpson and Britney Spears were listed by 38 percent of Americans as the people they heard most about, in comparison to George Bush, Hillary Clinton, Barack Obama, Alan Greenspan, Osama bin Laden, Rudy Giuliani, and Iranian president Mahmoud Ahmadinejad combined, who were listed by 34 percent of Americans.

In an environment of celebrity worship, Anna Nicole Smith, Britney Spears, and O. J. Simpson often receive more media coverage than all other political leaders combined. Media outlets are increasingly successful in directing public attention to Hollywood stories and other gossip. Approximately one-third of Americans reported following the exploits of Paris Hilton "fairly" or "very closely" in June 2007; Mel Gibson's drunk driving arrest was followed closely by 37 percent in July 2006; one-quarter of Americans followed the Eliot Spitzer prostitute scandal closely in March 2008; 13 percent paid close attention to O. J. Simpson's arrest in September 2007; 56 percent closely followed the Michael Jackson child molestation trial in November 2003; and 53 percent closely followed the Kobe Bryant sexual assault scandal.[30]

THE "KING OF POP" AS A CELEBRITY NEWS FIXATION

Coverage of Michael Jackson's death in 2009 was one of the most heavily reported celebrity news stories. Journalists displayed a proclivity for even the most mundane aspects of Jackson's life, as the following CNN and Fox News online stories from July 2009 demonstrate: "Michael's Daughter; 'Daddy has been the Best,'" "Goodbye Michael: Star, Brother, Friend, Father," "Jackson Still 'King of Pop' on Billboard Charts," "Jackson's Death Sparks Fierce Debate in Congress," "Doctor Denies Giving Jackson Sedative," and "Blanket Jackson Exposed."

Like Anna Nicole Smith's death, attention to Michael Jackson effectively competed with political news stories such as the Iranian election and protests of electoral fraud. For the week of June 22–28, coverage of Iran made up 19 percent of all mainstream news examined by the Project for Excellence in Journalism, whereas Jackson coverage accounted for 18 percent of all news. At the peak of coverage from June 25–26, stories on Jackson made up 60 percent of all news programming, with Iran coverage falling to just 7 percent. Twenty-nine percent of Americans reported paying attention to Jackson's death "most closely" out of all the stories that they followed, as compared to 20 percent and 11 percent respectively who followed the economy and health care reform.[31] In terms of celebrity deaths, Jackson's ranked among the most closely followed, garnering more public attention than the deaths of NBC's *Meet the Press* host Tim Russert, Anna Nicole Smith, Heath Ledger, and Paul Newman, but behind the deaths of John F. Kennedy Jr., Princess Diana, and "Crocodile Hunter" Steve Irwin.[32]

Though celebrity stories receive varying levels of news coverage, they are often among the *most* intensely followed of all issues. Table 9.2 demonstrates that the Smith, Spitzer, Simpson, and Jackson stories effectively compete with other major political stories for public attention. The arrest of former NFL quarterback Michael Vick on dogfight charges received more attention from the public than did domestic crises such as Hurricane Dean and Midwest flooding, and was more closely followed than the Iraq war or the 2008 presidential election.[33]

Celebrity news tends to be more popular with certain demographic groups than others. These stories are more popular among wealthier, younger audiences, as well as with women and minorities.[34] Celebrity stories that speak demographically to one group of Americans over another are more likely to be popular with that demographic group. The death of Michael Jackson, for example, was overwhelmingly more popular among African Americans than non-African Americans.[35]

Some academics rationalize the strong emphasis on entertainment programming by arguing that these programs empower the public. Doris Graber claims that "although 'lightweight' programming draws the wrath of many people . . . one can argue that their disdain constitutes intellectual snobbery. Who is to say that the mass public's tastes are inferior to those of elites? The contention that people would choose education programs over fluffy entertainment, if they had the chance, is false."[36]

Journalists are some of the strongest defenders of fluff news. In rationalizing intense coverage of Anna Nicole Smith, CNN's Wolf Blitzer declared that "her death was tabloid gold. . . . I know a lot of people are complaining [about the saturation coverage]. But a lot of people are also watching." CNN's Paula Zahn justified the coverage as driven by "America's fixation on celebrity, on tragedy, on sex, money, tabloid headlines and death."[37] Former CBS anchor Dan Rather portrays media as hostage to a domineering public: "Fear runs in every newsroom in the country right now, a lot of different fears, but one fear is common—the fear that if we don't do it [run celebrity news], somebody else will, and when they do it, they will get a few more readers, a few more listeners, a few

TABLE 9.2: Public Attention to Celebrity News and Traditional News Stories (% of All Respondents Who Paid the Most Attention to Each Story)

Story (Feb '07)	%	Story (Mar '08)	%	Story (Sept '07)	%	Story (Jul '09)	%
Iraq	26%	2008 Election	37%	O. J. Simpson's Arrest	17%	Michael Jackson's Death	29%
Anna N. Smith	16%	Eliot Spitzer Scandal	14%	Iraq Conflict	25%	Economy	20%
Winter Weather	16%	Stock Market Problems	11%	2008 Election	10%	Obama in Russia/Italy	12%
2008 Election	9%	Iraq	8%	Jena Six Conflict	15%	Sarah Palin's Resignation	8%
Iran	6%	Bottled Water Scandal	4%	Iraq Policy Debate	9%	Health Care Reform	11%
N. Korea	4%	UNC Student Shooting	7%	Mukasey's Nomination	2%	Riots in China	2%

Source: Pew Research Center

more viewers than we do. The Hollywoodization of the news is deep and abiding. . . . It has become pervasive, the belief that to be competitive, you must run a certain amount of celebrity news."[38]

The myth of a reluctant media that passively reports celebrity news in response to the demands of an empowered public should be rejected outright. On an institutional level, we can dismiss the claim that the public drives news consumption as a distortion of reality. The public plays no *active* role in controlling the means of media production; it merely passively decides whether or not to consume a product that is created by media corporations. No corporate executive, editor, or journalist ever bothers to ask the general public if they want to view more celebrity fluff; certainly, media executives do not seriously examine the surveys that are done regarding public opinion of celebrity news. If they did, they would see that the evidence clearly indicates that the public is dissatisfied with such coverage, and feels that celebrity news is produced in excess of their

TABLE 9.3: Anna Nicole Smith and Public Opposition to Celebrity News

Story in Question (Feb. 2007)	% Listing Story as "Deserving More of My Time"
Iraq Conflict	15%
2008 Election	12%
Iran Conflict	10%
North Korea Negotiations	8%
Weather	5%
Anna Nicole Smith	3%

Source: Pew Research Center

level of interest. Although the public plays an *indirect* role in influencing media content through measures such as the Nielsen ratings (which track public consumption of network programming) and through increased consumption of some programs and products over others, this role is extremely limited. It hardly represents democratic control or empowerment over the means of production for modern communication.

In the case of the Anna Nicole Smith story, although 38 percent of the public followed the story closely at the height of its coverage, 61 percent felt that the story "received too much coverage." Conversely, in the same survey, four times as many Americans felt that Iraq deserved more coverage than it received in national media, while two and a half times as many felt that the 2008 election deserved more attention.[39] When asked about the conflict in Afghanistan in June 2008, nearly eight times as many Americans felt that it did not receive enough attention as compared to those who felt it received too much.[40]

As reproduced in Table 9.3, when Americans were provided with a list of competing stories, Anna Nicole Smith's death ranked dead last of those seen as "deserving more of my time." Public dissatisfaction with celebrity news coverage also extends to a slew of stories receiving heavy attention.

A majority of Americans feel that celebrity news stories receive "too much" attention in almost every case (Table 9.4).

Excluding the Michael Vick dog fighting case, feelings that celebrity stories receive too much coverage outnumber conclusions that they received both "too little" and the "right amount" of coverage by double digits. In cases such as Michael Jackson's death, O. J. Simpson's arrest, the celebrity starlet scandals, and the Ellen Degeneres controversy over a

TABLE 9.4: Public Assessments of Celebrity News Stories

Story	(Reported on) Too Much	Too Little	Right Amount
O.J. Simpson Arrest/Robbery (2007)	62%	5%	26%
Eliot Spitzer Prostitute Case (2008)	53%	5%	35%
Don Imus Firing (2007)	57%	6%	37%
Michael Vick Dog Fighting Scandal (2007)	49%	6%	37%
Celebrity Starlet Scandals: B. Spears, P. Hilton, L. Lohan (2007)	87%	2%	8%
Ellen Degeneres Pet Adoption Controversy (2007)	58%	8%	20%
Michael Jackson's Death (2009)	64%	3%	29%

Source: Pew Research Center

dog adoption, twice as many people felt the stories received too much coverage, as compared to too little or the right amount of coverage.[41] If media executives were interested in democratically empowering the public, the first thing they would do is pay serious attention to these public opinion studies, and decrease coverage of celebrity gossip, while increasing attention to other types of stories.

The growth in prominence of junk food stories can be summarized as follows. This type of news receives increased attention in an era of journalistic cost-cutting; as a result of increased media attention to celebrity news, much of the general public recognizes celebrities and their exploits. In the end, however, most of the public negatively reacts to what they see, feeling that junk food news is overemphasized. When we talk of the general public as supportive of junk food news, the statement must be carefully qualified. Some are genuinely interested in celebrity news, and feel these stories should receive the current amount of attention or more. Statistical evidence confirms this reality, as news consumers who are strongly interested in celebrity news tend to pay attention to these stories with greater frequency than consumers with other priorities.[42] This devoted group of celebrity news consumers, however, represents a minority of the public. A sizable majority feels that celebrity stories receive too much attention, and many do not follow these stories with any frequency. However, due to sheer inundation with junk food news, many are unable to avoid hearing about these stories, despite their strong disinterest.

If most Americans feel that celebrity stories receive too much attention, then these stories cannot possibly be serving the general public's interest. Many may quietly follow such stories while claiming they are over covered, a pattern that makes the junk food news analogy so apt. Like those who consume fast food, consumers of celebrity news are reacting to their surrounding environment, which provides them with a steady diet of unhealthy stories. Many citizens may concurrently consume fluff news while admitting the stories are not in their best interest. However, they lack the necessary influence over media production to influence the decisions of media executives. Corporate executives—those who are more interested in making profits than educating the masses about important foreign policy issues—are hesitant to cut profitable celebrity stories. ABC executive producer Tom Bettag explains that following the end of the Cold War "everybody said it's time for the United States to tend to its own domestic problems." It was during this time that the "three blind mice" (ABC, NBC, and CBS) were taken over "by people who were only interested in making money. That was a great cover for saying, people are not interested in foreign news—and we can cover a domestic story for half the price that it costs to cover a foreign story. And so the accountants used that argument to push the idea that what people care about is domestic news."[43]

Many journalists are increasingly distraught over the decline of foreign reporting and the growth of profit motives in influencing reporters' priorities. Just over half of national journalists and 46 percent of local journalists surveyed in a 2004 Pew Research Center poll indicated that "journalism is going in the wrong direction." Sixty-six percent of national journalists and 57 percent of local journalists cited the "increased bottom line pressure" for profits as "seriously hurting" the production of the news.[44]

In large part, the public blames media corporations for putting profit ahead of education. To a significant degree, they reject media efforts to manufacture their consent, resisting attempts to divert public attention from political conflicts to stories featuring Britney Spears's haircut, O. J. Simpson's robberies, and Michael Vick's dogfighting. Despite their infrequent attention to foreign policy issues, much of the public successfully develops critical insight regarding conflicts such as the Iraq war. Most blame the media, rather than the public, for the increase in celebrity news. When questioned about who is to blame for fluff news, 54 percent point to the media, and only 32 percent blame the public. The power of media to socialize consumers, however, should not be underestimated. Young viewers who grew up in the celebrity news era are more susceptible to this programming. Those under thirty are more likely to blame the public, rather than the media, for the prevalence of gossip news, and those over thirty are more likely to blame media corporations instead of the public. Growing up at a time when celebrity news was *not* the norm, older demographic groups know the difference between serious news and news without substance, and they are reacting skeptically to the growth in fluff.[45]

IMPLICATIONS FOR THE CONSUMPTION OF CELEBRITY NEWS

The power of the mainstream media to socialize the young to favor celebrity news is accompanied by dramatic consequences. One major consequence is that people who consume greater amounts of celebrity news inevitably end up spending less time following political news. For example, those who consume online celebrity news are less likely to follow more traditional political news programs such as the evening newscasts for ABC, CBS, and NBC.[46] The focus on online consumption of celebrity gossip is particularly important, since online consumers are disproportionately young, and young viewers are generally more likely to follow celebrity news than older audiences.

The above evidence suggests that celebrity news is often successful in encouraging de-politicization and ignorance among the public. To say that media corporations create apathetic audiences, and that such apathy serves their profit motives, is not a conspiracy. The goal of any corporation is to make as much money as possible, and this is increasingly done through top-down transmission of inexpensive fluff news. This process inherently depends on passive consumers who fail to challenge the possible drawbacks of not only junk food news but the entire capitalist advertising system, which also encourages a passive, unquestioning fixation on fashionable consumption. Concern with celebrity news remains an important component of fashionable consumption, as citizens regularly digest a large volume of this diversionary form of "news" at the expense of political engagement. It may not be the primary goal of media corporations to create ignorant, de-politicized Americans, but this is certainly the consequence of single-minded profit motives that push celebrity news at the expense of political programming.

THE CONTINUED RELEVANCE OF PUBLIC OPINION

In a democratic society, it is the obligation of political leaders to pay serious attention to the wishes of the people. Reporting and editorializing that fail to include the public as a integral part of the policy debate are clearly propagandistic. At a time when the public strongly distrusts political and business leaders, public insights cannot be ignored by a government that relies on consent. Public skepticism of government is common in the post-Vietnam and post-Watergate era. Unlike journalists, Americans are willing to shed naïve assumptions that political leaders act only in altruistic ways and without any selfish interest in projecting global power.

Prior to the Vietnam War, public opinion in the United States was characterized by strong trust in government. Nearly 80 percent in 1964 trusted government "to do the right thing."[47] Over thirty years later, official behavior was viewed far more suspiciously, with only 34 percent of the public trusting government in 1998.[48] In a 1997 *New York Times*/CBS poll, 79 percent of Americans claimed that government is "pretty much run by a few big interests looking out for themselves."[49] High levels of distrust were again voiced prior to the 2006 midterm election, when the public threw out of office Republican majorities in Congress, in large part due to their support for an unpopular war in Iraq.[50] Approval ratings for specific institutions such as Congress and the presidency remain incredibly low, as numerous studies demonstrate.[51]

Common reasons given for public disapproval of leaders include: politicians are considered "dishonest crooks"; they are seen as "only out for themselves and for personal gain"; and they "say one thing and do another."[52] In the 2004 National Election Study, the public expressed serious misgivings about the bipartisan political system, contrary to mass media's reliance on that system. A mere 20 percent of respondents in this study felt that the two-party system "works well," contrasted with 76 percent who felt it had either "real problems" or was "seriously broken."[53]

The media appear to share in negative public ratings alongside political officials. Table 9.5 reproduces information from one 2006 study, showing that nearly 60 percent of Americans share a low level of trust in media, ranking it alongside other distrusted institutions and officials such as Congress, the executive branch, and business leaders.[54] Only friends and coworkers are seen as deserving high levels of trust by most Americans. Conversely, media outlets, the courts, the president, business leaders, and Congress benefit from high levels of trust from less than 30

TABLE 9.5: Public Trust in Various Social Institutions and Actors

Actor/Institution	% w/ Low Trust	Actor/Institution	% w/ High Trust
Congress	76%	Friends and Coworkers	75%
President	69%	Courts	29%
Business Leaders	69%	President	24%
Media	58%	Media	11%
Courts	33%	Business Leaders	7%
Friends and Coworkers	4%	Congress	3%

Source: Zogby polling organization: Zogby Interactive Poll, "United States Public Widely Distrusts its Leaders," 23 May 2006, http://www.zogby.com/News/ReadNews.cfm?ID=1116.

percent of Americans. This does not mean that people express no trust in media. Public opinion polls show that the public is often happy with the information they consume in the mass media and with the ability of journalists to report issues fairly.[55] Public trust in media, however, seems to vary among many Americans, depending on the specific news outlet in question and whether that outlet conforms to the liberal, conservative, or centrist ideology of readers and viewers. Trust in the mass media may also wax and wane over time, with news organizations enjoying more credibility during national crises and at the onset of major conflicts, and Americans increasingly challenging media credibility as these conflicts and their costs increase over the years.[56]

GLOBAL DISTRUST OF THE AMERICAN POLITICAL SYSTEM

U.S. reporting on Iraq and Iran neglects global public opinion, which is strongly critical of the United States' "humanitarian" motives in the Middle East. Chapter 1 of this book demonstrated the meager attention to global voices in stories on withdrawal from Iraq. Chapters 4 and 5 documented journalistic contempt for international voices that challenge official assumptions that Iraq and Iran are threats, and portrayals of the United States as acting reasonably to deter those threats. The mass media not only neglects the American public's moral challenges to the Iraq war, but international opinion is also off the radar, as these perspectives are seen as lacking in newsworthiness. Such contempt for global opinion should be rejected in an era of globalization, when the United States is more reliant on the rest of the world than ever before. Journalists ignore world opinion because it often resides outside of the ideologically narrow American political system. The parochialism of reporters, however, is increasingly dangerous as the United States grows more alienated from the rest of the world.

An entire literature exists documenting how states today are closely linked to one another—culturally, politically, economically, militarily, and ideologically—and how these processes have accelerated in recent decades.[57] In light of the strengthening of national relationships, Americans can no longer afford to be so ignorant about, or dismissive of global opinions that challenge the foundation of U.S. foreign policy. Globalization theorist Manfred Steger argues that in the post-Second World War period "novel technologies" effectively "facilitated the speed and intensity with which" ideas move "freely across national boundaries. This new sense of 'the global' that erupted within and onto the national began to undermine the normality and self-contained coziness of the modern nation-state—especially deeply engrained notions of community tied to a sovereign and clearly demarcated territory containing relatively homogeneous populations."[58] Steger's conclusions are relevant when assessing the U.S. mass media. Reporters can certainly ignore the perspectives and value systems that characterize world opinion, but they do so at their own peril when the United States is inextricably linked across so many different dimensions to the rest of the world.

An analysis of global opinion is instructive, primarily because it demonstrates the tremendous chasm between belief systems in the United States and the rest of the world. Reviewing the following evidence is vital for those who wish to know more about global public opinion:

- Much of the world does not distinguish between the violence and aggression of the United States and its enemies. Contrary to the distinctions made between the "moral" use of violence by the United States and Israel, and "immoral" violence by North Korea and Iran, respondents in a 27-nation survey placed all four countries at the top of their list of those with "mainly negative influence[s]" on the rest of the world. As Steven Kull, director of the Program on International Policy Attitudes, concludes: "It appears that people around the world tend to look negatively on countries whose profile is marked by the use or pursuit of military power."[59]

TABLE 9.6: Is the United States a Leading Global Threat?

% Viewing United States and Competing Country as a Threat "To World Peace and Stability"	
United States and Iran	49% v. 36%
United States and N. Korea	45% v. 39%
United States and China	50% v. 32%
United States and Russia	56% v. 25%
United States and Syria	52% v. 28%
United States and France	65% v. 15%
United States and al-Qaeda	33% v. 51%

Source: BBC, "What the World Thinks of America," Independent Communications and Marketing, 16 June 2003, http://www.bbc.co.uk/pressoffice/pressreleases/stories/2003/06_june/16/news_poll_america.shtml.

- By 2003, three in four in the United Kingdom no longer saw Iraq as a major danger. Iraq was seen as a threat by only 23 percent of those surveyed, whereas the United States was seen as a danger by 32 percent. Such apprehension toward the United States was reinforced in other surveys in following years. Another survey of Britain, Canada, and Mexico indicated that majorities found President Bush to be a "greater danger to world peace" than Kim Jong Il of North Korea, Mahmoud Ahmadinejad of Iran, and Hassan Nasrallah of Hezbollah (based in Lebanon). Table 9.6 reproduces data from a BBC global poll, comparing views of the United States and other countries commonly framed as a danger by American leaders.[60] With the exception of al-Qaeda, the United States is seen as a greater threat than all other factions or states listed in the survey. Despite the emphasis in the American press on Iran posing a major threat, with the United States simply reacting defensively, many throughout the world disagree. In fifteen countries surveyed in Europe, Asia, and Africa, "the continued presence [of the United States] in Iraq is frequently seen as a greater threat to world peace than the possibility of Iran having nuclear weapons."[61]

- Majorities in nine countries surveyed agree that "a world system dominated by a single world power [the United States] is not the best framework for ensuring peace and stability in the world."

Nearly eight in ten feel that the best system for ensuring peace is one "led by the United Nations" or "by a balance of regional powers," as contrasted with a system led by one power, as seen in the current system celebrated in U.S. political, economic, and media circles.[62] Most do not want the United States to disengage from world affairs; they simply feel the United States should not play the role of global policeman.[63]

- Minorities throughout countries surveyed accept the claim, popular in the U.S. press, that American power is vital to promoting the common global good. In an 18-country study, nearly 70 percent of respondents felt that the United States' projection of military power in the Middle East "provokes more conflict than it prevents," with only 17 percent concluding that the United States serves as a stabilizing force in the region—the latter being the dominant view among American journalists and political leaders.[64] In one BBC poll, 55 percent in countries surveyed disagreed that the United States "is a force for good in the world," with 41 percent agreeing. Twenty-five percent felt that "America's superior military power makes the world a safer place," with 52 percent disagreeing. Fifty-four percent disagreed that the "American military presence has helped bring about peace and stability" to the Middle East, with 38 percent agreeing. Finally, 74 percent felt that the United States can do more in Iraq to "avoid civilian casualties" with only 20 percent feeling it does enough.[65]

- In one global study, 43 of 47 countries polled supported a plan for withdrawal from Iraq. Majorities in just one country of 22 that were polled in another survey felt that the United States should not withdraw from Iraq until the security situation improves. In a final survey of 25 countries, three-fourths of respondents disapproved of American policies in Iraq. The specific reasons cited for U.S. unpopularity included its handling of detainees at Guantanamo Bay prison, unconditional support for Israel in its attacks on Lebanon in 2006, handling of Iran's nuclear program, and approach to managing the conflict with North Korea.[66]

This book described at length the media's disinterest in Iraqis' criticisms of the war. Journalists occasionally report on Iraqi opposition to the occupation—as seen in stories in the *New York Times*, *Washington Post*, and elsewhere—but chapter 2's content analysis revealed that such references rarely factor into media dialogue on withdrawal. Simply put, Iraqi public opinion does not enter into debate in the U.S. media. This pattern is unfortunate, since political elites who are interested in promoting Iraqi democracy would place Iraqi public opinion at the forefront of any debate about withdrawal. If journalists bothered to pay serious attention to Iraqi public opinion, they would learn some of the following facts:

- Eighty-four percent of Iraqis have little to no confidence in the United States military. Seventy-seven percent oppose American plans to maintain permanent military bases in Iraq, and three-quarters would "feel safer if United States and other foreign forces left." The vast majority of Iraqis support withdrawal from Iraq in less than a year and have felt this way for years. Seventy-one percent support a timetable of one year or less, with 65 percent supporting immediate withdrawal. Conversely, a mere 9 percent support a reduction of American forces "as the security situation improves." This is dramatically contrasted with the standard view in the U.S. media and among U.S. officials. Both opposed setting a timetable through late 2006, claiming that only a reduction of violence could set the stage for discussions of withdrawal.[67] As of late 2009, the Obama administration and military officials had not yet fully committed to a total withdrawal from Iraq.

- Grassroots protests in Iraq translate public opinion into action. Protests of tens of thousands of Iraqis demanding U.S. withdrawal are common in Iraq. Iraqi oil workers fiercely oppose U.S. efforts to privatize Iraq's oil. Iraq's Federation of Oil Unions undertook a strike against privatization efforts, pushing for oil to remain in the hands of the national government. Most Iraqis oppose privatization plans as well, with 63 percent preferring national over private development of petroleum resources.[68]

- As with the majority of Americans, most Iraqis rejected the Bush administration's claims—dutifully reported in the mainstream press—that the surge succeeded in improving the security situation in Iraq. Most strongly disagree with the view that the U.S.

occupation is the solution to, rather than the cause of Iraq's problems. A BBC poll released eight months after the onset of the February 2007 troop surge found that three-quarters of Iraqis felt that coalition forces have done a "very bad" or "quite bad" job in Iraq. Following the surge, most Iraqis rejected claims that their country turned a corner and sufficiently moved in a positive direction (see Table 9.7). Regarding the security situation, 71 percent felt the surge either made security worse or had no effect, with only 29 percent feeling it made the situation better. By a two-to-one ratio, Iraqis blamed the United States and former president Bush for the violence, rather than the Iraqi government, Iraqi army, Iraqi police, Sunni leaders and militias, and Shiite leaders and militias *combined*. Again, this contrasts dramatically with U.S. media editorials that frame Iraqi, rather than U.S. political leaders, as the major problem.[69]

- Finally, the occupation is seen by the people of Iraq as the fulfillment of U.S. neocolonial interests, rather than enabling Iraqi sovereignty. When asked in 2007 "who controls things in the country," 59 percent of Iraqis said it was the United States, with just 34 percent claiming it was the government of Iraq. Most, however, wanted to see security matters placed in the hands of Iraq's institutions: 61 percent expressed a "great deal" or "quite a lot" of confidence in Iraq's army, and 64 percent in Iraq's police. American forces, in contrast, received a vote of confidence from only 18 percent of Iraqis, with 82 percent holding little to no confidence in them.[70]

SOME FINAL NOTES ON MEDIA PROPAGANDA

The image of the mass media in this study differs dramatically from those presented by mainstream academics and journalists. I reject portrayals of the corporate press as independent or even semi-independent of government, portrayals of journalists as non-ideological, and depictions of media as "objective" or balanced in reporting major issues. For decades studies analyzed the extensive reliance of the mass media on official sources. Whether one concludes that the media is propagandistic, however, depends upon whether one feels that public debate should be limited to the views of the Democratic and Republican parties, or extended to

TABLE 9.7: Public Perceptions of Iraqi Life Under Occupation (Post-Surge, September 2007)

% Rating the Following Aspects of Life as...	"Very Good" or "Quite Good"	"Very Bad" or "Quite Bad"
Protection from Crime	40%	60%
Freedom of Movement	24%	75%
Clean Water Access	31%	69%
Medical Care Quality	31%	69%
Local School Quality	31%	69%
Job Availability	20%	79%
Electricity Access	13%	88%
Ability to Live Without Persecution	23%	77%

Source: BBC, "Iraq Poll September 2007" 10 September 2007, http://news.bbc.co.uk/2/shared/bsp/hi/pdfs/10_09_07_iraqpollaug2007_full.pdf.

include U.S., global, and Iraqi public opinion. Feelings about media propaganda are influenced by academic opinions on the "appropriate" limits of wartime criticisms. Unsurprisingly, many see no need to include in reporting moral criticisms of war, and are opposed to discussing media propaganda. Most scholars and reporters reject these broader expectations of media, claiming that they are unrealistic. Chapters 1, 4, 5, and 6, however, demonstrated that a plethora of media outlets throughout the world *do* transcend the narrow views presented in the U.S. press. These papers' coverage reinforce my central claim: for those interested in democracy, serious consideration of dissident domestic and international voices is absolutely vital.

Sadly, most academic studies of media are confined artificially to examining the American press. Examination of national media systems outside of the "core" of the capitalist world economic system yields important results. Those media not invested in the occupation of Iraq, and residing outside the global web of corporate media conglomeration, tend to benefit from a higher degree of freedom to question the foundations of American power (chapter 6).

Since U.S. journalists are unwilling to seriously challenge U.S. foreign policy in ways that the U.S. public, foreign publics, and foreign media do, we should stop referring to them as printing "all the news that's fit to print" or being "fair and balanced" in representing all political views. A more appropriate slogan for reporters might be "all the news that the parties allow us to print."

Media propaganda is not an inevitable fact of American life. Though it may be asking too much of media corporations to challenge the very state capitalist system upon which they rely, the U.S. public is subject to no such constraints. In the conclusion of my previous book, *Mass Media, Mass Propaganda*, I explored the role of an empowered public in ensuring that a diversity of voices is heard in societal deliberation. Media diversity may be established if the public succeeds in creating, maintaining, and protecting a truly public, non-corporate mass media—one that can effectively compete with corporate media outlets. Citizen and interest group involvement in, and decision-making power over such media are absolutely vital if an independent media is to emerge. Whether Americans are able to create such a system—in the face of strong government, business, and scholarly opposition—remains to be seen.

Before one can challenge government and media propaganda, one must know where to begin. A starting point could include a basic summary of the findings from this book, which will aid in informing others about the basic realities we face. First, this book provided evidence that the U.S. media is unwilling to transcend the bipartisan boundaries of debate that exists on foreign policy. Second, I presented evidence that debate in wealthy allied countries is subject to similar constraints, although there appears to be significantly more room for debate in countries such as the United Kingdom. On the other hand, media coverage in poorer, less developed countries is far more open to challenging the foundations upon which U.S. and allied policy in Iraq is based. In short, a country's position in the global capitalist economy, in addition to its investment in the conflict at hand (in this case Iraq), influences to a great extent the characteristics of the debate within media in each country.

I also stressed a few other points regarding public opinion. First, there is much room for optimism for those who worry about the negative effects of propaganda. I presented empirical evidence that, when confronted with narrow, parochial coverage of foreign conflicts such as Iraq, Americans are often successful in creating their own narratives that present not only pragmatic challenges to U.S. policy but substantive ones as well. Americans may be subject to manipulation in the short term at the onset of wars, but that vulnerability fades—in the case of Iraq rather quickly—in light of growing public hostility and distrust of government and mass media. Second, I explored the similarities between opinions of the

American public and people throughout the rest of the world—all of whom share a strong skepticism about U.S. unilateralism and military power. Although the media spend little time exploring these opinions, increased familiarity with global opposition is necessary if Americans are to gain a better understanding of our increasingly globalized world. I hope that this book will provide a first, but long overdue step in accomplishing this objective.

POSTSCRIPT

Media Coverage in the Age of Obama

Little of substance has changed in U.S. media coverage of the Middle East since the end of the Bush administration. Many new events were reported in the press, however, including the June 2009 election in Iran, President Barack Obama's attacks on Iran's nuclear power program, the planned de-escalation of war in Iraq, and the February 2009 surge of U.S. troops in Afghanistan. Discussion of these issues remains within the parameters of the bipartisan range of opinions, as expressed by members of the Democratic and Republican parties. Wars are celebrated as humanitarian interventions at their best and strategic blunders at their worst.

American media coverage of Iraq progressed through a number of stages in the conflict's first seven years. Framing of the invasion in news stories and editorials was overwhelmingly nationalistic and prowar in 2003 and 2004.[1] Coverage remained generally favorable to the war in late 2004, although many media outlets argued for a change in management in the executive branch, as editors often felt that John Kerry was better capable of successfully pursuing the war.[2] By the 2005 to 2008 period, a dramatic increase in violence in Iraq dominated media headlines and contributed to the public quickly turning against the war. The public opposed the war as early as November 2004, although it took liberal mainstream news outlets like the *Los Angeles Times* and *New York Times* until early to mid-2007 to editorially favor a timetable for withdrawal, claiming the war had become a quagmire.[3]

In response to growing criticism of the war among the public and the media, the Bush administration planned a surge of troops—sent to

Baghdad in early 2007—that effectively silenced many mainstream anti-war critics—at least in the short term. As violence in Iraq declined in late 2007 and early 2008, the war eventually fell out of the headlines.[4] Editorials and reporting framed the surge as an example of U.S. humanitarianism in action, as the Bush administration was congratulated for its alleged success in limiting Iraq's sectarian violence.[5] Despite celebrations of the surge's success, liberal journalists continued to support a withdrawal timetable.[6] Following the election of President Barack Obama in November 2008, editorials stressed the need to decrease troops in Iraq in order to fight terrorism in Afghanistan. Reporting was still cautious, however, in warning that Obama's withdrawal of troops from Iraqi cities could lead to an increase in sectarian violence.

Total withdrawal from Iraq is required—under the Status of Forces Agreement signed by the Bush administration and al-Maliki government—by the end of 2011. Withdrawal from urban areas began under Obama in July 2009, although this initiative was carefully qualified by claims from General George Casey that troops might remain in the country through at least 2019.[7] Journalistic discussions of de-escalation focused on claims that Iraq might further destabilize. The ***Washington Post***, for example, ran a June 26 story emphasizing that "Iraqi civilians" would "become less protected." The story referenced attacks in late June that killed dozens of Iraqis, and "heightened concern about the readiness of Iraq's security forces to operate with limited American assistance."[8] *USA Today* discussed the deaths of over four hundred Iraqis in June 2009 as raising "concerns about the readiness of Iraqi forces to take over their own security."[9] At the *New York Times*, the editors discussed the need "to help Iraqis prepare the withdrawal and to reduce the chances the country will unravel as American troops leave." This concern revolved around questions of "whether Iraq's army—still plagued by corruption, discipline problems, equipment shortages and security breaches—is ready to keep the peace in the cities."[10] Such concern was merely a reiteration of the old assumption—repeated by *New York Times* reporters—that the country could fall into civil war following withdrawal.[11]

Paternalism and contempt characterized *New York Times* reporting of the 2011 Iraq timetable. The paper warned that "before American troops can really go, Iraq's army will need to develop enough of [its] missing [military and governmental] capacities to be able to fight on its own. The United States is going to have to help Iraq build an air force and a navy so it can defend its own borders—an effort that will stretch far beyond the

2011 withdrawal deadline."[12] This rhetoric characterizes the United States as stabilizing Iraq and stands in contrast to the opinions of most Iraqis and Americans, who feel that the occupation is causing Iraq's deterioration, not its rejuvenation.[13] U.S. forces are strongly distrusted by Iraqis, who see Iraq's governing institutions as the legitimate actors in restoring order in the country.[14]

The June 12, 2009, election in Iran received tremendous attention in the United States. As with the country's nuclear program, election coverage was strongly critical of the regime of President Mahmoud Ahmadinejad and Supreme Leader Ayatollah Ali Khameni. Charges of the government's manipulation of the electoral process were common in U.S. media, with Ahmadinejad reportedly engaging in fraud to defeat reformist challenger Mir-Hossein Mousavi. Middle East scholars such as Juan Cole made a powerful case that electoral irregularities implied government fraud.[15] But mainstream media outlets like the *Washington Post* reported that no "hard evidence" of manipulation existed: "The case for a rigged outcome is far from ironclad, making it difficult for the United States and other Western powers to denounce the results as unacceptable. Indeed, there is also evidence that Mahmoud Ahmadinejad, the incumbent president deeply disliked in the West . . . simply won a commanding victory."[16] In this instance, the *Washington Post*'s reporters were referring to a poll finding that Ahmadinejad led his closest competitor by a two-to-one ratio three weeks before the election. This poll's predicted advantage was larger than Ahmadinejad's margin of victory on election day.[17]

A review of the media reaction to the election demonstrates a pattern of contempt for the Iranian government. Journalists overwhelmingly took a faith-based approach to Iran—assuming the worst about the country's electoral outcome, even when substantive evidence was lacking. A June 14 editorial in the *New York Times* bitterly condemned "the [Iranian] government's even more than usually thuggish reaction" to protests of Ahmadinejad's electoral victory.[18] The evidence for electoral fraud, the paper concluded, is seen in the large rallies at challenger Moussavi's campaign events, in addition to the publication of some polls suggesting that Moussavi would win over Ahmadinejad. These developments supposedly demonstrated that Ahmadinejad was poised for a major electoral defeat, not an overwhelming victory. The *Chicago Tribune* editorialized that "Iran staged a presidential election. . . . It wasn't real. It was more like a charade of an election, elaborately mounted to show the world that Iranians freely choose their leaders."[19] The *Washington Times* asserted that "the last thing [Iranian] rulers want is for the unvarnished, unfiltered voice of the people to be heard."[20] The *Los Angeles Times* published a "memo to the mullahs" that read: "If you're going to fake an election, at least make the results look plausible. According to the official tally in Iran's presidential race, incumbent Mahmoud Ahmadinejad didn't just beat his three opponents, he crushed them, winning 63% of the vote and a majority in all 30 provinces."[21] The *New York Times* spoke with disdain, understandably, about the Iranian government's crackdown on Iranians who protested the electoral outcome. "When protesters took to the streets in the fiercest demonstrations in a decade, the police beat them with batons. The government also closed universities in Tehran, blocked cell phones and text messaging and cut access to websites."[22]

This critical coverage of Iran in the media strongly influenced public opinion. A June 2009 CNN poll found that 82 percent of Americans thought the election results "were a fraud that were an attempt to steal the election," while just 10 percent felt that the results were "an accurate reflection of how Iranians voted." On a distant issue like Iran, journalists and political leaders enjoy a tremendous power to mold public opinion. Journalistic reactions to the election clearly played a major role in fostering public hostility toward Iran's government.

Coverage of Iran's nuclear program does not differ substantively in the age of Obama. Reporting is "faith based" in that it is not reliant on consultation with the intelligence record but on the dogmatic repetition of simplistic and propagandistic assumptions that Iran is a threat. This mindset is reflected in a June 2009 statement from Obama—which merely repeats the conventional view in Washington—that the United States is "going to be dealing with an Iranian regime that has historically been hostile to the United States, which has caused some problems in the neighborhood [Middle East], and is pursuing nuclear weapons."[23]

Nuclear fear mongering in the press continues under the Obama administration. The *New York Times* stokes American fears over "Iran's [nuclear] centrifuges," which "are still spinning," and its nuclear program, which is "advancing at an alarming rate."[24] The *Washington Post* discusses "Iran's nuclear weapons ambitions"—deemed "unacceptable" by American officials who see the United States and its allies as responsibly wielding, and even using or threatening to use such weapons for the greater good of humanity.[25]

Some news reports from 2008 and 2009 put reporting on Iran into better context. On November 20, 2008, the *New York Times* cited a report from global nuclear inspectors at the IAEA documenting "Iran's progress" in enriching "1,390 pounds of low-enriched uranium." The uranium, the paper conceded, could not be used to develop nuclear weapons since highly enriched uranium is required for this task. However, the story continued by uncritically citing "American intelligence agencies [that] have said Iran could make a bomb between 2009 and 2015."[26] The article failed to cite any specific intelligence report or agency making this claim, and the "finding" itself contradicted the *New York Times*'s own reporting that the U.S. National Intelligence Estimate concluded in 2007 that there is a high probability that Iran ended its nuclear weapons program.

One story from the *New York Times* on February 20, 2009, reported that U.S. "officials declared for the first time that the amount of uranium that Tehran has now amassed—more than a ton—was sufficient, with added purification, to make an atom bomb."[27] Similarly, the *Los Angeles Times* reported on the same day that "Iran has enough fuel for a nuclear bomb *if* it decides to take the drastic steps of violating its international treaty obligations, kicking out inspectors and further refining its supply."[28] No evidence, however, was provided that Iran was considering undertaking such steps. Even international inspectors are not beyond being co-opted into alarmist reporting. IAEA head Mohammed ElBaradei, for example, received prominent coverage in the *New York Times* when he shared his "gut feeling" that Iran's leaders wanted the technology to build nuclear weapons "to send a message to their neighbors, to the rest of the world: don't mess with us." The IAEA's actual conclusion—that there is no evidence of an Iranian nuclear weapons program—seemed at a disadvantage when competing with ElBaradei's "gut."[29] A final example of nuclear fear mongering in the *New York Times* appeared on May 21, 2009, when Iran "test-fired an upgraded surface-to-surface missile with a range of about 1,200 miles," which "would put it within striking distance of Israel and of American bases in the Persian Gulf."[30] The standard operating procedure in such stories is clear: promote worst-case scenarios while conceding a complete lack of documented evidence that Iran is a dire threat to the United States. Though this approach may not be substantiated by evidence, it has the advantage of pleasing American officials who demand sycophantic media coverage.

Editorializing from the elite press is similar in its demonization of Iran. Op-ed writer John Hannah, for example, wonders in the *Washington Post* whether Obama's "diplomatic engagement [can] persuade Iran to cease its efforts to develop nuclear weapons."[31] Similarly, the editors at the *New York Times* conclude that "the amount of uranium that Tehran now holds is sufficient to make an atom bomb," and a *Boston Globe* editorial claims that Iran's launching of a satellite into orbit "ostentatiously foreshadows the capability one day to deliver nuclear warheads on intercontinental ballistic missiles."[32] Iran's admission that it constructed a second nuclear facility in the city of Qum was also met critically by major papers, with the editors of the *New York Times* and *Washington Post* assuming the plant represents proof that Iran was developing nuclear weapons.[33] It should be noted, however, that the construction of the plant was openly declared by Iran to the IAEA prior to uranium production and in accord with Iran's legal requirements, and there was *no physical evidence* as of late 2009 that weapons grade uranium was being manufactured at the plant or at any other location in Iran.

American newspapers demonstrated their commitment to hypocrisy when the U.S. government openly announced, just five days after Obama's speech about the Iranian "threat," that it was moving forward, in violation of the Non-Proliferation Treaty, with its own plan to reconstitute nuclear weapons. As the Inter Press Service (IPS) reported on September 30, 2009: "The U.S. Department of Energy's National Nuclear Security Administration continues to push forward a program called Complex Modernization, which would expand two existing nuclear plants to allow them to produce new plutonium pits and new bomb parts out of enriched uranium for use in a possible new generation of nuclear bombs." The announcement was reported only by alternative-left news outlets such as *Truthout*, *Z Magazine*, and *Common Dreams* on October 1.[34]

Television coverage of U.S. plans for enrichment was non-existent. There was not a single reference to the U.S. Complex Modernization program anywhere in any of the news programs on ABC News, CBS, NBC, MSNBC, CNN, or Fox News in the week after the IPS report. References to Iranian "nuclear weapons" appeared, in contrast, in nearly four dozen stories in these television outlets in the same period. U.S. plans for nuclear enrichment received no headline, op-ed, or editorial coverage in the *New York Times*, *Washington Post*, *Washington Times*, *Chicago Sun-Times*, *Houston Chronicle*, *San Francisco Chronicle*, or the *Los Angeles Times* in the week following the disclosure.[35] In contrast, Iran's alleged nuclear weapons development was heavily discussed. A total of 66 news stories, op-eds, and/or editorials appeared in the same papers in the following order: nineteen pieces in the *New York Times*, eighteen in the *Washington Post*, seven in the *Houston Chronicle*, six in the *Washington Times*, six in the *Boston Globe*, five in the *Los Angeles Times*, four in the *Chicago Sun-Times*, and one story in the *San Francisco Chronicle*. A brief review of these stories demonstrates the extraordinarily propagandistic nature of reporting and commentary:

- From the *Washington Times*: "The Coming War with Iran; Real Question Is Not If, but When," "Righteous Indignation: Countdown to War and Armageddon," and "Big, Ominous Win for Iran; Buying Time to Continue Clandestine Work."

- From the *Washington Post*: "U.N. Chief Says Iran Must Prove Its Sincerity on Nuclear Issue," and "Nuclear Disarmament Is an Issue of Morality."

- From the *New York Times*: "Iran Agrees to Key Concessions on Uranium, but Doubts Linger," "Iran May Have All It Needs for Bomb, U.N. Agency Says; Functioning Nuke Is in Reach," "Challenge for Obama: Holding Iran to Its Word," "The Possibility of a Nuclear-Armed Iran Alarms Arabs," and "Answering Iran's Nuclear Challenge."

- From the *Los Angeles Times*: "Access Delay May Give Iran Time to Obscure Data."

- From the *Houston Chronicle*: "Iran Will Send Its Enriched Uranium to Russia; Concession a Win for West—If It's Not Hollow."

Noam Chomsky and Edward Herman argue in *Manufacturing Consent* that U.S. coverage of foreign elections is politicized to create favorable images of elections in repressive allied states while demonizing elections in enemy states.[36] In the case of elections in Iraq and Iran, there is strong evidence of the politicization of coverage to fit U.S. strategic interests in the Middle East. In question here is the June 2009 election in Iran—widely regarded as fraudulent in the United States, and the June 2003 local elections in Iraq, which were forcibly cancelled by the U.S. military. As the *Washington Post* reported in 2003: "U.S. military commanders ordered a halt to the local elections and self-rule in provincial cities and towns across Iraq, choosing instead to install their own hand-picked mayors and administrators." The motivation for the termination of elections derived from U.S. distrust of Iraqi Shiites (the majority in the country), who the Bush administration worried would win elections and establish a close relationship with Iran (which is also majority Shiite).[37] The *Washington Post*—reflecting Iraqi opinion in 2003—reported that "the decision to deny Iraqis a direct role in selecting municipal governments is creating anger and resentment among aspiring leaders and ordinary citizens, who say the U.S. led occupation forces are not making good on their promise to bring greater freedom and democracy to a country dominated for three decades by Saddam Hussein."[38]

The Bush administration's goal in Iraq was not originally to hold democratic elections, but to impose a caucus-style system whereby U.S. administrators would select local Iraqi notables who would then pick members of the legislature. The November 2003 plan issued by the Bush administration was condemned publicly by Iraqi religious leader Ayatollah Ali al-Sistani, who provided the spiritual inspiration for a mass non-violent rebellion against the caucus system.[39] There is good reason to expect that the U.S. media should have paid close attention to charges of electoral manipulation in *both* Iraq in 2003 and Iran in 2009. In both cases, a government repressed citizens who protested what they saw as the perversion of elections. In both cases, supporters of change were silenced in the electoral arena, and protests took to the streets as government actions incited massive public opposition. Both the U.S. and Iranian governments initially dismissed protestors as agitators, although in both cases sustained rebellion succeeded in drawing negative attention to government actions. Additionally, in both cases resistance was largely nonviolent in pushing for democratic elections and transparency. The major difference between both cases, however, is that one of these electoral manipulations was conducted by the United States, and the other by an enemy state. Another key difference is that the claims of manipulation of Iran's election were based primarily on suspicion and electoral irregularities, rather than hard evidence, whereas there is no question that the U.S. government defrauded the local Iraqi elections and refused to consider Iraqi public demands for a direct vote.

Although it is reasonable to expect that U.S. electoral fraud in Iraq would receive at least as much coverage as the Iranian election, the pattern is largely the opposite in reporting. U.S. media were enthusiastic in politicizing democratic elections in the Middle East by devoting massive coverage to Iran and downplaying U.S. electoral suppression in Iraq. The

New York Times devoted just thirteen stories, and the *Washington Post* only ten stories, to the cancelled Iraqi elections and subsequent protests of the planned caucus system in the one-month period from June 28 to July 28, 2003 (the cancellation of elections was first reported in the *Washington Post* on June 28, 2003). Conversely, both papers paid far greater attention to the June 12 elections in Iran and the subsequent government crackdown on protestors. During the one-month period from June 12 to July 12, 2009, the *New York Times* devoted seventy stories, and the *Washington Post* devoted forty-six stories to the Iran election and its aftermath. In other words, the *New York Times* dedicated nearly 5.5 times more coverage to Iran than Iraq, while the *Washington Post* dedicated over 4.5 times more coverage to Iran.

The words used to frame the elections in Iraq and Iran could not be more different. Critical assessments are applied to Iran to the near exclusion of similar assessments in Iraq—as measured by the key words below:

- The extent to which the crackdown on Iraqi elections, the imposition of the U.S. caucus plan in Iraq, and Iran's electoral results are "*disputed*" by opponents and the extent that manipulation of both elections is seen as a "*fraud*."

- The characterization of the crackdown on Iraqi elections, the imposition of the U.S. caucus plan, manipulation of the Iran election, and repression of Iranian protestors as fomenting "*unrest*," "*turmoil*," "*defiance*," and "*protest*."

- Descriptions of the crackdown on Iraqi elections, the imposition of the U.S. caucus plan, the manipulation of the Iran election, and repression of Iranian protestors as inciting a "*crisis*" marked by public rebellion and government repression.

As Table 10.1 demonstrates, these key words are used to frame the Iran election with far greater frequency than the election in Iraq.[40]

Reporting on the incidents in Iraq and Iran is heavily politicized. Coverage demonizes an official enemy of U.S. leaders—the Iranian theocracy—while downplaying U.S. activities in an occupation that claimed to promote the best interests of the Iraqi people. Negative framing of the Iranian election serves the purpose of legitimizing U.S. policy in the Middle East—particularly the belligerent rhetoric and threats made against Iran—while also directing attention away from controversial U.S. actions seen as threatening Iraqi democracy, human rights, self-determination, and sovereignty. In sum, coverage of the Middle East under Obama does not appear to be significantly different in substance to coverage under the Bush administration. In both periods, journalists worked to demonize officially designated enemies of state, while vindicating U.S. officials for their altruistic rhetoric. Criticisms of Obama do not extend beyond tactical criticisms of the costs of conflicts in which the United States is engaged.

A final area of interest in the study of media under Obama is the 2009 escalation of war in Afghanistan. In this conflict, Obama promised to crush al-Qaeda and defeat the Taliban by increasing the bombing campaigns in southern Afghanistan and Pakistan. By February 2009, Obama authorized the deployment of an additional 17,000 troops to Afghanistan, with the possible introduction of tens of thousands more by late 2009 to 2010. Unmanned Predator drone attacks were used in Pakistan, allegedly to target al-Qaeda and other Islamist militants.

American journalists see their role in foreign conflicts as dutifully reflecting the range of opinions expressed in Washington. In the case of Afghanistan, both Democrats and Republicans lent their support to escalating war as of early to mid 2009. "Responsible" criticisms were limited to questions of whether the war is unwinnable or too costly. The Obama administration paternalistically denigrated the Afghan government for complicity in corruption, ballot-tampering, collusion with warlords, narcotics dealing, and a lack of democratic responsiveness. These criticisms were echoed in news stories and editorials. The editors of the *Los Angeles Times* concluded that the government of Hamid Karzai needed to help the Afghan people ensure "security, honest governance, impartial justice, economic development with far less corruption, and protection of women's rights."[41] Reporting in the *New York Times* highlighted the inability of the Afghan government to provide resources to local governors to promote "security," medical care, educational resources, and advisement.[42] *New York Times* editors lambasted the August 2009 Afghan election as illegitimate, with "neither of the two main contenders offer[ing] serious solutions to the country's problems."[43] Seeing themselves as benevolent in their intentions, U.S. leaders reserved the "right" to sit in judgment of other governments seen as impure in their motives and actions.

By mid to late 2009, U.S. journalists blamed Afghan leaders for failing to ensure reconstruction of their country while exonerating U.S. officials

TABLE 10.1: Framing of Contested Elections in the Middle East
Iraq (June 28–July 28, 2003); Iran (June 12–July 12, 2009)
No. of Articles Using Key Word; Descriptions of Elections and Their Surrounding Events

New York Times		*Washington Post*	
"Protest" of Iranian Repression and U.S. Occupation			
Iraq (2003)	0	Iraq (2003)	2
Iran (2009)	57	Iran (2009)	45
The Election as "Disputed"			
Iraq (2003)	0	Iraq (2003)	0
Iran (2009)	45	Iran (2009)	29
The Election as "Fraud"			
Iraq (2003)	0	Iraq (2003)	0
Iran (2009)	29	Iran (2009)	24
"Unrest" Following the Election			
Iraq (2003)	0	Iraq (2003)	0
Iran (2009)	26	Iran (2009)	22
The Election as Accompanied by "Crisis"			
Iraq (2003)	1	Iraq (2003)	1
Iran (2009)	20	Iran (2009)	8
Public "Defiance" of the Electoral Outcome			
Iraq (2003)	0	Iraq (2003)	0
Iran (2009)	20	Iran (2009)	5
"Turmoil" within the Country			
Iraq (2003)	0	Iraq (2003)	0
Iran (2009)	7	Iran (2009)	5

Source: Lexis Nexis

for their disinterest in humanitarian aid. The editors of the ***Washington Post*** congratulated Obama for his serious commitment to "nation-building."[44] The *New York Times* editors concurred that Obama "must speed deployment of American civilians to help Afghan leaders carry out development projects."[45] Critics of the war asked what evidence existed—outside of Obama's rhetoric—that he was seriously committed to the reconstruction (rather than destruction) of Afghanistan. This question was generally neglected in the media.

Little has improved in Afghanistan under U.S. occupation. The country remains one of the poorest, worst-off countries in the world. Its 32 million people rank 174th of 178 countries in the United Nations Human Development Index. Afghanistan suffers from some of the world's highest infant mortality rates. Nearly two-thirds of children are unable to attend school, and less than a quarter enjoy clean drinking water.[46] The challenge these statistics pose to the narrative of U.S. humanitarianism is neglected in reports celebrating U.S. action in Afghanistan.

Available evidence raises serious questions about Obama's promise that humanitarian aid is a serious priority. The U.S. committed a mere $5 billion in reconstruction funds from 2002 to 2008, yet was spending by 2008 an average of $36 billion a year on military action in Afghanistan. As of 2008, the Afghan government concluded that it needed as much as $50 billion for adequate reconstruction over the next five years.[47] Barack Obama, in contrast, committed just $4 billion to reconstruction for 2010, but $68 billion for military activities. After looking at such figures, many critics concluded that the escalation of war was deemed far more important than reconstruction. This view was not shared by mainstream American journalists, as reflected in their reporting above.[48]

The American and Afghan publics were strongly opposed to the escalation.[49] It was not that widespread public opposition was always ignored in media reports; such opposition was simply not a serious concern for reporters and politicians. The editors at the *New York Times*, for example, conceded that "it is understandable that polls show that many Americans are tiring of the 8-year-old war."[50] This, however, did not prevent them from enthusiastically supporting the war as "the real front in the war on terrorism."[51] Although the *New York Times*'s reporters admitted in 2009 that southern Afghans were in "popular revolt" against Obama's escalation, "extra [U.S.] forces" were still seen as vital in defeating Taliban forces and "securing" the region.[52]

Almost all the major newspapers in the United States supported escalation in Afghanistan as of mid- to late 2009. The editors of the *New York Times, Wall Street Journal, Washington Post, Los Angeles Times,* and the *Washington Times* all supported the surge in troops as necessary to fight terrorism.[53] Editors at the *Wall Street Journal* agreed that "more U.S. troops will likely be needed," and a "proper counterinsurgency strategy" must be developed.[54] The *New York Times* reported that there was not "enough equipment for patrols" of the Iranian-Afghan border and that military commanders saw "their forces [as] insufficient to get the job done."[55] Opposition did appear in the *Boston Globe*, where reporters pondered whether the conflict was a "quagmire comparable to Vietnam."[56] Although this was the minority view in mid-2009, opposition to the war did begin to materialize in late September 2009. U.S. officials such as Democratic Vice President Joe Biden and President Barack Obama began to publicly announce the need to rethink the strategy of escalation in light of the economic crisis and the Afghan war's unpopularity. It was not until their public announcements appeared that the editors of the *New York Times* began to seriously reconsider their enthusiasm for escalation, addressing "Americans' doubts about the war" and discussing ways for the U.S. to "cut its losses in Afghanistan" in light of a war in which U.S. allies are "fighting and dying" and "looking for a way out."[57] Other papers such as the *Washington Post* continued editorially to echo the views of Republican officials that the war was necessary and just.[58] Such editorializing represented a classic case of media dependence on government, with the *New York Times* enthusiastically supporting escalation in August 2009 when Democrats and Republicans were largely united on the issue, and the paper beginning to criticize the conflict once Democrats began a critical reevaluation. Some critical questions arose when contemplating military escalation in Pakistan and Afghanistan—all of which were raised in 2009 by non-mainstream journalists reporting from Afghanistan and by scholars studying the Middle East. These views were generally ignored, however, by mainstream journalists and political officials. It is not that the U.S. media should be expected to provide definitive answers to these critical questions. But when media refuse to report the assessments of critical experts in the area, news consumers inevitably suffer from a curtailment of debate on the legitimacy of war.

A review of critical appraisals of the Afghan war that were made in 2009 adds depth to the public debate. Middle East specialist Juan Cole questioned the true extent of al-Qaeda's capabilities. They don't seem to have a presence in Afghanistan any more to speak of. What is called al-Qaeda in the northwest of Pakistan is often just Uzbek, Tajik, and Uighur political refugees who have fled their own countries in the region because their Muslim fundamentalism is not welcomed by those regimes. The old al-Qaeda of Bin Laden and al Zawahiri appears to have been effectively disrupted. Terrorist attacks in the West are sometimes planned by unconnected cells who are al Qaeda wannabes, but I don't see evidence of command and control capabilities by al Qaeda central.[59]

Cole also warns about the unrealistic military goals of the Obama administration and worries about a humanitarian crisis that may result from U.S. bombings:

What is the goal here in Afghanistan? If it is to wipe out the Taliban, the Taliban are a social movement that has a certain amount of support in the Pashtun areas and wiping them out would be a genocide. It's very unlikely to be accomplished and very brutal if it were done. If the goal is to establish a stable Afghan government that could itself deal with challenges like the remaining Taliban, that's state building on a large scale. Afghanistan's a mess; it's been through thirty years of war . . . it has no visible means of support, it's a fourth world country. . . . So there's a real question of whether Afghanistan actually has the resources to accomplish what the U.S. wants it to do.[60]

Non-mainstream reporters raised similar concerns. Christian Parenti—a reporter for the *Nation* magazine and recently returned from Afghanistan—explained:

I don't think the Obama administration thinks it's going to win militarily against the Taliban, and I don't think they're stupid enough to think the institutions of the Afghan state are going to function. It's considered one of the most corrupt governments in the world. . . . Nothing gets done, the Afghan government has very limited ability to raise taxes, 95 percent of its income comes from foreign aid [which again, is far from enough to cover the country's needs], and very little for the people of the society is produced from that.[61]

Extensive reliance on pragmatic criticisms of the Afghan war as a quagmire contributes to the marginalization of moral challenges to the war. More specifically, concern with Afghan civilian casualties is heavily neglected in news coverage. U.S. officials and media are careful to project a rhetorical concern with civilians killed in Afghanistan. At times, the *New York Times* stresses the thousands of Afghan civilians killed as "a decisive factor in souring many Afghans on the war."[62] The *Washington Post* reports that "Afghan civilian deaths present [the] U.S. with strategic problems." Such "mistakes" harm the United States' image and discredit official claims that "the Taliban is the main cause of suffering in the country."[63] Whether these deaths constitute a mistake, or are an entirely predictable form of criminal recklessness and negligence is a relevant question, though one that officials and media prefer not to ask. Journalists assume that U.S. policy utilizes precision-based attacks, as the *New York Times* uncritically quotes official promises that "success" in Afghanistan "will not be measured by the number of enemy killed" but by "the number of Afghans shielded from violence."[64] Civilian casualties may be tragic, as the *New York Times* reminds its readers, but they are a necessary price to be paid for progress in fighting terror in Afghanistan.

Reporting on Obama's Afghan escalation neglects the civilian casualties that result from U.S. bombing. Statistical studies, on the other hand, suggest that civilian casualties are climbing steadily. Afghan civilian casualties escalated by 40 percent in 2008 to a total of 2,100.[65] The 60 U.S. Predator drone strikes undertaken in Pakistan from January 2006 to April 2009 resulted in the alleged deaths of fourteen al-Qaeda leaders, but an additional 687 Pakistani civilians.[66] In other words, 94 percent of all deaths reportedly committed by the United States were innocent civilians. This reality is often omitted from reporting on the strikes. The *Los Angeles Times*, for example, ran a headline in March 2009 that read "U.S. Missile Strikes Said to Take Heavy Toll on al-Qaeda."[67] The story referenced the alleged members of al-Qaeda killed in U.S. attacks but omitted any reference to the number of civilians killed. Nowhere in the story were international legal scholars or antiwar critics quoted explaining that these attacks are a criminal act of aggression and a blatant violation of international law. This approach to reporting the Pakistan bombings is standard operating procedure. For example, the *New York Times* ran sixteen stories and the *Los Angeles Times* twelve stories on the U.S. bombings and aerial drone missions in Pakistan from January 1 to August 31, 2009. Not a single story in the *New York Times* and only one story in the *Los Angeles Times* emphasized the deaths of civilians from these attacks. These papers preferred to frame the attacks as targeting and killing al-Qaeda, the Taliban, and other militants, but not civilians.[68]

FIGURE 10.1: Public Opinion on Afghanistan

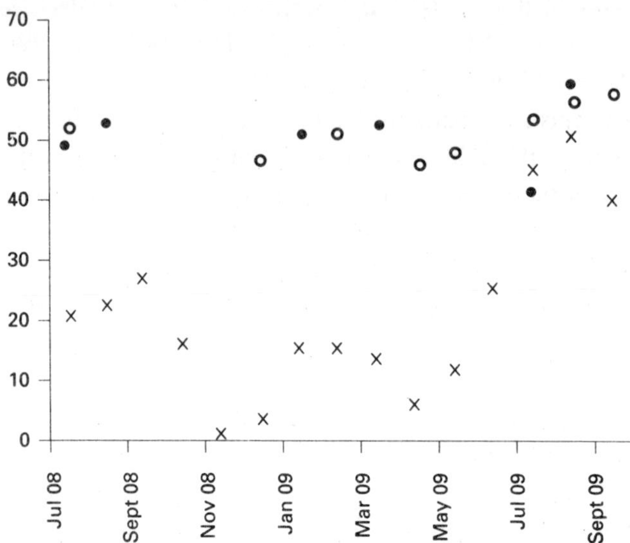

× U.S. Monthly Casualties

● % Feeling War is Going "Moderately or Very Badly"

o % of Public Opposing War

Source: www.pollingreport.com

Public opinion on the war in Afghanistan displayed some susceptibility to influence by media. Figure 10.1 demonstrates that a majority of Americans opposed the war in 2008, although Obama's defense of the February 2009 escalation was accompanied by an increase in public support.

The conclusion that the war was going "moderately or very badly" dropped from 52 percent in January to 43 percent in July 2009, likely in response to Obama's rhetorical defense of the surge and sympathetic media coverage. As in the case of Iraq, however, opposition to the war dramatically increased once American casualties escalated. Casualties reached an all-time high in July and August 2009, at 45 and 51 deaths respectively. Increased attention to these deaths in the news likely explains the massive increase in resistance to the war, as reflected in Figure 10.1.[69] Feelings that the war was going "moderately or very badly," for example, increased radically from 43 to 61 percent of the public in the single month from July to August. This sort of rapid, short-term change in public opinion is rarely seen in regards to public policy issues.

The findings in this Postscript confirm the themes expressed in the rest of the book. U.S. media outlets provide a charitable reading of U.S. foreign policy while largely disregarding those assessments that substantively challenge U.S. actions in Iraq, Iran, Afghanistan, and Pakistan. No conspiracy is at work here; rather, reporters simply see the world through the same lens as political leaders. This does not mean that the general public accepts such messages, hook, line, and sinker. As the public assessments of Afghanistan and Iraq demonstrate, opposition to war quickly materializes when costly conflicts contribute to increased destabilization and destruction in host countries. The American public, then, is not merely a passive vessel that accepts the dogmas proclaimed by officials and repeated by journalists. Public opinion is influenced by a number of social factors, of which media is only one.

Select Bibliography

Artz, Lee, and Yahya R. Kamalipour, eds. 2003. *The Globalization of Corporate Media Hegemony*. Albany, N.Y.: SUNY Press.

_____. 2007. *The Media Globe: Trends in International Mass Media*. Lanham, Md: Rowman and Littlefield Publishers.

Abrahamson, Mark. 2004. *Global Cities*. Oxford: Oxford University Press.

Agnew, John. 2005. *Hegemony: The New Shape of Global Power*. Philadelphia: Temple University Press.

Alger, Dean. 1998. *Megamedia: How Giant Corporations Dominate Mass Media, Distort Competition, and Endanger Democracy*. Lanham, Md: Rowman and Littlefield Publishers.

Almond, Gabriel A. 1962. *The American People and Foreign Policy*. New York: Praeger.

Ansolabehere, Stephen, and Shanto Iyengar. 1995. *Going Negative: How Political Advertisements Shrink and Polarize the Electorate*. New York: Free Press.

Apter, David E., ed. 1964. *Ideology and Discontent*. Glencoe, Ill.: Free Press of Glencoe.

Baker, C. Edwin. 2007. *Media Concentration and Democracy: Why Ownership Matters*. Cambridge: Cambridge University Press.

Bartels, Larry M. 2008. *Unequal Democracy: The Political Economy of the New Gilded Age*. Princeton: Princeton University Press.

Baum, Matthew A. 2003. *Soft News Goes to War: Public Opinion and American Foreign Policy in the New Media Age*. Princeton: Princeton University Press.

Baumgartner, Frank R., and Bryan D. Jones. 1993. *Agendas and Instability in American Politics*. Chicago: University of Chicago Press.

Ben-Zvi, Abraham. 1998. *Decade of Transition: Eisenhower, Kennedy, and the Origins of the American-Israeli Alliance*. New York: Columbia University Press.

Bennett, W. Lance. 2001. *News: The Politics of Illusion*. New York: Addison Wesley Longman.

Bennett, W. Lance, Regina G. Lawrence, and Steven Livingston. 2007. *When the Press Fails: Political Power and the News Media from Iraq to Katrina*. Chicago: University of Chicago Press.

Bennett, W. Lance, and David L. Paletz, eds. 1994. *Taken by Storm: The Media, Public Opinion, and U.S. Foreign Policy in the Gulf War*. Chicago: University of Chicago Press.

Berenger, Ralph D., ed. 2004. *Global Media Go to War: The Role of News and Entertainment Media During the 2003 Iraq War*. Spokane, Wash.: Marquette.

Berger, Peter L., and Thomas Luckmann. 1967. *The Social Construction of Reality: A Treatise in the Sociology of Knowledge*. New York: Anchor Books.

Bernays, Edward. 2005. *Propaganda*. Brooklyn, NY: IG Publishing.

Berry, Nicholas. 1990. *Foreign Policy and the Press: An Analysis of the New York Times' Coverage of U.S. Foreign Policy*. Westport, Conn.: Greenwood Publishing.

Borjesson, Kristina, ed. 2004. *Into the Buzzsaw: Leading Journalists Expose the Myth of a Free Press*. New York: Prometheus Books.

Borjesson, Kristina, ed. 2005. *Feet to the Fire: The Media After 9/11: Top Journalists Speak Out*. New York: Prometheus Books.

Brody, Reed. 1999. *Contra Terror in Nicaragua: A Fact-Finding Mission: September 1984–January 1985*. Boston: South End Press.

Brody, Richard A. 1991. *Assessing the President: The Media, Elite Opinion, and Public Support*. Stanford, Calif.: Stanford University Press.

Burnell, Peter, and Vicky Randall. 2008. *Politics in the Developing World*. Oxford: Oxford University Press.

Callaghan, Karen, and Frauke Schnell, eds. 2005. *Framing American Politics*. Pittsburgh: University of Pittsburgh Press.

Campbell, Angus, Phillip E. Converse, Warren E. Miller, and Donald E. Stokes. 1960. *The American Voter: Unabridged Edition*. Chicago: University of Chicago Press.

Cappella, Joseph N., and Kathleen Hall Jamieson. 1997. *Spiral of Cynicism: The Press and the Public Good*. Oxford: Oxford University Press.

Chandrasekaran, Rajiv. 2007. *Imperial Life in the Emerald City: Inside Iraq's Green Zone*. New York: Vintage.

Chang, Won Ho. 1989. *Mass Media in China: The History and the Future*. Ames: Iowa State University Press.

Chomsky, Noam. 1987. *On Power and Ideology: The Managua Lectures*. Boston: South End Press.

_____. 1991. *Deterring Democracy*. New York: Hill and Wang.

_____. 1993. *Rethinking Camelot: JFK, the Vietnam War, and U.S. Political Culture*. Boston: South End Press.

_____. 1996. *World Orders Old and New*. New York: Columbia University Press.

_____. 1999. *The New Military Humanism: Lessons from Kosovo*. Monroe, Me.: Common Courage Press.

Chomsky, Noam, and David Barsamian. 2003. *Imperial Ambitions: Conversations on the Post-9/11 World*. New York: Metropolitan Books.

_____. 2007. *What We Say Goes: Conversations on U.S. Power in a Changing World*. New York: Metropolitan Books.

Cirino, Robert. 1974. *Power to Persuade: Mass Media and the News*. New York: Bantam.

Cockburn, Patrick. 2006. *The Occupation: War and Resistance in Iraq*. London: Verso.

_____. 2008. *Muqtada: Muqtada al-Sadr, the Shia Revival, and the Struggle for Iraq*. New York: Scribner.

Cockburn, Alexander, and Jeffrey St. Clair. 2007. *End Times: The Death of the Fourth Estate*. Oakland, Calif.: A.K. Press.

_____. 1998. *Whiteout: The CIA, Drugs, and the Press*. London: Verso.

Cohen, Bernard C. 1993. *The Press and Foreign Policy*. Berkeley: IGS.

Cook, Timothy E. 1998. *Governing with the News: The News Media as a Political Institution*. Chicago: University of Chicago Press.

Croteau, David, and William Hoynes. 2001. *The Business of Media and the Public Interest*. Thousand Oaks, Calif.: Pine Forge Press.

Curran, James, and Myung-Jin Park, eds. 2000. *De-Westernizing Media Studies*. London: Routledge.

Dearing, James W., and Everett M. Rogers. 1996. *Agenda Setting*. Thousand Oaks, Calif.: Sage.

Delli Carpini, Michael X., and Scott Keeter. 1996. *What Americans Know about Politics and Why It Matters*. New Haven: Yale University Press.

DiMaggio, Anthony. 2008. *Mass Media, Mass Propaganda: Examining American News in the "War on Terror."* Lanham, Md.: Lexington.

Donald, Stephanie Hemeiryk, Michael Keane, and Yin Hong, eds. 2002. *Media in China: Consumption, Content, and Crisis*. London: Routledge.

Dorman, William A., and Mansour Farhang. 1987. *The U.S. Press and Iran: Foreign Policy and the Journalism of Deference*. Berkeley: University of California Press.

Edelman, Murray. 1988. *Constructing the Political Spectacle*. Chicago: University of Chicago Press.

Edwards, David, and David Cromwell. 2006. *Guardians of Power: The Myth of the Liberal Media*. Ann Arbor, Mich.: Pluto Press.

Entman, Robert. 2004. *Projections of Power: Framing News, Public Opinion, and U.S. Foreign Policy*. Chicago: University of Chicago Press.

Epstein, Edward Jay. 2000. *News from Nowhere: Television and the News*. Chicago: Ivan R. Dee.

Erlich, Reese. 2007. *The Iran Agenda: The Real Story of U.S. Policy and the Middle East*. Sausalito, Calif.: PoliPoint Press.

Esser, Frank, and Barbara Pfetsch, eds. 2004. *Comparing Political Communication: Theories, Cases, and Challenges*. Cambridge: Cambridge University Press.

Ewen, Stuart. 1996. *PR! A Social History of Spin*. New York: Basic Books.

Fallows, James. 2006. *Blind into Baghdad: America's War in Iraq*. New York: Vintage.

Fenton, Tom. 2005. *Bad News: The Decline of Reporting, the Business of News, and the Danger to Us All*. New York: Regan Books.

Fishman, Mark. 1980. *Manufacturing the News*. Austin: University of Texas Press.

Fisk, Robert. 2002. *Pity the Nation: The Abduction of Lebanon*. New York: Nation Books.

____. 2007. *The Great War for Civilisation: The Conquest of the Middle East*. New York: Vintage.

Flew, Terry. 2007. *Understanding Global Media*. New York: Palgrave.

Forgacs, David. ed. 2000. *The Antonio Gramsci Reader: Selected Writings 1916–1935*. New York: New York University Press.

Frenkel, Erwin. 1994. *The Press and Politics in Israel: The Jerusalem Post From 1932 to the Present*. Westport, Conn.: Greenwood Publishing.

Gamson, William A. 1996. *Talking Politics*. Cambridge: Cambridge University Press.

Gans, Herbert J. 1980. *Deciding What's News: A Study of CBS Evening News, NBC Nightly News, Newsweek, and Time*. New York: Vintage.

Gerbner, George, Hamid Mowlana, and Kaarle Nordenstreng, eds. 1993. *The Global Media Debate: Its Rise, Fall, and Renewal*. Norwood, N.J.: Ablex Publishing.

Gilbert, Dennis. 2003. *The American Class Structure in an Age of Growing Inequality*. Belmont, Calif.: Thomson Wadworth Publishing.

Ginsberg, Benjamin. 1986. *The Captive Public: How Mass Opinion Promotes State Power*. New York: Harper.

Gitlin, Todd. 1980. *The Whole World Is Watching: The Making and Unmaking of the New Left*. Berkeley: University of California Press.

Goffman, Erving, and Bennett Berger. 1986. *Frame Analysis: An Essay on the Organization of Experience*. Boston: Northeastern University Press.

Graber, Doris A. 2001. *Processing Politics: Learning from Television in the Internet Age*. Chicago: University of Chicago Press.

____. 2002. *Mass Media and American Politics*. Washington D.C.: CQ Press.

Gunther, Richard, and Anthony Mughan, eds. 2000. *Democracy and the Media: A Comparative Perspective*. Cambridge: Cambridge University Press.

Hachten, William A., and James F. Scotton. 2002. *The World News Prism: Global Media in an Era of Terrorism*. Ames: Iowa State University Press.

Hackworth, Jason. 2007. *The Neoliberal City: Governance, Ideology, and Development in American Urbanism*. Ithaca, N.Y.: Cornell University Press.

Hafez, Kai. 2007. *The Myth of Media Globalization*. Cambridge: Polity Press.

Hallin, Daniel C. 1989. *The Uncensored War: The Media and Vietnam*. Berkeley: University of California Press.

____. 1994. *We Keep America on Top of the World: Television Journalism and the Public Sphere*. London: Routledge.

Hallin, Daniel C., and Paolo Mancini. 2004. *Comparing Media Systems: Three Models of Media and Politics*. Cambridge: Cambridge University Press.

Herbst, Susan. 1998. *Reading Public Opinion: How Political Actors View the Democratic Process*. Chicago: University of Chicago Press.

Herman, Edward S. 1999. *The Myth of the Liberal Media*. New York: Peter Lang Publishing.

Herman, Edward S., and Noam Chomsky. 1988. *Manufacturing Consent: The Political Economy of the Mass Media*. New York: Pantheon.

_____. 2002. *Manufacturing Consent: The Political Economy of the Mass Media*. New York: Pantheon.

Herman, Edward S., and Robert W. McChesney. 1997. *The Global Media: The New Missionaries of Corporate Capitalism*. New York: Continuum.

Hertsgaard, Mark. 1988. *On Bended Knee: The Press and the Reagan Presidency*. New York: Farrar, Straus and Giroux.

Hoynes, William. 1994. *Public Television for Sale: Media, the Market, and the Public Sphere*. Boulder, Colo.: Westview Press.

Huntington, Samuel, Jodi Watanuki, and Michael Crozier. 1975. *The Crisis of Democracy: Task Force Report 8*. New York: New York University Press.

Iyengar, Shanto. 1991. *Is Anyone Responsible? How Television Frames Political Issues*. Chicago: University of Chicago Press.

Iyengar, Shanto, and Donald Kinder. 1987. *News That Matters: Television and American Opinion*. Chicago: University of Chicago Press.

Jamail, Dahr. 2007. *Beyond the Green Zone: Dispatches from an Unembedded Journalist in Occupied Iraq*. Chicago: Haymarket Books.

Jeffries, Leo W. 1997. *Mass Media Effects*. Prospect Heights, Ill.: Waveland.

Johnson, Dominic D. P., and Dominic Tierney. 2006. *Failing to Win: Perceptions of Victory and Defeat in International Politics*. Cambridge: Harvard University Press.

Katovsky, Bill, and Timothy Carlson. 2003. *Embedded: The Media at War in Iraq: An Oral History*. Guilford, Conn.: Lyons.

Keck, Margaret E., and Kathryn Sikkink. 1998. *Activists beyond Borders*. Ithaca, N.Y.: Cornell University Press.

Kennan, George F. 1999. *American Diplomacy*. Chicago: University of Chicago Press.

Kerbel, Matthew R. 2001. *If It Bleeds, It Leads: An Anatomy of Television News*. Boulder, Colo.: Westview Press.

Kiernan, V. G. 2005. *America, The New Imperialism: From White Settlement to World Hegemony*. London: Verso.

Kingdon, John W. 2003. *Agendas, Alternatives, and Public Policies*. New York: Addison Wesley Longman.

Kissinger, Henry. 1982. *Years of Upheaval*. New York: Little, Brown.

Klaehn, Jeffery, ed. 2005. *Filtering the News: Essays on Herman and Chomsky's Propaganda Model*. New York: Black Rose Books.

Klapper, Joseph. 1960. *The Effects of Mass Communication*. New York: Free Press.

Klare, Michael T. 2005. *Blood and Oil: The Dangers and Consequences of America's Growing Dependency on Imported Petroleum*. New York: Henry Holt.

Lang, Gladys Engel, and Kurt Lang. 1983. *The Battle for Public Opinion: The President, the Press, and the Polls during Watergate*. New York: Columbia University Press.

Lasswell, Harold. 1972. *Politics: Who Gets What, When, How*. New York: Meridian .

Lawson, Stephanie. 2003. *International Relations: A Short Introduction*. Cambridge: Polity Press.

Lazarsfeld, Paul, Bernard Berelson, and Hazel Gaudet. 1944. *The People's Choice*. New York: Columbia University Press.

Lewis, Justin. 2001. *Constructing Public Opinion: How Political Elites Do What They Like and Why We Seem to Go Along with it*. New York: Columbia University Press.

Lewis, Justin, Rod Brookes, Nick Mosdell, and Terry Threadgold. 2006. *Shoot First and Ask Questions Later: Media Coverage of the 2003 Iraq War*. New York: Peter Lang.

Lichter, Robert S., Stanley Rothman, and Linda S. Lichter. 1990. *The Media Elite: America's New Powerbrokers*. New York: Hastings.

Lindblom, Charles. 1977. *Politics and Markets: The World's Political-Economic Systems*. New York: Basic Books.

Lippmann, Walter. 1993. *The Phantom Public*. New Brunswick, NJ: Transaction Publishers.

_____. 1997. *Public Opinion*. New York: Free Press.

_____. 2008. *Liberty and the News*. Princeton: Princeton University Press.

Manza, Jeff, Fay Lomax Cook, and Benjamin I. Page, eds. 2002. *Navigating Public Opinion: Polls, Policy, and the Future of American Democracy*. Oxford: Oxford University Press.

McAdam, Douglas. 1999. *Political Process and the Development of Black Insurgency: 1930-1970*. Chicago: University of Chicago Press.

McChesney, Robert W. 1999. *Rich Media, Poor Democracy: Communication Politics in Dubious Times*. New York: New Press.

_____. 2004. *The Problem of Media: U.S. Communication Politics in the 21st Century*. New York: Monthly Review Press.

_____. 2007. *Communication Revolution: Critical Junctures and the Future of Media*. New York: New Press.

_____. 2008. *The Political Economy of Media: Enduring Issues, Emerging Dilemmas*. New York: Monthly Review Press.

McCombs, Maxwell. 2004. *Setting the Agenda: The Mass Media and Public Opinion*. Cambridge: Polity Press.

McFarland, Andrew S. 2004. *Neopluralism: The Evolution of Political Process Theory*. Lawrence: University Press of Kansas.

McManus, John H. 1994. *Market Driven Journalism: Let the Citizen Beware?* Thousand Oaks, Calif.: Sage.

McNair, Brian. 1994. *News and Journalism in the U.K.* London: Routledge.

Mermin, Jonathan. 1999. *Debating War and Peace: Media Coverage of U.S. Intervention in the Post-Vietnam Era.* Princeton: Princeton University Press.

Miller, David., ed. *Tell Me Lies: Propaganda and Media Distortion in the Attack on Iraq.* London: Pluto Press.

Miller, David, and William Dinan. 2008. *A Century of Spin: How Public Relations Became the Cutting Edge of Corporate Power.* Ann Arbor, Mich.: Pluto Press.

Mindich, David T. Z. 1998. *Just the Facts: How "Objectivity" Came to Define American Journalism.* New York: New York University Press.

Moghadam, Valentine. 2008. *Globalization and Social Movements: Islamism, Feminism, and the Global Justice Movement.* Lanham, Md.: Rowman and Littlefield.

Morris, Nancy, and Silvio Waisbord. 2001. *Media and Globalization: Why the State Matters.* Lanham, Md.: Rowman and Littlefield.

Mueller, John E. 1973. *War, Presidents, and Public Opinion.* New York: Wiley.

_____. 1994. *Policy and Opinion in the Gulf War.* Chicago: University of Chicago Press.

Nassar, Jamal R. 2004. *Globalization and Terrorism: The Migration of Dreams and Nightmares.* Lanham, Md.: Rowman and Littlefield.

Nerone, John C. 1995. *Last Rights: Revisiting Four Theories of the Press.* Urbana: University of Illinois Press.

Neuman, W. Russell, Mario R. Just, and Ann N. Crigler. 1992. *Common Knowledge: News and the Construction of Political Meaning.* Chicago: University of Chicago Press.

Nikoleav, Alexander G., and Ernest A. Hakanen, eds.. 2003. *Leading to the 2003 Iraq War: The Global Media Debate.* New York: Palgrave.

Norris, Pippa, Montague Kern, and Marion Just, eds. 2003. *Framing Terrorism: The News Media, the Government, and the Public.* London: Routledge.

Page, Benjamin I. 1996. *Who Deliberates? Mass Media in Modern Democracy.* Chicago: University of Chicago Press.

Page, Benjamin I., and Marshall M. Bouton. 2006. *The Foreign Policy Disconnect: What Americans want from Our Leaders but Don't Get.* Chicago: University of Chicago Press.

Page, Benjamin I., and Robert Y. Shapiro. 1992. *The Rational Public: Fifty Years of Trends in Americans' Policy Preferences.* Chicago: University of Chicago Press.

Parenti, Michael. 1992. *Inventing Reality: The Politics of the News Media.* New York: St. Martin's Press.

_____. 2002. *Democracy for the Few.* New York: St. Martin's Press.

Parry, Robert. 1999. *Lost History: Contras, Cocaine, the Press & "Project Truth."* Arlington, Va.: TMC Books.

Patterson, Thomas E. 1994. *Out of Order.* New York: Vintage.

_____. 2002. *The Vanishing Voter: Public Involvement in an Age of Uncertainty.* New York: Vintage.

Perse, Elizabeth M. 2001. *Media Effects and Society*. Mahwah, N.J.: Lawrence Erlbaum.

Phillips, Peter, and Andrew Roth, eds. 2008. *Censored 2008: The Top 25 Censored Stories of 2006–2007*. New York: Seven Stories Press.

Popkin, Samuel L. 1994. *The Reasoning Voter: Communication and Persuasion in Presidential Campaigns*. Chicago: University of Chicago Press.

Price, Monroe E. 2002. *Media and Sovereignty: The Global Information Revolution and Its Challenge to State Power*. Cambridge: MIT Press.

Protess, David L., and Maxwell McCombs. 1991. *Agenda Setting: Readings on Media, Public Opinion, and Policymaking*. Mahwah, N.J.: Lawrence Erlbaum.

Rabe, Stephen G. 1988. *Eisenhower and Latin America: The Foreign Policy of Anti-Communism*. Chapel Hill: University of North Carolina Press.

Ricks, Thomas E. 2007. *Fiasco: The American Military Adventure in Iraq*. New York: Penguin Books.

Ritter, Scott, and William Rivers Pitt. 2002. *War on Iraq: What Team Bush Doesn't Want You to Know*. New York: Context Books.

Roberts, J. Timmons, and Amy Bellone Hite, eds. 2007. *The Globalization and Development Reader: Perspectives on Development and Global Change*. Malden, Mass.: Blackwell.

Rojecki, Andrew. 1999. *Silencing the Opposition: Antinuclear Movements and the Media in the Cold War*. Chicago: University of Illinois Press.

Romano, Angela, and Michael Bromley, eds. 2005. *Journalism and Democracy in Asia*. London: Routledge.

Rosenau, James R. 1961. *Public Opinion and Foreign Policy*. New York: Random House.

Russett, Bruce, and John R. Oneal. 2001. *Triangulating Peace: Democracy, Interdependence, and International Organizations*. New York: W. W. Norton.

Sassen, Saskia. 2006. *Cities in a World Economy*. Thousand Oaks, Calif.: Pine Forge Press.

Schou, Nick. 2006. *Kill the Messenger: How the CIA's Crack-Cocaine Controversy Destroyed Journalist Gary Webb*. New York: Nation Books.

Schoultz, Lars. 1998. *Beneath the United States: A History of U.S. Policy toward Latin America*. Cambridge: Harvard University Press.

Schudson, Michael. 1973. *Discovering the News: A Social History of American Newspapers*. New York: Basic Books.

_____. 1995. *The Power of News*. Cambridge: Harvard University Press.

Semetko, Holli A., Jay G. Blumler, Michael Gurevitch, and David H. Weaver. 1991. *The Formation of Campaign Agendas: A Comparative Analysis of Party and Media Roles in Recent American and British Elections*. Mahwah, N.J.: Lawrence Erlbaum .

Shanahan, James, and Michael Morgan. 1999. *Television and Its Viewers: Cultivation Theory and Research*. Cambridge: Cambridge University Press.

Shapiro, Robert Y., and Lawrence Jacobs. 2000. *Politicians Don't Pander: Political Manipulation and the Loss of Democratic Responsiveness.* Chicago: University of Chicago Press.

Siebert, Fred S., Thedore Peterson, and Wilbur Schramm. 1974. *Four Theories of the Press: The Authoritarian, Libertarian, Social Responsibility, and Soviet Communist Concepts of What the Press Should Be and Do.* Chicago: University of Illinois Press.

Sigal, Leon V. 1973. *Reporters and Officials: The Organization and Politics of Newsmaking.* Lexington, Mass.: D.C. Heath.

Skinner, David, and Mike Gasher, eds. 2005. *Converging Media, Diverging Politics: A Political Economy of News Media in the United States and Canada.* Lanham, Md.: Lexington Books.

Sklar, Leslie. 2002. *Globalization: Capitalism and its Alternatives.* Oxford: Oxford University Press.

Sobel, Richard, ed. 1993. *Public Opinion in U.S. Foreign Policy: The Controversy Over Contra Aid.* Lanham, Md.: Rowman and Littlefield Publishers.

____. 2001. *The Impact of Public Opinion on U.S. Foreign Policy since Vietnam.* Oxford: Oxford University Press.

Soley, Lawrence. 2002. *Censorship Inc.: The Corporate Threat to Free Speech in the United States.* New York: Monthly Review Press.

Sparks, Colin. 2007. *Globalization, Development, and the Mass Media.* Thousand Oaks, Calif.: Sage.

Sparrow, Bartholomew H. 1999. *Uncertain Guardians: The News Media as a Political Institution.* Baltimore: Johns Hopkins University Press.

Squires, James D. 1993. *Read All About It! The Corporate Takeover of America's Newspaper.* New York: Times Books.

Steele, Jonathan. 2008. *Defeat: Why America and Britain Lost Iraq.* Berkeley: Counterpoint.

Steger, Manfred B. 2008. *Globalisms: The Great Ideological Struggle of the Twenty-first Century.* Lanham, Md.: Rowman and Littlefield.

Steger, Manfred B. 2008. *The Rise of the Global Imaginary: Political Ideologies from the French Revolution to the Global War on Terror.* Oxford: Oxford University Press.

Stiglitz, Joseph E. 2003. *Globalization and Its Discontents.* New York: W. W. Norton.

____. 2007. *Making Globalization Work.* New York: W. W. Norton.

____. 2008. *The Three Trillion Dollar War: The True Cost of the Iraq Conflict.* New York: W. W. Norton.

Stimson, James A. 2004. *Tides of Consent: How Public Opinion Shapes American Politics.* Cambridge: Cambridge University Press.

Switzer, Les, and Mohammed Adhikari, eds. 2000. *South Africa's Resistance Press: Alternative Voices in the Last Generation under Apartheid.* Athens, Ohio: Ohio University Center for International Studies.

Sylvester, Judith, and Suzanne Huffman. 2005. *Reporting from the Front: The Media and the Military.* Lanham, Md.: Rowman and Littlefield Publishers.

Thomas, Helen. 2006. *Watchdogs of Democracy? The Waning Washington Press Corps and How It Has Failed the Public*. New York: Scribner.

Thomas, Pradip N., and Zaharom Nain, eds. 2004. *Who Owns the Media? Global Trends and Local Resistance*. London: Zed Books.

Tomlinson, John. 1999. *Globalization and Culture*. Chicago: University of Chicago Press.

Traudt, Paul J. 2005. *Media, Audiences, Effects: An Introduction to the Study of Media Content*. New York: Pearson Longman.

Tuchman, Gaye. 1980. *Making News: A Study in the Construction of Reality*. New York: Free Press.

Tumber, Howard, and Frank Webster. 2006. *Journalists under Fire: Information War and Journalistic Practices*. Thousand Oaks, Calif.: Sage.

Tunstall, Jeremy. 2007. *The Media Were American: U.S. Mass Media in Decline*. Oxford: Oxford University Press.

Tye, Larry. 1998. *The Father of Spin: Edward L. Bernays and the Birth of Public Relations*. New York: Owl Books.

Uslaner, Eric M. 2002. *The Moral Foundations of Trust*. Cambridge: Cambridge University Press.

Walker Jr., Jack L. 2000. *Mobilizing Interest Groups in America: Patrons, Professions, and Social Movements*. Ann Arbor: University of Michigan Press.

Wallerstein, Immanuel. 2006. *World-Systems Analysis: An Introduction*. Durham, N.C.: Duke University Press.

Wolfsfeld, Gadi. 1997. *Media and Political Conflict: News from the Middle East*. Cambridge: Cambridge University Press.

____. 2004. *Media and the Path to Peace*. Cambridge: Cambridge University Press.

Yergin, Daniel. 2008. *The Prize: The Epic Quest for Oil, Money, and Power*. New York: Free Press.

Zaller, John R. 1992. *The Nature and Origins of Mass Opinion*. Berkeley: University of California Press.

Notes

INTRODUCTION: PROPAGANDA AND THE NEWS IN A TIME OF TERROR

1. For more information, see the National Election Study of November 2004: http://www.electionstudies.org/studypages/2004prepost/2004prepost.htm.
2. Editorial, "The Road Home," *New York Times*, 8 July 2007, http://www.nytimes.com/2007/07/08/opinion/08sun1.html.
3. Timothy Williams, "Iraq's War Widows Face Dire Need With Little Aid," *New York* Times, 22 February 2009, http://www.nytimes.com/2009/02/23/world/ middleeast/23widows.html; Reuters, "Iraq Conflict Has Killed Over a Million, Says Survey," 30 January 2008, http://www.alertnet.org/thenews/newsdesk/L30488579.htm.
4. Editorial, "The Road Home."
5. Edward Herman and Noam Chomsky, *Manufacturing Consent: The Political Economy of the Mass Media* (New York: Pantheon, 1988), xi.
6. Ibid., 298.
7. Anthony DiMaggio, *Mass Media, Mass Propaganda: Examining American News in the "War on Terror"* (Lanham, Md.: Lexington, 2008); Michael Ryan, "Framing the War Against Terrorism: U.S. Newspaper Editorials and Military Action in Afghanistan," *International Communication Gazette*66/5 (2004): 363–82.
8. George W. Bush, "Address to a Joint Session of Congress and the American People," White House website, September 2001, http://www.whitehouse.gov/news/releases/2001/09/20010920-8.html.
9. For more information, see Chapter 10 of: Anthony R. DiMaggio, *Mass Media, Mass Propaganda: Examining American News in the "War on Terror"* (Lanham, Md.: Lexington, 2009).
10. For more information on this poll, see the September 2001 survey from CBS, available through the *Inter-University Consortium for Political and Social Research* (http://www.icpsr.org).
11. The relationships discussed are all statistically significant. The relationship between two variables, in this case respondents' viewing of Bush's speech and their expressions of support for his policies, is said to be statistically significant if that relationship is unlikely to materialize due to chance variation in the population of

people sampled. The data regarding public exposure to Bush's speech and support for war is derived from a September 2001 CBS poll (see n. 9). Ordinary Least Squares regression analysis indicates that exposure to President Bush's speech to Congress is positively related to increased support for Bush's handling of the crisis, support for force, support for war, and support for a broader war outside of Afghanistan, after controlling for other demographic factors such as respondent age, sex, party identification, and race. The relationship between exposure to the president's speech and support for war is significant for the broader war question at the .01 percent level, and significant for the other three policy questions at the 1 percent level.

12. David Forgacs, ed., *The Antonio Gramsci Reader: Selected Writings 1916–1935* (New York: New York University, 2000), 422–23.
13. Ibid., 307.
14. Ibid., 424.
15. Robin Mansell, "Political Economy, Power, and New Media," *New Media and Society* 6/1 (2004): 102.
16. Peter L. Berger and Thomas Luckmann, *The Social Construction of Reality: A Treatise in the Sociology of Knowledge* (New York: Anchor, 1967); Gaye Tuchman, *Making News: A Study in the Construction of Reality* (New York: Free Press, 1980); Michael Parenti, *Inventing Reality: The Politics of the News Media* (New York: St. Martin's, 1992).
17. Robert W. McChesney, *Rich Media, Poor Democracy: Communication Politics in Dubious Times* (New York: New Press, 1999); Robert W. McChesney, *Communication Revolution: Critical Junctures and the Future of Media* (New York: New Press, 2007); Robert W. McChesney, *The Problem of Media: U.S. Communication Politics in the 21st Century* (New York: Monthly Review Press, 2004); Robert W. McChesney, *The Political Economy of Media: Enduring Issues, Emerging Dilemmas* (New York: Monthly Review Press, 2008).
18. Robert W. McChesney, "Journalism, Democracy . . . and Class Struggle," *Monthly Review* 52/6 (2000): 1–15.
19. Todd Gitlin, *The Whole World Is Watching: The Making and Unmaking of the New* Left (Berkeley: University of California, 1980), 11.
20. Although Gitlin does not explicitly argue (to my knowledge) that hegemony is defined by the debate over the best application of American power and promotion of capitalism, his claim that radical critiques of the media in times of war from those on the socialist left receive a hearing in the mass media is not supported by any empirical evidence from studies done on the Vietnam War or the Iraq war, including: Herman and Chomsky, *Manufacturing Consent*, 1988: and Daniel C. Hallin, *The Uncensored War: The Media and Vietnam* (Berkeley: University of California, 1989). Realistically, when Gitlin claims that hegemonic structures were contested during Vietnam through increasingly critical media dialogue, we have to examine what dialogue he is referring to. We are left with little, after undertaking this examination, than the dialogue of doves and hawks, who argued within the capitalist framework, over the wisest application of military force during the Cold War.
21. Gitlin, *The Whole World Is Watching*, 270.
22. Noam Chomsky, "Questions About the Propaganda Model," email to author, 14 October 2007.
23. Ibid.
24. Very few empirical works are dedicated to exploring U.S. media propaganda, following the 1988 publication of *Manufacturing Consent*. Few of these studies have

actually been published as major books: DiMaggio, *Mass Media, Mass Propaganda*, 2008; and Jeffery Klaehn, ed., *Filtering the News: Essays on Herman and Chomsky's Propaganda Model* (New York: Black Rose, 2005). Few works appear in the U.S. scholarly community outside of a few unpublished works such as Andrew Kennis, "The Propaganda Model: Evaluating a Theory on the Political Economy and Performance of the Mass Media," *Midwest Political Science Conference*, April 2006, http://www.allacademic.com/meta/p_mla_apa_research_citation/1/3/7/0/0/p137004_index.html; Mark Major, "Contesting Media Models: Propaganda vs. Cascading Activation," *Midwest Political Science Conference*, April 2006, http://www.allacademic.com/meta/p_mla_apa_research_citation/1/3/6/9/9/p136990_index.html.

25. Major works ignoring the propaganda model and Herman and Chomsky include Gadi Wolfsfeld, *Media and the Path to Peace* (Cambridge: Cambridge University, 2004); Gadi Wolfsfeld, *Media and Political Conflict: News from the Middle East* (Cambridge: Cambridge University, 1997); Shanto Iyengar, *Is Anyone Responsible? How Television Frames Political Issues* (Chicago: University of Chicago, 1991); Jonathan Mermin, *Debating War and Peace: Media Coverage of U.S. Intervention in the Post-Vietnam Era* (Princeton: Princeton University, 1999); John Zaller and Dennis Chiu, "Government's Little Helper: U.S. Press Coverage of Foreign Policy Crisis, 1945–1991," *Political Communication* 13/4 (1996): 385–405.
26. Herring and Robinson, "Too Polemical or Too Critical? Chomsky on the Study of the News Media and United States Foreign Policy," *Review of International Studies*, 2003, Vol. 29, 553-568.
27. John R. Zaller, "Elite Leadership of Mass Opinion," in *Taken By Storm: The Media, Public Opinion, and U.S. Foreign Policy in the Gulf War*, eds. W. Lance Bennett and David L. Paletz, (Chicago: University of Chicago, 1994), 202.
28. W. Lance Bennett, Regina G. Lawrence, and Steven Livingston, *When the Press Fails: Political Power and the News Media From Iraq to Katrina* (Chicago: University of Chicago, 2007), 14.
29. Doris A. Graber, "When the Press Fails: Political Power and the News Media from Iraq to Katrina" (book review), *Political Science Quarterly* 123/1 (2008): 167–68.
30. Gadi Wolfsfeld, "When the Press Fails: Political Power and the News Media From Iraq to Katrina" (book review), *Journal of Communication* 58/1 (2008): 198–99; Jonathan McDonald Ladd, "When the Press Fails: Political Power and the News Media From Iraq to Katrina" (book review), *Perspectives on Politics* 6/3 (2008): 601–2.
31. This is a typical definition provided by the Merriam-Webster Dictionary. See: http://www.merriam-webster.com/dictionary/independence.
32. Scott L. Althaus, "When News Norms Collide, Follow the Lead: New Evidence for Press Independence," *Political Communication* 20/4 (2003): 381–14.
33. W. Lance Bennett and Steven Livingston, "A Semi-Independent Press: Government Control and Journalistic Autonomy in the Political Construction of News," *Political Communication* 20/4 (2003): 359–62.
34. Kurt Lang and Gladys Engel Lang, "Noam Chomsky and the Manufacture of Consent for American Foreign Policy," *Political Communication* 21/1 (2004): 95.
35. Hallin, *We Keep America on Top of the World*, 12–13.
36. Herman and Chomsky, *Manufacturing Consent*, 226.
37. Timothy E. Cook, *Governing with the News: The News Media as a Political Institution* (Chicago: University of Chicago, 1998), 196.
38. W. Lance Bennett, *News: The Politics of Illusion* (New York: Longman, 2001), 3.

39. Mark Achbar and Peter Wintonick, dir., *Manufacturing Consent: Noam Chomsky and the Media* Zeitgeist Films, 1992.
40. Lang and Lang, "Noam Chomsky and the Manufacture of Consent," 95.
41. Stephanie Lawson, *International Relations: A Short Introduction* (Cambridge: Polity, 2003), 93; Peter Burnell and Vicky Randall, *Politics in the Developing World* (Oxford: Oxford University Press, 2008), 365.
42. Richard A. Brody, *Assessing the President: The Media, Elite Opinion, and Public Support* (Stanford: Stanford University Press, 1991), 7; Bruce Russett and John R. Oneal, *Triangulating Peace: Democracy, Interdependence, and International Organizations* (New York: W. W. Norton, 2001).
43. Lang and Lang, "Noam Chomsky and the Manufacture of Consent," 95.
44. Michael Schudson, *The Power of News* (Cambridge: Harvard University Press, 1995), 4.
45. Schudson, *The Power of News*, 16.
46. Edward Jay Epstein, *News from Nowhere: Television and the News* (Chicago: Ivan R. Dee, 2000), 201.
47. Ibid., 203–5; David T. Z. Mindich, *Just the Facts: How "Objectivity" Came to Define American Journalism* (New York: New York University, 1998), 8, 41.
48. Herman and Chomsky, *Manufacturing Consent*, 304.

1. WITHDRAWAL PAINS: IRAQ AND THE POLITICS OF MEDIA DEFERENCE

1. George W. Bush, "President Bush Rejects Artificial Deadline, Vetoes Iraq War Supplemental," *White House Website*, 1 May 2007, http://www.whitehouse.gov/news/releases/2007/05/20070501-6.html; Nizar Latif and Phil Sands, "Muqtada al-Sadr: The British are Retreating from Basra," *Independent*, 20 August 2007, http://news.independent.co.uk/world/middle_east/article2878776.ece
2. For more on Democratic support for the Iraq war during the 2003 to 2007 period, see my previous essay addressing this topic: Anthony R. DiMaggio, "There Are No Protestors Here: Media Marginalization and the Antiwar Movement," paper presented at the 2007 Conference for the Illinois Political Science Association.
3. "The Democratic Presidential Debate on MSNBC," *New York Times*, 26 September 2007, http://www.nytimes.com/2007/09/26/us/politics/26DEBATE-TRANSCRIPT.html?pagewanted=all.
4. Anthony R. DiMaggio, *Mass Media, Mass Propaganda: Examining American News in the "War on Terror"* (Lanham, Md.: Lexington, forthcoming April 2008), 113–14, 206–8.
5. Scott L. Althaus, "When News Norms Collide, Follow the Lead: New Evidence for Press Independence," *Political Communication* 20/4 (2003): 381–414; W. Lance Bennett and Steven Livingston, "A Semi-Independent Press: Government Control and Journalistic Autonomy in the Political Construction of News," *Political Communication* 20/4 (2003): 359–62; W. Lance Bennett, Regina G. Lawrence, and Steven Livingston, *When the Press Fails: Political Power and the News Media from Iraq to Katrina* (Chicago: University of Chicago Press, 2007), 46–71.
6. Benjamin I. Page, *Who Deliberates? Mass Media in Modern Democracy* (Chicago: University of Chicago Press, 1996).
7. For a small sample, see the following authors: Robert Entman, *Projections of Power: Framing News, Public Opinion, and United States Foreign Policy* (Chicago:

University of Chicago Press, 2004); Karen Callaghan and Frauke Schnell, eds., *Framing American Politics* (Pittsburgh: University of Pittsburgh Press, 2005); Shanto Iyengar and Donald Kinder, *News That Matters: Television and American Opinion* (Chicago: University of Chicago Press, 1987); Pippa Norris, Montague Kern, and Marion Just, eds., *Framing Terrorism: The News Media, the Government, and the Public* (New York: Routledge, 2003); Frank R. Baumgartner and Bryan D. Jones, *Agendas and Instability in American Politics* (Chicago: University of Chicago Press, 1993); Erving Goffman and Bennett Berger, *Frame Analysis: An Essay on the Organization of Experience* (Boston: Northeastern University Press, 1986).

8. Entman, *Projections of Power*. Emphasis added.
9. Murray Edelman, *Constructing the Political Spectacle* (Chicago: University of Chicago Press, 1988).
10. Ibid., 97.
11. Frank Baumgartner and Bryan Jones, *Agendas and Instability in American Politics* (Chicago: University of Chicago Press, 1993), 111.
12. John W. Kingdon, *Agendas, Alternatives, and Public Policies* (New York: Longman, 2003), 199–200.
13. Iyengar and Kinder, *News That Matters*, 1989.
14. Michael Parenti, *Inventing Reality: The Politics of the News Media* (New York: St. Martin's Press, 1992).
15. Edward Herman and Noam Chomsky, *Manufacturing Consent: The Political Economy of the Mass Media* (New York: Pantheon, 2002); Ben Bagdikian, *The New Media Monopoly* (New York: Beacon, 2004); Robert McChesney, *Rich Media, Poor Democracy: Communication Politics in Dubious Times* (New York: New Press, 2000).
16. Charles Lindblom, *Politics and Markets: The World's Political-Economic Systems* (New York: Basic Books, 1977), 229, 207.
17. Bennett, Lawrence, and Livingston, *When the Press Fails: Political Power and the News Media from Iraq to Katrina* (Chicago: University of Chicago Press, 2007), 72–107.
18. Daniel C. Hallin, *The Uncensored War: The Media and Vietnam* (Berkeley: University of California Press1986), 8, 10; Jonathan Mermin, *Debating War and Peace: Media Coverage of U.S. Intervention in the Post-Vietnam Era* (Princeton: Princeton University Press,1999), 5, 12, 151.
19. Daniel C. Hallin and Paolo Mancini, *Comparing Media Systems: Three Models of Media and Politics* (Cambridge: Cambridge University Press, 2004), 13.
20. Ibid., 212, 215–16.
21. Ibid., 16; Hetty Van Kempen, "Media–Party Parallelism and Its Effects: A Cross-National Comparative Study," *Political Communication* 2007, Vol. 24: No. 3, 303–320.
22. David Edwards and David Cromwell, *Guardians of Power: The Myth of the Liberal Media* (Ann Arbor, Mi.: Pluto Press, 2006); David Edwards and David Cromwell, *Newspeak in the 21st Century* (Ann Arbor, Mi.: Pluto Press, 2009). Edwards and Cromwell's analyses look at British media coverage across a wide number of foreign policy issues. The authors look at media framing of various issues such as the wars in Iraq and Afghanistan and highlight certain newscasts and stories, as well as correspondence between themselves and news reporters/editors, as evidence of propagandistic British media coverage. Although the authors' work remains an important exploratory contribution to the question of whether British media coverage is propagandistic, it does not systematically and empirically test news outlets in both the United Kingdom and United States. As a result, it is difficult to know for certain

whether British and American news coverage is equally propagandistic, or whether they are different in important respects. My own analysis in this book suggests that both the U.S. and British media are propagandistic, although the British press is relatively less propagandistic when compared to the U.S. press.

23. One of the few studies I have uncovered comparing British and American media covers the topic of media coverage of elections in both countries: Holli A. Semetko, Jay G. Blumler, Michael Gurevitch, and David H. Weaver, *The Formation of Campaign Agendas: A Comparative Analysis of Party and Media Roles in Recent American and British Elections* (Hillsdale, N.J.: Lawrence Erlbaum, 1991).
24. Editorial, "The Pelosi Plan for Iraq," *Washington Post*, 13 March 2007, 16(A).; Editorial, "The Phony Debate," *Washington Post*, 21 July 2007, 12(A).
25. Editorial, "The Road Home," *New York Times*, 8 July 2007, http://www.nytimes.com/2007/07/08/opinion/08sun1.html?_r=1&oref=slogin
26. In determining the number of minutes devoted to withdrawal, I utilized the Vanderbilt television news archive. The news abstracts were reviewed, searching for stories containing the words *Iraq* and *withdrawal.* The minutes for any stories containing these words were added up for the periods prior to and following the November 2006 election, and the average number of stories per month was calculated. Features on Iraq withdrawal were similarly calculated by simply counting the number of stories in the pre- and post-November 2006 election periods that mentioned the words Iraq and withdrawal.
27. Editorial, "Death in Basra," *Times*, 8 May 2006, 23.
28. Editorial, "Not So Fast," *Times*, 3 October 2007, 14.
29. The overlap percentages in Table 5 represent the correlations between each paper's coverage of withdrawal. These figures represent the percent of time (measured in months) in which each paper's coverage increases or decreases in accord with that of each other paper.
30. Editorial, "The United States and Britain Must Now Prepare an Orderly End to Their Occupation of Iraq," *Independent*, 17 May 2004, 28.
31. David E. Sanger, Michael R. Gordon, and John F. Burns, "Chaos Overran Iraq Plan in '06, Bush Team Says," *New York Times*, 2 January 2007, http://www.nytimes.com/2007/01/02/washington/02war.html; Robert Fisk, "Iraq Aftermath: Can't Blair See that This Country Is About to Explode? Can't Bush?" *Independent*, 1 August 2004, 11.
32. Fisk, "Iraq Aftermath."
33. Ibid.
34. Sources were categorized as antiwar if they were explicitly identified by reporters as members of the antiwar movement, or taking part in antiwar protests, activities, rallies, or marches.
35. Patrick Cockburn, "Revealed: The True Extent of Britain's Failure in Basra," *Independent*, 23 February 2007, 10.
36. Robert Fisk, "Baghdad Is a City that Reeks with the Stench of the Dead," *Independent*, 28 July 2004, 27.
37. John Roberts, "This Week at War," CNN, 24 March 2007, 19:00 ET.
38. Information about the Iraq Foundation and its many activities are available through the group's website: http://www.iraqfoundation.org/aboutus_overview.htm
39. John Roberts and Carol Lin, *This Week at War*, CNN, 28 October 2006, 19:00 ET.
40. Wolf Blitzer and Fredericka Whitefield, *This Week at War,* CNN, 25 June 2006, 13:00 ET.
41. John Roberts and Carol Lin, *This Week at War,* CNN, 30 September 2006, 19:00 ET.

42. John Roberts and Michael Ware, *This Week at War,* CNN, 17 September 2006, 13:00 ET.
43. John Roberts, *This Week at War,* CNN, 4 November 2006, 20:00 ET.
44. John Roberts and Carol Lin, *This Week at War,* CNN, 28 October 2006, 19:00 ET.; John Roberts, *This Week at War,* CNN, 24 February 2007, 19:00 ET.; John Roberts, *This Week at War,* CNN, 4 November 2006, 20:00 ET.
45. John Roberts and James Marks, *This Week at War,* CNN, 15 October 2006, 13:00 ET.
46. Kirk Semple, "Amid United States Buildup, Iraqis Seek Timetable for Pullout," *New York Times*, 12 May 2007.
47. The origins of stories were classified according to headlines. If the story origin was not determinable through the headline, the first two paragraphs were examined to discern whether specific individuals led the story, or whether it was based on specific events, or both. A second coder was used to verify the reliability of story origins, with over 90 percent reliability, after having reviewed all of the articles.
48. Kim Murphy, "Departing Blair Blasts Britain's 'Feral' Media," *Chicago Tribune*, 13 June 2007, 15.
49. Robert W. McChesney, *Rich Media, Poor Democracy: Communication Politics in Dubious Times* (New York: New Press, 1999); W. Lance Bennett, *News: The Politics of Illusion* (New York: Addison Wesley Longman, 2001); C. Edwin Baker, *Media Concentration and Democracy: Why Ownership Matters* (Cambridge: Cambridge University Press, 2007).
50. Brian McNair, *News and Journalism in the U.K.* (New York: Routledge, 1994), 158–59.
51. Timothy E. Cook, *Governing with the News: The News Media as a Political Institution* (Chicago: University of Chicago Press, 1998), 6.
52. Robert Fisk, "Covering the Middle East," in *Tell Me Lies: Propaganda and Media Distortion in the Attack on Iraq*, ed. David Miller (London: Pluto Press, 2004), 216–17.

2. THERE ARE NO PROTESTORS HERE: MEDIA MARGINALIZATION AND THE ANTIWAR MOVEMENT

1. Dahr Jamail, *Beyond the Green Zone: Dispatches From an Unembedded Journalist in Occupied Iraq* (Chicago: Haymarket, 2007), 125.
2. Rahul Mahajan, "Report From Fallujah: Destroying a Town in Order to Save It," *Common Dreams*, 12 April 2004, http://www.commondreams.org/views04/0412-01.htm.
3. Bernard C. Cohen, *The Press and Foreign Policy* (Westport, CT: Institute of Government Studies, 1993), 46.
4. Shanto Iyengar, *Is Anyone Responsible? How Television Frames Political Issues* (Chicago: University of Chicago Press, 1991), 2–3, 14.
5. Gaye Tuchman, *Making News: A Study in the Construction of Reality* (New York: Free Press, 1978), 86–87.
6. Andrew Rojecki, *Silencing the Opposition: Antinuclear Movements and the Media in the Cold War* (Chicago: University of Illinois Press, 1999), 160.
7. Ibid., 40.
8. Robert Entman, *Projections of Power: Framing News, Public Opinion, and United States Foreign Policy* (Chicago, University of Chicago Press, 2004), 139.
9. Todd Gitlin, *The Whole World Is Watching: Mass Media in the Making & Unmaking of the New Left* (Berkeley: University of California Press, 1980), 2.

10. Ibid., 11.
11. Ibid., 254.
12. Ibid., 271.
13. Ibid., 38.
14. Ibid., 39.
15. Edward Herman and Noam Chomsky, *Manufacturing Consent: The Political Economy of the Mass Media* (New York: Pantheon, 1988), 2.
16. Ibid., 22.
17. Gitlin, *The Whole World Is Watching*, 273–274. Emphasis added.
18. Ibid., 270.
19. Todd Gitlin, "From Put Down to Catch Up: The News and the Antiwar Movement," *American Prospect*, March 2003, 33–35.
20. It has been widely established that most Americans, since at least late 2004, are generally opposed to the war. This is seen clearly in the 2004 National Election Study, which found that 59 percent of Americans no longer thought the Iraq war was "worth it," as opposed to 38 percent that felt it was "worth it."
21. Susan Page, "Poll: USA Is Losing Patience in Iraq," *USA Today*, 12 June 2006, http://www.usatoday.com/news/washington/2005-06-12-poll_x.htm.
22. Anthony DiMaggio, *Mass Media, Mass Propaganda: Examining American News in the "War on Terror"* (Lanham, Md.: Lexington, 2008), 79–101, .
23. Noam Chomsky, *Rethinking Camelot: JFK, the Vietnam War, and United States Political Culture* (Boston: South End, 1993), 112.
24. Chomsky, *Rethinking Camelot*, 61.
25. Edward Herman, "The New York Times Versus the Civil Society," *Z Magazine*, December 2005, http://zmagsite.zmag.org/Images/herman1205.html.
26. Cindy Sheehan originally made these claims during the speaker portion of the march, prior to the march to the Capitol in which protestors were arrested attempting to enter the building.
27. Michelle Boorstein, V. Dion Haynes, and Allison Klein, "Dueling Demonstrations," *Washington Post*, 16 September 2007, 8(A); Natasha Altamirano, "Protestors Slam War," *Washington Times*, 16 September 2007, 7(A); Gabrielle Russon, "Thousands Hit Streets of D.C. to Protest War," *Chicago Tribune*, 16 September 2007, 1(A); Tina Marie Macias, "Thousands Demonstrate Against Iraq War in D.C.," *Los Angeles Times*, 16 September 2007, 16(A); David Johnston, "Dozens are Arrested in Antiwar Protest Near the Capitol," *New York Times*, 16 September 2007, 21(A). The *Washington Times* and *Washington Post* instead ran the stories on pages A7 and A8 respectively. Other major papers' coverage appeared as follows: the *New York Times* (A21), the *Los Angeles Times* (A16), the *Chicago Tribune* (A4), and the *Atlanta Journal Constitution* (A3).
28. Annie Gowen, "Brave New Boomers," *Washington Post*, 16 September 2007, 1(A); John Solomon and Matthew Mosk, "Hsu Cast Wide Net for Clinton Donors," *Washington Post*, 16 September 2007, 1(A); Ariana Eunjung Cha, "Pig Disease in China Worries the World," *Washington Post*, 16 September 2007, 1(A); Gary Emerling, "In Market for Change?" *Washington Times*, 16 September 2007, 1(A); Valerie Richardson, "Another Colorado Flock Leaves Episcopalian Fold," *Washington Times*, 16 September 2007, 1(A); Melissa Isaacson, "Illegal? Unethical? Or Strategy?" *Chicago Tribune*, 16 September 2007, 1(A).
29. Steven Lee Myers and Carl Hulse, "Bush Says Success Allows Limited Troop Cuts," *New York Times*, 14 September 2007, 1(A).
30. George W. Bush, "In Bush's Words: Assessing the War Today, and the Risks to

Avoid Tomorrow," *New York Times*, 14 September 2007, 8(A).

31. Peter Baker and Karen DeYoung, "Bush Tells Nation He Will Begin to Roll Back 'Surge,'" *Washington Post*, 14 September 2006, 1(A); Michael Tackett, "Bush Vows Troop Cuts," *Chicago Tribune*, 14 September 2007, sec. 1, 1; David Jackson, "Bush Ties Pullback to Success in Iraq," *USA Today*, 14–16 September 2007, sec. 1, 1.
32. Local DC News, *Channel 8*, 15 September 2007.
33. Suzanne Malveaux, *CNN Newsroom*, 15 September 2007, CNN.
34. Kimberly Guilfoyle, *Fox News Live*, 15 September 2007, Fox News.
35. Malveaux, 15 September 2007; Altamirano, "Protestors Slam War," 16 September 2007.
36. Boorstein, Haynes, and Klein, "Dueling Demonstrations"; Altamirano, "Protestors Slam War," 16 September 2007.
37. These estimations are derived from my own experiences at the protest, in assessing the approximate numbers of antiwar and counter-protestors at the march.
38. Macias, "Thousands Demonstrate Against Iraq War in D.C.," 16 September 2007; Johnson, "Dozens Are Arrested," 16 September 2007.
39. Boorstein, Haynes, and Klein, "Dueling Demonstrations," 16 September 2007.
40. Matthew R. Kerbel, *If It Bleeds, It Leads: An Anatomy of Television News* (Boulder: Westview, 2001), 131–132.
41. Malveaux, 15 September 2007; Local DC News, 15 December 2007.
42. Johnston, "Dozens Are Arrested in Antiwar Protest Near the Capitol," 16 September 2007; Boorstein, Haynes, and Klein, "Dueling Demonstrations," 16 September 2007.
43. Russon, "Thousands Hit Streets of D.C. to Protest War," 16 September 2007.
44. Johnston, "Dozens Are Arrested," 16 September 2007.
45. Altamirano, "Protestors Slam War," 16 September 2007.
46. Gitlin, *The Whole World Is Watching*, 42.
47. Russon, "Thousands Are Arrested in Antiwar Protest Near the Capitol," 16 September 2007.
48. Michael Parenti, *Inventing Reality: The Politics of the News Media* (New York: St. Martin's, 1993), 96, 175.
49. Johnston, "Dozens Are Arrested in Antiwar Protest Near the Capitol," 16 September 2007; Russon, "Thousands Hit Streets of D.C. to Protest War," 16 September 2007.
50. William F. Buckley, "Iraq: One More Time," *Washington Times*, 16 September 2007, 1(B).
51. Elton Gallegly, "Iraq Alternative," *Washington Times*, 16 September 2007, 4(B).
52. Ken Connor, "Battling Divisions Over the Surge," *Washington Times*, 16 September 2007, 5(B).
53. Wolf Blitzer, The Situation Room, 10 September 2007, CNN, 17:00 ET; Frank Salvato, "Accepting Thuggery," *Washington Times*, 16 September 2007, 5(B).
54. Wesley K. Clark, "The Next War," *Washington Post*, 16 September 2007, 1(B).
55. Henry A. Kissinger, "The Disaster of Hasty Withdrawal," *Washington Post*, 16 September 2007, 7(B).; Jim Hoagland, "From Hope to Fear in Iraq," *Washington Post*, 16 September 207, 7(B).
56. For examples of Matzzie's criticisms of the Iraq war, see the following stories: Tom Matzzie, "Which Way Iraq?" *Huffington Post*, 18 June 2007, http://www.huffingtonpost.com/tom-matzzie/which-way-iraq-a-huffpos_b_56734.html.
57. Michael Crowley, "Can Lobbyists Stop the War?" *New York Times*, 9 September 2007, http://www.nytimes.com/2007/09/09/magazine/09antiwar-t.html.

58. Michael Luo, "Antiwar Groups Use New Clout to Influence Democrats on Iraq," *New York Times*, 6 May 2007, 1(A).
59. Ibid.
60. For more information on the lack of attention to antiwar claims, see the following pieces. Elisabeth Bumiller, "Bush Says Leaving Iraq Now Would Be Wrong," *New York Times*, 24 August 2005, 6(A); Kirk Semple, "On Even of Nuclear Meeting, Thousands Stage a Protest," *New York Times*, 2 May 2005, 3(B). The second story by Semple is particularly noteworthy. Despite going into extensive detail about antiwar groups like UFPJ, the story does not contain one substantive antiwar claim.
61. Time, "Washington Memo: A Surge in Speculation," *Time*, 3 September 2007, 16.
62. Editorial, "After the Surge," *Chicago Tribune*, 17 June 2007, sec. 1, 6. Emphasis added.
63. Jonah Goldberg, "How About Those Liberals Flipping on Genocide?" *Chicago Tribune*, 9 July 2007, sec. 1, 23; Dennis Byrne, "Careful Reading of Report Shows Patience Required," *Chicago Tribune*, 17 July 2007, sec. 1, 15.
64. Editorial, "Tomorrow's Iraq," *Chicago Tribune*, 16 September 2007, sec. 2, 6.
65. Editorial, "The Iraq War Debate: The Great Denier," *New York Times*, 16 September 2007, http://www.nytimes.com/2007/07/21/opinion/21sat1.html; Justin Logan, "Would Leaving Iraq Damage United States Standing in the World?" *Chicago Sun Times*, 24 February 2007, sec. 1, 14.
66. Logan, "Would Leaving Iraq Damage United States Standing in the World?" 2007.
67. Pew Research Center, "More Say Iraq War Hurts Fight Against Terrorism," 21 July 2005, http://people-press.org/reports/display.php3?ReportID=251.
68. Editorial, "Bring Them Home," *Los Angeles Times*, 6 May 2007, http://www.latimes.com/news/opinion/editorials/la-ed-iraq6may06,1,4321136.story; Editorial, "The Road Home," *New York Times*, 8 July 2007, http://www.nytimes.com/2007/07/08/opinion/08sun1.html?pagewanted=print.
69. Michael Duffy, "How to Walk Away," *Time*, 30 July 2007, 26.
70. Frank Newport, "Support Exists for Both Troop Withdrawal Proposals," 3 October 2007, http://www.gallup.com/poll/28876/Americans-Favor-Both-Bushs-Democrats-Troop-Withdrawal-Proposals.aspx.
71. Inter-University Consortium for Political and Social Research, *New York Times*-CBS Poll, 14–16 September 2007.
72. Editorial, "After the Surge," *Chicago Tribune*, 17 June 2007, sec. 1, 6.
73. Editorial, "Progress? Not Enough," *Chicago Tribune*, 13 June 2007, sec. 1, 22.
74. Editorial, "Congress's Iraq Quagmire," *Washington Post*, 25 January 2007, 24(A).
75. Editorial, "World Spotlight: Iraqi Parliament Holiday," *Time*, 20 August 2007, 17.
76. Editorial, "Power Failure," *Chicago Tribune*, 27 August 2007, sec. 1, 16; Charles Krauthammer, "Fence-Sitting by al-Maliki Imperils Iraq," *Chicago Tribune*, 3 September 2007, sec. 119.
77. Editorial, "No Progress Report," *New York Times*, 13 July 2007, 20(A).
78. For this content analysis, a second coder analyzed 25 percent of all articles featuring the topic of Iraq withdrawal. Basic key words were used in order to determine whether a specific type of claim in support of, or opposed to withdrawal appeared. For substantive criticisms of withdrawal, key words such as "empire," "imperialism," "oil," "illegal" war or occupation, and "nationalism" had to appear in articles, and be used by those who are supportive of withdrawal. Procedural arguments against the war were similarly coded with key words. Sources had to argue or support withdrawal, while being quoted describing the war as "unwinnable," a "quagmire," or referencing the "cost" or "price" of the war as too high. Stories were coded

as referencing public opinion as opposed to the war if they explicitly mentioned a poll directing attention to the conflict. Articles were categorized as including pro-war claims if they contained similar key words, citing sources who opposed withdrawal while referencing the "troops," "soldiers," "men" or "women" in uniform, or referencing the dangers of "civil war," "insurgents," or "terror" or "terrorism" in Iraq. Intercoder reliability for these analyses were over 90 percent for all measures.

79. David E. Sanger, "In Strong Words, Bush Tries to Redirect Debate on Iraq," *New York Times*, 11 January 2006, 12(A).
80. Edward Wong and Sheryl Gay Stolberg, "A Draft Oil Bill Stirs Opposition From Iraqi Blocs," *New York Times*, 3 May 2007, 1(A).
81. Peter Baker, "Bush Says United States Pullout Would Let Iraq Radicals Use Oil as a Weapon," *Washington* Post, 5 November 2006, 6(A); Jennifer Loven, "Bush Gives New Reason for Iraq War," *Boston Globe*, 31 August 2005, http://www.boston.com/news/nation/articles/2005/08/31/bush_gives_new_reason_for_iraq_war/.
82. Kate Zernike, "On Iraq, Kerry Again Leaves Democrats Fuming," *New York Times*, 21 June 2006, 1(A).
83. Kate Zernike, "Senators Begin Debate on Iraq, Visions in Sharp Contrast," *New York Times*, 22 June 2006, 12(A).
84. Edward Wong, "6 in Iraq Cabinet Resign on Order of Shiite Cleric," *New York Times*, 17 April 2007, 1(A).
85. John M. Broder, "What Would the Democrats Do?" *New York Times*, 17 September 2006, 1(D); Richard G. Jones, "With Voters' Eyes on Iraq, Menendez Offers a Plan," *New York Times*, 6 September 2006, 7(B); John M. Broder, "In Call for More Troops, McCain Places His Bet on Iraq," *New York Times*, 14 November 2006, 18(A).
86. For more on the prominence of procedural criticisms, see Anthony DiMaggio, *Mass Media, Mass Propaganda: Examining the News in the "War on Terror"* (Lanham: Lexington, 2008), 79–101.
87. Carl Hulse, "Democrats Regroup After Veto, Seeking Unity on Iraq Plan," *New York Times*, 3 May 2007, 14(A).
88. Sheryl Gay Stolberg and Jeff Zeleny, "Bush Vetoes Bill Tying Iraq Funds to Exit Schedule," *New York Times*, 2 May 2007, 1(A).
89. Michael Luo and Sheryl Gay Stolberg, "Bush and Congress Easing Tone of Debate on War Bill," *New York Times*, 28 April 2007, 10(A).
90. Robin Toner, "In Trying to Steer the War in Iraq, Democrats Drive in Fits and Starts," *New York Times*, 10 March 2007, 1(A).
91. Robin Toner, "In Trying to Steer the War in Iraq, Democrats Drive in Fits and Starts," *New York Times*, 10 March 2007, 1(A). Emphasis added.
92. Patrick D. Healy, "Clinton Calls for Iraq Plan to Start Withdrawal by '06," *New York Times*, 30 November 2005, 6(B).
93. Kate Zernike and Carl Hulse, "Senate Democrats Urge Beginning of an Iraq Pullout this Year, but Avoid a Firm Schedule," *New York Times*, 20 June 2006, 8(A).
94. "The Democratic Presidential Debate on MSNBC," *New York Times*, 26 September 2007, http://www.nytimes.com/2007/09/26/us/politics/26DEBATE-TRANSCRIPT.html?bl&ex=1191211200&en=e97dbcb313b23329&ei=5087%0A
95. Richard W. Stevenson, "Staying the Course in Iraq: Acknowledging Difficulties, Insisting on a Fight to the Finish," *New York Times*, 29 June 2005, 12(A).
96. Elisabeth Bumiller, "Cheney Sees 'Shameless' Revisionism on War," *New York Times*, 22 November 2005, 1(A); Robin Toner and Marjorie Connelly, "Economy Lifts Bush's Support in Latest Poll," *New York Times*, 8 December 2005, 1(A).
97. Richard W. Stevenson, "Bush Says United States Needs Patience on Iraq War,

Admits Errors," *New York Times*, 15 December 2005, 24(A).

98. Elisabeth Bumiller, "For 3rd Day in a Row, Bush Says Withdrawal Now From Iraq Would Embolden Terrorists," *New York Times*, 25 August 2005, 10(A); Adam Nagourney, "McCain Says Democrats Play 'Small Politics' Over Iraq," *New York Times*, 12 April 2007, 18(A).
99. Sheryl Gay Stolberg and Jeff Zeleny, "Bush Vetoes Bill Tying Iraq Funds to Exit Schedule," *New York Times*, 2 May 2007, 1(A).
100. Sheryl Gay Stolberg, "Opposition Undercuts Troops, Cheney Says of Spending Bill, *New York Times*, 13 March 2007, 10(A).
101. *Manufacturing Consent: Noam Chomsky and the Media*, DVD, directed by Mark Achbar and Peter Wintonick (Zeitgeist, 1992).
102. Tuchman, *Making News*, 165–66,
103. Rojecki, *Silencing the Opposition*, 25.
104. Ibid., 18.
105. Doris Graber, *Processing Politics: Learning from Television in the Internet Age* (Chicago, University of Chicago Press, 2001), 2–3, 20.
106. Ibid., 31.
107. Ibid., 5–6.
108. Although both of the books cited here by Gitlin (*The Whole World Is Watching*) and Iyengar and Kinder (*News that Matters*) were published before the release of Herman and Chomsky's *Manufacturing Consent*, subsequent works by Gitlin and Iyengar released after *Manufacturing Consent* fail to incorporate the propaganda model as effective in explaining media reporting. Gitlin is well known as heavily antagonistic to Chomsky and Herman's views of indoctrination and propaganda in a democratic society. Similarly, Iyengar fails to cite Herman or Chomsky in subsequent books such as *Going Negative* and *Is Anyone Responsible?* Instead, he chooses to cite Gitlin and his work, *The Whole World Is Watching*.

3. WORTHY AND UNWORTHY VICTIMS: THE POLITICIZATION OF GENOCIDE AND HUMAN RIGHTS IN U.S. FOREIGN POLICY

1. Editorial, "Turkey, Armenia, and Denial," *New York Times*, 16 May 2006, http://www.nytimes.com/2006/05/16/opinion/16tue3.html.
2. Todd Gitlin, *The Whole World Is Watching* (Berkeley: University of California Press, 1980), 181.
3. Edward Herman and Noam Chomsky, *Manufacturing Consent: The Political Economy of the Mass Media* (New York: Pantheon, 1988), 37.
4. Ibid., 40–41.
5. Ibid., 43.
6. Noam Chomsky, *The New Military Humanism: Lessons From Kosovo* (Monroe, Me.: Common Courage, 1999), 32.
7. Editorial, "Inflaming the Turks," *Boston Globe*, 13 October 2007, 10(A).
8. Editorial, "A Dangerous Political Stunt," *Chicago Tribune*, 14 October 2007, sec. 1, 6.
9. Editorial, "Stay Out of This Dispute," *Chicago Sun-Times*, 24 October 2007, sec. 1, 41.
10. Editorial, "Worse than Irrelevant," *Washington Post*, 10 October 2007, 16(A).
11. Editorial, "Stay Out of This Dispute."
12. David Ignatius, "The Dignity Agenda," *Washington Post*, 14 October 2007, 7(B); Charles Krauthammer, "Pelosi's Armenian Gambit," *Washington Post*, 19 October

2007, 21(A); Richard Cohen, "Turkey's War on the Truth," *Washington Post*, 16 October 2007, 19(A); Victor Davis Hanson, "Congress Sticks Its Nose Where It Doesn't Belong," *Chicago Tribune*, 19 October 2007, sec. 1, 25.

13. Andrew Greeley, "Why Those Who Love America Are Feeling Brokenhearted," *Chicago Sun-Times*, 24 October 2007, sec. 1, 43; Georgie Anne Geyer, "Owning Up to the Past," *Chicago Tribune*, 19 October 2007, www.chicagotribune.com/news/opinion/chi-oped1019geyeroct19,0,2160570.story.
14. The seven stories analyzed from the *Boston Globe*, *New York Times*, and *Washington Post* were from October 10 to 12, 2007, and are as follows: Steven Lee Myers and Carl Hulse, "Vote By House Panel Raises Furor on Armenian Genocide," *New York Times*, 11 October 2007, 1(A); Sebenem Arsu, "Turkey Seethes at United States Over House Genocide Vote," *New York Times*, 12 October 2007, 12(A); Glenn Kessler, "White House and Turkey Fight Bill on Armenia," *Washington Post*, 10 October 2007, 1(A); Elizabeth Williamson, "Panel Labels Armenian Killings Genocide," *Washington Post*, 11 October 2007, 3(A); Molly Moore and Robin Wright, "Tensions Rise in Turkey on Two Fronts," *Washington Post*, 12 October 2007, 12(A); Farah Stockman, "Genocide Vote Sets a Face-Off with Bush," *Boston Globe*, 11 October 2007, http://www.boston.com/news/nation/articles/2007/10/11/genocide_vote_sets_a_face_off_with_bush/; Farah Stockman, "Turkey Swift to Admonish US Over Vote," *Boston Globe*, 12 October 2007, http://www.boston.com/news/world/articles/2007/10/12/turkey_swift_to_admonish_us_over_vote/.
15. United Press International, "Bush Calls Srebrenica Anniversary Reminder," 11 July 2005.
16. House of Representatives, "H. Res. 199," 27 June 2005, *GovTrack.us*, http://www.govtrack.us/congress/billtext.xpd?bill=hr109-199.
17. Angela Brkic, "The Wages of Denial," *New York Times*, 11 July 2005, 17(A).
18. Editorial, "Lessons From Bosnia Fading Too Fast," *Chicago Sun-Times*, 12 July 2005, sec. 1, 41; Patrick McCarthy, "A Decade of Sorrow," *St. Louis Dispatch*, 7 July 2005, 7(B).
19. Editorial, "Serbia Confronts an Awful Truth," *Chicago Tribune*, 9 June 2005, sec. 1, 26.
20. Ibid.
21. Brkic, "The Wages of Denial."
22. Louise Branson, "Srebrenica—Time to Own Up," *USA Today*, 12 July 2005, 15(A).
23. The LexisNexis search found any stories from June and July 2005 that contained the words "Bosnia" and "genocide." The search revealed that the Srebrenica was very prevalent in U.S. newspaper stories, op-eds, and editorials, considering this period marked the tenth-anniversary landmark.
24. Richard Holbrooke, "Was Bosnia Worth It?" *Pittsburgh Post Gazette*, 24 June 2005, 2(J); Richard Holbrooke, "Bosnia Was Worth the Effort," *New York Sun*, 20 July 2005, 9; Richard Holbrooke, "Was Bosnia Worth It?" *Washington Post*, 19 July 2005, 21(A).
25. Editorial, "Srebrenica, an Obligation Unfulfilled," *New York Times*, 14 July 2005, 24(A); Sabaa U. Saleem, "Being Muslim in a Mad, Sad World," *Washington Post*, 31 July 2005, 3(B); Editorial, "Remembering a Massacre," *Providence Journal*, 28 July 2005, 4(B).
26. Editorial, "Never Again," *St. Louis Dispatch*, 17 July 2005, 2(B).
27. Patrick McCarthy, "A Decade of Sorrow," *St. Louis Dispatch*, 7 July 2005, 7(B); Helle Dale, "Remember the Balkans," *Washington Times*, 29 June 2005, 21(A).

28. Gary Martin, "A Decade Later, the Specter of Genocidal War Remains," *San Antonio News*, 16 July 2005, 11(B).
29. Edward P. Joseph, "Bystanders to a Massacre," *Washington Post*, 10 July 2005, 4(B).
30. Herman and Chomsky, *Manufacturing Consent,* xxi.
31. Suna Erdem, "Turkey and Iraq Scramble for Diplomatic Solution Over Kurdish Rebels," (London) *Times*, 25 October 2007, http://www.timesonline.co.uk/tol/news/world/iraq/article2739398.ece.
32. Associated Press, "Turkish Jets Strike Kurdish Rebels," 26 December 2007, http://www.truthout.org/docs_2006/122607R.shtml.
33. Amit R. Paley and Dlovan Brwari, "Turkey Bombs Villages in N. Iraq," *Washington Post*, 5 February 2008, 15(A).
34. Karl Vick and Yesim Borg, "In Turkish Bombings, 'Who Benefits?'" *Washington Post*, 20 April 2006, 16(A).
35. BBC, "Kurdish Rebels Kill Turkey Troops," 8 April 2007, http://news.bbc.co.uk/2/hi/europe/6537751.stm
36. Amberin Zaman, "Rebel Kurds Asks Turkish Court to Spare His Life," *Washington Post*, 1 June 1999, 10(A).
37. Human Rights Watch, "Turkey: Human Rights Developments, 1999 World Report," 1999, http://www.hrw.org/worldreport99/europe/turkey.html; Amnesty International, "Amnesty International Report 2007: Republic of Turkey," 2007, http://www.amnesty.org/en/region/europe-and-central-asia/balkans/turkey
38. Tamar Gabelnick, William D. Hartung, and Jennifer Washburn, "Arming Repression: United States Arms Sales to Turkey during the Clinton Administration," *World Policy Institute*, October 1999, http://www.fas.org/asmp/library/reports/turkeyrep.htm.
39. Chomsky, *The New Military Humanism*, 54.
40. Ibid.; Human Rights Watch, "Human Rights Watch Briefing Paper," 4 October 2004, http://hrw.org/backgrounder/eca/turkey/2004/10/; Human Rights Watch, "Displaced and Disregarded: Turkey's Failing Village Return Program," October 2002, http://hrw.org/reports/2002/turkey/; Human Rights Watch, "Still Critical: Prospects in 2005 for Internally Displaced Kurds in Turkey," 2005, http://www.hrw.org/reports/2005/turkey0305/3.htm#_Toc97005223.
41. Amnesty International, "Amnesty International Report 2007: Republic of Turkey," 2007, http://www.amnesty.org/en/region/europe-and-central-asia/balkans/turkey.
42. Human Rights Watch, "Abolition of Capital Punishment and Prevention of Torture," 10 September 2002, http://hrw.org/press/2002/09/osce0910–stat.htm; John M. Goshko, "United States to Expand Relations With Turkey," *Washington Post*, 13 June 1993, 28(A); John Ward Anderson, "Kurdish Scar Unhealed in Turkey," *Washington Post*, 8 November 2000, 3(A).
43. Human Rights Watch, "Whatever Happened to the Iraqi Kurds?" 11 March 1991, http://www.hrw.org/reports/1991/IRAQ913.htm#12.
44. John Ward Anderson, "Kurd Wins Free Speech Case," *Washington Post*, 14 February 2002, 24(A).
45. A comprehensive analysis of LexisNexis was undertaken from the period of January 1, 1990, through December 31, 2007. Three key words, "Turkey," "Kurds," and "Terrorist," were used, so as to capture a sample of articles referencing both parties (Turkey's government and Kurdish rebels) and any terrorist acts that may be discussed in regards to either of the parties.
46. Searches of *Lexis Nexis* from March of 1988 (when Hussein gassed Iraqi Kurds at Halabja) through March of 2003 (at the time of the United States invasion) reveal

dozens of hits for stories framing Iraq's attacks on the Kurds as a tragedy, massacre, atrocity, or genocide. As this article has shown, no similar inflammatory language is directed at the government of Turkey, despite the existence of numerous human rights reports that have condemned the regime for torture, kidnapping, and killing of thousands of civilians.

47. Steven R. Weisman, "The Struggle for Iraq: Chemical Atrocity," *New York Times*, 16 September 2003, http://query.nytimes.com/gst/fullpage.html?res=9903E1D9163Af935A2575AC0A96569C8B63; Editorial, "Kurd's Way," *Washington Post*, 1 October 1999, 32(A).
48 Seanna Adcox, "McCain Fighting Iraq Withdrawal Timeline," *Washington Post*, 28 July 2007, http://www.washingtonpost.com/wp-dyn/content/article/2007/07/28/AR2007072800681.html?tid=informbox.
49. Claims that Iraq's repression of the Kurds amounts to genocide have received much attention, as this study demonstrates. For examples of political and dissident classifications of Turkish behavior as genocide, see Blaine Harden, "Turkish Kurds' Revolt Sparks Wide Violence," *Washington Post*, 25 March 1992, 25(A); Leyla Zana, "On Trial for Being a Kurd," *Washington Post*, 5 December 1994, 23(A); Thomas W. Lippman, "Turkey Catches Flak in Congress," *Washington Post*, 23 March 1995, 24(A); Dan Morgan, "Plan to Delay Aid to Turkey Is Rejected," *Washington Post*, 16 June 1995, 11(A).
50. Ann Scott Tyson and Robin Wright, "United States Helps Turkey Hit Rebel Kurds in Iraq," *Washington Post*, 18 December 2007, 1(A).
51. Foxnews.com, "Iraqi Officials Protest Turkish Jets Bombing Kurdish Rebel Positions," 17 December 2007, http://www.foxnews.com/story/0,2933,317095,00.html; BBC News, "'United States Backed' Turkish Raids on Iraq," 16 December 2007, http://news.bbc.co.uk/2/hi/europe/7147271.stm.
52. Editorial, "Even Closer to the Brink," *New York Times*, 23 October 2007, 28(A).
53. Ibid.
54. Editorial, "Turkey's Wise Hesitation," *Washington Post*, 23 October 2007, 18(A).
55. Andrew Roth, Zoe Huffman et al., "Covering War's Victims," in *Censored 2008: The Top 25 Censored Stories of 2006–07*, ed. Peter Phillips and Andrew Roth (New York: Seven Stories, 2007), 253–71.
56. Michael Duffy, "How to Walk Away," *Time*, 30 July 2007, 28.
57. For more information on the estimated one million Iraqis killed and for U.S. responsibility, see the following studies: Opinion Research Business, "September 2007: More than 1,000,000 Iraqis Murdered," September 2007, http://www.opinion.co.uk/Newsroom_details.aspx?NewsId=78; and Michael Schwartz, *War Without End: The Iraq War in Context* (Chicago: Haymarket, 2008), 120-122.
58. Kevin Young, "What Would a Withdrawal Mean?" *Counterpunch*, 5–6 January 2008, http://www.counterpunch.org/young01052008.html.
59. Editorial, "21st-Century Barbarism," *Washington Post*, 16 August 2007, 14(A).
60. John Podesta, Lawrence J. Korb, and Brian Katulis, "Strategic Drift," *Washington Post*, 15 November 2007, 25(A).
61. Michael Gerson, "Another Test in Iraq," *Washington Post*, 22 August 2007, 17(A).
62. Iraq Body Count.org, "A Dossier of Civilian Casualties in Iraq 2003–2005," 19 July 2005, http://www.iraqbodycount.org/analysis/reference/press-releases/12/
63. Lily Hamourtziadou, "How the West Values Civilian Lives in Iraq," Iraq Body Count.org, 12 November 2007, http://www.iraqbodycount.org/analysis/beyond/the-price-of-loss/.
64. Sarah Boseley, "100,000 Iraqi Civilians Dead, Says Study," *Guardian*, 29 October

2004, http://www.guardian.co.uk/Iraq/Story/0,2763,1338749,00.html.

65. Sarah Boseley, "655,000 Iraqis Killed since Invasion," *Guardian*, 11 October 2006, http://www.guardian.co.uk/Iraq/Story/0,,1892888,00.html.
66. Opinion Research Business, "More Than 1,000,000 Iraqis Murdered," September 2007, http://www.opinion.co.uk/Newsroom_details.aspx?NewsId=78.
67. Anthony DiMaggio, "Damage Control," *Z Magazine*, 17 October 2006, http://www.zmag.org/content/showarticle.cfm?ItemID=11201; see also Anthony DiMaggio, *Mass Media, Mass Propaganda: Examining American News in the "War on Terror"* (Lanham, Md.: Lexington, 2008), chap. 8, 179–215.
68. Tony Karon, "Iraq Civilian Casualties? Who Knew?" *Time*, 8 December 2004, http://www.time.com/time/columnist/karon/article/0,9565,933405,00.html.
69. Carol Lin and John Roberts, *This Week at War (TWAW)*, CNN, 4 November 2006, 20:00 ET.
70. TWAW, 10 September 2006, 13:00 ET.
71. TWAW, 24 February 2007, 19:00 ET.
72. TWAW, 8 October 2006, 13:00 ET.
73. TWAW, 25 November 2006, 19:00 ET.
74. Carol Lin and Tom Foreman, *TWAW*, CNN, 26 August 2006, 18:00 ET.
75. John Roberts, *TWAW*, CNN, 24 September 2006, 13:00 ET.
76. Ibid., 15 October 2006, 13:00 ET.
77. Carol Lin and John Roberts, *TWAW*, CNN, 18 November 2006, 19:00 ET.
78. John Roberts, *TWAW*, CNN, 29 July 2006, 19:00 ET.
79. Ibid., 29 July 2006, 19:00 ET; Carol Lin and John Roberts, *TWAW*, CNN, 2 September 2006, 19:00 ET; Carol Lin and Tom Foreman, *TWAW*, CNN, 26 August 2006, 18:00 ET; Carol Lin and John Roberts, *TWAW*, CNN, 25 November 2006, 19:00 ET.
80. Carol Lin and John Roberts, *TWAW*, CNN, 18 November 2006, 19:00 ET.
81. TWAW, 21 October 2006, 18:00 ET.
82. Carol Lin and Wolf Blitzer, *TWAW*, CNN, 10 June 2006, 19:00 ET.
83. Ibid., 10 June 2006, 19:00 ET.
84. Carol Lin and John Roberts, *TWAW*, CNN, 17 June 2006, 19:00 ET.
85. TWAW, 8 July 2006, 19:00 ET.
86. John Roberts, *TWAW*, CNN, 15 October 2006, 13:00 ET.
87. Fox News, "Officials Believe 'Azzam' is Gadahn," 29 October 2004, http://www.foxnews.com/story/0,2933,137087,00.html.
88. John Roberts, *TWAW*, CNN, 17 September 2006, 13:00 ET.
89. Brian Ross, "Alleged American al Qaeda Warns of US Attacks," ABC News, 28 October 2004, http://abcnews.go.com/WNT/story?id=206661.

4. JOURNALISTIC NORMS AND PROPAGANDA: IRAQ AND THE WAR ON TERROR

1. Timothy E. Cook, "The News Media as a Political Institution: Looking Backward and Looking Forward," *Political Communication* 23/2 (April–June 2006).
2. David Michael Ryfe, "Guest Editor's Introduction: New Institutionalism and the News," *Political Communication* 23/2 (April–June 2006): 137.
3. Ryfe, "Guest Editor's Introduction," 138; Todd Gitlin, *The Whole World Is Watching: Mass Media in the Making & Unmaking of the New Left* (Berkeley: University of California, 1980), 11–12.

4. Bernard C. Cohen, *The Press and Foreign Policy* (Berkeley, Ca.: IGS, 1993), 25–36.
5. Ryfe, "Guest Editor's Introduction," 138.
6. David T. Z. Mindich, *Just the Facts: How "Objectivity" Came to Define American Journalism* (New York: New York University, 1998), 5; Michael Schudson, *Discovering the News: A Social History of American Newspapers* (New York: Basic Books, 1973), 7.
7. Bartholomew H. Sparrow, "A Research Agenda for an Institutional Media," *Political Communication* 23/2 (April-June 2006): 148, 151.
8. Ibid., 147.
9. Bartholomew H. Sparrow, *Uncertain Guardians: The News Media as a Political Institution* (Baltimore: John Hopkins, 1999), 68, 60, 56.
10. Ibid., 76, 80; Dean Alger, *Megamedia: How Giant Corporations Dominate Mass Media, Distort Competition, and Endanger Democracy* (Lanham, Md.: Rowman and Littlefield, 1998), 163–64; Robert Cirino, *Power to Persuade: Mass Media and the News* (New York: Bantam, 1974), 109; S. Robert Lichter, Stanley Rothman, and Linda S. Lichter, *The Media Elite: America's New Powerbrokers* (New York: Hastings, 1990), 29; Greg Mitchell, "Readers Support Bush, Say Coverage Was Good," *Editor and Publisher*, 6 November 2000, 7–9.
11. Gaye Tuchman, *Making News: A Study in the Construction of Reality* (New York: Free Press, 1978), 210.
12. Mark Fishman, *Manufacturing the News* (Austin: University of Texas, 1980), 27.
13. Tuchman, *Making News*, 212.
14. Herbert J. Gans, *Deciding What's News: A Study of CBS Evening News, NBC Nightly News, Newsweek, and Time* (New York: Vintage, 1980), 42–48.
15. Leon V. Sigal, *Reporters and Officials: The Organization and Politics of Newsmaking* (Lexington, Mass.: D. C. Heath, 1973), 124.
16. Timothy E. Cook, *Governing With the News: The News Media as a Political Institution* (Chicago: University of Chicago, 1998), 90, 15, 105, 112.
17. Ibid., 106.
18. Ibid., 102.
19. Anne Plummer Flaherty, "Whose Side Is CNN On?" *Chicago Sun Times*, 24 October 2006, sec. 1, 28; FAIR, "Is Media Filtering Out Good News From Iraq?" 28 October 2003, http://www.fair.org/index.php?page=1840.
20. For more on the vacuous nature of claims that the mass media is reporting violence in Iraq out of proportion with the reality on the ground, see Anthony DiMaggio, "From Bush to Obama: Seven Years of Wartime Propaganda," *Counterpunch*, 27 February 2009, http://www.counterpunch.org/dimaggio02272009.html.
21. Cook, *Governing with the News*, 128.
22. Gary Webb, "The Mighty Wurlitzer Plays On," in *Into the Buzzsaw: Leading Journalists Expose the Myth of a Free Press*, ed. Kristina Borjesson (Amherst, N.Y.: Prometheus, 2004), 142–43.
23. Peter Kornbluh, "The Storm Over 'Dark Alliance,'" *Columbia Journalism Review*, January/February 1997, http://www.gwu.edu/~nsarchiv/NSAEBB/NSAEBB2/storm.htm.
24. Doug Ireland, "The Tragedy of Gary Webb," *In These Times*, 10 October 2006, http://www.inthesetimes.com/article/2839/.
25. Nick Schou, *Kill the Messenger: How the CIA's Crack-Cocaine Controversy Destroyed Journalist Gary Webb* (New York: Nation, 2006), 128, 131–132.
26. Alexander Cockburn and Jeffrey St. Clair, *End Times: The Death of the Fourth Estate* (Oakland, Calif.: A.K., 2007), 120.
27. Robert Parry, *Lost History: Contras, Cocaine, the Press & 'Project Truth'* (Arlington,

Va.: TMC, 1999), 224; Schou, *Kill the Messenger*, viii.

28. Ireland, "The Tragedy of Gary Webb"; Alexander Cockburn and Jeffrey St. Clair, *Whiteout: The CIA, Drugs, and the Press* (London: Verso, 1998), 35.
29. Mark Hertsgaard, *On Bended Knee: The Press and the Reagan Presidency* (New York: Farrar, Straus and Giroux, 1988), 5.
30. Hertsgaard, *On Bended Knee*, 5, 20.
31. Ibid., 30, 27, 34, 45, 52.
32. Ibid., 9, 35, 40, 47.
33. Ron Suskind, "Faith, Certainty and the Presidency of George W. Bush," *New York Times Magazine*, 17 October 2004, http://www.nytimes.com/2004/10/17/magazine/17BUSH.html.
34. Mark Memmott, "Reporters in Iraq Under Fire There, and from Critics," *USA Today*, 22 March 2006, http://www.usatoday.com/news/world/iraq/2006-03-22-media-criticism_x.htm.
35. Robert Fisk, "Censorship of the Press," *Z Magazine*, 11 June 2003, http://www.zmag.org/znet/viewArticle/10283.
36. Borzou Daragahi and Mark Mazzetti, "United States Military Covertly Pays to Run Stories in Iraqi Press," *Los Angeles Times*, 30 November 2005, http://articles.latimes.com/2005/nov/30/world/fg-infowar30.
37. Andrew Buncombe, "Bush 'Planted Fake News Stories on American TV'" *Independent*, 29 May 2006, http://www.independent.co.uk/news/world/ americas/bush-planted-fake-news-stories-on-american-tv-480172.html.
38. Dan Rather, "The Patriot and the Censor's Necklace," in Borjesson, *Into the Buzzsaw,* 39, 41.
39. Helen Thomas, "Grande Dame, Persona Non Grata," in *Feet to the Fire: The Media After 9/11: Top Journalists Speak Out*, ed. Kristina Borjesson (Amherst, N.Y.: Prometheus, 2004), 123–142; Helen Thomas, *Watchdogs of Democracy? The Waning Washington Press Corps and How It Has Failed the Public* (New York: Scribner, 2006), 53–55; James S. Brady, "Press Conference of the President," *The White House*, March 2006, http://www.whitehouse.gov/news/releases/2006/03/20060321-4.html.
40. Thomas, *Watchdogs of Democracy?*, 61.
41. Editorial, "To Be a Journalist in Iraq," *New York Times*, 24 October 2007, http://www.nytimes.com/2007/10/24/opinion/24wed2.html.
42. Committee to Protect Journalists, "Iraq: Journalists in Danger," 2008, http://www.cpj.org/Briefings/Iraq/Iraq_danger.html.
43. Laura Rozen, "Journalists Take Flak in Iraq," *Nation*, 12 January 2004, http://www.thenation.com/doc/20040112/rozen.
44. Jeff Cohen, *Cable News Confidential: My Misadventures in Corporate Media* (Sausalito, Calif.: PoliPoint, 2006), 125.
45. Tom Yellin, "Inside the Ratings Vise," in Borjesson, *Feet to the Fire*, 52–53.
46. Barton Gellman, "Accountability's Coroner," in Borjesson, *Feet to the Fire*, 199–200.
47. Scott Ritter and William Rivers Pitt, *War on Iraq: What Team Bush Doesn't Want You to Know* (New York: Context, 2002).
48. CNN.com, "Transcript of Blix's United Nations Presentation," 7 March 2003, http://www.cnn.com/2003/US/03/07/sprj.irq.un.transcript.blix/index.html.
49. Seth Ackerman, "The Great WMD Hunt," July/August 2003, *Extra!* http://www.fair.org/index.php?page=1150; CNN.com, "Transcript of ElBaradei's United Nations Presentation," 7 March 2003, http://www.cnn.com/2003/US/03/07/sprj.irq.un.transcript.elbaradei/.

50. David Martin, "Sound Bite's Truth," in Borjesson, *Feet to the Fire*, 258.
51. For more information, see Anthony R. DiMaggio, *Mass Media, Mass Propaganda: Examining American News in the "War on Terror"* (Lanham, Md.: Lexington, 2008), 65–66.
52. John MacArthur, "Everybody Wants to Be at Versailles," in Borjesson, *Feet to the Fire*, 96–97, 112.
53. Daniel Chomsky, "'Wild' or 'Crazy': The New York Times, and the Logic of War in Iraq," Annual Meeting of the American Political Science Association, September 2004.
54. Amy Goodman and David Goodman, "The Corporate Media in Wartime," *International Socialist Review* (May–June 2005), 52.
55. *Uncovered: The War on Iraq*, DVD, dir. Robert Greenwald (Cinema Libre, 2004).
56. Scott L. Althaus and Devon M. Largio, "When Osama Became Saddam: Origins and Consequences of the Change in America's Public Enemy #1," *Political Science & Politics* 37/4 (October 2004): 795–99.
57. Bill Katovsky and Timothy Carlson, *Embedded: The Media at War in Iraq: An Oral History* (Guilford, Conn.: Lyons, 2003), 49.
58. Joe Strupp, "Study: Media Self-Censored on Iraq," *Editor & Publisher*, 18 March 2005, http://www.alternet.org/story/21538.
59. Judith Sylvester and Suzanne Huffman, *Reporting from the Front: The Media and the Military* (Lanham, Md.: Rowman and Littlefield, 2005), 66; Cohen, *Cable News Confidential*, 137.
60. Sylvester and Huffman, *Reporting From the Front*, 135.
61. Journalism.org, "Journalists in Iraq—A Survey of Reporters on the Front Lines," 28 November 2007, http://journalism.org/node/8621.
62. See DiMaggio, *Mass Media, Mass Propaganda*, chap. 9, 217–52; Michael Pfau, Elaine M. Wittenberg, Carolyn Jackson, Phil Mehringer, Rob Lanier, Michael Hatfield, and Kristina Brockman, "Embedding Journalists in Military Combat Units: How Embedding Alters Television News Stories," *Mass Communication and Society* 8/3 (July 2005): 179–95; Michel M. Haigh, Michael Pfau, Jamie Danesi, Robert Tallmon, Tracy Bunko, Shannon Nyberg, Bertha Thompson, Chance Babin, Sal Cardella, Michael Mink, and Brian Temple, "A Comparison of Embedded and Nonembedded Print Coverage of the United States Invasion and Occupation of Iraq," *Harvard International Journal of Press/Politics* 11/2 (2006): 139–53; Greg Mitchell, "New Study Calls 'Embed' Program for United States Media in Iraq a 'Victory'—for the Pentagon," *Editor & Publisher*, 14 May 2008, http://www.editorandpublisher.com/eandp/news/article_display.jsp?vnu_content_id=1003803787.
63. Jim Wolf, "United States Media Curtail Iraq War Coverage: Study," Reuters, 20 August 2007, http://www.reuters.com/article/newsOne/idUSN1923063520070820.
64. PBS, "As Iraq War Pushes On, Media Coverage Shifts," 24 March 2008, http://www.pbs.org/newshour/bb/middle_east/jan-june08/media_03-24.html.
65. Howard Tumber and Frank Webster, *Journalists Under Fire: Information War and Journalistic Practices* (Thousand Oaks, Calif.: Sage, 2006), 55.
66. Richard Sambrook, "The Poliak Lecture Given at Columbia University, America," BBC, 27 October 2004, http://www.bbc.co.uk/pressoffice/speeches/stories/sambrook_poliak.shtml.
67. Tara Conlan, "Telegraph Leads Reporting on Global Conflicts," *Guardian*, 14 December 2006, http://www.guardian.co.uk/media/2006/dec/14/pressandpublishing.thedailytelegraph.
68. Sambrook, "The Poliak Lecture," 2004.

69. Peter Foster, "Objectivity, in a Manner of Speaking," *Telegraph*, 4 April 2008, http://www.telegraph.co.uk/telegraph/search/sitesearch.do?queryText=objectivity+manner+speaking&action=doBasicSearch&advSearch=false&Go=Go&ch=news&selectedChannel=News.
70. Wolfgang Donsbach and Bettina Klett, "Subjective Objectivity: How Journalists in Four Countries Define a Key Term of their Profession," *International Communication Gazette* 51/1 (1993): 53–83.
71. Neil Tickner, "Media Coverage of WMD Issue Gets a Failing Grade: UM Study," *University of Maryland*, 9 March 2004, http://www.newsdesk.umd.edu/sociss/release.cfm?ArticleID=889.
72. Craig Murray, Katy Parry, Piers Robinson, and Peter Goddard, "Reporting Dissent in Wartime: The British Press, the Antiwar Movement and the 2003 Iraq War," *European Journal of Communication* 23/1(2008): 7–27; Piers Robinson and Peter Goddard, "Measuring Media Autonomy in Wartime: An Analysis of United Kingdom T.V. News Coverage of the 2003 Iraq War," International Studies Association Convention, March 2006.
73. John Pilger, "An Interview by David Barsamian," *Progressive*, November 2002, http://www.thirdworldtraveler.com/Pilger_John/Pilger_interview.html.
74. Rajiv Chandrasekaran, *Imperial Life in the Emerald City: Inside Iraq's Green Zone* (New York: Vintage, 2007); James Fallows, *Blind Into Baghdad: America's War in Iraq* (New York: Vintage, 2006); Thomas E. Ricks, *Fiasco: The American Military Adventure in Iraq* (New York: Penguin, 2007).
75. Robert Fisk, *The Great War for Civilisation: The Conquest of the Middle East* (New York: Vintage, 2007); Robert Fisk, *Pity the Nation: The Abduction of Lebanon* (New York: Nation, 2002); Jonathan Steele, *Defeat: Why America and Britain Lost Iraq* (Berkeley: Counterpoint, 2008); Patrick Cockburn, *The Occupation: War and Resistance in Iraq* (New York: Verso, 2006); Patrick Cockburn, *Muqtada: Muqtada al-Sadr, The Shia Revival, and the Struggle for Iraq* (New York: Scribner, 2008).
76. Justin Lewis, Bob Franklin, Andrew Williams, James Thomas, and Nick Mosdell, "The Quality and Independence of British Journalism: Working Paper," Cardiff School of Journalism, 1 February 2008, http://www.mediawise.org.uk/files/uploaded/Quality%20and%20Independence%20of%20British%20Journalism.pdf
77. David Edwards and David Cromwell, *Guardians of Power: The Myth of the Liberal Media* (London: Pluto, 2006), 13–31, 56–62, 81.
78. John Pilger, "The BBC and Iraq: Myth and Reality," *New Statesman*, http://www.lewrockwell.com/orig4/pilger1.html.
79. Justin Lewis and Rod Brookes, "Reporting the War on British Television," in *Tell Me Lies: Propaganda and Media Distortion in the Attack on Iraq*, ed. David Miller (London: Pluto, 2004), 135.
80. Justin Lewis, "Facts in the Line of Fire," *Guardian*, 6 November 2003, http://www.guardian.co.uk/media/2003/nov/06/broadcasting.politicsandthemedia.
81. Justin Lewis, Rod Brookes, Nick Mosdell, and Terry Threadgold, *Shoot First and Ask Questions Later: Media Coverage of the 2003 Iraq War* (New York: Peter Lang, 2006), 84–85, 116.

5. IRAN, NUCLEAR WEAPONS, AND THE POLITICS OF FEAR

1. *Time*, "Intimidation in Tehran," 10 September 2007, 43–45.
2. Damien McElroy, "Bush Warns of Iran 'Nuclear Holocaust," *Telegraph*, 29 August 2007, http://www.telegraph.co.uk/news/worldnews/1561535/Bush-warns-of-

Iran-%27nuclear-holocaust%27.html.

3. Robin Wright, "Iran a Nuclear Threat, Bush Insists," *Washington Post*, 21 March 2008, 14(A).
4. Dave Newbart, "Obama: Iran Threatens All of Us," *Chicago Sun-Times*, 3 March 2007, sec. 1, 6; Ewen MacAskill, Daniel Nasaw, and Suzanne Goldberg, "Clinton Makes Threat Against Iran as Voters Go to Polls," *Guardian*, 22 April 2008, http://www.guardian.co.uk/world/2008/apr/22/hillaryclinton.barackobama3; David E. Sanger and William J. Broad, "U.S. and Allies Warn Iran Over Nuclear 'Deception,'" *New York Times*, 26 September 2009, http://www.nytimes.com/2009/09/26/world/middleeast/26nuke.html
5. Mark Silva, "Cheney: United States Prefers Diplomacy, but Has Military Option on Iran," *Chicago Tribune*, 24 February 2007, sec. 1, 9; Ewen MacAskill and Julian Borger, "Cheney Pushes Bush to Act on Iran," *Guardian*, 16 July 2007, http://www.guardian.co.uk/world/2007/jul/16/usa.iran/
6. Michael Abramowitz, "Cheney Says United States Is Sending 'Strong Signal' to Iran," *Washington Post*, 29 January 2007, 2(A).
7. Julian Borger, "Britain Took Part in Mock Iran Invasion," *Guardian*, 15 April 2008, http://www.guardian.co.uk/politics/2006/apr/15/uk.military.
8. Reuters, "Cheney Mulled Israeli Strike on Iran: Newsweek," 23 September 2007, http://www.reuters.com/article/newsOne/idUSN2323126720070923
9. Peter Baker, Dafna Linzer, and Thomas E. Ricks, "United States Is Studying Military Strike Options on Iran," *Washington Post*, 9 April 2006, 1(A); Seymour M. Hersh, "Shifting Targets: The Administration's Plans for Iran," *The New Yorker*, October 2007, http://www.truthout.org/article/seymour-hersh-shifting-targets-new-plans-iran.
10. Sarah Baxter, "Pentagon: 'Three-Day' Blitz for Iran," *Sunday Times*, 2 September 2007, http://www.timesonline.co.uk/tol/news/world/asia/article2369001.ece; Philip Sherwell and Tim Shipman, "Bush Setting America Up for War with Iran," *Telegraph*, 17 September 2007, http://www.telegraph.co.uk/news/worldnews/1563293/Bush-setting-America-up-for-war-with-Iran.html.
11. Gabriel Ronay, "America 'Poised to Strike at Iran's Nuclear Sites' from Bases in Bulgaria and Romania," *Sunday Herald*, 28 January 2007, http://www.commondreams.org/headlines07/0128-05.htm.
12. Ramin Mostaghim and Jeffrey Fleishman, "Iran Claims Uranium Enrichment Progress," *Chicago Tribune*, 3 September 2007, sec. 1, 17; Associated Press, "Iranian Warns Against Added Nuclear Sanctions," *New York Times*, 6 June 2007, http://www.nytimes.com/2007/06/06/world/middleeast/06iran.html.
13. Anne Penketh, "The Big Question: Is Iran Developing a Nuclear Bomb, and If So, Should It Be Stopped," *Independent*, 9 May 2006, http://www.independent.co.uk/news/world/middle-east/the-big-question-is-iran-developing-a-nuclear-bomb-and-if-so-should-it-be-stopped-477426.html.
14. John Ward Anderson and Joby Warrick, "IAEA: Iran Cooperating in Nuclear Investigation," *Washington Post*, 31 August 2007, 10(A); Chicago Tribune, "Tehran Agrees to Nuclear Inspection Demands," 14 July 2007, sec. 1, 10.
15. Peter Slevin and Dafna Linzer, "United Nations Agency Rebukes Iran on Nuclear Activity," *Washington* Post, 19 June 2004, 1(A).
16. Farideh Farhi, "Politics of Reporting on IAEA Reports," *Informed Comment*, 16 November 2007, http://icga.blogspot.com/2007/11/politics-of-reporting-on-iaea-reports.html.
17. Gareth Porter, "U.S. Story on Iran Nuke Facility Doesn't Add Up: The Qom Site,"

Counterpunch, 30 September 2009; Paul Craig Roberts, "Another War in the Works: Fabricating a Case Against Iran," *Counterpunch*, 30 September 2009, http://www.counterpunch.org/roberts09302009.html#

18. Dafna Linzer, "Iran Is Judged 10 Years from Nuclear Bomb," *Washington Post*, 2 August 2005, 1(A).
19. Joby Warrick and Glenn Kessler, "Iran had Secret Nuclear Program, United Nations Agency Says," *Washington Post*, 11 November 2003, 1(A); Dafna Linzer, "No Proof Found of Iran Arms Program," *Washington Post*, 23 August 2005, 1(A).
20. George Jahn, "Nuclear Agency Praises Tehran," *Chicago Tribune*, 31 August 2007, sec. 1, 12; George Jahn, "Uranium Pullback Observed in Iran," *Chicago Tribune*, 10 July 2007, sec. 1, 7.
21. Agence-France Presse, "Hersh: CIA Analysis Finds Iran Not Developing Nuclear Weapons," *Agence France-Presse*, 19 November 2006, http://www.truthout.org/article/hersh-cia-analysis-finds-iran-not-developing-nuclear-weapons; Mark Mazzetti, "United States Says Iran Ended Atomic Arms Work," *New York Times*, 3 December 2007, http://www.nytimes.com/2007/12/03/world/middleeast/03cnd-iran.html?ref=world; Dafna Linzer and Joby Warrick, "United States Finds that Iran Halted Nuclear Arms Bid in 2003," *Washington Post*, 4 December 2007, 1(A).
22. Robin Wright, "Iranian Unit to Be Labeled 'Terrorist,'" *Washington Post*, 15 August 2007, 1(A).
23. Dafna Linzer, "Troops Authorized to Kill Iranian Operatives in Iraq," *Washington Post*, 26 January 2007, 1(A); Anthony DiMaggio, "U.S. Media and the British Iranian Standoff," *Z Magazine*, 11 April 2007, http://www.zmag.org/znet/viewArticle/1613.
24. Tribune News Services, "Pace Questions Claim on Iran," *Chicago Tribune*, 14 February 2007, sec. 1, 14.
25. Alireza Jafarzaedh, "Al-Maliki Encourages Iran's Growing Presence in Iraq," *Chicago Tribune*, sect. 1, 19 August 2007, 7.
26. Robin Wright and Nancy Trejos, "United States Troops Raid 2 Iranian Targets in Iraq," *Washington Post*, 12 January 2007, 16(A); James Glanz, "G.I.s in Iraq Raid Iranian's Offices," *New York Times*, 12 January 2007, 1(A); Dafna Linzer, "Troops Authorized to Kill Iranian Operatives in Iraq," *Washington Post*, 26 January 2007, 1(A).
27. Bay Fang, "Sanctions Reflect United States Frustration," *Chicago Tribune*, 26 October 2007, sec. 1, 14.
28. Helene Cooper and David E. Sanger, "Strategy on Iran Stirs New Debate at White House," *New York Times*, 16 June 2007, http://www.nytimes.com/2007/06/16/washington/16diplo.html.
29. Gareth Porter, "Iran Pushes for Talks with United States on Nukes, Security," *Inter Press Service*, 1 May 2006, http://ipsnews.net/news.asp?idnews=33070; Gareth Porter, "How a 2003 Secret Overture from Tehran Might Have Led to a Deal on Iran's Nuclear Capacity—If the Bush Administration Hadn't Rebuffed It," *Amerian Prospect*, 21 May 2006, http://www.prospect.org/cs/articles?articleId=11539.
30. Elise Labott, "Rice Blasts Iran, Says United States Will Pursue Tough Diplomacy," CNN.com, 3 June 2008, http://edition.cnn.com/2008/POLITICS/06/03/rice.aipac/index.html; Sheryl Gay Stolberg and Marc Santora, "Bush Declares Iran's Arms Role in Iraq Is Certain," *International Herald Tribune*, 15 February 2007, http://www.iht.com/articles/2007/02/15/america/web.0215prexy.php; CNN.com, "Bush Slams Syria, Iran Over Hezbollah, 22 July 2006, http://www.cnn.com/2006/POLITICS/07/22/Bush.radio/index.html; Yair Ettinger,

"Bush: Hezbollah, Hamas, Al-Qaida Are All the Same," *Haaretz*, 16 May 2008, http://www.haaretz.com/hasen/spages/983468.html.

31. Chris Floyd, "A Prism for the New Paradigm," *Counterpunch*, 5 November 2008, http://www.counterpunch.org/floyd11052008.html.
32. William A. Dorman and Mansour Farhang, *The United States Press and Iran: Foreign Policy and the Journalism of Deference* (Berkeley: University of California, 1987), 33–34.
33. Dorman and Farhang, *The United States Press and Iran*, 70, 153, 163, 174, 157.
34. Rupert Cornwell, "Iraq Is the Only Topic of Conversation as the US and Iran Finally Meet," *Independent*, 29 May 2007, http://www.independent.co.uk/news/world/middle-east/iraq-is-the-only-topic-of-conversation-as-the-us-and-iran-finally-meet-450845.html.
35. The data for this analysis was gathered by the author from the Vanderbilt Television News Archive. All stories that mentioned Iran's nuclear program or alleged nuclear weapons in their synopses were included.
36. Reese Erlich, *The Iran Agenda: The Real Story of U.S. Policy and the Middle East Crisis* (Sausalito, Ca.: Polipoint, 2007), 18.
37. Floyd Kalber, *NBC Evening News*, 23 June 1974, NBC, 5:30PM; Tom Brokaw, *NBC Evening News*, 24 April 1984, NBC, 5:30PM.
38. Howard Kurtz, "The Post on Weapons of Mass Destruction: An Inside Story," *Washington Post*, 12 August 2004, 1(A).
39. Editorial, "The Times and Iraq," *New York Times*, 26 May 2004, http://www.nytimes.com/2004/05/26/international/middleeast/26FTE_NOTE.html?ex=1231822800&en=8e376fe2a5c0e91f&ei=5070.
40. DiMaggio, *Mass Media, Mass Propaganda*, 57–76.
41. Sayed Salahuddin, "United States Show of Force in Gulf Alarming: Afghan Paper," Reuters, 26 May 2007, http://www.reuters.com/article/topNews/idUSISL20608020070526.
42. BBC, "World Press Weighs Iran Nuclear Standoff," 17 January 2006, http://news.bbc.co.uk/2/hi/middle_east/4620668.stm.
43. Editorial, "Wanted: A Foreign Policy," *Chicago Tribune*, 2 August 2007, sec. 1, 16.
44. Editorial, "Stalling for Time," *Chicago Tribune*, 4 September 2007, sec. 1, 16; Editorial, "Arming Tehran," *Chicago Tribune*, 22 January 2007, sec. 1, 18.
45. Editorial, "Tehran's Tentacles," *Chicago Tribune*, 14 June 2007, sec. 1, 24.
46. Richard S. Williamson, "United States Can't Just Talk while Iran Builds Nuclear Weapon," *Chicago Sun-Times*, 20 November 2006, 39(A).
47. Ali Akbar Dareini, "United States Can't Afford Another War: Iran," *Chicago Sun-Times*, 25 February 2007, 22(A).
48. Clarence Page, "Ahmadinejad's Real Agenda," *Chicago Tribune*, 26 September 2007, sec. 1, 21.
49. Victor Davis Hanson, "Here's Who's Afraid of an Iranian Bomb," *Chicago Tribune*, 26 October, 2007, sec. 1, 29.
50. Editorial, "Keep the Pressure on Iran," *Chicago Tribune*, 9 December 2007, sec. 2, 10.
51. Georgie Anne Geyer, "Harder Line with Iran Reduces Options," *Chicago Tribune*, 17 August 2007, sec. 1, 27.
52. Jimmy Carter, "Mixed Message on Nuclear Weapons," *Chicago Tribune*, 9 September 2007, sec. 1, 7.
53. Economist.com "What to Do about Iran?" 12 November 2007, http://www.economist.com/world/international/displaystory.cfm?story_id=10125367; Economist.com, "Iran's Nuclear Dossier," 22 November 2007, http://www.econo-

mist.com.hk/research/articlesBySubject/PrinterFriendly.cfm?story_id=10191788; Economist.com, "They Think They Have Right on Their Side," 22 November 2007, http://www.economist.com/world/mideast-africa/displaystory.cfm?story_id=10181134.

54. Economist.com, "Iran's Nukes: Less Scary than We Thought?" 4 December 2007, http://www.economist.com/world/mideast-africa/displaystory.cfm?story_id=10238608; Economist, "Pressure Works," 4 December 2007, 13; Economist, "Nuclear Fallout," 4 December 2007, 38.
55. Economist.com, "What's Not to Celebrate?," 8 December 2007, 54.
56. New Statesman, "Will the United States Now Attack Tehran?" 27 September 2004, http://www.newstatesman.com/200409270001.
57. Andrew Stephen, "Iran—This, Mr. President, Is How Wars Start," *New Statesman*, 19 February 2007, http://www.newstatesman.com/politics/2007/02/iran-iraq-bush-war; Katharine Gun, "Iran: Don't Let It Happen," *New Statesman*, 17 April 2006, http://www.newstatesman.com/200604170003.
58. John Pilger, "Iran: The War Ahead," *New Statesman*, 16 April 2007, http://www.newstatesman.com/politics/2007/04/iran-pilger-iraq-british-blair; John Pilger, "Iran: The War Begins," *New Statesman*, 5 February 2007, http://www.newstatesman.com/politics/2007/02/iran-iraq-pilger-israel.
59. Pilger, "The War Begins," 2007.
60. Kevin Sullivan, "Blair Reshuffles Cabinet after Election Losses," *Washington Post*, 6 May 2006, 11(A).
61. CNN.com, "Blair: Iran Sponsors Terrorism," 8 February 2005, http://www.cnn.com/WORLD/meast/02/08/blair.iran/; Matthew Tempest, "Military Action Against Iran Not Off Table, Says Blair," *Guardian*, 6 February 2007, http://www.guardian.co.uk/politics/2007/feb/06/foreignpolicy.uk.
62. Tim Shipman, "Gordon Brown 'Will Back Airstrikes on Iran,'" *Telegraph*, 10 August 2007, http://www.telegraph.co.uk/news/1565410/Gordon-Brown-'will-back-air-strikes-on-Iran'.html.
63. Dale Van Atta, "World's Most Dangerous Leaders," *Reader's Digest*, July 2007, http://www.rd.com/your-america-inspiring-people-and-stories/worlds-most-dangerous-leaders-/article40554.html.
64. Christopher Dickey, "Flunking Iran," *Newsweek*, 15 November 2007, http://www.newsweek.com/id/70679.
65. Thomas Omestad, "Taking Aim at Iran," *United States News and World Report*, 16 September 2007, http://www.usnews.com/articles/news/world/2007/09/16/think-tank-buzz-is-building-on-the-chances-of-war-with-iran.html.
66. Michael Hirsh, "Another Turn of the Screw," *Newsweek*, 27 October 2007, Tony Karon, "Why the Tough Talk on Iran?" *Newsweek*, 20 September 2007, http://www.newsweek.com/id/62306.
67. Jonathan Alter, "Before We Bomb Iran . . . " *Newsweek*, 22 October 2007, http://www.newsweek.com/id/43363; "Time to Change Tacks on Iran," *Newsweek*, 5 November 2007, http://www.newsweek.com/id/68464.
68. Massimo Calabresi, "Iran's Nuclear Threat," *Time*, 8 March 2003, http://www.time.com/time/printout/0,8816,430649,00.html; Tony Karon, "Why Iran Will Go Nuclear," *Time*, 12 February 2005, http://www.time.com/time/columnist/karon/article/0,9565,1027246,00.html.
69. Intercoder reliability for each category examined in the MSNBC analysis ranges between 90 to 100 percent. Intercoder reliability refers to the accuracy of the findings from Table 5.3, after comparing the content analyses undertaken by the authors.

70. Associated Press, "Rice: Cheney Not Pushing for War With Iran," MSNBC, 1 June 2007; Associated Press, "Ahmadinejad: West Can't Stop Iran's Nukes," MSNBC, 5 June 2007.
71. Associated Press, "United Nations Official: 'Madness to Attack Iran,'" MSNBC, 14 June 2007. Emphasis added.
72. Associated Press, "IAEA Sending Nuclear Team to Iran," MSNBC, 25 June 2007.
73. Associated Press, "United States Ready to Talk to Iran about Iraq," MSNBC, 17 July 2007; Associated Press, "Iran OKs High-Level Talks with United States," MSNBC, 18 July 2007.
74. John Seigenthaler, "Nuclear Crisis Growing in Iran, North Korea," *NBC Nightly News*, 20 July 2003.
75. Tom Brokaw and Andrea Mitchell, "The Development of Nuclear Weapons in Iran Most Immediate Foreign Policy Problem for President Bush," *NBC Nightly News*, 19 November 2004.
76. Brian Williams and Jim Miklaszewski, "United Nations Says It Found Uranium in Environmental Samples Takes From Iran," NBC, 18 July 2003.
77. John Siegenthaler and Dana Priest, *NBC Nightly News*, 1 April 2006.
78. Amy Robach and Rehema Ellis, *NBC Nightly News*, 17 September 2005; John Seigenthaler and Kevin Corke, *NBC Nightly News*, 23 December 2006.
79. Brian Williams and Andrea Mitchell, "United States, Allies Deliver Incentive Package to Iran to Stop Nuclear Program," *NBC Nightly News*, 6 June 2006.
80. John Seigenthaler and Jonathan Alter, "Iran Refuses to Give Up Rights to Pursue Nuclear Program," *NBC Nightly News*, 1 May 2005; Campbell Brown and Andrea Mitchell, "Iran Retaliates by Telling International Inspectors to Pull Out Cameras and Other Surveillance Equipment," *NBC Nightly News*, 6 February 2006; Andrea Mitchell, "Iran Begins Processing Uranium which Could Be Used to Make Several Bombs," *NBC Nightly News*, 21 September 2004; Brian Williams and Jim Miklaszewski, "US Threatens Iran with Pre-Emptive Strikes If They Continue Developing Nuclear Capabilities," *NBC Nightly News*, 16 March 2006; Tim Russert and Robin Wright, *Meet the Press*, NBC, 19 November 2006, http://www.msnbc.msn.com/id/15751399/page/4/.
81. Scott Pelley, *60 Minutes*, CBS, 23 September 2007.
82. Charles Gibson, *World News With Charles Gibson*, ABC, 20 November 2007.
83. Bob Schieffer, *Face the Nation*, CBS, 11 November 2007.
84. Steve Rendall, "What National Intelligence Estimate?" *Fairness and Accuracy in Reporting*, March/April 2008, 9–10.
85. Katie Couric and David Martin, "United States Military Ready to Send Message to Iranians," CBS, 29 April 2008.
86. George Stephanopoulos, *This Week*, ABC, 9 December 2007.
87. Under international law, there are only two cases under which force is considered legitimate. States using force must show that they are doing so in the pursuit of immediate self-defense against an ongoing or immenent attack and with explicit approval from the United Nations Security Council. The U.S. invasion of Iraq, U.S. and Israeli threats to bomb Iran, and Israel's 1982 bombing of Iraq all failed to meet these preconditions, hence they are illegal under international law.
88. Bob Simon, *60 Minutes*, CBS, 27 April 2008.
89. Borzou Daragahi, "Iran Has Enough Fuel for a Nuclear Bomb, Report Says," *Los Angeles Times*, 20 February 2009, http://articles.latimes.com/2009/feb/20/world/fg-iran-nuclear20.
90. William J. Broad and David E. Sanger, "Iran Has More Enriched Uranium than

Thought," *New York Times*, 19 February 2009, http://www.nytimes.com/2009/02/20/world/middleeast/20nuke.html.

91. Editorial, "Launching Dialogue with Iran," *Boston Globe*, 9 February 2009, 12(A).
92. Intercoder reliability for the analysis of the *Washington Post* ranged between 90 and 100 percent for all categories analyzed for the 25 percent of stories examined by a second coder.
93. Reuters, "Iran's Missiles Can Now Hit Europe, Ex-Official Says," *Washington Post*, 6 October 2004, 21(A); Reuters, "Iran Completes Testing of Long-Range Missile," *Washington Post*, 8 July 2003, 13(A); Glenn Kessler, "Iran Launches Nine Test Missiles, Says More Are Ready," *Washington Post*, 10 July 2007, 1(A).
94. Dana Milbank and Peter Slevin, "Bush Details Plan to Curb Nuclear Arms," *Washington Post*, 12 February 2004, 1(A); Robin Wright, "Showdown over Nuclear Plans Awaits Election Winner," *Washington Post*, 29 October 2004, 10(A).
95. Peter Baker, "Iran's Defiance Narrows United States Options for Response," *Washington Post*, 13 April 2006, 18(A).
96. Federation of American Scientists, "The Reliable Replacement Warhead Program: Background and Current Developments: CRS Report for Congress," 19 May 2008, http://www.fas.org/sgp/crs/nuke/RL32929.pdf.
97. Walter Pincus, "House Vote Stops Appropriation for New Generation of Nuclear Weapons," *Washington Post*, 20 June 2007, 20(A); Walter Pincus, "Nuclear Warhead Cut from Spending Bill," *Washington Post*, 18 December 2007, 2(A).
98. Simon Tisdall, "Iran's Secret Plan for Summer Offensive to Force United States Out of Iraq," *Guardian*, 22 May 2007, 1.
99. Media Workers Against War, "The Guardian and Iraq: Bad News," 23 May 2007, http://www.mwaw.net/2007/05/23/watershed/; David Edwards and David Cromwell, "Forum," 25 May 2007, http://www.medialens.org/forum/viewtopic.php?t=2367.
100. Juan Cole, "Informed Comment," Juancole.com, 22 May 2007, http://www.juan-cole.com/2007/05/parliament-building-shelled-iraqi.html.
101. Intercoder reliability for all categories of analysis of the *Guardian* were between 90 and 100 percent, for the 25 percent of stories analyzed by a second coder.
102. *Guardian*, "Leading Article: Iran's Nuclear Ambitions: Fuelling the Crisis," 5 January 2006, 28.
103. Hilary Benn and Hazel Blears, "Iraq Questions," *Guardian*, 21 February 2007, 6; Lee Glendinning, "Front: Iran 'Six Months From Mass Uranium Enrichment,'" *Guardian*, 20 February 2007, 3; Michael White, "Politics: Political Briefing Tony Brown and the Nuclear Deterrent," *Guardian*, 7 February 2007, 13; Richard Norton-Taylor and Ewen MacAskill, "Renewing Trident: Countering Nuclear Threats and Anti-Nuclear Agreements," 5 December 2006, *Guardian*, 6.
104. Michael White, "National: Blair Forced to Rely on Tories for Victory in Trident Vote," *Guardian*, 12 March 2007, 6; Will Woodward and Richard Norton-Taylor, "Nuclear Debate: Brown's Trident Pledge Angers Backbenchers and the Military," *Guardian*, 23 June 2006, 12; Sam Jones, "Reaction: 'A Colossal Waste of Money,'" *Guardian*, 22 June 2006, 4; Richard Norton-Taylor, "United States Still Has 110 Nuclear Weapons in United Kingdom," *Guardian*, 10 February 2005, 2.
105. Simon Tisdall, "Tehran Accuses US of Nuclear Double Standard," *Guardian*, 28 July 2005, 14; Ewen MacAskill, "United Kingdom Changes Tack in Nuclear Talks," *Guardian*, 6 September 2005, 15.
106. Richard Norton-Taylor, "Analysis: A Most Dangerous Message: Contradictory United States and British Nuclear Proliferation Policies Will Lead Other States to

Conclude that Nuclear Weapons Earn Respect and Deter Attack," *Guardian*, 13 April 2005, 23.

107. Intercoder reliability for all the categories in Table 3 range from 90 to 100 percent for the 25 percent of articles analyzed by a second coder.
108. Editorial, "Iran's Bomb," *Washington Post*, 22 September 2003, 22(A).
109. Editorial, "Countering Iran," *Washington Post*, 13 April 2008, 6(B).
110. Robert M. Kimmitt, "Iran: Time for Europe to Lead," *Washington Post*, 4 September 2003, 21(A).
111. Charles Krauthammer, "Today Tehran, Tomorrow the World," *Time*, 3 April 2006, 96.
112. Robert Samuelson, "Nuclear Nightmare," *Washington Post*, 20 October 2004, 27(A). Emphasis added.
113 Ed Henry, "Analysis: Bush Won't Back Down on Iran," CNN.com, 4 December 2007, http://www.cnn.com/2007/POLITICS/12/04/bush.presser/index.html.
114. Rasoul Movahedian, "Iran Is a Force for Peace: Instead of Demonising, the US Must Accept that We Have Every Right to a Civil Nuclear Programme," *Guardian*, 22 February 2007, 32.
115. Hamid Babaei, "Response: Iran's Energy Needs Will Not Be Met by Oil Alone: The International Pressure Over Our Nuclear Plants is Unfair and Unjustified, Says Hamid Babaei," *Guardian*, 20 January 2006, http://www.guardian.co.uk/world/2006/jan/20/iran.uk.
116. Editorial, "Next Step on Iran," *Washington Post*, 27 May 2007, 6(B); Editorial, "Rogue Regulator," *Washington Post*, 5 September 2007, 20(A).
117. Muhammad Sahimi, "Nuclear Options," *Guardian*, 2 June 2008, http://www.guardian.co.uk/commentisfree/2008/jun/02/nuclearoptions.
118. Ian Williams, "Déjà Vu All Over Again," *Guardian*, 3 November 2007, http://www.guardian.co.uk/commentisfree/2007/nov/03/dejavualloveragain.
119. George F. Will, "The Iran Dilemma," *Washington Post*, 23 September 2004, 29(A); David Ignatius, "Tehran's Two Worlds," *Washington Post*, 8 September 2006, 17(A).
120. Jim Hoagland, "The One-Sentence Iran Policy," *Washington Post*, 6 February 2005, 7(B).
121. Robert Kagan, "It's the Regime, Stupid," *Washington Post*, 29 January 2006, 7(B).
122. Jonathan Freedland, "The Problem Is: Iran Does Pose a Threat in Every Way Iraq Did Not: The G8 Leaders Can Exploit Tehran's Fear of International Isolation to Get a Nuclear Deal," *Guardian*, 26 April 2006, 25.
123. Tariq Ali, "This High-Octane Rocket-Rattling Against Tehran is Unlikely to Succeed: Ringed by Nuclear States, Iran's Atomic Programme is Scarcely Unreasonable. So Why Has Washington Manufactured this Crisis?" *Guardian*, 3 May 2006, 30.
124. Jonathan Steele, "If Iran Is Ready to Talk, the United States Must Do So Unconditionally: It Is Absurd to Demand That Tehran Should Make Concessions Before Sitting Down with the Americans," *Guardian*, 2 June 2006, 33; Roger Howard, "Neither Sanctions Nor Bombs Will End the Iran Nuclear Crisis: If Bush Really Wants a Safer Middle East, He Should Stop Giving Tehran Compelling Reasons to Acquire Nuclear Weapons," *Guardian*, 11 January 2007, 31; Dan Plesch, "Next Target Tehran: All the Signs Are that Bush Is Planning for a Neocon-Inspired Military Assault on Iran," *Guardian*, 15 January 2007, 30.
125. George Monbiot, "We Lie and Bluster about Our Nukes—and Then Wag Our Fingers at Iran," *Guardian*, 29 July 2008, 25.
126. Tony Benn, "Atomic Hypocrisy: Neither Bush Nor Blair Is in a Position to Take a

High Moral Line on Iran's Nuclear Programme," *Guardian*, 30 November 2005, 30; *Guardian*, "The Treaty Wreckers: In Just a Few Months, Bush and Blair Have Destroyed Global Restraint on the Development of Nuclear Weapons," 2 August 2005, 19; George Monbiot, "Building Bigger Nuclear Weapons Will Make Us Even Less Secure," *Guardian*, 24 January 2006, 27; Roy Hattersley, "A Complete Fantasy: Nuclear Deterrence Worked during the Cold War, But Replacing Trident Is an Expensive Nonsense," *Guardian*, 4 December 2006, 29; Simon Jenkins, "MPs Are Voting for a White Elephant," *Guardian*, 14 March 2007, 35.

127. George Monbiot, "Proliferation Treaty: Of Course Iran Wants to Develop Nuclear Weapons—and Has the Legal Entitlement to Do So," *Guardian*, 21 September 2004, 23.
128. Fareed Zakaria, "Talk to Tehran," *Washington Post*, 16 August 2005, 13(A).
129. Reese Erlich, *The Iran Agenda: The Real Story of United States Policy and the Middle East* (Sausalito, Calif.: PoliPoint, 2007), 54–58.
130. Noam Chomsky and David Barsamian, *Imperial Ambitions: Conversations on the Post-9/11 World* (New York: Metropolitan, 2005), 150.
131. Herbert J. Gans, *Deciding What's News: A Study of CBS Evening News, NBC Nightly News, Newsweek, and Time* (New York: Vintage, 1980), 183.

6. MEDIA, GLOBALIZATION, AND VIOLENCE: VIEWS FROM AROUND THE WORLD

1. "Truth Was First Casualty in Iraq War: Study," *Nation*, 23 January 2008.
2. Editorial, "Bush in Middle East," *Nation*, 10 January 2008.
3. Ghulam Asghar Khan, "Unleashing Armageddon on Iran," *Nation*, 2 October 2007.
4. Ibid.
5. Frank Esser and Barbara Pfetsch, eds., *Comparing Political Communication: Theories, Cases, and Challenges* (Cambridge: Cambridge University Press, 2004), 3.
6. Alexander G. Nikoleav and Ernest A. Hakanen, *Leading to the 2003 Iraq War: The Global Media Debate* (New York: Palgrave, 2003), 4.
7. James Curran and Myung-Jin Park, "Beyond Globalization Theory," in James Curran and Myung-Jin Park, *De-Westernizing Media Studies* (London: Routledge, 2000), 3.
8. Daniel C. Hallin and Paolo Mancini, *Comparing Media Systems: Three Models of Media and Politics* (Cambridge: Cambridge University Press, 2004); Richard Gunther and Anthony Mughan, *Democracy and the Media: A Comparative Perspective* (Cambridge: Cambridge University Press, 2000).
9. Fred S. Siebert, Theodore Peterson, and Wilbur Schramm, *Four Theories of the Press: The Authoritarian, Libertarian, Social Responsibility, and Soviet Communist Concepts of What the Press Should Be and Do* (Urbana: University of Illinois, 1974), 16, 27.
10. Ibid., 123, 141.
11. Ibid., 67.
12. Ibid., 51, 44.
13. Ibid., 51.
14. Ibid., 73–74.
15. John C. Nerone, "Revisiting Four Theories of the Press," in Nerone, *Last Rights: Revisiting Four Theories of the Press* (Urbana: University of Illinois, 1995), 29.

16. Curran and Myung-Jin Park, *De-Westernizing Media Studies,* 4.
17. Andre Gunder Frank, "The Development of Underdevelopment," in *The Globalization and Development Reader: Perspectives on Development and Global Change*, ed. J. Timmons Roberts and Amy Bellone Hite (Malden, Mass.: Blackwell, 2007), 77.
18. Immanuel Wallerstein, "The Rise and Demise of the World Capitalist System: Concepts for Comparative Analysis," in Roberts and Hite, *The Globalization and Development Reader,* 95–113.
19. Immanuel Wallerstein, *World-Systems Analysis: An Introduction* (Durham, N.C.: Duke, 2006), 10.
20. Walt W. Rostow: "The Stages of Economic Growth: A Non-Communist Manifesto," in Roberts and Hite, *The Globalization and Development Reader*, 47.
21. Curran and Myung-Jin Park,"Beyond Globalization Theory," in Curran and Park, *De-Westernizing Media Studies*, 5; Daniel C. Hallin and Paolo Mancini, "Americanization, Globalization, and Secularization," in Esser and Pfetsch, *Comparing Political Communication,* 25–26.
22. Sean MacBride and Colleen Roach, "The New International Information Order," in *The Global Media Debate: Its Rise, Fall, and Renewal*, ed. George Gerbner, Hamid Mowlana, and Kaarle Nordenstreng (Ablex, N.J.: Norwood, 1993), 6.
23. Colin Sparks and Philip Schlesinger, "British Press Coverage," in Gerbner, *The Global Media Debate: Its Rise, Fall, and Renewal*, 129–34.
24. Lee Artz and Yahya R. Kamalipour, eds., *The Globalization of Corporate Media Hegemony* (Albany, N.Y.: SUNY, 2003).
25. William A. Hachten and James F. Scotton, *The World News Prism: Global Media in an Era of Terrorism* (Ames: Iowa State University Press, 2002), 32.
26. Ibid., 168, 174.
27. Edward S. Herman and Robert W. McChesney, *The Global Media: The New Missionaries of Corporate Capitalism* (New York: Continuum, 1997), 1.
28. Ibid., 8–9.
29. Ibid., 1.
30. Nancy Morris and Silvio Waisbord, "Introduction: Rethinking Media Globalization and State Power," in *Media and Globalization: Why the State Matters*, ed. Nancy Morris and Silvio Waisbord (New York: Rowman and Littlefield, 2001), x.
31. Monroe E. Price, *Media and Sovereignty: The Global Information Revolution and Its Challenge to State Power* (Cambridge: MIT Press, 2002), 3; Curran and Myung-Jin Park, eds., *De-Westernizing Media Studies*, 12.
32. Daniel C. Hallin and Paolo Mancini, *Comparing Media Systems: Three Models of Media and Politics* (Cambridge: Cambridge University Press, 2004), 8, 13, 26.
33. Mehdi Semati, "Paradigm Loss: Frameworks for Global Media Analysis" *Journal of Broadcasting and Electronic Media* 48/3 (2004): 518–24.
34. Colin Sparks, *Globalization, Development, and the Mass Media* (Thousand Oaks, Calif.: Sage, 2007), 116.
35. Sparks, *Globalization, Development, and the Mass Media*, 120–21.
36. Terry Flew, *Understanding Global Media* (New York: Palgrave, 2007), 205; John Tomlinson, *Globalization and Culture* (Chicago: University of Chicago Press, 1999), 106–49.
37. Flew, *Understanding Global Media*, 66–97.
38. Flew, *Understanding Global Media*, 181–184.
39. Kai Hafez, *The Myth of Media Globalization* (Cambridge: Polity Press, 2007), 25.
40. Hafez, *The Myth of Media Globalization*, 31.

41. Jeremy Tunstall, *The Media Were American: U.S. Mass Media in Decline* (Oxford: Oxford University Press, 2008).
42. Lee Artz, "The Corporate Model from National to Transnational," in Lee Artz and Yahya R. Kamalipour, *The Media Globe: Trends in International Mass Media* (Lanham, Md.: Rowman and Littlefield, 2007), 141.
43. Pradip N. Thomas, "Agendas for Research and Strategies for Intervention," in *Who Owns the Media? Global Trends and Local Resistance*, ed. Pradip N. Thomas and Zaharom Nain (New York: Zed Books, 2004), 293.
44. Dal Yong Jin, "Transformation of the World Television System Under Neoliberal Globalization, 1983–2003," *Television and New Media* 8/3 (August 2007): 179–96.
45. Claudia Padovani and Kaarle Nordenstreng, "From NWICO to WSIS: Another World Information and Communication Order?" *Global Media and Communication* 1/3 (2005): 264–72.
46. Jean K. Chalaby, "American Cultural Primacy in a New Media Order: A European Perspective," *International Communication Gazette* 68/1 (2006): 33–51.
47. Peter Wilkin, "Global Communication and Political Culture in the Semi-Periphery: The Rise of the Globo Corporation," *Review of International Studies* 34 (2008): 93–113.
48. George F. Kennan, "Policy Planning Study 23: Review of Current Trends in United States Foreign Policy," in *Foreign Relations of the United States: 1948*, vol. 1, 1948, 509–29.
49. Tariq Ali, "A Naked Display of Military Power…" *Newsweek*, 10 March 2003, http://www.newsweek.com/id/58628; Bashir Abu-Manneh, "Israel in the United States Empire," *Monthly Review*, March 2007, http://www.monthlyreview.org/0307abu-manneh.htm.
50. Michael T. Klare, *Blood and Oil: The Dangers and Consequences of America's Growing Dependency on Imported Petroleum* (New York: Henry Holt, 2005), 36.
51. Daniel Yergin, *The Prize: The Epic Quest for Oil, Money, and Power* (New York: Free Press, 2008), 409.
52. David McNeil, "McNeil Interview With Noam Chomsky," *Z Magazine*, 31 January 2005, http://www.zmag.org/znet/viewArticle/6970; Lars Schoultz, *Beneath the United States: A History of U.S. Policy toward Latin* America (Cambridge: Harvard University Press, 1998), 345; Stephen G. Rabe, *Eisenhower and Latin America: The Foreign Policy of Anti-Communism* (Chapel Hill: University of North Carolina Press, 1988), 70; Abraham Ben-Zvi, *Decade of Transition: Eisenhower, Kennedy, and the Origins of the American-Israeli Alliance* (New York: Columbia University Press, 1998), 80.
53. Noam Chomsky, "Chomsky: 'There Is No War on Terror,'" Truthout.org, 14 January 2006, http://www.truthout.org/article/chomsky-there-is-no-war-terror.
54. Noam Chomsky, *World Orders Old and New* (New York: Columbia University Press, 1996), 192.
55. Henry Kissinger, *Years of Upheaval* (New York: Little, Brown, 1982), 862.
56. Henry Kissinger, "Seizing Arab Oil," *Harper's*, March 1975, http://harpers.org/SeizingArabOil.html.
57. V. G. Kiernan, *America, The New Imperialism: From White Settlement to World Hegemony* (London: Verso, 2005), 369.
58. Jimmy Carter, "Presidential Directive/NSC-63," The White House, 15 January 1981, http://www.fas.org/irp/offdocs/pd/pd63.pdf.
59. "Selling the Carter Doctrine," *Time*, 18 February 1980, http://www.time.com/time/magazine/article/0,9171,921819-1,00.html; Stuart Malawer, "Reagan's Law

and Foreign Policy: Reagan Corollary to International Law," *Harvard Law Review* (1988); Fred Lawson, "The Reagan Administration in the Middle East," *Middle East Research and Information Project*, November–December 1984, 27–34.

60. Ronald Reagan, "United States National Security Strategy," The White House, 20 May 1982, http://www.fas.org/irp/offdocs/nsdd/nsdd-032.htm.
61. George H. W. Bush, *National Security Strategy of the United States: 1990–1991* (Dulles, Va.: Potomac Books, 1990).
62. PBS, "Excerpts From 1992 Draft 'Defense Policy Guidance,'" http://www.pbs.org/wgbh/pages/frontline/shows/iraq/etc/wolf.html.
63. George H. W. Bush, "National Security Directive 26: United States Policy toward the Persian Gulf," The White House, 2 October 1989, http://www.fas.org/irp/offdocs/nsd/nsd26.pdf
64. George H. W. Bush, "Responding to Iraqi Aggression in the Gulf," The White House, 15 January 1991, http://www.fas.org/irp/offdocs/nsd/nsd_54.htm.
65. William J. Clinton, "A National Security Strategy of Engagement and Enlargement," The White House, February 1996, http://www.fas.org/spp/military/docops/national/1996stra.htm.
66. George Wright, "Wolfowitz: Iraq War Was about Oil," *Guardian*, 4 June 2003.
67. Ray McGovern, "We Need the Oil, Right? So What's the Problem?" *Common Dreams*, 16 February 2005, http://www.commondreams.org/views05/0216- 20.htm.
68. BBC, "Weapons of Mass Destruction Emphasis Was Bureaucratic," 29 May 2003, http://news.bbc.co.uk/2/hi/middle_east/2945750.stm
69. Michael Schwartz, "U.S. Eyes Still on the Iraqi Prize," *Asia Times*, 7 May 2007, http://www.atimes.com/atimes/Middle_East/IE09Ak01.html
70. Peter Baker, "Bush Says U.S. Pullout Would Let Iraq Radicals Use Oil as a Weapon," *Washington* Post, 5 November 2006, 6(A); Jennifer Loven, "Bush Gives New Reason for Iraq War," *Boston Globe*, 31 August 2005, http://www.boston.com/news/nation/articles/2005/08/31/bush_gives_new_reason_for_iraq_war/.
71. David E. Sanger and Steven R. Weisman, "Bush's Aides Envision New Influence in Region," *New York Times*, 10 April 2003, 11(B).
72. Greg Muttitt, "Crude Designs: The Rip-Off of Iraq's Oil Wealth," *Global Policy*, November 2005, http://www.globalpolicy.org/security/oil/2005/crudedesigns.htm.
73. Antonia Juhasz, "Oil for Sale: Iraq Study Group Recommends Privatization," *Alternet*, 7 December 2006, http://www.alternet.org/story/45190/.
74. Ann Wright, "What Congress Really Approved: Benchmark No. 1: Privatizing Iraq's Oil for United States Companies," Truthout.org, 26 May 2007, http://www.truthout.org/article/ann-wright-what-congress-really-approved-benchmark-no-1-privatizing-iraqs-oil-us-companies.
75. Andrew E. Kramer, "Deals With Iraq Are Set to Bring Oil Giants Back," *New York Times*, 19 June 2008, http://www.nytimes.com/2008/06/19/world/middleeast/19iraq.html.
76. Brian Dominick, "United States Forgives Iraq Debt to Clear Way for IMF Reforms," *New Standard*, http://www.globalpolicy.org/security/issues/iraq/reconstruct/2004/1219uscancelled.htm.
77. Antonia Juhasz, "The Handover that Wasn't," *Alternet*, 21 August 2004, http://www.alternet.org/story/19293/
78. Juhasz, "The Handover that Wasn't," 2008.
79. Michael Meacher, "My Sadness at the Privatisation of Iraq," *Times*, 12 August 2005, http://www.timesonline.co.uk/tol/comment/columnists/guest_contributors/article554318.ece.

80. For a brief summary of these orders, see Juhasz, "The Handover that Wasn't." For a specific listing of the different orders and what they entail, see Coalition Provisional Authority, "CPA Official Documents: Orders," http://www.iraqcoalition.org/regulations/#Orders.
81. Thomas J. Nagy, "The Secret Behind the Sanctions: How the United States Intentionally Destroyed Iraq's Water Supply," *Progressive*, September 2001, http://www.progressive.org/mag/nagy0901.html.
82. Former secretary of state Madeleine Albright conceded that this many Iraqis may have died under the sanctions, when questioned about the issue by Lesley Stahl on CBS's *60 Minutes*.
83. Estimates vary regarding Iraqi deaths, but studies have suggested that between hundreds of thousands to more than one million Iraqis have died under the occupation, possibly hundreds of thousands directly as a result of United States attacks and bombing campaigns. For more information, see Rob Stein, "100,000 Civilian Deaths Estimated in Iraq," *Washington Post*, 29 October 2004, 16(A); Sabrina Tavernise, "Iraqi Dead May Total 600,000, Study Says," *New York Times*, 11 October 2006, http://www.nytimes.com/2006/10/11/world/middleeast/11casualties.html; Tina Susman, "Poll: Civilian Death Toll in Iraq May Top 1 Million," *Los Angeles Times*, 14 September 2007, http://www.latimes.com/news/printedition/asection/la-fg-iraq14sep14,1,1207545.story.
84. Ellen Knickmeyer, "United States Has End in Sight on Iraq Rebuilding: Documents Show Much of Funding Diverted to Security, Justice System, and Hussein Inquiry," *Washington Post*, 2 January 2006, 1(A).
85. Knickmeyer, "United States Has End in Sight on Iraq Rebuilding," 2006.
86. Dana Hedgpeth, "Inspector General Details Failures of Iraq Reconstruction," *Washington Post*, 22 March 2007, 18(A).
87. James Glanz and Campbell Robertson, "As Iraq Surplus Rises, Little Goes into Rebuilding," *New York Times*, 8 June 2008, http://www.nytimes.com/2008/08/06/world/middleeast/06surplus.html.
88. Amy Goodman and David Bacon, "Iraqi Oil Workers Fight Privatization and Occupation," *Democracy Now!* 13 June 2005, http://www.democracynow.org/2005/6/13/iraqi_oil_workers_fight_privatization_and#
89. Ben Terrall, "Iraq Oil Workers Strike to Stop Privatization," *Dissident Voice*, 15 May 2007, http://www.dissidentvoice.org/2007/05/iraq-oil-workers-strike-to-stop-privatization/.
90. Aaron Glantz, "Poll: Iraqis Oppose Oil Privatization," *Common Dreams*, http://www.commondreams.org/archive/2007/08/08/3061/.
91. The overlap percentages in Table 6.3 represent the correlations between each paper's coverage of Iraq. These figures represesnt the percent of the time (measured in months) in which each paper's coverage increases or decreases in accord with that of each other paper.
92. Rodney Benson and Daniel C. Hallin, "How States, Markets and Globalization Shape the News: 1965-97," *European Journal of Communication* 22/1 (2007): 27–48.
93. Frank E. Dardis, "Military Accord, Media Discord: A Cross-National Comparison of United Kingdom vs. United States Press Coverage of Iraq War Protest," *International Communication Gazette* 68/5–6 (2006): 409–26.
94. Tim Hames, "Iraq—The Biggest, and Best, Story of the Year," *Times*, 17 December 2007, 19.
95. Michael Evans, "British Legacy in Basra Is Hope, Despite Crumbling Services and Street Violence," *Times*, 17 December 2007, 7.

96. Anjana Ahuja, "Could 650,000 Iraqis Really Have Died Because of the Invasion?" *Times*, 5 March 2007, 36.
97. Thom Shanker and Steven Lee Myers, "United States Asking Iraq for Wide Rights in Fighting War," *New York Times*, 25 January 2008, 1(A); David M. Herszenhorn, "After Veto, House Passes a Revised Military Policy Measure," *New York Times*, 17 January 2008, 28(A).
98. James Glanz, "United States Agency Finds New Waste and Fraud in Iraqi Rebuilding Projects," *New York Times*, 1 February 2007, 8(A); Mark Mazzetti, "Analysis Is Bleak on Iraq's Future," *New York Times*, 3 February 2007, 1(A); Mark Mazzetti, "United States Says Iran Ended Atomic Arms Work," *New York Times*, 3 December 2007, http://www.nytimes.com/2007/12/03/world/middleeast/03cnd-iran.html?partner=rssnytandemc=rss; Eric Schmitt and David Rohde, "Report Assails State Department on Iraq Security," *New York Times*, 23 October 2007, http://www.nytimes.com/2007/10/23/washington/23contractor.html; David Stout, "Slow Progress Being Made in Iraq, Petraeus Tells Congress," *New York Times*, 10 September 2007, http://www.nytimes.com/2007/09/10/washington/10cnd-policy.html.
99. Martin Hirst and Robert Schutze, "Allies Down Under? *The Australian* at War and the 'Big Lie,'" in *Global Media Go to War: The Role of News and Entertainment Media during the 2003 Iraq War*, ed. Ralph D. Berenger (Spokane, Wash.: Marquette, 2004), 173–89.
100. Daniela V. Dimitrova, "The War in Iraq: A View from Australia," in *Leading to the 2003 Iraq War*, ed. Alexander G. Nikoleav and Ernest A. Hakanen (New York: Palgrave, 2006), 120–22.
101. Pamela Bone, "The Left Is on Side of Hate," *Australian*, 1 February 2007, 12; Janet Albrechtsen, "Protector of the Free World Deserves Better," *Australian*, 14 February 2007, 12; Nick Cohen, "Liberals Are Now the Appeasers of Hate," *Australian*, 17 February 2007, 24.
102. See chap. 2 and chap. 6, "Free Speech Fatalities," in Anthony R. DiMaggio, *Mass Media, Mass Propaganda: Examining American News in the "War on Terror"* (Lanham, Md.: Lexington, 2008), 135–58.
103. Richard Gunther, Jose Ramon Montero, and Jose Ignacio Wert, "The Media and Politics in Spain: From Dictatorship to Democracy," in *Democracy and the Media: A Comparative Perspective*, ed. Richard Gunther and Anthony Mughan (Cambridge: Cambridge University Press, 2000), 33–34, 45.
104. Editorial, "A Favor de la Retirada," *El Pais*, 29 March 2007, 14; Editorial, "Britanicos en Retirada," *El Pais*, 25 February 2007, 14.
105. Editorial, "La Estrategia Sobre Iran," *El Pais*, 5 February 2007, 14.
106. David Skinner and Mike Gasher, "So Much by So Few: Media Policy and Ownership in Canada," in *Converging Media, Diverging Politics: A Political Economy of News Media in the United States and Canada*, ed. David Skinner, James R. Compton, and Michael Gasher (Lanham, Md.: Lexington, 2005), 54.
107. Editorial, "Canada Must Stay the Course," *Globe and Mail*, 22 September 2007, 24(A).
108. Lea Mandelzis and Chanan Naveh, "American Crisis–Israeli Narrative: The Role of Media Discourse in the Promotion of a War Agenda," in *Leading to the 2003 Iraq War*, ed. Alexander G. Nikoleav and Ernest A. Hakanen (New York: Palgrave, 2006), 187.
109. Erwin Frenkel, *The Press and Politics in Israel: The Jerusalem Post From 1932 to the Present* (Westport, Conn.: Greenwood, 194, 151–12.
110. Barry Rubin, "Identifying America's Top Mideast Priority," *Jerusalem Post*, 12 June 2007, 16.

111. Ibid.; Hilary Leila Krieger, "Bush: Stymie Nuclear Iran or Face World War III," *Jerusalem Post*, 18 October 2007, 1.
112. Daniel Pipes, "Can the IAF Take Out Iran's Nukes?" *Jerusalem Post*, 14 June 2007, 16; Editorial, "It's All About Iran," *Jerusalem Post*, 26 October 2007, 13; Hilary Leila Krieger, "Cheney: We Won't Allow Iran to Have Nukes," *Jerusalem Post*, 22 October 2007; Hilary Leila Krieger, "Iran Could Trigger Nuke Race in Mideast Beckett Warns," *Jerusalem Post*, 28 June 2007.
113. Editorial, "About-Turn Confirms All Is Lost," *New Zealand Herald*, 14 July 2007.
114. Editorial, "Blair Legacy: Prosperity and Honor," *New Zealand Herald*, 14 May 2007.
115. Mike Houlahan, "Clark Claims Iraq Invasion Has Made World Less Safe," *New Zealand Herald*, 1 October 2008, http://www.nzherald.co.nz/world/news/article.cfm?c_id=2andobjectid=10400858; Patrick Walters, "Kevin Rudd Hammers John Howard's Iraq War Judgment," *Australian*, 3 June 2008, http://www.theaustralian.news.com.au/story/0,25197,23801099-5013946,00.html.
116. Sallie Hughes, *Newsrooms in Conflict: Journalism and the Democratization of Mexico* (Pittsburgh: University of Pittsburgh, 2006), 59–62, 77–78, 208.
117. Gabriel Guerra Castellanos, "Republicanos al Borde de un Ataque de Nervios," *Reforma*, 4 September 2007, 2.
118. Jorge Ramos Avalos, "Yo No Soy Bush," *Reforma*, 1 January 2008, 7; Gabriel Guerra Castellanos, "Iran: el Segundo Frente de Bush," *Reforma*, 9 October 2007, 2.
119. Ezra Shabot, Iraq: Sin Salidas," *Reforma*, 28 July 2007, 2.
120. Robert H. Horwitz, "'Negotiated Liberalization': The Politics of Communications Sector Reform in South Africa," in *Media and Globalization: Why the State Matters*, ed. Silvio Waisbord and Nancy Morris (New York: Rowman and Littlefield, 2001).
121. Mohamed Adhikari, "You Have the Right to Know," in *South Africa's Resistance Press: Alternative Voices in the Last Generation under Apartheid*, ed. Les Switzer and Mohamed Adhikari (Athens, Ohio: Ohio University Center for International Studies, 2000).
122. Christine Buchinger, Herman Wasserman, and Arnold de Beer, "Nowhere to Hide: South African Media Seek Global Perspective on Iraq War," in Berenger, *Global Media Go to War*, 215, 220.
123. Ronie Mamoepa, "SA Will Stick by its Principles," *Star*, 5 March 2007, 8.
124. Allister Sparks, "Bush's Losing Battle Continues," *Star*, 22 April 2007, 14.
125. David Gardner, "Heroic War Tales Nothing but Pack of Lies," *Star*, 25 April 2007, 15.
126. Allister Sparks, "Bush's Losing Battle Continues," *Star*, 22 April 2007, 14; Moulana Ebrahim Bham, "Hidden Costs of the War in Iraq," *Star*, 11 September 2007, 8.
127. Singapore's media has traditionally ranked extremely low on the press freedom rankings of international organizations such as Reporters Without Borders, due to high levels of government censorship and control over media. For more information, see: http://www.rsf.org/article.php3?id_article=24025.
128. Alastair McIndoe, "Security Panel and Charter Top ASEAN Agenda in Manila," *Straits Times*, 28 July 2007; Derwin Pereira, "No-Show by US Leaders Hints at Shift in Focus on White House," *Straits Times*, 19 July 2007.
129. Editorial, "Debating Iraq Responsibly," *Straits Times*, 18 July 2007.
130. Cheong Suk-Wai, "Knocking Iran Out of Iraq," *Straits Times*, 15 September 2007.
131. Laikwan Pang, "The Global-National Position of Hong-Kong Cinema in China," in *Media in China: Consumption, Content, and Crisis*, ed. Stephanie Hemeiryk Donald, Michael Keane, and Yin Hong (New York: Routledge, 2002), 55–58.

132. Won Ho Chang, *Mass Media in China: The History and the Future* (Ames: Iowa State University, 1989).
133. Joseph M. Chan and Clement Y. K. So, "The Surrogate Democracy Function of the Media," in *Journalism and Democracy in Asia*, ed. Angela Romano and Michael Bromley (New York: Routledge, 2005), 66–80; Paul S. N. Lee, "Democracy, the Press, and Civil Society in Hong Kong," in *Journalism and Democracy in Asia*, ed. Angela Romano and Michael Bromley (New York: Routledge, 2005), 81–95.
134. Editorial, "Humbled Bush Needs to Work with Congress," *South China Morning Post*, 1 February 2007, 14. Editorial, "United States Can Prevent Wrong by Getting Intelligence Right," *South China Morning Post*, 3 March 2007, 14.
135. Doug Bandow, "Reining in American Foreign Policy," *South China Morning Post*, 27 February 2007, 13.
136. Michael Chugani, "Bush's Crumbling Wall of Deceit," *South China Morning Post*, 2 May 2007, 15.
137. Nina L. Kruschcheva, "The Liars' Club Last Reunion," *Nation*, 4 June 2007.
138. Max Hastings, "West Losing Moral Authority after Iraq Fallout," *Nation*, 28 March 2007.
139. Anna Husarska, "US Should Lead Action on Iraq's Refugee Crisis," *Nation*, 30 April 2007.

7. PUBLIC RATIONALITY, POLITICAL ELITISM, AND OPPOSITION TO WAR

1. Andrew Kohut, "Washington Leaders Wary of Public Opinion," Pew Research Center, 17 April 1998, http://people-press.org/reports/pdf/92.pdf
2. Benjamin I. Page and Marshall S. Bouton, *The Foreign Policy Disconnect: What Americans Want from Our Leaders but Don't Get* (Chicago: University of Chicago Press, 2006).
3. James Devitt, "Politicians Disregard Public Opinion Polls, Says Political Scientist Shapiro in New Book," *Columbia University Record* 26/4 (25 September 2000), http://www.columbia.edu/cu/record/archives/vol26/vol26_iss4/2604_Shapiro_Book_Politicians.html; Robert Y. Shapiro and Lawrence Jacobs, *Politicians Don't Pander: Political Manipulation and the Loss of Democratic Responsiveness* (Chicago: University of Chicago Press, 2000).
4. Public support for Obama and opposition to McCain increased dramatically in late September to early October 2008, at the same time that the media outlets were reporting on the collapse of American banking and investment firms, in addition to the collapse of the housing and derivatives industries. Opposition to McCain was likely driven by disenchantment at government at the onset of the recession, as reflected in anger directed against former president Bush's political party. For more on these events, see: BBC, "Q&A: Lehman Brothers Bank Collapse," 16 September 2008, http://news.bbc.co.uk/2/hi/7615974.stm; Peter S. Goodman, "Economic Memo: Credit Enters a Lockdown," *New York Times*, 25 September 2008, http://www.nytimes.com/2008/09/26/business/26assess.html; Lori Montgomery and Paul Kane, "Sweeping Bailout Bill Unveiled," *Washington Post*, 29 September 2008, http://www.washingtonpost.com/wp-dyn/content/article/2008/09/28/AR2008092800064.html; Chris Isidore, "Buffett: My Fix for the Economy," *MoneyCNN.com*, 2 October 2008, http://money.cnn.com/2008/10/02/news/newsmakers/buffett.fortune/index.htm.

5. Phillip Converse, "Information Flow and the Stability of Partisan Attitudes," *Public Opinion Quarterly* 26/4 (Winter 1962): 578–99; Angus Campbell, Phillip E. Converse, Warren E. Miller, and Donald E. Stokes, *The American Voter: Unabridged Edition* (Chicago: University of Chicago Press, 1960), 542–543.
6. Gabriel A. Almond, *The American People and Foreign Policy* (New York: Praeger, 1962), 69.
7. James R. Rosenau, *Public Opinion and Foreign Policy* (New York: Random House, 1961), 35–40.
8. Michael X. Delli Carpini and Scott Keeter, *What Americans Know about Politics and Why It Matters* (New Haven: Yale University Press, 1996), 162–71.
9. John E. Mueller, *War, Presidents, and Public Opinion* (New York: Wiley, 1973), 124–25.
10. G. William Domhoff, "The Power Elite, Public Policy, and Public Opinion," in *Navigating Public Opinion: Polls, Policy, and the Future of American Democracy*, ed. Jeff Manza, Fay Lomax Cook, and Benjamin I. Page (Oxford: Oxford University Press, 2002), 136–37, 124.
11. Gladys Engel Lang and Kurt Lang, *The Battle for Public Opinion: The President, the Press, and the Polls During Watergate* (New York: Columbia University Press, 1983), 21–22.
12. Ibid., 301.
13. Andrew S. McFarland, *Neopluralism: The Evolution of Political Process Theory* (Lawrence: University Press of Kansas, 2004), 63–64. For more on the interaction between the civil rights movement and government institutions, also see Douglas McAdam, *Political Process and the Development of Black Insurgency: 1930–1970* (Chicago: University of Chicago Press, 1999).
14. Jack L. Walker Jr. *Mobilizing Interest Groups in America: Patrons, Professions, and Social Movements* (Ann Arbor: University of Michigan Press, 2000), 12.
15. Margaret E. Keck and Kathryn Sikkink, *Activists Beyond Borders* (Ithaca, N.Y.: Cornell University Press).
16. William M. LeoGrande, "Did the Public Matter? The Impact of Opinion on Congressional Support for Ronald Reagan's Nicaragua Policy," in *Public Opinion in United States Foreign Policy: The Controversy over Contra Aid*, ed. Richard Sobel (Lanham, MD.: Rowman and Littlefield, 1993).
17. Reed Brody, *Contra Terror in Nicaragua: A Fact Finding Mission: September 1984–January 1985* (Boston: South End Press, 1999).
18. John E. Mueller, *Policy and Opinion in the Gulf War* (Chicago: University of Chicago Press, 1994); Andrew Rosenthal, "Standoff in the Gulf," *New York Times*, 19 December 1990, query.nytimes.com/gst/fullpage.html?res=9C0CE2D8123BF93AA2571C1A966958260&sec=&spon=&pagewanted=all.
19. Richard Sobel, *The Impact of Public Opinion on United States Foreign Policy since Vietnam* (Oxford: Oxford University Press, 2001), 62.
20. Philip Converse, "The Nature of Belief Systems in Mass Publics," in *Ideology and Discontent*, ed. David E. Apter (New York: Free Press, 1964), 243–45; John R. Zaller, *The Nature and Origins of Mass Opinion* (Cambridge: Cambridge University Press, 1992).
21. Zaller, *The Nature and Origins of Mass Opinion*, 43, 159, 19.
22. Ibid., 21.
23. Ibid., 16, 18.
24. Ibid., 86, 95, 98, 115.
25. Sobel, *The Impact of Public Opinion on United States Foreign Policy*, 20–21.

26. John R. Zaller, "Elite Leadership of Mass Opinion," in W. Lance Bennett and David L. Paletz, *Taken by Storm: The Media, Public Opinion, and United States Foreign Policy in the Gulf War* (Chicago: University of Chicago Press, 1994), 186.
27. Ibid., 191.
28. Zaller, *The Nature and Origins of Mass Opinion*, 102–4.
29. Benjamin I. Page and Marshall M. Bouton, *The Foreign Policy Disconnect: What Americans Want from Our Leaders but Don't Get* (Chicago, University of Chicago Press, 2006), 16.
30. James A. Stimson, *Tides of Consent: How Public Opinion Shapes American Politics* (Cambridge: Cambridge University Press, 2004), 155.
31. Benjamin I. Page and Robert Y. Shapiro, *The Rational Public: Fifty Years of Trends in Americans' Policy Preferences* (Chicago: University of Chicago Press), 1992, 48–49.
32. Ibid., 60, 32, 53; Ole R. Holsti, *Public Opinion and American Foreign Policy* (Ann Arbor: University of Michigan Press, 1999), 78.
33. William A. Gamson, *Talking Politics* (Cambridge: Cambridge University Press, 1996), 4, 11.
34. Samuel L. Popkin, *The Reasoning Voter: Communication and Persuasion in Presidential Campaigns* (Chicago: University of Chicago Press, 1994), 7–13, 17, 20.
35. W. Russell Neuman, Mario R. Just, and Ann N. Crigler, *Common Knowledge: News and the Construction of Political Meaning* (Chicago: University of Chicago Press, 1992), 81, 92.
36. Doris A. Graber, *Processing Politics: Learning from Television in the Internet Age* (Chicago: University of Chicago Press, 2001), 58.
37. Ibid., 61.
38. Matthew A. Baum, *Soft News Goes to War: Public Opinion and American Foreign Policy in the New Media Age* (Princeton: Princeton University Press, 2003), 126.
39. Ellen Knickmeyer, "United States Has End in Sight on Iraq Rebuilding," *Washington Post*, 2 January 2006, 1(A).
40. Knickmeyer, "United States has End in Sight on Iraq Rebuilding," 2006.
41. Reuters, "Iraq: Unemployment and Violence Increase Poverty," 17 October 2006, http://www.alertnet.org/thenews/newsdesk/IRIN/c14c2cc0f6c99e87f284df922a039cad.htm; Ahmed Ali and Dahr Jamail, "Iraq's Unemployment Epidemic," *Common Dreams*, February 21, 2008, http://www.commondreams.org/archive/2008/02/21/7211; Mark Tran, "Iraq Report: Job Prospects Would Combat Insurgency," *Guardian*, 26 June 2008, http://www.guardian.co.uk/world/2008/jun/26/iraq.usa1?gusrc=rss&feed=networkfront.
42. Agence France Presse, "Iraq Says Power Grid Not Fully Restored until 2011," 24 December 2008; Knickmeyer, "United States Has End in Sight on Iraq Rebuilding"; Michael Schwartz, "Wrecked Iraq: What Good News from Iraq Really Means," TomDispatch.com, 23 October 2008, http://www.tomdispatch.com/post/174993/michael_schwartz_iraq_in_hell; James Glanz, "Report Finds Iraq Water Treatment Project to Be Late, Faulty and Over Budget," *New York Times*, 27 October 2008, http://www.nytimes.com/2008/10/27/world/middleeast/27reconstruct.html?ref=world.
43. Chris Shumway, "Iraqis Endure Worse Conditions than under Saddam," *Z Magazine*, 19 May 2005, http://www.zmag.org/content/showarticle.cfm?SectionID=15&ItemI-D=7894; UNICEF, "Iraq's Water and Sanitation Crisis Adds to Dangers Faced by Children and Families," 19 March 2008, http://www.unicef.org/infobycountry/iraq_43232.html.

44. Shumway, "Iraqis Endure Worse Conditions than under Saddam," 2005; UNICEF, "Iraq's Children 2007: A Year in Their Life," 2007, http://www.unicef.org.uk/campaigns/publications/pdf/iraq_07.pdf; Karl Vick, "Children Pay Cost of Iraq's Chaos," *Washington Post*, 21 November 2004, 1(A).
45. Patrick Cockburn, "UN Warns of Five Million Iraqi Refugees," *Independent*, 10 June 2007, http://www.independent.co.uk/news/world/middle-east/un-warns-of-five-million-iraqi-refugees-452522.html.
46. Leonard Doyle, "US Surge Sees 600,000 More Iraqis Abandon Home," *Independent*, 25 August 2007, http://www.independent.co.uk/news/world/americas/us-surge-sees-600000-more-iraqis-abandon-home-462926.html.
47. Iraq Body Count, 2008, http://www.iraqbodycount.org/; BBC, "Iraq Death Toll 'Soared Post-War,'" 29 October 2004, http://news.bbc.co.uk/2/hi/middle_east/3962969.stm; John Tirman, "Study: More than 600,000 Dead in Iraq, *Alternet*, 11 October 2006, http://www.alternet.org/waroniraq/42867/; Peter Beaumont and Joanna Walters, "Greenspan Admits Iraq Was about Oil, as Deaths Put at 1.2 Million," *Guardian*, 16 September 2007, http://www.guardian.co.uk/world/2007/sep/16/iraq.iraqtimeline.
48. I conclude that claims of the surge's success are exaggerated at best and deceitful at worst in Anthony DiMaggio, "From Bush to Obama: Seven Years of Wartime Propaganda," 7 February 2009, *Counterpunch*, http://www.counterpunch.org/dimaggio02272009.html. To more thoroughly explore the issue of the surge's alleged success, see these reports from journalists and experts: John Hendren, "'Sunni Awakening': Insurgents Are Now Allies," ABC News, 23 December 2007, http://abcnews.go.com/International/Story?id=4045471&page=1; Jim Lehrer, Nir Rosen, and Robert Kagan, "As Violence Peaks and Dips, Debate Over 'Surge' Persists," PBS, 11 March 2008, http://www.pbs.org/newshour/bb/middle_east/jan-june08/surge_03-11.html; Michael Shwartz, *War Without End* (Chicago: Haymarket, 2008); Saul Landau, "Whining about Winning in Iraq," *Counterpunch*, 24 October 2008, http://www.counterpunch.org/landau10242008.html; CNN.com, "Al Sadr Calls Off Fighting, Orders Compliance with Iraqi Security," 30 March 2008, http://www.cnn.com/2008/WORLD/ meast/03/30/iraq.main/index.html; CNN.com, "Sources: Iran Helped Prod Al-Sadr Ceasefire," 31 March 2008, http://www.cnn.com/2008/WORLD/meast/ 03/31/iraq.main/index.html; Patrick Cockburn, "The Big Questions about Iraq," *Counterpunch*, 26 August 2008, http://www.counterpunch.org/patrick08262008. html; Patrick Cockburn, "What's Really Happened during the Surge?" *Counterpunch*, 12 December 2007, http://www.counterpunch.org/patrick 12122007.html; Juan Cole, "A Social History of the Surge," *Informed Comment*, 24 July 2008, http://www.juancole.com/2008/07/social-history-of-surge.html; Nir Rosen, "Inside the Surge," *Nation*, 3 April 2008, http://www.thenation.com/ doc/20080421/rosen; Nir Rosen, "Myth of the Surge," *Rolling Stone*, 6 March 2008, http://www.rollingstone.com/politics/story/18722376/the_myth_of_the_surge/print.
49. Iraq Body Count, "The Baghdad 'Surge' and Civilian Victims," 2008, http://www.iraqbodycount.org/analysis/numbers/baghdad-surge/.
50. The public opinion information provided in Figure 7.1 is derived from time series public opinion questions asked by various news organizations, including: CNN, Pew Research Center, ABC News, and the *Washington Post*.
51. This data again was drawn from various polling organizations, including *CNN*, *Pew Research Center*, *ABC News*, and the *Washington Post*. The information is available from http://www.pollingreport.com. By running a simple statistical correlation test,

one sees that each question in Figure 7.1 is strongly correlated with the other questions. Altogether, there are six separate pairs of questions, for which I provide the correlations in this endnote: the correlation between support for withdrawal and support for troop reductions is .88; the correlation between support for withdrawal and opposition to the war as "not worth it" is .94; the correlation between support for withdrawal and opposition to Bush's handling of the Iraq war is .93; the correlation between opposition to the war as "not worth it" and support for troop reductions is .69; the correlation between support for troop reductions and opposition to Bush's handling of the Iraq war is .6; and the correlation between opposition to the war as "not worth it" and opposition to Bush's handling of the Iraq war is .96.

52. Scott Sigmund Gartner, "The Multiple Effects of Casualties on Public Support for War: An Experimental Approach," *American Political Science Review*, Vol. 102/1 (2008): 105.
53. Richard K. Herrmann, Philip E. Tetlock, and Penny S. Visser, "Mass Public Decisions to Go to War: A Cognitive-Interactionist Framework," *American Political Science Review* 93/3 (1999): 553–73.
54. Richard C. Eichenberg, "Victory Has Many Friends: United States Public Opinion and the Use of Military Force, 1981–2005," *International Security* 30/1 (2005): 140–77.
55. John Mueller, "The Iraq Syndrome," *Foreign Affairs*, November/December 2005, http://www.foreignaffairs.org/20051101faessay84605-p20/john-mueller/the-iraq-syndrome.html.
56. Christopher Gelpi and John Mueller, "The Cost of War," *Foreign Affairs*, January/February 2006, http://www.foreignaffairs.org/20060101faresponse85114/christopher-gelpi-john-mueller/the-cost-of-war.html.
57. CNN.com, "Poll: Most in United States Say Iraq War Not Worthwhile," 3 March 2005, http://www.cnn.com/2005/US/05/03/iraq.poll/; Gary Langer, "Poll: Americans Conflicted about Iraq War," *ABC News*, 15 March 2005, http://abcnews.go.com/Politics/PollVault/Story?id=582744&page=1.
58. Dan Froomkin, "The Trust is Gone," *Washington Post*, 23 November 2005, http://www.washingtonpost.com/wp-dyn/content/blog/2005/11/23/BL2005112301195_pf.html.
59. PIPA, "Americans Want to Begin Drawdown of Troops in Iraq but Not a Quick Pullout," WorldPublicOpinion.org, 15 March 2006, http://www.worldpublicopinion.org/pipa/articles/international_security_bt/178.php?lb=btis&pnt=178&nid=&id=.
60. Tom Regan, "Polls Show Opposition to Iraq War at All-Time High," *Christian Science Monitor*, 1 September 2006, http://www.csmonitor.com/2006/0901/dailyUpdate.html.
61. PIPA.org, "United States Public Opinion in Line with Iraq Study Group's Proposals," WorldPublicOpinion.org, 5 December 2006, http://www.worldpublicopinion.org/pipa/articles/brunitedstatescanadara/283.php?nid=&id=&pnt=283&lb=brusc.
62. Dalia Sussman, "Poll Shows Opposition to Iraq War at All-Time High," *New York Times*, 24 May 2007, http://www.truthout.org/article/poll-shows-opposition-iraq-war-all-time-high.
63. Jon Cohen and Dan Balz, "Poll Finds Democrats Favored on War," *Washington Post*, 24 July 2007, 1(A).
64. Amy Belasco, "The Cost of Iraq, Afghanistan, and Other Global War on Terror Operations Since 9/11," Congressional Research Service, 15 October 2008, http://www.fas.org/sgp/crs/natsec/RL33110.pdf; David R. Francis, "Iraq War Cost Estimates Run into the Trillions," *Christian Science Monitor*, 10 March 208,

http://www.csmonitor.com/2008/0310/p16s01-wmgn.html; Joseph Stiglitz, *The Three Trillion Dollar War: The True Cost of the Iraq Conflict* (New York: W. W. Norton, 2008).

65. I have employed time-series data related to public opposition to the war. Opposition to the war as "not worth it" is drawn from month-by-month public opinion polling from ABC News, and is available from: http://www.pollingreport.com/iraq.htm. I employ ordinary least squares regression to measure the relationships among media coverage, American casualties, violence in Iraq, and opposition to the war. Controlling for other independent variables such as monthly military casualties and critical monthly media coverage (measured in the number of monthly stories in the *New York Times* discussing withdrawal), we see that monthly attacks in Iraq are strongly associated with increased opposition to the war. The correlation coefficient for increased monthly attacks and its relation to increased opposition to the war as a "mistake" is a strong .689, and highly statistically significant at the .1 percent level. The correlation coefficient for increased monthly attacks and its relation to increased opposition to Bush's handling of the Iraq war is again strong at .601, and highly statistically significant at the .1 percent level. Finally, the correlation coefficient for increased monthly attacks and its relation to increased opposition to the war as "not worth it" is a strong .694, and statistically significant at the .1 percent level. American casualties are also a significant factor associated with opposition to the war as not "worth it" and opposition to Bush's handling of the Iraq war (although not for the question of whether the war is a mistake), but the casualty variable is much weaker than the monthly attacks variable. The casualty variable coefficients are .216 and .260 for opposition to the war as not "worth it" and opposition to Bush's handling of the war respectively. Critical media coverage is not significant for any of the three policy questions. The entire model (including media coverage, monthly attacks, and monthly casualties) retains an R^2 of .611, .695, and .781 respectively for policy questions viewing the war as a mistake, criticizing Bush's handling of the war, and depicting the war as "not worth it."

66. For information on the entire American public, see the following: PIPA, "United States Public Opinion in Line with Iraq Study Group's Proposals," *World Public Opinion*, 5 December 2006, http://www.worldpublicopinion.org/pipa/articles/brunitedstatescanadara/283.php.

67. For more information on the definition of statistical significance, see endnote 11 from the Introduction to this book.

68. My model for measuring opposition to the war includes three independent variables: monthly attacks in Iraq, monthly American casualties, and critical monthly coverage in the *New York Times*. Unfortunately, the financial cost of the war cannot be effectively measured in a regression that measures month-by-month changes in opinion, since budgets for the war are allocated on a more infrequent basis. Increased opposition to Bush's handling of the Iraq war and increased opposition to the war as "not worth it" are both positively related to increased monthly American casualties in Iraq. The relationship between casualties and opposition to Bush's handling of the war is significant at the 5 percent level. The relationship between opposition to the war as "worth it" and increased casualties is also significant at the 5 percent level.

69. Monthly deaths reached their height in 2004 and 2005, when 71 soldiers died on average per month in both years, as opposed to 52 deaths on average per month in 2003, 69 deaths per month in 2006, and 75 deaths per month in 2007.

70. The correlation coefficient for a simple bivariate regression between the percent

change in monthly military casualties and the percent change in monthly media coverage in the *New York Times* is .7, with a significance level of 5 percent. However, this single variable is not all that powerful in explaining changes in media coverage on casualties, as the models R^2 is a weak .13. The weakness of casualties themselves in explaining public reactions to increased American deaths is related to official dominance of media reporting. This point is discussed at greater length within the chapter.

71. However, the relationship between monthly media reporting of casualties and opposition to the war as a "mistake," opposition to Bush's handling of the war, and opposition to the war as "not worth it" is not statistically significant. Possible reasons for this are provided at greater length in this chapter.
72. Victor Davis Hanson, "2,000 Dead, in Context," *New York Times*, 27 October 2005, 31(A).
73. The data from the Pew Research Center was drawn from three surveys: Pew Research Center, "April 2006 News Interest Index," April 2006, http://people-press.org/dataarchive/; Pew Research Center, "February 2007 Political Survey," 2 February 2007, http://people-press.org/dataarchive/; Pew Research Center, "December Political and Economic Survey," 3 December 2008, http://people-press.org/dataarchive/.
74. For more information on the decline in news on Iraq in late 2007 and 2008, see Reuters, "Decline in Iraq News May Have Boosted U.S. Opinion," December 19, 2007, http://www.reuters.com/article/politicsNews/idUSN1846357720071219; CNN.com, "U.S. Deaths in Iraq Down 66 Percent from Last Year," 30 December 2008, http://www.cnn.com/2008/WORLD/meast/12/30/iraq.main/index.html.
75. A multivariate regression analysis of the 2006, 2007, and 2008 surveys finds a number of important results regarding respondents' demographic backgrounds and their knowledge of military casualties. For the 2006 survey, logistic regression analysis finds that older Americans, men, those of higher education, whites (compared to non-whites) and those who consumed more news on Iraq were all more likely to accurately provide the number of U.S. military casualties. Logistic analysis of the 2007 survey also found that older Americans, men, wealthier Americans, O'Reilly viewers, NPR listeners, and Limbaugh listeners were better able to estimate the number of dead. Finally, logistic analysis of the 2008 survey finds that older Americans and the more highly educated are better able to estimate the number of dead.
76. This statistic is derived from a review of the headlines in the *New York Times* pulled from the LexisNexis database from a two-year sample period from March 2003 to January 2005.
77. I used a simple bivariate OLS regression model to estimate the relationship between increased coverage of violence in Iraq by the *New York Times* and increased public opposition to Bush's handling of the war, and opposition to the war as "not worth it." The total data period I analyzed runs from May of 2003 through July of 2007. The relationship between increased coverage of violence and increased opposition to Bush's handling of the war is statistically significant at the .01 level. The relationship between increased coverage of violence and increased opposition to the war as "not worth it" is statistically significant at the five percent level. Figure 7.8 does not include data from mid 2005 through mid 2007 because there are larger sequence gaps in the public opinion data between months, making it more difficult to discern the relationships between coverage and opposition to war by the naked eye. For more information on the public opinion data used for this figure, please see endnote 50 from this chapter.

78. Probably the most compelling evidence that the media is not driven by a partisan antiwar agenda is the fact that the Democratic Party—which the media allegedly supports—is *not* antiwar. Upon assuming office, Barack Obama gave no indication that he would end the Iraq war, only that he would de-escalate the conflict by removing troops. At the same time, Obama indicated he favored *expanding* the war in Afghanistan, and like the Bush administration before him, continued with American military strikes in Pakistan. It is difficult to interpret this history of militarism as "antiwar" by any stretch of the term.
79. Peter Hart, "Spinning the Surge: Iraq and the Election," FAIR, September/October 2008, http://www.fair.org/index.php?page=3611; FAIR, "Debating the Iraq 'Surge' on PBS," 10 January 2007, http://www.fair.org/index.php?page=3029.

8. MEDIA EFFECTS ON PUBLIC OPINION: PROPAGANDA, INDOCTRINATION, AND MASS RESISTANCE

1. Data for this study is derived from the University of Michigan's Inter-University Consortium for Political and Social Research. Statistical data is derived, among other sources, from the 2002 and 2004 National Election Studies.
2. In testing whether increased consumption of media and electoral attentiveness are associated with higher levels of trust in media, I employ multivariate, ordinary least squares regression. After controlling for relevant demographic factors such as respondent age, income, education, sex, and race, I find positive, statistically significant relationships between increased media consumption and trust. The correlation coefficient between attention to media and elections and trust in media is statistically significant for all respondents at the 1 percent level, and for conservative respondents at the 5 percent level, although not significant for liberal respondents.
3. Increased attention to television news stories on the election and trust in media is statistically significant at the 5 percent level for all respondents; the relationship is not significant for conservatives, but significant for liberals at the 5 percent level. Increased attention to magazine articles on the election and trust in media is statistically significant at the 5 percent level for all respondents; the relationship is not significant for liberal and conservative subgroups.
4. Increased trust in media and trust in government is statistically significant at the 0.1 percent level for all respondents, significant at the 0.1 level for conservative respondents and significant at the 1 percent level for liberal respondents.
5. In analyzing public opinion on Iraq, Afghanistan, and the war on terror, the statistical tests in this chapter utilize logisitic regression in estimating the probability of various demographic groups supporting or opposing government policies. Figures depicting differences between citizens based on education, media consumption, and electoral attentiveness are statistically significant, after controlling for other relevant demographic variables such as age, sex, race, income, and ideology.
6. Bush's job approval rating, according to Fox News, rose from 55 percent in February to 71 percent in April of 2003; for more information, see: http://www.washingtonpost.com/wp-srv/politics/interactives/nationdivided/ index.html.
7. Editorial, "The Iraq Dossier," *New York Times*, 10 January 2003, 22(A).
8. Editorial, "Small Effort," *Boston Globe*, 19 February 2003, 18(A); Editorial, "Bush's Challenges," *Boston Globe*, 29 January 2003, 14(A).
9. Increased education is positively associated with increased opposition to the invasion of Iraq. Correlations are statistically significant for all respondents at the 0.1

percent level, for liberals at the 0.1 percent level, and for conservatives at the 5 percent level.

10. Higher levels of electoral attentiveness are positively associated with feelings that the Iraq war has increased the threat of terrorism. This correlation is statistically significant at the 5 percent level. Increased political attentiveness for liberals is also positively associated with feelings that the war has increased the terror threat, and this relationship is statistically significant at the 0.1 percent level. There is no statistically significant correlation between attentiveness and feelings about the terror threat among conservatives.
11. The relationship between higher education and opposition to shorter timetables for withdrawal is statistically significant for all respondents at the one percent level. The relationship between education and opposition to short-term withdrawal is also significant for conservatives at the 0.1 percent level, but not significant for liberals.
12. Opposition to a short timetable for withdrawal is present not only among all respondents and conservatives. Highly educated moderates were also more likely to resist short-term withdrawal. The relationship between education and feelings on withdrawal among moderates is statistically at the one percent level.
13. Greater electoral attentiveness and attention to greater attention to radio news covering the election are positively associated with feelings that the Iraq war was worth it. This correlation is statistically significant for all respondents at the 5 percent level, for conservatives at the 5 percent level, but not significant for liberals.
14. The positive relationship between greater electoral attentiveness and identification of terrorist motives is statistically significant for the support for Israel explanation at the 0.1 percent level, for views of the United States as an immoral power at the 5 percent level, and for desire for religious war at the 5 percent level.
15. Strong support for the United States presence abroad is discernible across all categories in this analysis. Statistically, doves and hawks surveyed in the 2004 ANES study are not more or less likely to support or oppose a strong American role abroad based upon their ideological differences.
16. For more information on this development, see Anthony DiMaggio, *Mass Media, Mass Propaganda: Examining American News in the "War on Terror"* (Lanham, Md.: Lexington, 2008), chap. 4.
17. Greater attention to newspaper articles and greater attention to electoral politics are both correlated with increased disapproval of President Bush for all respondents questioned, and the relationships are statistically significant at the 5 and 1 percent levels respectively. News and electoral attention and disapproval of Bush are positively related and significant for liberals at the 5 and 1 percent levels respectively. Increased approval of the president among conservatives is associated with increased electoral attention, and this relationship is significant at the 5 percent level. There is no significant relationship, however, between greater attention to news and approval of Bush among conservatives. Higher education (amongst all respondents, and amongst liberals particularly) is positively associated with disapproval for the president. These relationships are both statistically significant at the 0.1 percent level. There is no significant relationship between education and presidential approval for conservatives.
18. Greater interest in political campaigns is positively associated with disapproval of Bush's handling of relations with foreign countries for all respondents and for liberals. The relationship for all respondents and for liberals is statistically significant at the 5 percent level. Greater interest in political campaigns is positively associated with increased support for Bush's handling of relations with foreign countries for

conservatives. This relationship is significant at the 5 percent level.

19. Higher formal education is positively associated with increased support for the Afghan war as "worth it" among all respondents, and for conservatives. The relationship is statistically significant for all respondents at the 1 percent level, and for conservatives at the 5 percent level. There is no statistically significant relationship between education and support for the Afghan war for liberals surveyed.

20. Increased attention to the 2004 election on television is positively associated with support for the war in Afghanistan among all respondents and for conservatives. The relationship is statistically significant for all respondents at the 5 percent level, and for conservatives at the 0.1 percent level. There is no statistically significant relationship between attention to news and the election, and support for the Afghan war, amongst liberal respondents.

21. Increased opposition to Bush's handling of the war on terror is positively associated with attention to news articles, and is significant for all respondents at the 1 percent level. For liberals, increased opposition is positively related to greater attention to news at the 5 percent level. There is no significant relationship between support for Bush and consumption of news among conservatives. Increased opposition to Bush's handling of the war on terror is positively associated with greater interest in the 2002 election, and is significant for all respondents at the 5 percent level. For liberals, increased opposition is positively related to greater electoral interest at the 5 percent level. For conservatives, support for Bush is positively related to electoral interest at the 5 percent level as well.

22. Maxwell McCombs, *Setting the Agenda: The Mass Media and Public Opinion* (Cambridge: Polity Press, 2004), 125; Bernard C. Cohen, *The Press and Foreign Policy* (Princeton: Princeton University Press, 1963), 13; Shanto Iyengar and Donald R. Kinder, *News That Matters: Television and American Opinion* (Chicago: University of Chicago Press, 1988); G. Ray Funkhouser, "The Issues of the Sixties: An Exploratory Study in the Dynamics of Public Opinion," *Public Opinion Quarterly* 37/1 (1973): 62–75; James W. Dearing and Everette M. Rogers, *Agenda Setting* (Thousand Oaks, Calif.: Sage, 1996); Paul J. Traudt, *Media, Audiences, Effects: An Introduction to the Study of Media Content and Audience Analysis* (New York: Pearson, 2005); David L. Protess and Maxwell McCombs, *Agenda Setting: Readings on Media, Public Opinion, and Policymaking* (Hillsdale, N.J.: Lawrence Erlbaum, 1991).

23. McCombs, *Setting the Agenda*, 2004, 5.

24. Paul Lazarsfeld, Bernard Berelson, and Hazel Gaudet, *The People's Choice* (New York: Columbia University Press, 1944); Joseph Klapper, *The Effects of Mass Communication* (New York: Free Press, 1960).

25. Iyengar, *News that Matters*, 1988.

26. Shanto Iyengar, *Is Anyone Responsible? How Television Frames Political Issues* (Chicago: University of Chicago Press, 1991).

27. Joseph N. Cappella and Kathleen Hall Jamieson, *Spiral of Cynicism: The Press and the Public Good* (Oxford: Oxford University Press, 1997), 84–85, 159.

28. Donald L. Jordan and Benjamin I. Page, "Shaping Foreign Policy Opinions: The Role of TV News," *Journal of Conflict Resolution* 36/2 (1992): 227–41.

29. Doris Graber, *Processing Politics: Learning from Television in the Internet Age* (Chicago: University of Chicago Press, 2001); W. Russell Neuman, Marion R. Just, and Ann N. Crigler, *Common Knowledge: News and the Construction of Political Meaning* (Chicago, University of Chicago Press, 1992).

30. Stephen Ansolabehere and Shanto Iyengar, *Going Negative: How Political*

Advertisements Shrink and Polarize the Electorate (New York: Free Press, 1995); Thomas Patterson, *Out of Order* (New York: Vintage, 1994); Thomas Patterson, *The Vanishing Voter: Public Involvement in an Age of Uncertainty* (New York: Vintage, 2002).

31. James Shanahan and Michael Morgan, *Television and Its Viewers: Cultivation Theory and Research* (Cambridge: Cambridge University Press, 1999); Leo W. Jeffries, *Mass Media Effects* (Prospect Heights, Ill.: Waveland Press, 1997).
32. Douglas M. McLeod and Benjamin H. Detenber, "Framing Effects of Television News Coverage of Social Protest," *Journal of Communication* 49/3 (1999): 3–23; Douglas M. McLeod and James K. Hertog, "The Manufacture of 'Public Opinion' by Reporters: Informal Cues for Public Perceptions of Protest Groups," *Discourse and Society* 3/3 (1992): 259–75.
33. Shanto Iyengar and Adam Simon, "News Coverage of the Gulf Crisis and Public Opinion: A Study of Agenda-Setting, Priming, and Framing," in *Taken by Storm: The Media, Public Opinion, and United States Foreign Policy in the Gulf War* (Chicago: University of Chicago Press, 1994), 167–85.
34. Zhongdang Pan and Gerald M. Kosicki, "Voters' Reasoning Processes and Media Influence during the Persian Gulf War," *Political Behavior* 16/1 (1994): 117–56.
35. Seok Kang, "Impact of Television News on Public Opinion about the Iraq War: An Assessment of Second-Level Agenda Setting and Framing," International Communication Association Annual Meeting, 26 June 2006, 16.
36. Carrie Cihasky, Lara Grusczynski, Jennifer Luse, and Jung-Yeop Woo, "The Media, Public Opinion, and Iraq: The Roles of Tone and Coverage in Public Misperceptions," Southern Political Science Association Meeting, 6 January 2005, 28.
37. Robert M. Entman, "How the Media Affect What People Think: An Information Processing Approach," *Journal of Politics* 51/2 (1989): 347–70; Justin Lewis, *Constructing Public Opinion: How Political Elites Do What They Like and Why We Seem to Go Along with It* (New York: Columbia University Press, 2001), 101.
38. Larry M. Bartels, "Messages Received: The Political Impact of Media Exposure." *The American Political Science Review* 87/2 (1993): 267–85.
39. Matt Guardino and Danny Hayes, "Whose Views Made the News? Media Coverage and the March to War in Iraq," Midwest Political Science Conference, April 2008; Cihasky, "The Media, Public Opinion, and Iraq."
40. Anthony R. DiMaggio, *Mass Media, Mass Propaganda: Examining American News in the "War on Terror"* (Lanham, Md.: Lexington, 2008), 57–76; Anthony R. DiMaggio, "Saddam Hussein, the Mass Media, and the Social Construction of Good and Evil," Working Paper, 2008; Guardino and Hayes, "Whose Views Made the News?"
41. DiMaggio, *Mass Media, Mass Propaganda*.
42. As mentioned in the chapter, this analysis is based on the ABC-*Washington Post* poll conducted immediately following the Bush administration's 2003 State of the Union address. The relationship between increased consumption of government-media propaganda and increased support for the war is statistically significant across all six policy questions examined here. All six OLS regressions examining associations between media consumption and policy opinions on Iraq are highly statistically significant at the 0.1 percent level. Unfortunately, demographic variables such as respondent religion, education, income, and race were not controlled for in these regressions, because such questions were not asked in the polls examined. However, respondents' sex and political party (as a representation of their ideology) were included in the poll, and are included in my analysis. The positive

relationship between exposure to presidential rhetoric and support for the Iraq war remains, after controlling for the individual respondent's ideology/party label.

43. PIPA, "Misperceptions, the Media, and the Iraq War," *World Public Opinion*, 2 October 2003, http://www.worldpublicopinion.org/pipa/articles/international_security_bt/102.php.
44. PIPA, "Most Americans Believe Bush Administration Is Still Saying Iraq Had a Major Weapons of Mass Destruction Program," *World Public Opinion*, 13 April 2006, http://www.worldpublicopinion.org/pipa/articles/brunitedstatescanadara/188.php?nid=&id=&pnt=188&lb=brusc.
45. Editorial, "Off Course in Iraq," *New York Times*, 21 July 2005, 28(A).
46. Editorial, "The Deluder in Chief," *New York Times*, 7 December 2008, http://www.nytimes.com/2008/12/07/opinion/07sun2.html.
47. Editorial, "Iran and the Bomb," *New York Times*, 13 January 2006, 20(A).
48. See the Iran section of http://www.pollingreport.com.
49. See the Iran section of http://www.pollingreport.com.
50. PIPA, "Russians and Americans Agree Iran Is Trying to Develop Nuclear Weapons, but Disagree on Economic Sanctions," *World Public Opinion*, 30 May 2006, http://www.worldpublicopinion.org/pipa/articles/international_security_bt/201.php?nid=&id=&pnt=201&lb=breu.
51. Zogby, "Bush Job Approval Rating Unchanged at Inauguration: Public Doubts Democracy Possible in Iraq; Large Majorities Oppose Military Intervention in Iran," 24 January 2005, http://www.zogby.com/news/ReadNews.dbm?ID-95; Reuters, "Americans Favor Diplomacy on Iran," 28 September 2006, http://elections.us.reuters.com/top/news/usnN27288539.html; for information on the CBS polls, see http://www.pollingreport.com.
52. See the Iran section of http://www.pollingreport.com.
53. Pew Research Center, "Iran a Growing Danger," 7 February 2006, http://people-press.org/reports/display.php3?ReportID=269.
54. The evidence for this Figure was gathered from a CBS-*New York Times* poll in May of 2006 and from a CBS-*New York Times* Poll in February 2005. As with much of the data from this chapter, these surveys were pulled from the University of Michigan's Inter-University Consortium for Political and Social Research (ICPSR) website. Perceptions of a threat based upon media consumption of Iran stories is significant at the 5 percent level for the May 2006 poll, and perceptions that Iran possesses weapons of mass destruction and is a threat based upon media consumption of Iran stories is highly statistically significant at the 0.1 percent level for the February 2005 poll. Respondent philosophy is not a relevant variable in influencing perceptions of a threat from Iran. In other words, in contrast to earlier discussion in this chapter, there is no difference between liberal and conservative elites in regard to perceptions of a threat. Threats from Iran seem to be consistent across liberal and conservative philosophies as consumption of stories on Iran's nuclear program increases.
55. All of the basic information cited here regarding public opinion and Iran is available in summary form via http://www.pollingreport.com.
56. Robert Entman, *Projections of Power: Framing News, Public Opinion, and United States Foreign Policy* (Chicago: University of Chicago Press, 2004), 10, 142.
57. Benjamin I. Page and Robert Y. Shapiro, "Effects of Public Opinion on Policy," *American Political Science Review* 77/1 (March 1983): 175–90; Matthew Baum and Tim Groeling, "Iraq and the 'Fox Effect': An Examination of Polarizing Media and Public Support for International Conflict," American Political Science Conference,

August 2007, http://www.allacademic.com/meta/p210432_index.html; Brian Anse Patrick and A. Trevor Thrall, "Beyond Hegemony: Bush Media Strategy and the War in Iraq," *Mass Communication and Society* 10/1 (2007): 95-118.

58. Pew Research Center, "Public Wants Proof of Iraqi Weapons Programs," 16 January 2003, http://people-press.org/report/170/public-wants-proof-of-iraqi-weapons-programs.

59. PIPA, "Three in Four Americans Say If Iraq Did Not Have Weapons of Mass Destruction or Support al-Qaeda, United States Should Not Have Gone to War," *World Public Opinion*, 28 October 2004, http://www.pipa.org/OnlineReports/Iraq/IraqPresElect_Oct04/IraqPresElect_Oct04_pr.pdf.

60. In the same model described in notes 64 and 67 in chap. 7, three independent variables are included: monthly casualty figures, critical media coverage, and monthly attacks in Iraq. There is no statistically significant relationship between critical media coverage and opposition to the war, although, as explained earlier, monthly casualties and attacks are significantly related to increased opposition.

61. For further exploration of the positions of mainstream newspapers by 2007, see Anthony DiMaggio, "The *New York Times* and the 'Antiwar' Turn," *Z Magazine*, 9 July 2007, http://www.zmag.org/znet/viewArticle/15003.

62. Editorial, "Waiting for a President," *New York Times*, 3 November 2004, 18(A).

63. Editorial, "President Bush's Speech about Iraq," *New York Times*, 29 June 2005, http://www.nytimes.com/2005/06/29/opinion/29wed1.html.

64. Rod Nordland and Michael Hirsh, "Fighting Zarqawi's Legacy," *Newsweek*, 19 June 2006, http://www.newsweek.com/id/52372; James Carney, "After Zarqawi: A Drawdown of Troops?," *Time*, 11 June 2006, http://www.time.com/time/magazine/article/0,9171,1202938-1,00.html.

65. Editorial, "Death of a Terrorist," *New York Times*, 9 June 2006, http://www.nytimes.com/2006/06/09/opinion/09fri1.html; Editorial, "A Good Day in Iraq," *Washington Post*, 9 June 2006, 22(A); John Gibson, "The Big Story: Al-Zarqawi Dead," Fox News, 8 June 2006; Kyra Phillips, "Al Zarqawi Killed," CNN, 8 June 2006, 1:37 p.m.

66. The public opinion data regarding Zarqawi's death was derived from a CBS poll from June of 2006. Increased consumption of news regarding Zarqawi's death is positively related to increased support for beliefs that Iraqi sectarian violence is on the decline and the country is moving toward more stabilization. The relationship is statistically significant for both questions at the 0.1 percent level. However, as with other surveys discussed in this chapter, there is also an ideological polarization at work between hawks and doves. Those liberal doves who consumed more news on Zarqawi were less likely to accept promises that Iraq was stabilizing and violence was declining. Conservative hawks who consumed more news were more likely to accept promises that Iraq was stabilizing and violence was declining. Even after controlling for political philosophy (which is significant at the 0.1 percent level), media coverage still exercised an independent effect in terms of reinforcing administration propaganda. As with all other regressions in this chapter, demographic variables such as respondent sex, race, religion, education, and income are controlled for.

67. For more information on pro-surge framing, see Peter Hart, "Spinning the Surge: Iraq and the Election," *Fairness and Accuracy in Reporting*, September/October 2008, http://www.fair.org/index.php?page=3611.

68. Public opinion information regarding the troop surge was derived from two surveys, a CBS poll from January 2007 and a CBS-*New York Times* poll from May

2007. Exposure to Bush's January surge speech was *not* associated with increased confidence in Bush's abilities in Iraq, increased support for the surge, feelings that the surge would be successful, increased support for Bush's reconstruction program in Iraq, increased support for initiation of the surge without congressional authorization, or increased expectations that democracy will soon emerge in Iraq following the surge. No statistically significant relationship exists between exposure to the president's speech and support for the surge, after controlling for demographic variables for respondents including sex, income, education, political ideology, and race.

69. Peter L. Berger and Thomas Luckmann, *The Social Construction of Reality: A Treatise in the Sociology of Knowledge* (New York: Anchor Books, 1966); Susan Herbst, *Reading Public Opinion: How Political Actors View the Democratic Process* (Chicago: University of Chicago Press, 1998).
70. Justin Lewis, *Constructing Public Opinion: How Political Elites Do What They Like and Why We Seem to Go Along with It* (New York: Columbia University Press, 2001), 18, 20.
71. Benjamin Ginsberg, *The Captive Public: How Mass Opinion Promotes State Power* (New York: Harper, 1986), 82.
72. For an excellent sample of such questions, see polling aggregations on Iraq from the website pollingreport.com
73. This question was specifically asked by ABC News and the *Washington Post* in a number of polls conducted in 2004 and 2005.
74. In all of the years I examined public opinion surveys of Iraq, I never saw questions in any polls regarding the questions of whether the United States was motivated by oil in Iraq, whether it is imperialistic, whether Americans are concerned with Iraqi civilian deaths, or whether the war is immoral. Although it seems unlikely, some of these questions may have been asked at some point, in some extremely limited fashion, but they have certainly never appeared with any frequency.
75. For more on the extensive literature regarding public opposition to "unwinnable" wars, see Nicholas Berry, *Foreign Policy and the Press: An Analysis of the New York Times' Coverage of United States Foreign Policy* (Westport, Conn.: Greenwood, 1990); Dominic D. P. Johnson and Dominic Tierney, *Failing to Win: Perceptions of Victory and Defeat in International Politics* (Cambridge: Harvard University Press, 2006); Richard A. Brody, *Assessing the President: The Media, Elite Opinion, and Public Support* (Stanford: Stanford University Press, 1991); John Mueller and Christopher Gelpi, "How Many Casualties Will Americans Tolerate?" 2006; Scott Althaus, Nathaniel Swigger, Christopher Tiwald, Svitlana Chernykh, David Hendry and Sergio Wals, "Marking Success, Criticizing Failure, and Rooting for 'Our' Side: The Tone of American War News from Verdun to Baghdad," Midwest Political Science Conference, April 2008, http://www.allacademic.com/meta/p266614_index.html.
76. Zaller, "Elite Leadership of Mass Opinion"; John R. Oneal, Brian Lian, and James H. Joyner Jr., "Are the American People 'Pretty Prudent'? Public Responses to United States Use of Force, 1950–1988," *International Studies Quarterly* 40/2 (1996): 261–80; Adam J. Berinsky, "Assuming the Costs of War: Events, Elites, and American Public Support for Military Conflict," *Journal of Politics* 69/4 (2007): 975–97.
77. PIPA, "Comprehensive Analysis of Polls Reveals Americans' Attitudes on US Role in the World," *World Public Opinion*, 3 August 2007, http://www.worldpublicopinion.org/pipa/articles/brunitedstatescanadara/383.php?lb=brusc&pnt=383&nid=&id.

78. Susan Page and William Risser, "Many Americans Don't Mind Much if United States Seen as Losing," *Chicago Sun Times*, 9 May 2007, 40.
79. PIPA, "United States Public Opposes Permanent Military Bases in Iraq, but Majority Thinks United States Plans to Keep Them," *World Public Opinion*, 15 March 2006, http://www.worldpublicopinion.org/pipa/articles/international_security_bt/177.php?lb=btis&pnt=177&nid=&id=.
80. PIPA, "United States Public Rejects Using Military Force to Promote Democracy," *World Public Opinion*, 29 September 2005, http://www.worldpublicopinion.org/pipa/articles/brunitedstatescanadara/77.php?lb=btgov&pnt=77&nid=&id=; also see the CBS-*New York Times* survey from December 2006, available from the International Consortium for Political and Social Research.
81. When asked, the largest segment of respondents indicated that the war was "neither humanitarian nor immoral." Those who saw the war as "fundamentally wrong and immoral," however, far outnumbered those who felt the war was "humanitarian in its goal and mission."
82. These phrases represent the standard way in which the conflict is examined in major polls undertaken by ABC News, the *Washington Post*, *USA Today*, Gallup, CBS, and the *New York Times*, among other polling organizations. For more information on summaries of this language, see http://www.pollingreport.com/iraq.htm.
83. In analyzing headlines in the *New York Times*, I examined a sample of stories from 2005 to 2007, accounting for any story that explicitly referenced Iraqi or American dead. The lopsided findings again reinforce the media's general lack of interest in the civilian casualties for which American forces are responsible.

9. PROPAGANDA, CELEBRITY GOSSIP, AND THE DECLINE OF NEWS

1. David Miller and William Dinan, *A Century of Spin: How Public Relations Became the Cutting Edge of Corporate Power* (Ann Arbor, Mich.: Pluto Press, 2008), 14–15; Larry Tye, *The Father of Spin: Edward L. Bernays and the Birth of Public Relations* (New York: Owl Books, 1998); Stuart Ewen, *PR! A Social History of Spin* (New York: Basic Books, 1996).
2. Edward L. Bernays, *Propaganda* (New York: IG Publishing, 2005), 37, 109, 39, 47, 39, 83, 84, 91.
3. Walter Lippmann, *Public Opinion* (New York: Free Press, 1997), 195, 157, 158; Walter Lippmann, *The Phantom Public* (New Brunswick, N.J.: Transaction, 2003), 145.
4. Harold Lasswell, *Politics: Who Gets What, When, How* (New York: World Publishing, 1972), 19, 31, 37.
5. Lasswell's comments are cited in Noam Chomsky, *Deterring Democracy* (New York: Hill and Wang, 1991), 368.
6. George F. Kennan, *American Diplomacy* (Chicago: University of Chicago Press, 1984), 93.
7. Samuel P. Huntington, "Political Development and Political Decay," *World Politics* 17/3 (1965): 386–430.
8. Samuel Huntington, Jodi Watanuki, and Michael Crozier, *The Crisis of Democracy: Task Force Report #8* (New York: New York University Press, 1975).
9. Edward L. Bernays and Howard Walden Cutler, *The Engineering of Consent* (Oklahoma City: University of Oklahoma, 1955).
10. Edward Herman and Noam Chomsky, *Manufacturing Consent: The Political Economy of the Mass Media* (New York: Pantheon, 2002), 16, 17.

11. Bartholomew H. Sparrow, *Uncertain Guardians: The News Media as a Political Institution* (Baltimore: Johns Hopkins University Press, 1999), 79; James D. Squires, *Read All about It! The Corporate Takeover of America's Newspapers* (New York: Times Books, 1993); C. Edwin Baker, *Advertising and a Democratic Press* (Princeton: Princeton University Press, 1994); Lawrence Soley, *Censorship Inc.: The Corporate Threat to Free Speech in the United States* (New York: Monthly Review Press, 2002); John H. McManus, *Market-Driven Journalism: Let the Citizen Beware?* (Thousand Oaks, Calif.: Sage, 1994); William Hoynes, *Public Television for Sale: Media, the Market, and the Public Sphere* (Boulder, Colo.: Westview, 1994); Dean Alger, *Megamedia: How Giant Corporations Dominate Mass Media, Distort Competition, and Endanger Democracy* (Lanham, Md.: Rowman and Littlefield, 1998), 163–64.
12. *Manufacturing Consent: Noam Chomsky and the Media*, DVD, directed by Mark Achbar and Peter Wintonick (Zeitgeist, 1992); *The Corporation*, DVD, directed by Mark Achbar, Jennifer Abbott, and Joel Bakan (Zeitgeist, 2005).
13. For a discussion of stagnating wages, see Dennis Gilbert, *The American Class Structure: In an Age of Growing Inequality* (Belmont, Calif.: Thomson Wadworth, 2003); Larry M. Bartels, *Unequal Democracy: The Political Economy of the New Gilded Age* (Princeton: Princeton University Press, 2008).
14. Bureau of Labor Statistics, "Union Members Summary," 25 January 2008, http://www.bls.gov/news.release/union2.nr0.htm.
15. Saskia Sassen, *Cities in a World Economy* (Thousand Oaks, Calif.: Pine Forge Press, 2006); Mark Abrahamson, *Global Cities* (Oxford: Oxford University Press, 2004).
16. Timothy Rusch, "New Report Details How American Families Rely on Credit Card Debt to Make Ends Meet," *Common Dreams*, 7 November 2007, http://www.commondreams.org/news2007/1107-09.htm.
17. David Shaw, "Foreign News Shrinks in Era of Globalization," *Los Angeles Times*, 27 September 2001, http://www.commondreams.org/headlines01/0927-03.htm.
18. John Hughes, "United States Media Can't Cover the News If They Don't Cover the World," *Christian Science Monitor*, 7 February 2007, http://www.csmonitor.com/2007/0207/p09s01-cojh.html.
19. Tom Fenton, *Bad News: The Decline of Reporting, the Business of News, and the Danger to Us All* (New York: Regan Books, 2005), 160.
20. Doris Graber, *Mass Media and American Politics* (Washington D.C.: CQ Press, 2002), 343.
21. Barbara Crossette, "On Foreign Affairs, United States Public Is Nontraditional," *New York Times*, 22 December 1997, http://query.nytimes.com/gst/fullpage.html?res=9507E6DD1731F93BA15751C1A961958260&sec=&spon.
22. Pew Research Center, "Public Opinion Six Months Later," 7 March 2002, http://people-press.org/commentary/?analysisid=44.
23. Pew Research Center, "Foreign Policy Attitudes Now Driven by 9/11 and Iraq," 18 August 2004, http://people-press.org/report/?pageid=863.
24. See the following Pew study for more on attention to Iraq, as compared to environmental disasters such as hurricanes: Pew Research Center, "Michael Vick Case Draws Large Audience," 28 August 2007, http://peoplepress.org/report/352/michael-vick-case-draws-large-audience.
25. Pew Research Center, "Younger Americans and Women Less Informed," 28 December 1995, http://people-press.org/report/134/younger-americans-and-women-less-informed-one-in-four-americans-follow-national-news-closely.

26. Project for Excellence in Journalism, "State of the News Media 2007," 2007, http://www.stateofthenewsmedia.org/2007/narrative_cabletv_audience.asp?cat=2&media=6; Pew Research Center, "News Audiences Increasingly Politicized," 8 June 2004, http://people-press.org/report/?pageid=834.
27. Pew Research Center, "Too Much Celebrity News, Too Little Good News," 12 October 2007, http://people-press.org/report/362/too-much-celebrity-news-too-little-good-news.
28. Mark Jurkowitz, "Iraq Dominates PEJ's First Quarterly NCI Report," *Project for Excellence in Journalism*, 25 May 2007, http://www.journalism.org/node/5716; Pew Research Center, "Iraq Most Closely Followed and Covered News Story," 23 February 2007, http://people-press.org/report/306/iraq-most-closely-followed-and-covered-news-story.
29. Pew, "Iraq Most Closed Followed and Covered News Story," 2007.
30. Pew Research Center, "Paris Hilton Becomes a National News Story," 14 June 2007, http://people-press.org/report/338/paris-hilton-becomes-a-national-news-story.
31. Pew Research Center, "Americans Remain Focused on Michael Jackson," 15 July 2009, http://people-press.org/report/529/americans-remained-focused-on-michael-jackson.
32. Pew Research Center, "Coverage of Jackson's Death Seen as Excessive," 1 July 2009, http://people-press.org/report/526/coverage-of-jackson-death-seen-excessive.
33. Pew Research Center, "Michael Vick Case Draws Large Audience," 28 August 2007, http://pewresearch.org/pubs/580/michael-vick.
34. Evidence for popularity of celebrity news among these demographics is derived from my regression analysis of an April 2006 CBS public opinion poll that questions respondents on news consumption habits. The data is taken from the University of Michigan's Inter-University Consortium on Political and Social Research website. OLS regression demonstrates that there are statistically significant differences between women (compared to men), minorities (compared to whites), younger audiences (compared to older ones), and wealthier people (compared to those with less money).
35. Pew, "Americans Remain Focused on Michael Jackson."
36. Graber, *Mass Media and American Politics*, 35.
37. Journalism.org, "Iraq Dominates PEJ's First Quarterly NCI Report: Anna Nicole Smith," *Project for Excellence in Journalism*, 25 May 2007, http://www.journalism.org/node/5716.
38. David Croteau and William Hoynes, *The Business of Media: Corporate Media and the Public Interest* (Thousand Oaks, Calif.: Pine Forge, 2001), 161–62.
39. Pew Research Center, "Too Much Anna Nicole, but the Saga Attracts an Audience," 16 February 2007, http://pewresearch.org/pubs/413/too-much-anna-nicole-but-the-saga-attracts-an-audience; Pew, "Iraq Most Closely Followed and Covered News Story."
40. Pew Research Center, "Interests in Floods Increases," 25 June 2008, http://people-press.org/report/432/interest-midwest-floods.
41. Pew Research Center, "Public Tunes Out Ellen Degeneres Controversy," 25 October 2007, http://people-press.org/report/365/public-tunes-out-ellen-degeneres-controversy.
42. This statistical evidence is derived from my regression analysis of the 2006 CBS poll described in endnote 34.
43. Fenton, *Bad News*, 141.
44. Pew Research Center, "Bottom Line Pressures Now Hurting Coverage," 23 May 2004, http://people-press.org/report/214/.
45. Pew Research Center, "Public Blames Media for Too Much Celebrity Coverage," 2

August 2007, http://people-press.org/report/346/public-blames-media-for-too-much-celebrity-coverage.

46. This statistical evidence is derived from my regression analysis of the 2006 CBS poll described in endnote 34.
47. Eric M. Uslaner, *The Moral Foundations of Trust* (Cambridge: Cambridge University Press, 2002), 148.
48. Pew Research Center, "How Americans View Government," 10 March 1998, http://people-press.org/report/95/.
49. Michael Parenti, *Democracy for the Few* (New York: St. Martin's Press, 2002), 211.
50. Zogby Interactive Poll, "United States Public Widely Distrusts Its Leaders," 23 May 2006, http://www.zogby.com/News/ReadNews.cfm?ID=1116.
51. Jeffrey M. Jones, "Congress Approval Rating Matches Historical Low," Gallup Polling Organization, 21 August 2007, http://www.gallup.com/poll/28456/ Congress-Approval-Rating-Matches-Historical-Low.aspx; Lydia Saad, "Congressional Approval Hits Record Low 14%," Gallup Polling Organization, http://www.gallup.com/poll/108856/Congressional-Approval-Hits-RecordLow-14.aspx; *Washington Post*, "President Bush's Approval Ratings," 11 October 2008, http://www.washington post.com/wp-dyn/content/custom/2006/02/02/CU2006020 201345.html. For time series data on long-standing disapproval of Congress and the President, see http://www.pollingreport.com/BushJob.htm and http://www.pollingreport.com/CongJob.htm.
52. Pew, "How Americans View Government."
53. Information on the 2004 NES was pulled from the University of Michigan's website, Inter-University Consortium for Political and Social Research (http://www.icpsr.org).
54. Zogby, "United States Public Widely Distrusts Its Leaders."
55. I explore the split nature of public opinion and trust in media in detail in chapter I of my book, *Mass Media, Mass Propaganda: Examining American News in the "War on Terror."*
56. The strong effects of the mass media on the public during the early years of conflicts are explored in chaps. 7 and 8. Similarly, the public's rejection of media propaganda in later years is also addressed in those chapters.
57. Jamal R. Nassar, *Globalization and Terrorism: The Migration of Dreams and Nightmares* (Lanham, Md.: Rowman and Littlefield, 2004); Manfred B. Steger, *Globalisms: The Great Ideological Struggle of the Twenty-first Century* (Lanham, Md.: Rowman and Littlefield, 2008); John Tomlinson, *Globalization and Culture* (Chicago: University of Chicago Press, 1999); Valentine Moghadam, *Globalization and Social Movements: Islamism, Feminism, and the Global Justice Movement* (Lanham, Md.: Rowman and Littlefield, 2008); Joseph E. Stiglitz, *Globalization and Its Discontents* (New York: W. W. Norton, 2003); Joseph E. Stiglitz, *Making Globalization Work* (New York: W. W. Norton, 2007); Leslie Sklar, *Globalization: Capitalism and Its Alternatives* (Oxford: Oxford University Press, 2002).
58. Manfred B. Steger, *The Rise of the Global Imaginary: Political Ideologies from the French Revolution to the Global War on Terror* (Oxford: Oxford University Press, 2008), 10–11.
59. BBC, "Israel and Iran Share Most Negative Ratings in Global Poll," *World Public Opinion*, 22 March 2007, http://www.worldpublicopinion.org/pipa/articles/views_on_countriesregions_bt/325.php?nid=&id=&pnt=325&lb=btvoc.
60. CNN.com, "Poll: United States More a Threat than Iraq," 11 February 2003, http://edition.cnn.com/2003/WORLD/europe/02/11/british.survey/; Julian Glover, "British Believe Bush is More Dangerous than Kim Jong-Il," *Guardian*, 3 November 2006, http://www.guardian.co.uk/uk/2006/nov/03/terrorism.northko-

rea; BBC, "What the World Thinks of America," *Independent Communications and Marketing*, 16 June 2003, http://www.bbc.co.uk/pressoffice/pressreleases/stories/2003/06_june/16/news_poll_america.shtml.

61. Tom Regan, "United States in Iraq Greatest Danger to Global Peace?" *Christian Science Monitor*, 15 June 2006, http://www.csmonitor.com/2006/0615/dailyUpdate.html.
62. PIPA, "Poll of 9 Major Nations Finds All, Including United States, Reject World System Dominated by Single Power in Favor of Multipolarity," *World Public Opinion*, 12 June 2006, http://www.worldpublicopinion.org/pipa/articles/views_on_countriesregions_bt/208.php?nid=&id=&pnt=208&lb=btvoc.
63. PIPA, "World Publics Reject United States Role as the World Leader," *World Public Opinion*, 17 April 2007, http://www.worldpublicopinion.org/pipa/articles/views_on_countriesregions_bt/345.php?nid=&id=&pnt=345&lb=btvoc.
64. PIPA, "World View of United States Role Goes from Bad to Worse," *World Public Opinion*, 22 January 2007, http://www.worldpublicopinion.org/pipa/articles/international_security_bt/306.php?nid=&id=&pnt=306&lb=btis.
65. BBC, "What the World Thinks of America."
66. Jim Lobe, "United States Image Abroad Still Sinking," *Inter Press Service*, 27 June 2007, http://www.commondreams.org/cgi-bin/print.cgi?file=/headlines05/0624-05.htm; PIPA, "Global Poll: Majority Wants Troops Out of Iraq within a Year," *World Public Opinion*, 6 September 2007, http://www.worldpublicopinion.org/pipa/articles/international_security_bt/394.php?lb=btis&pnt=394&nid=&id=; Kevin Sullivan, "Views on United States Drop Sharply in Worldwide Opinion Poll," *Washington Post*, 23 January 2007, 14(A).
67. PIPA, "Most Iraqis Want United States Troops Out within a Year," *World Public Opinion*, 27 September 2006; Amit R. Paley, "Most Iraqis Favor Immediate United States Pullout, Polls Show," *Washington Post*, 27 September 2006, 22(A).
68. Edward Wong, "Huge Protests in Iraq Demand United States Withdraw" *New York Times*, 10 April 2007, http://www.nytimes.com/2007/04/10/world/middleeast/10iraq.html; David Bacon, "Iraq's Workers Strike to Keep Their Oil," *Truthout*, 9 June 2007, http://www.truthout.org/article/iraqs-workers-strike-keep-their-oil; Oil Change International, "Iraqis Oppose Oil Development Plans, Poll Finds," *Global Policy*, 6 August 2007, http://www.globalpolicy.org/security/ issues/iraq/poll/2007/0806oildevt.htm.
69. BBC, "Iraq Poll September 2007," 10 September 2007, http://news.bbc.co.uk/2/shared/bsp/hi/pdfs/10_09_07_iraqpollaug2007_full.pdf.
70. BBC, "Iraq Poll September 2007," 2007.

POSTSCRIPT: MEDIA COVERAGE IN THE AGE OF OBAMA

1. Steve Rendall and Tara Broughel, "Amplifying Officials, Squelching Dissent: FAIR Study Finds Democracy Poorly Served by War Coverage," *Extra!*, May/June 2003, http://www.fair.org/index.php?page=1145; see also Anthony DiMaggio, *Mass Media, Mass Propaganda: Examining American News in the "War on Terror"* (Lanham, Md.: Lexington, 2008), chaps 3 and 4.
2. See DiMaggio, *Mass Media, Mass Propaganda,* chap. 4.
3. Anthony DiMaggio, "A Begrudging Reversal: The *New York Times* and the "Anti-War" Turn," *Counterpunch*, 10 July 2007, http://www.counterpunch.org/dimaggio07102007.html.
4. Richard Pérez-Peña, "U.S. Coverage in Iraq Plummets," *New York Times*, 24 March 2008, http://www.nytimes.com/2008/03/24/technology/24iht24press.11368053.html; Mark Jurkowitz, "Why News of Iraq Didn't Surge," Project for Excellence in

Journalism, 26 March 2008, http://pewresearch.org/pubs/775/iraq-news.

5. Peter Hart, "Spinning the Surge: Iraq and the Election," *Extra!*, September/October 2008, http://www.fair.org/index.php?page=3611.
6. Editorial, "The First Deadline," *New York Times*, 29 June 2009, http://www.nytimes.com/2009/06/30/opinion/30tue1.html.
7. Maya Schenwar, "Iraq Vote Could Oust U.S. Troops Early," Truthout.org, 2 July 2009, http://www.truthout.org/070209J.
8. Ernesto Londoño, "U.S. Troops, Civilians to Become Less Protected on July 1," *Washington Post*, 26 June 2009, http://www.washingtonpost.com/wp-dyn/content/article/2009/06/25/AR2009062503942.html.
9. Associated Press, "U.S. Troops to Remain Active in Iraq after Pullback," *USA Today*, 15 March 2009, http://www.usatoday.com/news/world/iraq/2009-03-15-combat-troops_N.htm.
10. Editorial, "The First Deadline," *New York Times*, 29 June 2009, http://www.nytimes.com/2009/06/30/opinion/30tue1.html.
11. Sheryl Gay Stolberg, "Biden Warns Iraq of Return to Ethnic Fights," *New York Times*, 3 July 2009, http://www.nytimes.com/2009/07/04/world/middleeast/04iraq.html.
12. Editorial, "The First Deadline," *New York Times*, 29 June 2009, http://www.nytimes.com/2009/06/30/opinion/30tue1.html.
13. For more on Iraqi and American public opposition to war, see chap. 9 of this book, and DiMaggio, *Mass Media, Mass Propaganda*, chap. 8.
14. Anthony DiMaggio, "A Perilous Path: Iraq and the Language of De-Escalation," *Counterpunch*, 3 July 2009, http://www.counterpunch.org/dimaggio07032009.html.
15. Juan Cole, "Stealing the Iran Election," *Informed Comment*, 13 June 2009, http://www.juancole.com/2009/06/stealing-iranian-election.html .
16. Glenn Kessler and Jon Cohen, "Signs of Fraud Abound, but Not Hard Evidence," *Washington Post*, 16 June 2009, 1(A).
17. Reuters, "Pre-Election Iranian Poll Showed Ahmadinejad Support," 15 June 2009, http://www.reuters.com/article/worldNews/idUSTRE55E3RO20090615.
18. Editorial, "Neither Real Nor Free," *New York Times*, 14 June 2009, http://www.nytimes.com/2009/06/15/opinion/15mon1.html.
19. Editorial, "A Mock Election in Iran," *Chicago Tribune*, 1 July 2005.
20. Editorial, "Incursion into Iran," *Washington Times*, 19 August 2009, http://www.washingtontimes.com/news/2009/aug/19/incursion-into-iran/print/.
21. Editorial, "What Now on Iran?," *Los Angeles Times*, 16 June 2009, http://articles.latimes.com/2009/jun/16/opinion/ed-iran16.
22. Editorial, "Neither Real Nor Free," *New York Times*, 14 June 2009, http://www.nytimes.com/2009/06/15/opinion/15mon1.html.
23. Jeff Zeleny and Helene Cooper, "Obama Warns Against Direct Involvement by U.S. in Iran," *New York Times*, 16 June 2009, http://www.nytimes.com/2009/06/17/us/politics/17prexy.html.
24. Editorial, "Neither Real Nor Free," *New York Times*, 14 June 2009, http://www.nytimes.com/2009/06/15/opinion/15mon1.html.
25. Editorial, "Neither Free Nor Fair," *Washington Post*, 15 June 2009, http://www.washingtonpost.com/wp-dyn/content/article/2009/06/14/AR2009061402399.html.
26. William J. Broad and David E. Sanger, "Iran Said to Have Enough Nuclear Fuel for One Weapon," *New York Times*, 20 October 2008, http://www.nytimes.com/2008/11/20/world/africa/20iht-20nuke.17986277.html

27. William J. Broad and David E. Sanger, "Iran Has More Enriched Uranium than Thought," *New York Times*, 19 February 2009, http://www.nytimes.com/2009/02/20/world/middleeast/20nuke.html.
28. Borzou Daraghi, "Iran Has Enough Fuel for a Nuclear Bomb, Report Says," *Los Angeles Times*, 20 February 2009, http://articles.latimes.com/2009/feb/20/world/fg-iran-nuclear20. Emphasis added.
29. Alan Cowell, "U.N. Atomic Energy Chief Says Iran Wants Bomb Technology," *New York Times*, 17 June 2009, http://www.nytimes.com/2009/06/18/world/18nuke.html.
30. David E. Sanger and Nazila Fathi, "Iran Test-Fires Missile with 1,200 Mile Range," *New York Times*, 20 May 2009, http://www.nytimes.com/2009/05/21/world/middleeast/21iran.html.
31. John P. Hannah, "Stopping an Iranian Bomb," *Washington Post*, 19 May 2009, http://www.washingtonpost.com/wp-dyn/content/article/2009/05/18/AR2009051802583.html.
32. Editorial, "Launching Dialogue with Iran," *Boston Globe*, 9 February 2009, 12(A).
33. Editorial, "The Big Cheat," *New York Times*, 25 September 2009, http://www.nytimes.com/2009/09/26/opinion/26sat2.html; Editorial, "Another Nuclear Plant," *Washington Post*, 26 September 2009, 16(A).
34. Matthew Cardinale, "U.S. Nukes Agency Pushes New Bomb Production," *Truthout*, 30 September 2009, http://www.truthout.org/093009R#; Matthew Cardinale, "U.S. Nukes Agnecy Pushes New Bomb Production," *Common Dreams*, 1 October 2009, http://www.commondreams.org/headline/2009/10/01-2.
35. My search of Lexis Nexis found that there were no headlines, op-eds, or editorials in any of the papers mentioned covering the U.S. announcement. The keywords "U.S." and "nuclear" were used to search for stories on the announcement. Using the words "Iran" and "nuclear," I found sixty headlines, editorials, and op-eds from these same papers covering Iran and the nuclear controversy.
36. Edward S. Herman, *Demonstration Elections: U.S. Staged Elections in the Dominican Republic, Vietnam, and El Salvador* (Boston: South End, 1984); Edward S. Herman and Noam Chomsky, *Manufacturing Consent: The Political Economy of the Mass Media* (New York: Pantheon, 2002).
37. Rajiv Chandrasekaran and Peter Finn, "U.S. Clamps Down on Iraqi Resistance," *Washington Post*, 1 July 2003, 1(A).
38. William Booth and Rajiv Chandrasekaran, "Occupation Forces Halting Elections Throughout Iraq," *Washington Post*, 28 June 2003, 20(A).
39. Jonathan Steele, "Why the U.S. Is Running Scared of Elections in Iraq," *Guardian*.
40. A simple process was used in order to determine the number of articles employing the key words in question. My search of LexisNexis from June 28 to July 28, 2003, was for articles that included the words "Iraq" and "election," in addition to the seven key words in question. Similarly, analysis of Iran from June 12 to July 12, 2009 looked for articles that included the words "Iran," and "election," in addition to the seven key words in question.
41. Editorial, "Karzai and the Friends He Keeps," *Boston Globe*, 20 August 2009, http://www.boston.com/bostonglobe/editorial_opinion/editorials/articles/2009/08/20/karzai_and_the_friends_he_keeps/.
42. Richard A. Oppel Jr., "Marines Fight Taliban with Little Aid from Afghans," *New York Times*, 22 August 2009, http://www.nytimes.com/2009/08/23/world/asia/23marines.html.
43. Editorial, "After Afghanistan's Vote," *New York Times*, 20 August 2009, http://www.nytimes.com/2009/08/29/opinion/29sat1.html.

44. Editorial, "The Price of Realism," *Washington Post*, 28 March 2009, 12(A).
45. Editorial, "After Afghanistan's Vote," *New York Times*, 20 August 2009, http://www.nytimes.com/2009/08/29/opinion/29sat1.html.
46. Suzi Emmerling, "U.S. Aid to Afghanistan by the Numbers," *Center for American Progress*, 14 August 2008, http://www.americanprogress.org/issues/2008/08/left_behind.html.
47. Kenneth Katzman, "Afghanistan: Post-Taliban Governance, Security, and U.S. Policy," *Congressional Research Service*, 14 August 2009, http://www.fas.org/sgp/crs/row/RL30588.pdf; Suzi Emmerling, "U.S. Aid to Afghanistan by the Numbers," *Center for American Progress*, 14 August 2008, http://www.americanprogress.org/issues/2008/08/left_behind.html.
48. Karen DeYoung and Greg Jaffe, "U.S. Ambassador Seeks More Money in Afghanistan," *Washington Post*, 12 August 2009, http://www.washingtonpost.com/wp-dyn/content/article/2009/08/11/AR200908 1103341.html.
49. Anthony DiMaggio, "An Unpopular War: What Obama Isn't Telling You about Afghanistan," *Counterpunch*, http://www.counterpunch.org/dimaggio08312009.html.
50. Editorial, "After Afghanistan's Vote," *New York Times*, 29 August 2009, http://www.nytimes.com/2009/08/29/opinion/29sat1.html.
51. Editorial, "The First Deadline," *New York Times*, 29 June 2009, http://www.nytimes.com/2009/06/30/opinion/30tue1.html.
52. Carlotta Gall, "U.S. Faces Resentment in Afghan Region," *New York Times*, 2 July 2009, http://www.nytimes.com/2009/07/03/world/asia/03helmand.html; Oppel, "Marines Fight Taliban with Little Aid from Afghans."
53. A LexisNexis search finds that all of the outlets mentioned published editorials in 2009 supporting escalation of U.S. war in Afghanistan.
54. Editorial, "Barack Obama's Afpakia," *Wall Street Journal*, 17 February 2009, http://online.wsj.com/article/SB123482632399795061.html.
55. Elisabeth Bumiller, "With Boots in Iraq, Minds Drift to Afghanistan," *New York Times*, 31 July 2009, http://www.nytimes.com/2009/08/01/world/middleeast/01memo.html; Helene Cooper, "G.O.P. Support May Be Vital to Obama on Afghan War," *New York Times*, 2 September 2009, http://www.nytimes.com/2009/09/03/world/asia/03policy.html.
56. Greg Wayland, "Is Afghanistan Becoming a Military Quagmire?," *Boston Globe*, 23 July 2009, http://multimedia.boston.com/m/25439192/is-afghanistan-becoming-a-military-quagmire.htm.
57. Editorial, "What Mr. Obama Said, and Didn't Say," *New York Times*, 23 September 2009, http://www.nytimes.com/2009/09/24/opinion/24thu1.html.
58. Editorial, "Wavering on Afghanistan? President Obama Seems to Have Forgotten His Own Arguments for a Counterinsurgency Campaign," *Washington Post*, 22 September 2009, 18(A).
59. Juan Cole, "Obama Defends Afghanistan War," *Informed Comment*, 18 August 2009, http://www.juancole.com/2009/08/obama-defends-afghanistan-war.html.
60. Juan Cole, "Interview on Media Matters with Robert McChesney," *Illinois Public Media WILL AM 580,* 1 March 2009, http://will.illinois.edu/mediamatters/P24/.
61. Christian Parenti, "Interview on Media Matters with Robert McChesney," *Illinois Public Media WILL AM 580,* 9 August 2009, http://will.illinois.edu/mediamatters/.
62. Carlotta Gall, "Civilian Deaths Imperil Support for Afghan War," *New York Times*, 6 May 2009, http://www.nytimes.com/2009/05/07/world/asia/07afghan.html.
63. Greg Jaffe, "Afghan Civilian Deaths Present U.S. with Strategic Problem," *Washington Post*, 8 May 2009, http://www.washingtonpost.com/wp-dyn/content/

article/2009/05/07/AR2009050702833.html.

64. Eric Schmitt and Thom Shanker, "U.S. Report Finds Error in Afghan Airstrikes," *New York Times*, 2 June 2009, http://www.nytimes.com/2009/06/03/world/asia/03military.html.

65. Col. Sam Gardiner and Erik Leaver, "Planning for Failure in Afghanistan," *Foreign Policy in Focus*, 30 March 2009, http://www.fpif.org/fpiftxt/6000.

66. Juan Cole, "Pakistan: U.S. Drones Have Killed 687 Innocents," *Informed Comment*, 12 April 2009, http://www.juancole.com/2009/04/pakistan-us-drones-have-killed-687.html.

67. Greg Miller, "U.S. Missile Strikes Said to Take Heavy Toll on Al Qaeda," *Los Angeles Times*, 22 March 2009, http://articles.latimes.com/2009/mar/22/world/fg-pakistan-predator22.

68. My analysis using the LexisNexis database finds that there were sixteen stories in the *New York Times* from January 1 to August 31, 2009, covering U.S. bombings and aerial drone flights in Pakistan. These stories were chosen from a list of stories including the key words "al Qaeda" and "Pakistan." In analyzing, I wanted to determine whether the stories emphasized civilian deaths. A story was categorized as emphasizing such deaths if they were mentioned in the headline or within the first five sentences. All sixteen stories emphasized that the attacks were either aimed at or killed al Qaeda, Taliban, and/or other militants within the first five sentences of each story. In contrast, not a single article contained any reference to civilians killed by these attacks within the first five sentences. The evidence here suggests that civilian casualties are ignored in the single-minded focus on killing militants.

69. The data from Figure 10.1 on opposition to the war is drawn from polls by CNN and Gallup.

Index